BUDDHA
IN
GANDHARA

Sunita Dwivedi is a Silk Road traveller and author. A keen photographer and an independent researcher, she has authored three travelogues—*Buddhist Heritage Sites of India* (2006, reprint 2017), *Buddha in Central Asia: A Travelogue* (2014) and *In Quest of the Buddha: A Journey on the Silk Road* (2009). This book (her fourth), *Buddha in Gandhara*, delves into the historico-cultural heritage of Pakistan and Afghanistan, which forms the ancient region of Gandhara.

Her work involves travelling and photographing Buddhist sites on the Silk Road's Asian circuit. So far, her work has taken her along ancient routes through China, Bangladesh, India, Pakistan, Afghanistan and the Central Asian Republics, from Turkmenistan to Kazakhstan. Besides authoring books, she has to her credit several articles on the Silk Road in reputed journals.

Praise for the Book

With this fine book, Sunita Dwivedi reclaims the ancient and lost world of Gandharan Buddhism. Combining keen observation with a deep knowledge of history, she will delight you with travel writing at its best. Her book will broaden your cultural horizons and deepen your understanding of religion and culture.
—**Frederick Starr**, Chairman, Central Asia-Caucasus Institute,
American Foreign Policy Council, Washington and author of
Lost Enlightenment: Central Asia's Golden Age

Both scholars and ordinary readers will find this book equally interesting. The information about the 'Asian Highway or Super Expressway' is fascinating. Tracing close relations of the Buddha with the ancient land of Gandhara through ancestry and spirituality is another commendable effort. I recommend this book to be part of all libraries in universities and research institutions throughout the world.
—**M.H. Khan Khattak**, Chief Editor,
Frontier Archaeology, Peshawar

This book gives comprehensive information about the rich Buddhist heritage of Gandhara. It covers the Buddhist art and culture of Gandhara and its systematic spread from the land of its origin to Pakistan, Afghanistan and Central Asia. I recommend this book as it gives a complete picture on the spread of Buddhist culture in the region.
—**Mohammad Fahim Rahimi**,
Director of National Museum of Afghanistan

This work is an account of the vibrant relations of Magadh and the classical land of Gandhara, the land of [ga] that was the gateway for the flourishing [dhara] of cultural, commercial and political relations of the Indian mainland with the Iranian and Greek kingdoms. The book is an accessible narrative of the first millennium when the Indian, Iranian and Hellenic cultures shared their best to create a world of harmony.

—**Lokesh Chandra**,
Director, International Academy of Indian Culture

This book is a unique effort towards recreating a journey on the Buddha's trail along the ancient highroads of Asia to the once-thriving cities of Gandhara. It sheds light on the remnants of monastic centres and the artistic genius of its craftsmen. Sunita Dwivedi deftly delves into the historico-cultural heritage of Pakistan and Afghanistan, which forms the ancient region of Gandhara.
—**Kapila Vatsyayan**, Chairperson, IIC-International Research Division;
Founder, Academic Director, Indira Gandhi National Centre of the Arts;
Member, UNESCO Executive Board; Former Secretary,
Department of Arts, Government of India

BUDDHA
IN
GANDHARA

SUNITA DWIVEDI

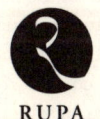
RUPA

Published by
Rupa Publications India Pvt. Ltd 2020
7/16, Ansari Road, Daryaganj
New Delhi 110002

Sales Centres:
Allahabad Bengaluru Chennai
Hyderabad Jaipur Kathmandu
Kolkata Mumbai

Copyright © Sunita Dwivedi 2020

The views and opinions expressed in this book are the author's own and the facts are as reported by her which have been verified to the extent possible, and the publishers are not in any way liable for the same.

All rights reserved.

No part of this publication may be reproduced, transmitted, or stored in a retrieval system, in any form or by any means, electronic, mechanical, photocopying, recording or otherwise, without the prior permission of the publisher.

ISBN: 978-93-89967-43-2

First impression 2020

10 9 8 7 6 5 4 3 2 1

Printed at Parksons Graphics Pvt. Ltd., Mumbai

The moral right of the author has been asserted.
This book is sold subject to the condition that it shall not, by way of trade or otherwise, be lent, resold, hired out, or otherwise circulated, without the publisher's prior consent, in any form of binding or cover other than that in which it is published.

To my husband Rakesh who has been my pillar of support on my journey through Buddhaland

CONTENTS

Preface	*ix*
Introduction	*xiii*
1. Buddha's Connection with Gandhara	1
2. Buddhism in Gandhara	16
3. On Buddha's Trail in Pakistan	31
4. Buddhist Cities on Delhi–Lahore Route	36
5. Road to Manikyala	44
6. Stupa of Manikyala	51
7. Taxila: Celebrated City of Uttarapath	59
8. On the Road to Taxila	71
9. Monasteries of Taxila	78
10. Dazzle of Peshawar	89
11. The Monastic Centres of Mardan	113
12. Buddhist Heritage of Afghanistan	148
13. Monasteries of Nagarhara	156
14. Kabul and Its Surroundings	168
15. Monasteries of Kapisa	179
16. Cave Monasteries of Bamiyan	186
17. Monastery of Kunduz	197
18. The Naubahar of Balkh	205
19. Monasteries and Deva Temples in Ghazni	215
20. Asokan Edicts at Kandahar	225

21. Art of Gandhara	232
22. Buddha and Bodhisattvas of Gandhara	240
23. 'Gandhara in Jataka' and 'Jataka in Gandhara'	264
24. Decline of Buddhism in Gandhara	275
Epilogue	287
Acknowledgements	291
Index	293

PREFACE

ON THE ASIAN HIGHWAY

The seed of my travels in Gandhara was sown in Andijan, a small city in the Ferghana Valley of Uzbekistan. This is the rich and prosperous valley in which even Alexander, the Macedonian, found it difficult to station his garrison in the fourth century BC, and spent nearly two years trying to conquer the fearless Ferghanians. Travellers and traders of Ancient India who came to the valley to buy the best wine, 'heavenly' horses and 'atlas' silk, also brought along their own gods and goddesses. I first stepped into this valley nearly a decade and a half ago—the place where pre-Islamic gods and goddesses such as Sridevi, Manjushri and Kubera were worshipped by inhabitants, and the Buddha colossi of Kuva stood guard over the flourishing valley. About 30 km from Ferghana, at the site of the local museum of Kuva, there is an array of Indian deities found during excavations at the site, and I was lucky enough to witness this during my visit to Uzbekistan.

Centuries of trade along the Wakhan Corridor directly into the Pamirs through the Khunjerab Pass via Kashgar closely connected Gandhara and Ferghana. As proof of the links between the two regions, there are carvings of horses—the famous flying Ferghanian breed that was sent to Ancient India in thousands—and inscriptions of pilgrims who travelled to the Gandharan Buddhist sites. Thus, it should come as no surprise to learn that while building the great stucco Buddha colossi of Kuva, moulds were produced in the ateliers of Gandhara, a region famous for its stucco artists.

When Islam became the dominant religion, the valley garnered fame anew from medieval heroes. Zahiruddin Muhammad Babur was one of them. Reams were written about him and a huge statue of Babur adorns the Bagh-e Babur in Andijan even today. His mausoleum built using soil brought all the way from Agra and Kabul—where he lies buried at Charbagh—can be seen at the Bagh-e Babur.

I first met the octogenarian professor Zakirjan Mashrobov in 2007 at Anjijan while reconnoitering the regions along the Amu Darya and Syr Darya rivers. He was raring to go on a motor rally through the extensive empire of Babur and his Mughal descendants, generally following the northern Silk Road along the valley of the Oxus and the old Grand Trunk Road through Kabul and Peshawar. Zakirjan, as head of the Babur Expedition titled 'In the Footsteps of Babur', had ridden along the Grand Trunk Road several times from Ferghana to Dhaka in search of historical records of the Mughal dynasty, in general, and of Babur, in particular.

I do not know whether like Babur, Zakirjan too hunted mountain goat, deer and boar in the thick forests along the riverbanks of the Ilamish River while on his expedition to India, or if he ran after pheasants, hares and foxes in the small wooded hills. Whether like Babur, he ate Nasukh melons called Ismail Shaykhi and whether he tasted, as Babur may have done, the juiciest pomegranates and apricots of Khojend and Margilan, on his way to India. I do not know all this. However, what I am certain of is that, like Babur, he thoroughly investigated every part of the 'road to India'.

Having said this, Zakirjan and I were looking at the history of this region differently. While I belonged to the ancient—the Gandharan period when Buddhism was the religion of the land now covering Pakistan and Afghanistan—Zakirjan was engrossed in the medieval era. Sharing his passion for travel, I had taken the same route, but I was following the Buddha's footprints and remnants of Buddhist establishments in Pakistan, Afghanistan and the republics of Central Asia. I wanted to explore the highway from Delhi to Peshawar and then across into Afghanistan, and later adding the stretch from Chittagong through Comilla and Dhaka into Kolkata and onwards to Delhi on the same road. Barring the short strife-torn stretch from the Khyber Pass up to Jalalabad, I would cover the entire Royal Road, an ancient highway, running from East Bengal (present-day Bangladesh) up to the Afghan border at Hairatan near the Friendship Bridge on the Oxus (present-day Amu Darya River) that led to the village of Arytam near Termez, in Uzbekistan.

My travels along the Asian Highroad from Chittagong to Balkh was aimed at experiencing first-hand the connectivity of the Buddhist sites falling along this great route, running from Bangladesh through northern India and the foothills of the Himalayas into Taxila, Peshawar and onwards to Kabul, Bamiyan, Samangan and across the Oxus to Termez and further into the countries of Central Asia and the Xinjiang region of China. As early as the sixth century BC, several celebrated travellers such as Trapussa and Bhallika, followed the same route along the Northern Highroad through Lahore, Taxila, Peshawar, Kabul and Bamiyan up to the Afghan borders at Balkh after having met the Buddha at the Deer Park in Sarnath. Scholars and pilgrims in search of sacred texts and knowledge disseminated from the renowned Mahaviharas, journeyed this long, arduous 2,000 km-long terrain that included plains, river valleys and mountains.

The monasteries and antiquities dug during archaeological excavations at the ancient cities along the 'Uttarapath', or Northern Highroad, are preserved in museums across Asia and Europe and still hold great attraction for world tourism. Several UNESCO World Heritage Sites lie in the countries of the Uttarapath—Afghanistan, Pakistan, India, Nepal and Bangladesh. Some of the famous sites along the route are Samangan, Bamiyan, Mes Aynak, Peshawar, Mardan, Taxila, Sanchi, Sravasti, Sarnath, Bodhgaya, Nalanda, Jagjivanpur, Murshidabad, Rajshahi, Mahasthangarh, Comilla and various sites in the Chittagong Hill Tracts, which have become icons of Asian tourism.

This book is a humble effort towards recreating a journey on the Buddha's trail along the Lahore–Peshawar and Kabul–Samangan routes to the once-thriving cities of Gandhara, a name synonymous with Buddha's *Dhamma* (doctrine) and the emblem of spellbinding Gandharan art. It sheds light on the remnants of monastic centres and the brilliant artistic genius of its craftsmen who embellished them. Braving time, nature's fury and human greed, the remains of these monasteries and their antiquities remind us of Asia's splendid heritage and stand as symbols of peace and scholarship in times of strife and ignorance.

INTRODUCTION

CENTRALITY OF GANDHARA ON THE ASIAN SILK ROAD CIRCUIT

Gandhara, comprising the Northwest Frontier regions of Pakistan and eastern and north-eastern Afghanistan, has been part of the colossal Buddhist corridor that connected the Bay of Bengal with Balkh through the ancient Uttarapath—the Northern Highroad, known as the Sher Shah Suri Marg during medieval times and the present-day Grand Trunk Road. (See maps)

The main route running along the foothills of the Himalayas and the Gangetic plains, across the river valleys and Doab regions of Punjab, crossed the Indus River near Hund. Then, following the course of the Peshawar Valley reached Kabul and in a north-westerly direction passed through Bamiyan before finally reaching Balkh.

Today, the freshly tarred Grand Trunk Road meandering through northern and north-western Pakistan and eastern and northern Afghanistan conceals under its glistening surface, the ancient Uttarapath from the Bay of Bengal to Kabul that was once the flourishing trade route from India through Gandhara to various countries of Asia and Europe. Since time immemorial, many a great traveller treaded the route to cross into the subcontinent seeking to acquire wealth through conquest, build empires or attain knowledge in the ancient universities of Taxila, Nalanda, Vikramshila, Odantapura, Jagaddala, Somapura and others.

The road covered the entire northern India from Bengal in the east to Gandhara in the north-west and from the Himalayas in the north to the Vindhyas in the south. The 'Dakshinapath', or the Southern Highroad, covered the southern regions of India.

This great Bengal–Afghan corridor had its network all over India with one branch going in the south-west direction, and one to the south. The former connected present-day Rajasthan, Gujarat and Maharashtra, while the latter passed through Kausambi and Ujjain (as the Dakshinapath), connecting present-day regions of Karnataka, Andhra Pradesh, Kerala and Tamil Nadu. It connected land routes to south India and to Sri Lanka along the sea. From the eastern coastal regions of India, it went up to Southeast Asia across the Bay of Bengal. Thus, foreign ships from Southeast Asia landed at Nagapattinam on the east coast and goods could be carried along coastal routes through Orissa and Bengal on to the Uttarapath that ran up to Afghanistan. It can therefore be said that the great Northern Highroad connected countries of Southeast Asia across the Bay of Bengal with Central Asia across the Oxus.

According to historian Romila Thapar, the main trade routes were along the Ganges River itself, going from Rajgriha as far as Kausambi, and then via Ujjain to Bhrigukachchha (present-day Bharuch) on the Narmada estuary, which grew into a major port for overseas trade with the West. Another route from Kausambi, up the Doab, went across Punjab to Taxila; this was the outlet for the overland western trade.[1]

The principal route from India passed through Taxila and Peshawar along the 45-km-long Khyber Pass through the Safed Koh and Sulaiman Ranges to Bamiyan and across the Hindukush to Balkh in Afghanistan. However, it was possible to take any of the three passes—Khyber, Gomal or Bolan—through the Sulaiman Mountain. The second route into Afghanistan led westwards from Mathura through Jaipur and Jaisalmer and running north-west into Quetta through the Bolan Pass before crossing into Kandahar in Afghanistan. The third road took the Gomal Pass midway between Khyber and Bolan to cross into Ghazni.

It is said that until the arrival of Islam, the most precious commodity being ferried along this corridor, and its branches into Central Asia and China, was the religion of the Buddha. Around the fifth century BC, the Buddha himself was travelling along and preaching in the ancient cities of this great corridor. In the present day, this region is what constitutes Bihar, Uttar Pradesh and Nepal, and possibly, Punjab and Gandhara, where the kings Rudrayana

---

[1] Romila Thapar, *The Penguin History of Early India: From the Origins to AD 1300*, Penguin India, Delhi, 2002, p.160.

and Puskarasarin accepted the Buddha's doctrines. Balkh traders, Trapussa and Bhallika, were travelling along the Bengal–Balkh route with their caravans on their way to Sarnath when they met the Buddha after his Enlightenment.

This road was witness to both war and peace. On the one hand, it witnessed the journeys of Asoka's missionaries, the *dhammadutas*, on their way to the Greek kingdoms as well as Buddhist scholars such as Jinagupta, who were on their way to the courts of the Western Turks and the Chinese emperors to preach and translate texts. On the other, it saw the movement of Indo-Greek, Yuechi (Kushan), and Turk and Arab invaders. On this path, saints and conquerors rubbed shoulders with each other.

After Asoka's reign, missionaries continued to travel along the Gandharan routes under the patronage of Greek and Kushan rulers. It was through this great Buddhist corridor of Gandhara that the new religion is believed to have reached Central Asia by the first century BC, giving rise to great Buddhist centres. Buddhism slowly spread through the oases towns on the fringes of the Taklamakan. Grottoes embellished with murals, stone sculptures and clay images of the Buddha and Buddhist deities have been excavated not only in the foothills of the Tien Shan and the Kunlun mountains but all along the Gansu Corridor at the remote sites of Majishan, Binglingsi, Anxi and Magao.

Most cities lying on this route running from the Bay of Bengal to the Oxus valley and even across the Oxus, in Turkmenistan, Uzbekistan and Tajikistan and further down the Chuy river valley, have a Buddhist past and began as halts for traders. Travelling along this route in the foothills of the Himalayas, across the Gangetic plains and the Doab of Punjab rivers, Buddhist missionaries came into contact with caravan leaders called *sarthavas*, who were members of the merchant's guild, or *nigam*, as well as artists and craftsmen, all treading the same caravan routes, resting at the same halts, sometimes for the entire *varshavasa*, or the rainy season, waiting to accompany the next caravan. We often hear of the merchant guild of Taxila and horse-dealers from Peshawar arriving in Mathura and

Varanasi. It was with the patronage of these guilds and local rulers that the missionaries gradually set up monasteries around trade halts, in nearby forests, hills and along river valleys. Over the years, the halts became village settlements with large Buddhist establishments. In fact, Asoka is believed to have set up his pillar and rock inscriptions not in isolation but at one of the flourishing trade halts along the corridor of the ancient Uttarapath in order to reach a wide audience for the propagation of his *Dhamma*.

The chain of Buddhist sites along the Grand Trunk Road from Bengal to Balkh is an indication of the large numbers of Buddhist missionaries and trade caravans who took this route. The monastic cities along the route offered shelter to the travelling monks. Chinese and Korean pilgrims on their way to and from India between the fourth and eighth centuries are known to have halted at the monasteries of Badakhshan, Kunduz, Balkh, Bamiyan, Kapisa, Hadda, Peshawar and Taxila in the western and north-western part of the corridor.

Today, a traveller on the Grand Trunk Road from Delhi through Haryana and Punjab to the cities of Lahore and Rawalpindi up to Peshawar, Kabul and Samangan will find ruins of numerous Buddhist establishments along the route. Many of these have been excavated, while many are still high mounds waiting to see the light of day.

Lahore, Taxila, Peshawar, Charsadda and Kabul were the chief trade entrepôts on the Northern Highroad, which wound its way to Peshawar, the premier city of the Northwest Frontier from where caravans left for the trading hubs of Kabul in Afghanistan and from Hairatan across the Oxus to the trading marts of Bukhara and Samarkand in Uzbekistan. (See maps)

The Delhi–Kabul route up to Ambala passes through Haryana, which until 1966 was a part of Punjab. Famous cities on this route include Panipat, Sirhind, Ludhiana and Amritsar. From Ambala up to Amritsar is now east Punjab on the Indian side and from Lahore up to Manikyala forms west Punjab in Pakistan. (See maps)

Ancient routes from Central Asia passed into Gandhara at several points through the territories of Uzbekistan (at Termez and Arytam), through Tajikistan (at Ushtur Mullo, Aivaz, Ishkashim), through Tarim Basin (via the Wakhjir Pass), through Turkmenistan (along the Murghab Valley into Badghis in north-western Afghanistan) and through Iran (at Herat in western and Zaranj in south-western Afghanistan). All routes met at Kabul and passed along the Uttarapath into the Peshawar Valley and across the Indus into Punjab. Following the course of the Ganges river valley, the highway led up to the Bay of Bengal. Routes from Herat could also lead to Kandahar and Ghazni and thereafter drop into the Bolan and Gomal valleys to lead into the Lower Indus region and western India.

BUDDHIST PILGRIM ROUTES

Famous Indologists P.C. Bagchi, B.N. Puri and Saroj Kumar Chaudhari have given the names of several Gandharan monks who travelled to Central Asia and China using the Gandharan routes. Records of their journeys to and from Gandhara present us with a choice of pilgrim routes that were available to Buddhist pilgrim and missionaries since the third century BC. (See maps)

Route to the Mediterranean

In his book, *India in Greece or, Truth in Mythology*, Edward Pococke discusses a possible Indian colonization of Greece. He writes that in the ancient past, a powerful body of Buddhistic adherents came from the 'extreme north-westerly boundaries of the Punjab and the frontiers of Thibet [Tibet]'[2] and settled around Thessaly in Greece. He goes on to show that dynasties disappearing from the western and north-western regions of India appeared in Greece and even points to identical localities in Greece where 'the Oriental tribes flowed like a mighty tide towards the West and South, enriching the lands with its current of civilisation.'[3]

If this is true, then it can be said that even in the great antiquity

---

[2] Edward Pococke, *India in Greece or, Truth in Mythology*, John Jay Griffin and Co., London, 1851, pp.98–99.

[3] Pococke, *India in Greece or, Truth in Mythology*, pp.12–19.

there must have been land or sea routes to the Mediterranean taken by this tide of Indian emigrants from Punjab and north-west India (present-day Northwest Frontier Province, now in Pakistan) onwards to Greece.

The discovery of a gravestone with a wheel and trident in Alexandria[4] attests to the fact that the western route to the shores of the Mediterranean was available to Indian migrants, who in turn, brought their religions with them. Close linkages with Greek rulers of West Asia were evident even during the Mauryan Emperor Bindusara's reign. It is said that Bindusara, who ruled from Pataliputra, could maintain cordial relations with the Syrian king Antiochus I along the Lamghan route.

There were routes leading up to the shores of the Mediterranean. We learn of a highway running through West Asia to the Mediterranean. This is indicated by two Lamghan Edicts of Asoka mentioning several places, their distances and directions. Written in Aramaic on a rock slab, an inscription dated to 260 BC was found in the Lamghan valley of eastern Afghanistan, which is said to have been a compulsory halt on the main trade route from India to Palmyra in Syria.[5]

The Asokan Edicts RE XIII mention the Mauryan emperor's *Dhamma* campaigns of the third century BC to the Greek kingdoms. His *dhammadutas* could have taken this route to reach the five Yavana kings—the Greek kings of Syria, Egypt, Macedonia, Cyrene and Epirus—who are explicitly mentioned as rulers of areas beyond Asoka's realm.[6] Earlier in the fourth century BC, the western route to Persis (Persia) was available to Alexander on his return journey from Taxila to Macedonia when a *samana* or *sramana* (meaning ascetic) named Kalanos (or Kalyan) had accompanied him. However, due to extreme ill health Kalanos or the 'naked philosopher' of Taxila

---

[4] Demetrios Th. Vassiliades, *The Greeks in India: A Survey in Philosophical Understanding*, Munshiram Manoharlal Publishers, Delhi, 2000, p.79.

[5] Ranabir Chakravarti, *Exploring Early India up to c. AD 1300*, Primus Books, Delhi, 2016, p.166.

[6] D.C. Ahir, *Asoka the Great*, B.R. Publishing Corporation, New Delhi, 1995, p.54.

committed himself to the flames on reaching Persis.[7] Around the first century BC, another Buddhist monk Zarmanos from Barygaza on the Narmada, not far south of the Indus districts, had travelled in an embassy as far as Antioch in ancient Syria and had committed himself to the flames at Athens.[8]

Merv Route

Another route running towards West Asia, Syria and shores of the eastern Mediterranean followed the valleys of the rivers Murghab and Tejen. This route could have been taken by the celebrated Parthian monks on their eastwards journey, through Balkh or Herat in Afghanistan, to China. An Shih-kao or Lokottama, a Parthian prince, abdicated the Arsacid royal throne and reached China c.AD 148 after taking the eastern highway. Other Parthian monks—unrivalled scholars of Sanskrit and Chinese—including An Hsuan (second century AD) and An Fachin (third century AD)[9] probably also took the same eastern highway to reach China to translate Buddhist texts. This eastern highway was none other than the caravan route leading eastwards through Balkh and the Oxus valley to the fertile Zerafshan Valley and further into China.[10]

Oxus Valley Route into Balkh

The Oxus valley route was the favoured route not only for pilgrims but also traders and invaders. The Chinese Scholar Xuanzang himself took this route while coming from the direction of the Issyk-Kul Lake

---

[7] Valerio Massimo Manfredi, *Alexander Vol.3: The End of the Earth* (translated from Italian by Iain Halliday), Macmillan, London, 2001 and Pan Books, London 2002, p.533.
[8] E.H. Warmington, *The Commerce between the Roman Empire and India*, Munshiram Manoharlal Publishers, Delhi, 1995, pp.36–37.
[9] Saroj Kumar Chaudhuri, *Lives of Early Buddhist Monks*, Abha Prakashan, Delhi, 2008, pp.47–56. See also P.C. Bagchi, *India and China*, Saraswat Library, Kolkata, 1981, p.113. See also, B.N. Puri, *Buddhism in Central Asia*, Motilal Banarsidass Publishers, Delhi, 2000, p.101.
[10] Y.F. Buryakov, K.M. Baipakov, K.H. Tashbaeva and Y. Yakubov, *The Cities and Routes of the Silk Road*, Sharg, Tashkent, 1999, p.23.

through the Chuy Valley up to Sairam (also called Ispijiab) and then along the Oxus Valley route up to Termez. But, he did not cross the river to enter Balkh. He had many more monasteries to check along the whole course of the Oxus and its tributaries in the land that is now Tajikistan.

Balkh-Surkhandarya Route

This was an extension of the pilgrim route leading from Balkh through Old Termez along the Surkhandarya to several Buddhist cities, namely Arytam and Dalverzin Tepe. This brings our attention to the other side of the Oxus river from Afghanistan and very close to Balkh. Excavations at the ancient Buddhist city of Dalverzin Tepe, near Termez across the Oxus in the Surkhandarya Valley, revealed a remarkable treasure of 115 items of gold jewellery and gold bars with inscriptions in Kharosthi.[11] This suggests that Gandharan pilgrims could have visited the Dalverzin Tepe Monastery with gold bars having Kharosthi inscription mentioning their weight not only for trade but possibly for pilgrimage too. This route also joined the Kafirnigan Valley (the valley of the kafirs—the non-believers or the Buddhists) running north-east to another monastic centre of Kafirnigan.

Another crossing on the Oxus lay at the ford of Awwaj or Uzaj, the present Aivaj, which was a port city wherein lay the renowned Buddhist centre of the now-collapsed Ushtur Mullo. It served as a ford to Kunduz city of Afghanistan and was the route into Gandhara from Kunduz. Near the mouth of the Vakhsh, a tributary of Oxus, was the well-known crossing of Mela; this was a three-day journey from Balkh, and two *farsakhs* (an old measure of length which is equal to about 5–5.5 km) from Tirmidh. In the thirteenth century AD, this place was called Panjab.[12] Perhaps, there existed a colony of Indians at Mela or Panjab. This route along the Vakhsh led to the

---

[11] B.A. Litvinsky, *Cities and Urban Life in the Kushan Kingdom*, Vol. II (The History of Civilizations of Central Asia), UNESCO, New Delhi, 1994 and Motilal Banarsidass Publishers, Delhi, 1999, p.297.

[12] W. Barthold, *Turkestan Down to the Mongol Invasion*, E.J.W. Gibb Memorial Trust, Oxford, UK, 1928 (reprints 2012), p.71.

famous monastery of Ajina Tepe from where the largest Reclining Buddha of Central Asia from the seventh or eighth century AD has been excavated.

Xuanzang writes in his memoirs about a spate of monasteries along the right bank of the Oxus. In order to visit these monasteries he did not cross into Balkh at Termez. Instead, he turned to the right bank of the Oxus from Termez and followed the pilgrim route into a series of Buddhist centres. The travel records of Xuanzang show that after he crossed the land of Termez (also called Tami or Termed), he found 10 *sangharamas* with about 1,000 monks. The pilgrim travelling eastwards crossed into the region of Chaganian where he found five *sangharamas* containing a few monks. He then travelled further eastwards towards Garam. Here, he found two convents and about 100 monks. Going further east, he arrived at the country of Suman and Kulab, where he also saw two convents and a few monks. In Kobadian, Xuanzang again found three convents and about 100 monks. Still eastwards lay the country of Vakhsh, which took its name from the Vakhsh River and then he moved on to Khuttal, which is bordered on the east by the Tsungling Mountains (present-day Pamirs).

Wakhan Corridor Route into Badakhshan

Xuanzang followed the 300-km-long Wakhan Corridor route in the north-eastern part of Afghanistan on his return journey to China, as did many other well-known pilgrims entering or exiting Gandhara. This route was the shortest for Indian, Gandharan and Parthian scholars on their way to China.

The corridor is a narrow Afghan territory that separates Tajikistan and Pakistan. Through this corridor ran an artery pilgrim route into Tarim Basin, and was a vital east–west link between China and the eastern Mediterranean region. The corridor was used not only as a route of commerce between the regions of Badakhshan and Yarkand but also as a pilgrim route to the monasteries of Gandhara and others built along the northern and southern Silk Road running along the foothills of Tienshan and Kunlun mountains in Xinjiang.

That this was a pilgrim route can be ascertained by the discovery of Chinese inscriptions, which are actually 'pilgrim inscriptions', as mentioned by E. Rtveladze.[13] According to him, more than 10 Chinese inscriptions mentioning names of merchants, pilgrims and royal envoys were found near Gilgit in the upper reaches of the Indus River, the territory directly adjacent to the Pamirs which points to the Indus Valley route through Gilgit into the Tarim Basin. One inscription mentions an ambassador Gu Wei-Long from the court of the Great Wei (despatched between AD 443 and AD 453) to Mimi (also known as Maimurgh), which lay south-east of Samarkand. This indicates a circuitous route via the Wakhan Corridor into Tokharistan that met the route coming from Samarkand via the Iron Pass at Derbent.[14]

In AD 518, Chinese pilgrims Sung Yun and Hu-sheng travelled by the southern Silk Road to Khotan[15] and then through the Wakhan Corridor to Badakhshan and Balkh from where they took up the route into Gandhara. Xuanzang also took this route while returning to China from Afghanistan in AD 645. The route led him from Bannu and Ghazni to Kunduz and Badakhshan and through the Wakhan Corridor to Kashgar, from where he travelled to Yarkand and Khotan and took the southern Silk Road to reach Xian.

In AD 673, Chinese pilgrims I-Ching travelled from Canton by the southern sea route to Tamralipti and travelled across India and Gandhara.[16] He returned to China by the Wakhan Corridor route onto the southern Silk Road via Yarkand and Khotan.

Hye Ch'o, a Korean pilgrim from Hsin-lo, also arrived by sea route in AD 724 into India, but after visiting Gandhara he left by the Badakshan route. Both Hye Ch'o and his predecessor I-Ching travelled by the southern sea route from Canton and landed

---

[13] Edvard Rtveladze, *Civilizations, States and Cultures of Central Asia*, Forum of Culture and Arts of Uzbekistan Foundation, Tashkent, 2009, p.279.
[14] Rtveladze, *Civilizations, States and Cultures of Central Asia*, p.279.
[15] Han-Sung Yang, Jan Yun-Hua Yang, Lida Shotaro and Lawrence Preston (eds and trans), *Hye Ch'o Diary: A Memoir of the Pilgrimage to the Five Regions of India*, Asian Humanities Press, Berkeley, CA, 1984, p.9.
[16] Yang et al., *Hye Ch'o Diary*, p.12.

at a port in eastern India, probably at Tamralipti on the Bay of Bengal. Travelling through a number of Central Asian states, Hye Ch'o went east to Samarkand and then arrived in Ferghana. From Ferghana, he reached Khuttal (in present-day Tajikistan) and then went on to Tokharistan, before arriving at Wakhan city. He followed the Wakhan Corridor route to Tashkurgan and Kashgar, and finally took the northern route to Anxi and Kucha at the end of AD 727.[17]

Buddist monk Faxian's travels from AD 399 to AD 412 took him along the southern Silk Road up to Khotan, from where instead of taking the Badakhshan route via Wakhan, he entered the Tsungling Mountains (Onion Mountains or the Kunluns) to Kheecha. He is supposed to have crossed the Indus at Skardo in Ladakh.[18]

Karakoram Highway

This ancient pilgrim route from Taxila to Kashgar, which was evidently a branch of the Silk Route, runs along the Indus River and into Hunza Valley. It enters the Xinjiang region of Tashkurgan at Khunjerab Pass. During the construction of the Karakoram Highway (the highest elevated road in the world), the existence of a much earlier route following similar directions was found. The location of Asokan Edicts at Mansehra and Shahbazgarhi marked a logical area for the start of such a route. According to Romila Thapar, inscriptions in Brahmi, Kharosthi and Bactrian and engravings of Buddhist images and themes along the way date the earlier route to the start of the Christian era.[19] The occasional depiction of horses would indicate an early horse trade with Central Asia.[20] At the time of Xuanzang's travels on this road to Tashkurgan in AD 644, the region was populated by Buddhists.[21]

---

[17] Yang et al., *Hye Ch'o Diary*, pp.14–15.
[18] James Legge (trans.), *A Record of Buddhistic Kingdoms Being an Account of the Chinese Monk Fa-Hein of Travels in India and Ceylon [AD 399–414] in Search of the Buddhist Books of Discipline*, Munshiram Manoharlal Publishers, Delhi, 1998, p.22.
[19] Romila Thapar, *The Penguin History of Early India*, 2002, p.222.
[20] Thapar, *The Penguin History of Early India*, p.222.
[21] Jonathan Tucker, *Silk Road Art and History*, Timeless Books, Delhi, 2003, p.189.

To the south of Tashkurgan, the modern road follows the course of the old Silk Road. After about 30 km, the road bifurcates—one enters the Wakhan Corridor and the other enters the Khunjerab Pass, following the course of the Khunjerab and Hunza rivers. The latter route is the Karakoram Highway. South of Gilgit, the road follows the Indus River right down as far as Thakot and then makes a gentle descent towards Taxila and Islamabad, the capital of Pakistan.

To date, 30,000 petroglyphs and 5,000 inscriptions in more than 10 different languages have been identified along the Karakoram Highway. The Sacred Rock of Hunza has inscriptions in Kharosthi (referring to Prince Kujula Kadphises from the first century AD) and Chinese (referring to the embassy of Gu Wei-long from the sixth century AD).[22]

At Kargah, 10 km from Gilgit, a massive figure of the Buddha from the seventh or eighth century AD has been found carved on the cliff face. Nearby are the ruins of a monastery with stupas from where a large number of manuscripts from the fifth century AD were discovered in the 1930s. This set of manuscripts is known as the Gilgit Manuscript.

The biggest concentration of petroglyphs and inscriptions, mostly in Brahmi, can be seen on rocks beside the Indus River at Shatial and Chilas. Of these, the earliest is dated between first and second century AD. At Chilas in northern Pakistan, a petroglyph depicting the Buddha seated beneath the Bodhi Tree and a stupa from the eighth century AD were found. At Shatial, inscriptions in Sogdian have been found in large numbers.[23]

Leh-Yarkand Route

Gandhara was also connected with Kashmir via the Jhelum Valley through routes running from the Zoji La to Ladakh. From here onwards, the north-bound Leh–Yarkand–Khotan route provided links with the southern Silk Road in Xinjiang. This in turn led to Dunhuang and the Gansu Corridor of China. The route from Leh to Yarkand was a journey of 779 km over the Khardung La, the

---

[22] Tucker, *Silk Road Art and History*, pp.191–93.
[23] Tucker, *Silk Road Art and History*, pp.197–98.

Sasser La and the Karakoram passes. Once in Yarkand, the caravan turned left for Kashgar and right for Khotan on the southern arm of the Silk Road along the Kunlun Mountains. Eastwards from Leh lay the route to Tibet through Rudok, the frontier post of Tibet. It crossed Mariom La, the highest pass to reach Lhasa. Faxian, who left the southern arm of the Silk Road at Khotan in Xinjiang, is said to have turned south towards Kheecha (believed to be Skardo in Ladakh). He could have either taken the ancient Karakoram Pass or the Leh–Yarkand route.

This is the most direct and important route starting from Ladakh into the Xinjiang region of China. There is also evidence of transportation of celebrated Buddhist bronze idols and written manuscripts in Brahmi along this route to places as far as the monastery of Krasnaya Rechka, near Bishkek. Caravans on the Leh–Yarkand route not only consisted of traders and explorers but also Buddhist pilgrims, scholars and missionaries as is evident from the numerous monasteries along the route from Leh along the Indus, Zanskar, Shyok and Nubra rivers that form a network of routes criss-crossing the entire region of Ladakh.

It was this route that linked the Taklamakan and Gobi desert regions located to the north of the Himalayan ranges with the regions of Punjab, Himachal Pradesh and Uttarakhand located in the south of the ranges. It thus gave the Leh–Yarkand route a strategic position on the Asiatic circuit of the Silk Road across Central Asia, China and India.

Northwest Frontier Passes

Khyber Pass was an integral part of the Silk Road connecting Torkham at the Afghan border with Peshawar Valley at Jamrud by traversing a part of the Safed Koh mountains. This has been a trade route from India to Afghanistan and Central Asia. The passing Buddhist missionaries left an indelible mark in the form of stupas and monasteries along the Khyber Pass.

The historic pass (now NH5) is the great northern route, an extension of the Grand Trunk Road from Peshawar to Kabul. The

Pass begins at Jamrud, 17 km west of Peshawar, and pierces through the Khyber Hills for 53 km till it is debouched at the village of Dakka in Afghanistan. The important points on this route are Ali Masjid, a village fort, 17 km from Jamrud; Landi Kotal, the summit of the Pass; and Torkham, where the Pass enters Afghanistan, about 10 km from Landi Kotal. From Landi Kotal, the Pass descends to Landi Khana, where it traverses another gorge and enters Afghanistan at the village of Dakka.[24]

Pilgrims and trade caravans not only took the Kabul Valley route through the Khyber Pass but also travelled along the Gomal Valley into Ghazni through the Gomal Pass. They could also take a third route running through the Bolan Pass into Kandahar. The three Passes in the Northwest Frontiers of the subcontinent were crucial in commerce between India, Afghanistan, Persia and the Trans-Caspian region. Xuanzang used this route while on his return journey through Bannu (in Pakistan) into Ghazni (in Afghanistan).

While the 70-km Khyber Pass connected Kabul with Peshawar, the Bolan Pass, an 89-km stretch of the Bolan river valley running through the Toba Kakar Range of Baluchistan connected Kandahar with Quetta and Sibi. It was used as a gateway to and from South Asia. It was also the nearest route into southern Afghanistan through Jaisalmer, Sibi, Quetta, Kandahar and Herat into Persia. On the northern side, the Kandahar road ran through Ghazni to Kabul up to Kunduz and Balkh.[25]

The Chinese pilgrim Xuanzang's route to Ghazni was through Fa-La-Na (Bannu in Pakistan in the direction south-east of Ghazni). Fa-La-Na is identified by Thomas Watters as Varana or Varna.[26] V. de

---

[24] *The Imperial Gazetteer of India*, v. 15, p.299. Available at <http://dsal.uchicago.edu/reference/gazetteer/pager.html> (last date of access: 8 February 2020).

[25] Sarina Singh, Lindsey Brown, Owen Bennet Jones, John Mock, Kimberly O'Neil and Ameena Yasmeen, *Pakistan and the Karakoram Highway*, Lonely Planet Guides, Lonely Planet Publications, Australia, USA, UK, 1981 (rev. ed. 2004), pp.112–13.

[26] Thomas Watters, *On Yuan Chwang's Travels in India*, Munshiram Manoharlal Publishers, Delhi, 2012, p.262.

St Martin in his memoir points out that the country corresponded to the modern Vanen in the middle part of the river Gomal's course.[27] Cunningham identified Varana with Bannu in the Kurram river district.[28] So, did the pilgrim follow the Bannu route through the Gomal Pass into Ghazni or through the Tochi Pass, which connects Bannu with Gazni? Tochi Valley is one of the few places where inscriptions in Bactrian language have been found indicating its antiquity.[29]

Once the trade routes dropped from Kashgar over the Karakoram into Taxila or ran through Balkh, Bamiyan and the Kabul Valley to Peshawar, they were met by the highroad which connected all of India through its northern (Uttarapath) and southern (Dakshinapath) arteries.

HERITAGE CORRIDOR

Known as the Asian Highway or Super Expressway, this 2,000-km-long corridor joining Bangladesh, India, Pakistan and Afghanistan is the heritage corridor that contains all major Buddhist sites of South Asia. It starts from Chittagong through Comilla, Dhaka, Bikrampur, Bogra and Rajshahi in Bangladesh, through the states of West Bengal and Bihar in India, onwards to Lahore, Taxila, Charsadda and Peshawar in Pakistan and finally passes through Kabul, Bamiyan, Samangan and Balkh in Afghanistan.

The Gandharan cities on this east–west corridor are an important source of history that narrates enthralling stories of trade and commerce, of plunder and conquest, of peace and religion, and of great art and scholarship in the region. Instrumental in bringing together people from different regions, different faiths and having different styles of art as well as ideas, this route assimilated and absorbed them to all create new styles, new ideas and a cosmopolitan outlook towards life. The philosophy of *vasudevay kutumbakam*,

---

[27] Watters, *On Yuan Chwang's Travels in India*, p.262.
[28] Watters, *On Yuan Chwang's Travels in India*, p.262.
[29] Hugh Chisholm (ed.), *Tochi Valley*, Encyclopaedia Britannica, 11th edition, Cambridge University Press, London, 1911.

meaning 'the world is one family', was the motto of the times that enabled people from separte parts of the world, following distinct faiths and speaking different languages to live and work together. Along this corridor in Gandhara existed some of the biggest centres of Buddhist learning such as Taxila, Peshawar, Kabul, Kapisa, Nagarhara, Wardak, Samangan, Balkh and Kunduz. Long galleries with vaulted roofs and meditation cells attached with courtyards for assembly of monks and scholars can today be seen among the monastic ruins of Takht-i-Bahi near Mardan and Takht-i-Rustam in Haibak near Samanagan. At the Kanishka Vihara in Peshawar, Chinese pilgrim Xuanzang records the existence of chambers for scholars. There was a time when pilgrims, instead of coming straight into India, halted at the monastic centres of Afghanistan, such as in Kunduz and Balkh, for special studies in Buddhism. Xuanzang stayed at the monastic centre of Naubahar in Balkh for a month. Other renowned Buddhist centres were created in the deserts of the Karakum at Merv, in the lap of the Hindukush at Bamiyan, on the road to India at Kapisa.

Xuanzang's travelogue tells us of Kapisa as a renowned centre of Buddhist studies where scholars lived, and where congregations were held and important questions regarding the Buddhist doctrine were discussed and debated. A five-day religious congregation was held in the temple of Sholokia (believed to be at Shotorak). In this convent lived three great Buddhist priests—Master of three Pitakas, Manojaghosh; Aryaverma of the Sarvastivadin School; and another priest, Gunabhadra. Xuanzang participated in the congregation along with monk Prajnakara and also addressed the congregation and answered all questions regarding the Buddhist doctrine.

According to Xuanzang, Dharmasinha, known to be well-versed in *Vibhasha Sastra* and considered the most revered scholar monk at the monastic centre in Kunduz, was the head and resided there with his many disciples. Considered the 'artisan of law' or the lawmaker, Dharmasinha was renowned among the priests of Kashgar, Khotan and Yutien and had travelled to India for Buddhist studies.[30]

---

[30] Hwui Li (Translated by Samuel Beal), *The Life of Hieun-Tsiang*, D.K. Publishers, Delhi, 2001, p.48.

Nava Vihara was the main monastery at Balkh and the centre of higher Buddhist study for all of Central Asia. Hwui Li in *The Life of Hieun-Tsiang* tells us that three eminent Buddhist scholars resided at the Navasangharama—one was Prajnakara, whose fame had spread throughout India and the other two being Dharmapriya and Dharmakara who were also staying at the monastery; they were well-versed in the texts of the 'Little Vehicle'.[31] Xuanzang remained at the monastery for a month to study the *Vibhasha Sastra*.

Scholars travelled to the university at Taxila, known to be the oldest in the world, and is said to have existed even before the time of the Buddha and before the occupation of the Taxila Valley by the Achaemenid rulers in sixth–fifth century BC.[32]

As early as the ninth century BC, debaters from east India were travelling to the Northwest Frontier regions of Gandhara to study and for research. One such Indian researcher was Uddalaka, who worked on his philosophy of 'evolution' in Kubha (present-day Kabul). The Buddhist text *Uddalaka-Jataka* (No. 487) also mentions that Uddalaka journeyed to Takshashila (present-day Taxila) and studied under a renowned teacher. Wandering scholars from India too were travelling to Gandhara from far and wide to participate in scholastic debates. As late as the tenth century AD, the Kanishka Monastery at Peshawar was still flourishing as a place of Buddhist education, and scholars travelled to the Kanishka Vihara to gain knowledge. Prince Vira Deva of Magadh was also sent there to benefit from instruction by the resident teachers who were famous for their piety.[33]

Considering the heavy traffic that rolled along this corridor, Asoka, who was viceroy of Taxila during his early days, planted shady banyan trees and provided all kinds of amenities for travellers. Over the centuries, seeds from those very trees have sprouted, grown, died and regrown through several generations. Groves of old banyan trees

---

[31] Hwui Li, *The Life of Hieun-Tsiang*, p.51.
[32] B.N. Puri, Buddhism in Central Asia, p.105.
[33] Vincent A. Smith, *History of India*, Vol. II, Cosimo Classics, New York, 2008, p.230.

that can still be seen lining the Grand Trunk Road are reminders of the benevolence of the great Mauryan emperor. They continue to provide shelter and shade to travellers who take the same road—many perhaps for the same purpose of trade. Only difference is instead of horse riders, camel safaris, palanquins, today there is a cavalcade of motorcars. The shiny new road running almost parallel to the Grand Trunk Road has been aptly named the 'motorway'. In conclusion, this 2,000-km-long Buddhist corridor has immense potential for heritage tourism in the countries located on the Uttarapath, namely Afghanistan, Pakistan, India and Bangladesh.

Chapter 1

BUDDHA'S CONNECTION WITH GANDHARA*

Scholars are generally of the opinion that the Buddha's field of activities lay in the region of the present states of Uttar Pradesh and Bihar in India and the low-lying regions of Nepal. However, there are historical records that point not only to the Buddha's connection with Gandhara but also to the possibility of his visit to Gandhara.

There is evidence that Buddha had 'accurate' knowledge about the 'relatively egalitarian' Greek society living in the frontier regions of India. References in Buddhist literature trace back the Yonas (supposed Greeks in Pali) to the time of the Buddha. There is evidence drawn by Thanissaro Bhikkhu and Greek scholar of Indian philosophy, Demetrios Th. Vassiliades, from the *Assalayana Sutta* of *Majjhima Nikaya* (MN 93) of the Buddha entering into a debate with a brahmin on whether one's worth as a person is determined by birth or by behaviour.

On the occasion of a discourse between the Buddha and a young brahmin named Assalayana, the Buddha speaks about the countries of the Yonas and Kambojas, who did not follow the four-fold caste division, but recognized only two classes, namely, slaves and free men.[1]

---

*For a more detailed study, see E. Pococke's *India in Greece*; John McCrindle's *Ancient India as Described by Megasthanese and Arrian* and K.L. Hazra's *Rise and Decline of Buddhism in India*.

[1] Demetrios Th. Vassiliades, *The Greeks in India, A Survey in Philosophical Understanding*, Munshiram Manoharlal Publishers, New Delhi, 2000, p.29. See also dhammatalks.org (Talks, Writings and Translations of Thanissaro Bhikkhu), *With Assalayana Assalayana Sutta* (MN 93).

It is said that Assalayana, a master of the three vedas, approached the Buddha at Jetavana Monastery (present-day Sravasti) and challenged him on his teachings about purity of the four castes and the non-superiority of brahmins. Assalayana, a proud brahmin, was urged by a large group of brahmins, who were rivals of the Buddha, to take him on.

Buddha is quoted to have said:

What do you think, Assalayana? Have you heard that in Yona and Kamboja and other outlying countries there are only two castes—masters and slaves—and that having been a master one can become a slave, and that having been a slave one can become a master?[2]

BUDDHA'S ANCESTRY IN GANDHARA

Tracing the Buddha's ancestry to Gandhara, scholar Edward Pococke[3] mentions the story of the Buddha's ancestor, the Sakyan Okkakamukho, who belonged to the Gandhara region around the Indus River. Taxila was among his 19 capital cities. Referring to a custom of intermarrying with their sisters among the Ptolemises, pursued right up to the time of Caesar, Pococke cites the practice running up to the ancient era of 'Okka'ko, the Icshwaca [Icskwaku] of the Hindus', one of the venerable Buddhas of antiquity. Pococke states that the origin of this custom amongst the *sakyans* (Buddhist princes) is of antiquity, as it proceeds from an authentic Buddhist source, furnished by the most distinguished Pali scholar of his time.[4]

Pococke presents the following information from the *Tika*, containing the names of the capitals at which different dynasties reigned at the time. He also provides a distinct account of Okkako

---

[2] Thanissaro Bhikkhu (translated from Pali), *Assalayana Suttam: With Assalayana*, Majjhima Nikaya II. Majjhima Panasa 5. Brahmana Vagga, Sutta 93. 2010. Available at <obo.genaud.net> (last date of access: 6 February 2020).
[3] Edward Pococke, *India in Greece*, John J. Griffin and Co., London, 1852, pp.192–96.
[4] Pococke, *India in Greece*, p.192.

(Icskwaku of Indus) and of his descendants, as well as the derivation of the royal patronymic *sakya* to which, he says, 'no clue could be obtained in Hindu annals but which is nearly identical with the account extracted by Csoma de Koros from the Tibetan "Kahgyur", and published in the Bengal Asiatic Journal of August, 1833.'[5] The eldest son of Okkako was Okkakamukho. The portion of the royal dynasty from Okkakamukho to Sudhodano (the father of Gautam Buddha), who reigned at Kapilavastu, was called the Okkako Dynasty. According to the story, Okkako had five consorts; the eldest had four sons and five daughters. After giving birth to these nine children, she died, and the king then raised a lovely and youthful princess to the station of queen consort who bore him a son. The delighted monarch promised to grant any prayer of the queen consort. She, having consulted her relations, prayed that the sovereignty might be passed on to her son.

Following this—the nine children of the deceased queen led by Okkakamukho—the eldest announced their intention to quit the capital, and with the blessings of the king himself moved to the frontier of Himawanto to seek a site for their city.

At that period, we learn that a brahmin by the name of Kapila, lived in the Himawanto country in a *pannasala* (leaf hut), in a Sal forest. Out of compassion for the princes, he permitted them to raise their city at the site of his *pannasala*. Building a *pannasala* for Brahmin Kapila in a corner, the princes founded their city, giving it the name of Kapilanagar and settled there. From that time up to the period of King Sudhodano, we learn that all who descended from their alliances were also called *sakya*.[6]

Basant Bidari, former chief of the Lumbini Development Authority, mentions in his book that the Buddha not only studied Sanskrit but also Kharoshti,[7] the language of the Northwest (Gandhara).

---

[5] Pococke, *India in Greece*, p.192.

[6] E. Pococke, *India in Greece*, p.194.

[7] Bidari Basant, *Kapilvastu: The World of Siddhartha*, Hill Side Press, Kathmandu, 2004, p.164.

BUDDHA'S CONTEMPORARIES

During the Buddha's own time, in the sixth–fifth century BC, Buddhism as a religion was already spreading in Gandhara and was patronized by the rulers, some of whose names have come down to us. Buddhologist Kanai Lal Hazra writes that King Pukkusati (Puskarasarin), who was a contemporary of the Buddha, ruled over Gandhara in the middle of the sixth century BC.[8] At the time, Gandhara roughly corresponded to the modern districts of Peshawar (Purushapur) and Rawalpindi in the north-western Punjab and Kashmir. Pukkusatis' capital was Taxila.

He further states that King Pukkusati took keen interest in Buddhism through the efforts of Bimbisara, the king of Magadh, with whom he had friendly relations. There existed close cultural ties between them. The latter is known to have sent ambassadors with valuable gifts including an inscribed golden plate which had the description of the three sacred jewels (Buddha, *Dhamma* and Sangha) and various tenets relating to the Buddha's teachings. After reading the inscription on the plate, the king joined the Sangha and became a Buddhist monk. He even came to Rajagaha to pay homage to the Buddha, who preached to him the *Dhatuvibhanga Sutta*. The king became an ardent follower of Buddhism and played an active part in popularizing Buddhism in his kingdom.[9] It does not seem unlikely that Pukkusati invited the Buddha to Gandhara and that he actually went there to preach to the Gandharans.

Scholar poets of the first century such as Asvaghosa also inform us that the Buddha converted the lord of Gandhara, Puskara, who is said to have immediately abandoned his royal glory on hearing the Law.[10]

---

[8] K.L. Hazra, *The Rise and Decline of Buddhism in India*, Munshiram Manoharlal Publishers, Delhi, 1995 (3rd edition, 2009), p.16.
[9] Hazra, *The Rise and Decline of Buddhism in India*, p.16.
[10] E.H. Johnston, *Asvaghosa's Buddhacharita or Acts of the Buddha*, Munshiram Manoharlal Publishers, Delhi, 1936 (reprint 1995), p.56, canto xxi 'Progress of the Mission', No. 4.

Likewise, Rudrayana occupied the throne of Roruka in Sovira (or the Lower Indus Valley) in the days of the Buddha. He first received news of the Buddha in Magadha from Bimbisara. This shows the connection of Bimbisara with Gandhara's neighbouring regions on the Indus. The latter also sent him an inscribed plate which contained some of the cardinal tenets of Buddhism. On seeing these, the king joined the Buddhist Sangha as a monk. During the lifetime of the Buddha, Buddhism established itself in the kingdom of Rudrayana, who conquered the Punjab, Sind, Baluchistan, Afghanistan, Himavatkuta, Nepal and Kashmir. He probably extended his kingdom up to Mysore in the south and in the north-west up to the borders of Persia.[11] He also could have invited the Buddha and the Sangha to the Indus region.

Other converts to the faith included the Naga kings, a tribe in Punjab and the Northwest beyond. Historian Ahmad H. Dani points to the Takshak rulers of Taxila (modern-day Taka tribe) whose name originated from their worship of Takila, the serpent. The Naga chief Nagadanta, occupying the hilly regions and river valleys of the Northwest was subdued by the teachings of the Buddha. 'Then in the Gandhara country the snake Apalala, with his senses tamed by the Rule, passed beyond evil.'[12]

The road from Balkh to Bodhgaya was active during the sixth century BC. We know of the merchants Trapussa and Bhallika,[13] who were the first two lay disciples of the Buddha and natives of the kingdom of Balkh. They had gone to India for trade, and happened to be at Bodhgaya when the Buddha had just attained his Enlightenment. They offered him cakes and honey out of their provision and became his first disciples. Buddha, at the time of their departure, gave them his hair and nail cuttings. On their return home, they built stupas on these relics. Xuanzang mentions these stupas near the city of Balkh.

---

[11] Hazra, *The Rise and Decline of Buddhism in India*, p.16 Dipavamsa: 550ff.
[12] Samuel Beal, *Si-Yu-Ki: Buddhist Records of the Western World*, Book II, Low Price Publications, Delhi, 1884, pp.93–94. See also, Ahmad H. Dani, 'History in Taxila: Prehistoric Taxila of Takshaka Rulers'. Available at http://www.heritage.gov.pk (last date of access: 6 February 2020)
[13] P.C Bagchi, *India and China*, Saraswat Library, Kolkata, 1981, p.31.

BUDDHA'S SOJOURN IN PUNJAB

Historian Charles Eliot writes that for about 45 years, the Buddha moved about Kosala, Magadh and Anga visiting the two capitals Savatthi (Sravasti) and Rajagaha (Rajgriha/Rajgir) and going as far west to the country of the Kurus (located until recently in Punjab, now in Haryana).[14] He further goes on to write that the 'Vinay of the Mulasarvastivadins' made the Buddha visit north-west India and Kashmir; however, Pali texts do not represent him as travelling further west than the country of the Kurus. According to Eliot, there is nothing impossible in it, particularly as there are periods in the Buddha's long life filled by no incidents.[15]

French historian Hans Loeschner also puts forward the '... possibility that [the] Buddha preached in Gandhara prior to the incorporation of this region into the Achaemenid Empire in 520 BCE. [Behistun epigraph of Darius dated 520–518 BCE].' According to Hans, this was the time when Siddhartha Gautam was leaving Kapilvastu at the age of 29 years. Enlightened after six years of harsh asceticism, he started preaching the Four Noble Truths when he was 35 years of age [the 532 BCE]. 'The last Gandharan king Pukkusati is said to have sent an embassy and letter to Bimbisara of Magadh [543–491 BCE]. There is a narration that Pukkusati became a Buddhist monk and a junior contemporary of Buddha.'[16]

FUGITIVE SAKYANS IN GANDHARA

During Buddha's life, four expatriated Sakyans settled in Gandhara or chose to travel to Gandhara after being expelled from Kapilavastu. Possibly because their Sakyan brethren were already settled not only

---

[14] Charles Eliot, *Hinduism and Buddhism: An Historical Sketch*, Vol. I, Bibliotheca Indo-Buddhica No. 54, Sri Satguru Publications, Delhi, 1988, p. 149.
[15] Eliot, *Hinduism and Buddhism*, p.301.
[16] Hans Loeschner, 'Kanishka in Context with the Historical Buddha and Kushan Chronology' in Vidula Jayaswal (ed.), *Glory of the Kushans: Recent Discoveries and Interpretation*, Aryan Books International, Delhi, 2012, p.163.

BUDDHA'S CONNECTION WITH GANDHARA ◆ 7

in Gandhara but all along the Uttarapath—the highway running along the foothills of the Himalayas from Rajgriha to Sravasti and leading to Taxila and onwards to different cities of Gandhara.

The expatriated Sakyans became kings of different regions of Gandhara and their rule continued uninterrupted up to the time when Xuanzang visited Gandhara[17] and mentioned the country of Himotolo. This leads us to the possibility that the expatriated Sakyans were absorbed in their own kingdom in Gandhara and this was the reason that the Buddha himself visited Gandhara to meet his clansmen.

Xuanzang relates the story of the fugitive Sakyan and how he became king of Udyayana (present-day Swat, in Pakistan) after killing the ruling king.[18] The expatriation of the Sakyans to Gandhara followed the attack on Kapilavastu by Virudhaka. Four Sakyans were engaged in ploughing their field between the watercourses and offered resistance to the warring army of Virudhaka and scattered them. In doing so however, the four brave Sakyans were punished and banished by their clansmen from Kapilavastu for bringing disgrace on the Sakyan family by acting 'cruelly and impetuously and without patience to kill and slay'.[19]

These banished Sakyans went to the north to the 'Snowy Mountains'; one became the king of Bamiyan, one of Udyayana, one of Himotolo and one of Sambi. These kings transmitted their kingly authority from generation to generation without any interruption.

The importance of Gandhara can be gauged from the fact that the fourth patriarch of the Buddhist Sangha, the great Sanakavasa, sometimes identified with Yasa,[20] who came a 100 years after Buddha, also lived in a monastery at Bamiyan. His begging bowl and *sanghati*

---

[17] Bidari, Kapilvastu: *The World of Siddhartha*, p.164.
[18] Samuel Beal, *Si-Yu-Ki: Buddhist Records of the Western World*, Book III, Low Price Publications, Delhi, 1884, pp.128–31, p.133.
[19] Bidari, Kapilvastu, p.164. See also, Samuel Beal, *Si-Yu-Ki: Buddhist Records of the Western World*, Book IV, Low Price Publications, Delhi, 1884, pp.20–21.
[20] Samuel Beal, *Si-Yu-Ki: Buddhist Records of the Western World*, Book I, Low Price Publications, Delhi, 1884, p.53 n.

(monastic robe) were seen by Xuanzang when he visited the Bamiyan monastery.[21]

SAKYAN KING OF SWAT

If Xuanzang's story is to be believed, Buddha visited his clansmen in Swat just before his death at Kusinagar.[22] After the death of the Sakya king in Swat, his son succeeded under the name of Uttarasena. Immediately after he came to power, his mother lost her sight. On returning from the subjugation of the Naga Apalala from Nagarhara, Buddha is said to have alighted in the palace of Uttarasena who was out hunting. Buddha preached a short sermon to his mother. Having heard the sermon from the mouth of the holy one, she recovered her sight insantly.

Buddha spoke to Uttarsena's mother:

This son of yours belongs to my family; he need only hear the truth to believe it and understand it. If he were not my relative I would remain to instruct his heart, but now I go. On his return, tell him that Tathagata has gone from this to Kusinagara (Keu-shi), where between the Sala trees he is about to die, and let your son come for a share of the relics to honour them.[23]

On returning from hunting and having heard these words, the king uttered cries of lamentation, and fell prostrate on the ground motionless. Coming to himself, he collected his cortege and went to the twin-trees, where Buddha had already died. Then the kings of the other countries treated him scornfully, and were unwilling to give him a share of the much-prized relics they were taking to their own countries. On seeing this, a great assembly of devas acquainted them with the Buddha's wishes, at which the kings divided the relics equally among themselves, beginning with Uttarsena.

---

[21] Beal, *Si-Yu-Ki*, Book I, pp.52–53.
[22] Beal, *Si-Yu-Ki*, Book III, p.128, p.131, pp.132–133.
[23] Beal, *Si-Yu-Ki*, Book III, p.128, p.131, pp.132–133.

SAKYAN SCHOLARS FROM SWAT

Monks Vimoksasena and Subhakarsimha were scholars belonging to the Sakyan families from Swat. Both travelled to China to translate Buddhist texts into Chinese. Vimoksasena was the son of the king of Udyayana and went to China with Gautama Prajnaruci and translated Buddhist texts in AD 541. Subhakarsimha reached Ch'ang-ngan in AD 716 by the Central Asian route, translated five works between AD 716 and AD 724 and remained in China till his death in AD 740 at the age of 99. Sinologist P.C. Bagchi informs us about another Sakyan scholar Buddhabhadra, who claimed descent from the Sakya family of Kapilavastu, and reached South China in AD 421 and stayed most of the time at Nanking.[24]

BUDDHA'S GANDHAKUTI

Is it no coincidence that Buddha's residence at all the rainy season retreats retained the name of Gandhara in some way. Gandhara, which is believed to have derived from Sanskrit, and literally means perfumed, was represented in the *gandhakutis* of Buddha wherever he resided.

Gandhakuti, the hut of fragrance at Jetavana Vihara, was the name given to the special apartment occupied by the Buddha and was used later in reference to his other residences as well. Gandhakuti of Lumbini (Mayadevi Temple) is the main sacred spot of the archaeological garden. Structural remains have identified its antiquity from Pre-Mauryan to Pala Sena period (approximately up to the twelfth century AD.[25] Likewise, we learn of the Mula-Gandhakuti of Sarnath, the Vajrasana-vrahad-Gadhakuti of Bodhgaya and the *gandhakutis* on the Griddhakuta Hill at Rajgir and that of the Ghositrama Monastery at Kausambi.

---

[24] Bagchi, *India and China*, p. 58, p.258 and p.275.
[25] Basant Bidari, *Lumbini: A Haven of Sacred Refuge*, Hill Side Press, Kathmandu, 2002, p.117.

JATAKAS SET IN GANDHARA

Whether during his life or in earlier incarnations, Buddha had lived in the region of Gandhara, where many a Jataka stories had taken roots. Travel records of Chinese pilgrim Xuanzang contain anecdotes about the Buddha travelling to the region of Gandhara where his Sakyan kins lived. He also mentions several stories of the Buddha and bodhisattvas that have their setting in Gandhara. For instance, the stories of Dipankar Buddha and Naga Gopala, Chandraprabha who cut off his head, Raja Sibi, Sarvadata Raja, Kshanti Rishi, Sudana, Ekasringa rishi, Samaka Jataka and the Mother of Demons, Hariti—all these are set in Gandhara. Most Buddhist stories mentioned were carved in stone by the artistes of Gandhara and the mystery of the 'Begging Bowl' of the Buddha was also set in Gandhara.

All this indicates that Buddha had a close connection with Gandhara where lay his ancestors and, where many of his clansmen were settled. In the eighth century AD, Sakyan scholars from Gandhara are known to have visited China for translation work.

FOREST ASCETICS OF GANDHARA

Another view in favour of the Buddha visiting Gandhara is that like Sarnath where ascetics congregated to discuss philosophy, Gandhara too was the land of great thinkers and philosophers. It was renowned for its forest wanderers, debaters and researchers who debated and ideated about the origin of matter, evolution and the concept of God. Scholars from the East travelled along the foothills of the Himalayas to participate in debates or study under learned teachers of Gandhara. Many scholars worked on new theories of existence and natural phenomenon and developed their philosophical thought.

It was thus natural for the Buddha to propagate his doctrine of Middle Path with Gandharan philosophers. In *Indian Buddhism*, A.K. Warder writes that scholar Uddalaka, who probably lived around the ninth century BC, worked out his philosophy in the region of Kubha (present-day Kabul), the most ancient centre of Vedic tradition.[26] He propounded the theory of evolution and natural science, elaborating that there is no supernatural, external agency that gave rise to everything in the universe. He further says:

> The original matter of the universe, the 'being' itself out of which everything comes and back into which everything goes…The laws of gods give way to natural law, a concept which becomes all powerful later, when Buddhism and other extra-Vedic philosophy develop.[27]

The Buddhist text *Uddalaka-Jataka* (No. 487) also mentions that Uddalaka journeyed to Takshashila (present-day Taxila), and studied there under the guidance of his guru, Vyasa. In the tradition of wandering scholars who went around the country engaging in debates and discussions, Uddalaka too participated in discourses held in the far-off Gandhara and other northern regions.[28]

Around the sixth century BC, Greek historian Herodotus mentions the ascetics of Gandhara as 'another set of Indians' whose customs are very different. He further mentions how they refuse to put any live animal to death, they sow no corn and have no dwelling houses. Vegetables are their only food. 'There is a plant which grows wild in their country bearing seeds [possibly wild rice] and having boiled it, calyx and all, to use it for food.'[29]

Between the fourth and third century BC, Megasthanes, in his book *Indica*, wrote about the worshippers of the Buddha. He referred to the ascetics he saw wandering in the north-western kingdom of Chandragupta Maurya in Gandhara as *sarmanas*.

---

[26] A.K. Warder, *Indian Buddhism*, Motilal Banarsidass Publishers, Delhi, 1991, p.239.
[27] Warder, *Indian Buddhism*, pp.32–33.
[28] Warder, *Indian Buddhism*, p.27.
[29] Herodotus, *The Histories*, George Rawlinson (trans.), Everyman's Library, USA, 1910 (1997), pp.271–73. See also: Vincent Willian, *The Commerce and Navigation of the Ancients in the Indian Ocean*, Vol. I: The Voyage of Nearchus, Asian Educational Service, Delhi, 1998, p.274, st.100.

Connected with the Sarmanai are the philosophers called the Hylobioi who neither live in cities nor even in houses. They clothe themselves with the bark of trees, and subsist upon acorns, and drink water by lifting it to their mouth with their hands. They neither marry nor beget children. Among the Indians are those philosophers also who follow the precepts of Boutta [Buddha] whom they honour as a god on account of his extraordinary sanctity.[30]

Thus, it can be said that Buddhists were found to be living in Gandhara in the fourth century BC.

This was also the time of Alexander's campaign in Gandhara. It is said of Alexander that wherever he went, he was in the habit of seeking out the local intelligentsia in order to understand cultures different from his own. In India, just as he had done in Egypt and Babylon, the king was anxious to meet philosophers about whom he had heard so much during his two-month stay at Taxila.[31] While on his march along the corridor in the Kabul Valley and across the region of the Indus, Alexander encountered some wandering ascetics in the thickly wooded jungles of the Uttarapath near Taxila. He had dialogues with them on the nature of life and God. Alexander was so fascinated by the ascetics who roamed about naked, carefree in the jungles that he enticed one such ascetic to come away with him on his return journey to Greece.

The story goes that when Alexander arrived in Taxila, he saw the Indian gymnosophists and desired to have one of these men brought into his presence, because he admired their endurance. The eldest of these sophists, with whom 15 others lived as disciples, was named Dandamis (Mandanis).

When Alexander learnt about such sophists, he sent Onesikrates to fetch Dandamis. Messengers from Alexander invited Dandamis,

---

[30] John W. McCrindle, *Ancient India as Described by Megasthanese and Arrian*, Fragment XLIII: Of Philosophers of India, Munshiram Manoharlal Publishers, Delhi, 2008), p.105.

[31] Alan Fildes and Joann Fletcher, *Alexander: The Great Son of God*, Duncan Baird Publishers, London, 2004, pp.122–23.

the chief of the ascetics, to go to the 'son of Zeus'—meaning Alexander—with the promise of gifts if he complied and threats of punishment, if he refused. But Dandamis, without as much as even raising his head, refused to go, saying:

> Alexander was not the son of Zeus for he was not so much as master of the larger half of the world. As for himself, he wanted none of the gifts of a man whose desires nothing could satiate; and as for his threats, he feared them not: for if he lived, India would supply him with food enough, and if he died, he would be delivered from the body of flesh now afflicted with age, and would be transported to a better and purer life. Alexander expressed admiration for the man and let him have his own way.[32]

Alexander, however won over Kalanos, one of the sophists of Taxila, also a disciple of Dandamis, who followed Alexander on his return to the west. Dandamis and his other disciple sophists, however, condemned Kalanos for having gone to serve a master other than God. 'Kalanos is despised and trodden upon by us and contemptuously cast out as unprofitable.'[33]

Alexander and Kalanos remained close friends until the philosopher's death in Susa in 324 BC.[34] It is said that when Kalanos was taken ill at the end of his life he burnt himself on a funeral pyre in the presence of the whole Macedonian army without evincing any symptom of pain. His last prophetic words to Alexander 'we shall meet in Babylon' came true when Alexander himself died of severe infection from his wounds at Babylon.[35]

Later, also in the fourth century BC, the Greek envoy Megasthenes was sent by Seleukos Nikator on a mission to Sandrakottos

---

[32] McCrindle, *Ancient India as Described by Megasthanese and Arrian*, Fragment XLIV: Of Kalanos and Mandanis, p.107.
[33] McCrindle, *Ancient India as Described by Megasthanese and Arrian*, Fragment LV, p.123.
[34] Fildes and Fletcher, *Alexander: The Great Son of God*, p.122.
[35] Valerio Massimo Manfredi, *Alexander*, Vol. 3: The End of the Earth (Translated from Italian by Iain Halliday), Pan Books, London, 2002, pp.532–33.

(Chandragupta, the Mauryan emperor of Ancient India whose capital was at Pataliputra in present-day Patna). He was probably sent after the peace treaty had been signed between Seleukos and Chandragupta *c.*303 BC[36] and friendship had been struck between the two kings. Megasthenes is said to have passed through Gandhara not once but frequently as Seleukos's ambassador.[37] He took the route through the Kabul Valley, crossed the Indus and went through Punjab. He reached Pataliputra by travelling along the Royal Road,[38] which was the then Mauryan highway or Uttarapath, and is the present-day Grand Trunk Road.

Several scholars think that the *sarmanas* of Megasthenes are the equivalent of the Sanskrit *sramanas*. Historian Radhakumud Mookerji thinks that they were probably brahmins of the third and fourth *asramas* of life, and he mentions them as Parivrajakas and Samnyasis.[39] But, according to German Indologist E. Hultzsch, they were Buddhist monks.[40]

In *The Commerce between Roman Empire and India*, E.H. Wharmington writes that another forest ascetic or gymnosophist called Zarmanos had travelled from the Indus region, neighbouring Barygaza, to Athens where, like Kalanos in Susa, he committed himself to the flames. It is said that several Indian embassies were received by the first Roman emperor Augustus around the first century BC. In this regard, one Nicolaos of Damascus, met at Antioch in Syria three members of an Indian embassy sent by a 'sovereign of six hundred kings, named Poros or Pandion', with a letter granting to Augustus

---

[36] Vincent Smith, *History of India*, Vol. II, Cosimo Classics, New York, 2008, p.108.
[37] McCrindle, *Ancient India as Described by Megasthanese and Arrian*, p.14.
[38] McCrindle, *Ancient India as Described by Megasthanese and Arrian*, p.15.
[39] Hazra, *The Rise and Decline of Buddhism in India*, p.34, citing Radhakumud Mookerji, *Chandragupta Maurya and His Times*, Meyer Lectures, Madras University, 1943. See also, McCrindle, *Ancient India as Described by Megasthanese and Arrian*, Fragment XLIII: Of the Philosophers of India, pp.104–05.
[40] Hazra, *The Rise and Decline of Buddhism in India*, p.34, citing Sten Konow Corpus Inscriptionum Indicarum, I, Introduction, I. See also, McCrindle, *Ancient India as Described by Megasthanese and Arrian*, Fragment XLIII: Of the Philosophers of India, pp.104–05.

free passage through Indian territory. The *sramana* Zarmanos had accompanied this embassy.[41]

During my travel, I did not meet an ascetic. Not the kind who walks around the woods naked and subsists on the bare necessities that nature provides. Though I am no Alexander of Macedon, my fascination for these ascetics is as immense as his. Interestingly, a captivating Gandharan relief in stone, dated from the second–third century AD, which is on display at the Archaeological Museum of Milan, is a telling commentary on the life of such forest ascetics who roamed the jungles of Gandhara. Perhaps the stone carver drew from the description provided by the Greek envoy Megasthanes.

---

[41] E.H. Warmington, *The Commerce between the Roman Empire and India*, Munshiram Manoharlal Publishers, Delhi, 1995, pp.35–36. See also McCrindle, *Ancient India as Described by Megasthanese and Arrian*, Fragment XLV Arr. VIII. ii. 3–9, p.116.

Chapter 2

BUDDHISM IN GANDHARA

Buddhism as a religion became entrenched in Gandhara under the patronage of rulers from the period of the Mauryan Emperor Asoka in the third century BC to the period of the Indo-Greek kings Demetrius and Menander in the second century BC and finally the Kushan King Kanishka in the first–second century AD. Thus, a period of 500 years beginning from the third century BC to the second century AD is considered crucial for understanding the massive propagation of Buddhism in Gandhara and its spread to the countries of Central Asia and China.

However, it is on record that the first stupas were built in the region of Balkh, in northern Afghanistan, during the lifetime of the Buddha himself, and Pukkusati and Rudrayana, who were rulers of Gandhara and the Indus region, became interested in Buddhism as early as the sixth century BC.

During the rule of Chandragupta Maurya in the fourth century BC, Buddhist monks were already scouring the jungles of Gandhara, which is where the Greek historian and diplomat Megasthanes first saw them. Megasthanes was travelling from Arachosia (present-day Kandahar) along the Royal Road to Pataliputra as an envoy to the court of Chandragupta Maurya in 303 BC, following a treaty between Chandragupta Maurya and the Greek ruler Seleucus I Nicator. Megasthanes writes in *Indica*, his famous book on Ancient India, 'Among the Indians are those philosophers also who follow the precepts of Boutta [Buddha] whom they honour as a god on account of his extraordinary sanctity.'[1]

By the early centuries of our era, hundreds of viharas and *mahaviharas* came up along the river valleys of Gandhara and

---

[1] John W. McCrindle, *Ancient India as Described by Megasthanese and Arrian*, Munshiram Manoharlal Publishers, Delhi, 2008 (3rd ed.), p.105.

neighbouring valleys of Murghab and Oxus. From the viharas emerged missionaries and scholars who, armed with the knowledge of Buddhist texts and languages, treaded their way along the Asian trade routes, disseminating the faith and compiling, commenting and translating Buddhist texts in the language of the people.

From the monasteries of the Murghab Valley emerged the great Parthian scholar, An Shih-kao or Lokottama, who abdicated the Arsacid royal throne and reached China c.AD 148. Apart from him, there were also other Parthian monks—'unrivalled scholars' of Sanskrit and Chinese—such as An Hsuan (second century AD) and An Fachin (third century AD).[2] From the Oxus Valley emerged great scholars such as Dharmasinha, Prajnakara, Dharmapriya and Dharmakara whom the Chinese pilgrim Xuanzang personally met in AD 629.[3]

There are references to several monks from Kabul who translated Buddhist canonical works into Chinese around the fourth century AD. Among these, a few notable names are Gautam Sanghdeva (AD 383), Vimalaksha (AD 406), Sanghabhuti (AD 381–385), Punyatrata (AD 399–415) and Dharmayasa (AD 407–415).[4]

Indologist P.C. Bagchi brings to us the names of several other reputed Gandharan scholars from the third to the eighth century AD. Among these are Buddhabhadra, Buddhatrata, Buddhapala, Danapala, Narendrayasa, Dharmagupta, Meghasikha, Prajna, Vimoksasena and Vinitaruci.[5] Kumaralata from Taxila was founder of the Sautrantika School of Buddhism in the third century AD. He wrote many treatises including the famous *Kalpnamanditika*.[6] As late as the sixth century AD, one of the most sought-after scholars from Gandhara was monk

---

[2] B.N. Puri, *Buddhism in Central Asia*, Motilal Banarsidass Publishers, Delhi, 2000, p.101. See also, Saroj Kumar Chaudhuri, *Lives of Early Buddhist Monks*, Abha Prakashan, Delhi, 2008, pp.47–56; P.C. Bagchi, *India and China*, Saraswat Library, Kolkata, 1981, p.113.

[3] Samuel Beal (trans.), *Hwui Li: The Life of Hiuen-Tsiang*, Low Price Publications 2001, p.48 and p.51.

[4] Puri, *Buddhism in Central Asia*, pp.103–04.

[5] Bagchi, *India and China*, pp.255–77. See also, P.C. Bagchi, *India and Central Asia*, National Council of Education, Kolkata, 1955, p.33.

[6] Bagchi, *India and Central Asia*, p.43.

Jinagupta, who went to China in AD 557. He lived among the Turks till AD 582 and propagated the faith.[7] Under royal patronage, the great monastic centres of Gandhara, especially those at Kabul, Bamiyan, Peshawar, Mardan and Taxila functioned as universities and renowned scholars resided there. Buddhist manuscripts written in Kharosthi script that was prevalent in Gandhara, have been recovered from several places along the Asian trade routes. Fragments of manuscripts continue to be unearthed in Bamiyan. The texts dating from about the first century AD or even earlier are believed to be the oldest Buddhist manuscripts yet discovered. The enormous volume of manuscripts recovered can be gauged from the fact that many libraries around the world are engaged in researching on the subject of these manuscripts and the various Buddhist sects which contributed to their writings. One such collection, the Schoyen Collection, adorns the library of the National Museum of Afghanistan at Kabul today.

MAURYAN EMPEROR ASOKA IN GANDHARA

In the third century CE, Mauryan Emperor Asoka, who was well aware of the volatile conditions of the Northwest Frontier regions (now in Pakistan) that formed a part of Gandhara, was eager to spread the doctrine of peace and non-violence in these lands.

Asoka was well aware of the prevailing conditions in Gandhara during the fourth and third centuries BC since the rule of his grandfather Chandragupta Maurya. Asoka was in charge of this crucial frontier province being stationed at the headquarters of Taxila, before he came to the throne after Bindusara. He had been sent there as viceroy by Bindusara to subdue a revolt by the Taxilians, which could not be suppressed by his brother Susima. Asoka is believed to have suppressed the revolt without the use of arms.[8]

---

[7] Margit Koves, *Buddhism among the Turks of Central Asia*, International Academy of Indian Culture and Aditya Prakashan, Delhi, 2009, p.9. See also, Bagchi, *India and China*, p.59.
[8] Radhakumud Mookerji, *Asoka*, Motilal Banarsidass Publishers, Delhi, 2007, p.51.

Historical records confirm that a large foreign population of Greeks and Persians was already living in Gandharan cities since pre-Alexandrian times. Herodotus mentions in *The Histories* that the Ionian states of Asia Minor together with the north-west regions of India were included in the list of the 20 satrapies of Persian Achaemenid ruler Darius in the sixth century BC. We read of the Gandharians in the seventh satrapy and Indians in the twentieth satrapy from whom Darius derived his revenues. Herodotus also informs that Indian troops formed part of the expedition of Xerxes I against Greeks in the battles of Thermopylae (480 BC) and Plataiae (479 BC).[9]

Names of some Greek cities founded in the region of Gandhara have come down to us, such as Alexandria in Arachosia (present-day Kandahar) and Alexandria in Caucasus (present-day Begram)—both in Afghanistan today. Alexander laid the foundation of two new cities by the Jhelum River; he named them Nicaea (after his victory over Porus) and Alexandria Bucephala (in fond remembrance of his faithful horse, Bucephala).[10] A third city along the Indus was Alexandria-in-Opiene located at the confluence of the Indus and the Acesines rivers. Then, there were also the towns of Sogda and Pattala on the Indus.[11]

Apart from the Greeks and Persians, the inhabitants of the Greek cities of Gandhara were also warriors who had accompanied Alexander on his Indian campaign of the fourth century BC. As a result, there was very close interaction between the Greeks, Persians and Indians bringing about a new spirit of cultural exchange.

History tells us that the rule of satraps posted by Alexander in the various provinces of Kabul and the Indus Valley was short-lived owing to Alexander's early death. Yet, according to historians A.H. Dani and P. Bernard, Alexander succeeded in 'bridging the rift between the Greek and the Persian worlds' and bringing 'the two

---

[9] Herodotus, *The Histories* (Translated by George Rawlinson), Everyman's Library, USA, 1910 (rev. ed. 1997), pp.271–272, p.582 and p.685.
[10] Alan Fildes and Joann Fletcher, *Alexander: The Great Son of God*, Duncan Baird Publishers, London, 2004, p.117.
[11] Fildes and Fletcher, Alexander, p.123.

under one imperial system'.[12]

After Alexander, the House of Seleucus sent regular embassies to the Mauryan court at Pataliputra and both Chandragupta and his son and successor, Bindusara, had Greek ambassadors in their courts— Megasthenes to Chandragupta and Daimachos from Antiochos I (the successor of King Seleucus of Syria) to Bindusara. Ptolemy Philadelphus, the Greek ruler of Egypt, also sent an embassy to the court of the Mauryas.[13]

The presence of foreigners in India was noticed by Megasthenes, who was the ambassador of Seleucus I Nicator at the Mauryan court in 302–298 BC. He tells us of the existence of a separate department in Chandragupta's government that looked after foreigners. Megasthanes also mentions in *Indica* about a board of officers set up to look into the affairs of foreigners—presumably Persians and Greeks. They were responsible for their lodging, arrangements for their daily lives, entertainment and property, and they also escorted them when they left the country.[14] Bindusara, the son and successor of Chandragupta and Asoka's father, even sent a letter to King Antiochos I of Syria, requesting figs, sweet wine and a sophist to teach him how to debate.[15]

ASOKA'S CONQUEST BY *DHAMMA*

It is said that soon after the bloody war for the conquest of Kalinga in 262 BC, Asoka was filled with remorse at the horrifying massacre of people and vowed to renounce conquest by arms. Instead, he launched his 'Conquest by *Dhamma*'. This was a concerted campaign for the diffusion of *Dhamma* by having the *Dhamma* instructions

---

[12] A.H. Dani and P. Bernard, *Alexander and His Successors in Central Asia*, Vol. II: History of Civilizations of Central Asia, UNESCO, New Delhi, 1994 and Motilal Banarsidass Publishers, Delhi, 1999, p.87.
[13] R.C. Majumdar, *Ancient India*, Motilal Banarsidass Publishers, Delhi, 2013, p.106.
[14] McCrindle, *Ancient India as Described by Megasthanese and Arrian*, p.87.
[15] Ranabir Chakravarti, *Exploring Early India up to c. AD 1300*, Primus Books, Delhi, 2016, p.152.

engraved on rocks and pillars throughout his empire. In addition to this, he appointed a new category of high officials known as *Dhamma Mahamatras*, whose primary duty was to preach and propagate *Dhamma* among the people of all faiths and religions.[16]

It was after the Third Buddhist Council that Asoka decided to send religious missions to various countries to popularize the *Dhamma*. The land of the Yavanas (Ionian Greeks), Gandhara, Kashmir and the Himalayan regions in the north were among the recipients of Asokan missions. Of the foreign kings, whose dominions thus received the Buddha's message of peace and non-violence, five are mentioned in the inscriptions of Asoka by name. They are Antiochus Theos, king of Syria and Western Asia; Ptolemy Philadelphus of Egypt; Antigonus Gonatas of Macedonia; Magas of Cyrene and Alexander of Epirus.[17]

In addition to the missions, Asoka also put up his 'Dhamma Edicts' (also known as Asokan Edicts) on rocks and pillars. Historian Irfan Habib mentions 14 Asokan inscriptions found at eight different places in Gandhara. Two were found at Shahbazgarhi (Peshawar district) and Mansehra (Hazara district), respectively. Two short inscriptions, written in Aramaic script, have also been found. Of these, one is in Taxila and the other in Jalalabad district of Afghanistan. A bilingual inscription, written in Greek and Aramaic, has been found on a rock at Shar-i-Kuna near Kandahar in Afghanistan. Another similar record has also been found in the same locality. Four Asokan Edicts were found in 1969 at a site between the villages of Shalatak and Oargha in the province of Lamghan in Afghanistan. One of these is in Aramaic, and the other is in 'an old Indic language' (perhaps Prakrit) written in the Kharosthi script.[18]

---

[16] D.C. Ahir, *Buddhist Sites and Shrines in India: History, Art and Architecture*, Sri Satguru Publications, Delhi, 2003, p.69.
[17] P.V. Bapat, *2500 Years of Buddhism, Chapter: Asoka and the Expansion of Buddhism*, Publications Division, Ministry of Information and Broadcasting, Government of India, 2012, p.52.
[18] Irfan Habib and Vivekanand Jha, *Mauryan India*, The People's History of India series (no.5), Tulika Books, Delhi, 2013, pp.60–61 and p.142.

Radhakumud Mookerji opines that a bilingual inscription in Greek and Aramaic, brought to light in 1958 during some excavations in Kandahar, suggests the Greeks who settled there had good knowledge of Asoka's *Dhamma*.[19] Thus, it may be said that Greeks were already settled in the eastern portion of the Syrian Emperor Seleucus' empire comprising the regions of Gedrosia (present-day Baluchistan), Arachosia (present-day Kandahar), Aria (present-day Herat) and Paropamisadae (present-day Hindukush), when it was annexed by the Indian king Chandragupta Maurya *c.*304 BC.[20]

As a result of Asoka's efforts, Buddhism 'which until then was a small sect confined only to particular localities...' was transformed into a world religion, writes historian Mohammad Ashraf Khan.[21] Asoka's *Dhamma Mahamatra* engaged with all sects among the Greeks, Iranians, Gandharans, Rastrikas, Pitinikas and other kingdoms from the West. Asoka expressed the wish that all sects should live everywhere and that all sects are to be tolerated and encouraged to spread everywhere in the world.[22]

Asokan Rock Edicts at Shahbazgarhi RE XII speaks of the commendable value of 'concord.' According this edict:

> How should there be the growth of the essential elements of all religious sects...the root of it is restraint of speech, that is, there should not be honour of one's own sect and condemnation of others' sect without any ground... Hence concord alone is commendable, in the sense that all should listen and be willing to listen to the doctrines professed by others.[23]

---

[19] Radhakumud Mookerji, Asoka, p.283.
[20] Mookerji, *Asoka*, p.286.
[21] Muhammad Ashraf Khan and Abdul Ghafoor Lone, *Gandhara Geography, Antiquity, Art and Personalities*, Department of Archaeology and Museums, Pakistan, 2012, p.57.
[22] A.K. Warder, *Indian Buddhism*, Motilal Banarsidass Publishers, Delhi, 1991, p.258.
[23] Mookerji, *Asoka*, pp.158–61.

ASOKAN STUPAS

To make Buddhism physically accessible to the entire population, Asoka is said to have built 84,000 pagodas all over his empire.[24] Of these, many Asokan stupas were seen and recorded by the Chinese pilgrim Xuanzang in the seventh century AD when he passed through Gandhara while on his way to India through Nagarhara (present-day Jalalabad) and Sakala (present-day Sialkot). A reading of the Books II, III and IV of the *Si Yu Ki: Buddhist Records of the Western World* mentions as many as 18 colossal stupas ranging between 200 and 300 feet in height that were built by Asoka over the relics of the Buddha as early as the third century BC in Gandhara.[25] These are located at Nagarhara, Pushkalavati (present-day Charsadda), Udyayana (present-day Swat), Taxila, Simhapura, Kashmir and also at Sialkot.

Asoka was instrumental in simplifying the teachings of Buddhism into stories and artistic presentation in sculpture and painting, along with the use of symbols such as lotus, tree, wheel and pagoda while representing the life of the Buddha.[26]

Many historians have commented that Asoka's *Dhamma* was the *Dhamma* of the Buddha. Buddhologist D.C. Ahir says, 'Like a pious Buddhist, Asoka revers the Buddha, adopts the Dhamma as a way of life, and shows respect and reverence to the Sangha.'[27]

INDO-GREEKS KINGS DEMETRIUS AND MENANDER

History informs that after the decline of Mauryans, Greeks from Bactria conquered Gandhara and Punjab in 185–180 BC, and an independent Indo-Greek kingdom was formed. Demetrius (Devmitra) and Menander (Milind) were the famous Indo-Greek kings who had their capital cities at Pushkalavati, Taxila and later at Sagala. Since

---

[24] Warder, *Indian Buddhism*, p.266.
[25] Beal, *Si-Yu-Ki: Buddhist Records of the Western World*.
[26] Warder, *Indian Buddhism*, p.266.
[27] D.C. Ahir, *Asoka the Great*, B.R. Publishing Corporation, Delhi, 1995, p.35 and p.69.

both Demetrius and Menander were interested in Buddhism,[28] they contributed to its expansion in Afghanistan, Bactria and neighbouring Parthia.[29] According to Indologist B.N. Puri, the kingdom unified under one political state the north Indian regions, Afghanistan and several parts of western Turkestan (located in present-day Kazakhstan), making it congenial for the Buddhist missionaries to convey the message of the Buddha outside the boundaries of this kingdom.[30] The existence of the Bactrian Greek kingdom is corroborated by the archaeological traces of the Greek cities of Ai Khanoum (in northern Afghanistan) and Kampyrtepa (in southern Uzbekistan) in the Oxus river valley. Interestingly, both have been designated 'Alexandria on Oxus'.

According to British historian W.W. Tarn, Demetrius is supposed to have attacked India to punish the Brahmin Sunga ruler, Pusyamitra Sunga for his anti-Buddhist activities and persecution of Buddhist monks. Demetrius was known as Dharmamita—his name modified to include the word 'Dharma' and thereby signify 'Friend of Justice'. Dharmamita was reminded of (or was akin to) the ideal 'King of Justice or Dharmaraja'.[31] Demetrius punished the brahmin ruler for killing of Buddhists. Thus, the Indo-Greek Demetrius became known as Dharmamita.

It is generally accepted that Demetrius was a devotee of the Buddha and certain symbols like the stupa on the coins of Agathocles, as also legends on the coins of Menander are in agreement with the theory of infiltration of Buddhism in the realm of Indo-Greek or Bactrian rulers.[32]

A series of square bronze coins from the period 190–180 BC issued by the Indo-Greek king Agathocles Dikaios—believed to be son of Demetrius—was recovered, with Prakrit legend and Buddhist

---

[28] Puri, *Buddhism in Central Asia*, p.91.
[29] Puri, *Buddhism in Central Asia*, p.91.
[30] Puri, *Buddhism in Central Asia*, pp.91–92.
[31] W.W. Tarn, *The Greeks in Bactria and India*, Munshiram Manoharlal Publishers, Delhi, 1980, p.175 and p.178.
[32] Puri, *Buddhism in Central Asia*, p.91.

symbols of a stupa on the reverse and a tree in a rail on the obverse is believed to be the Bodhi Tree and its enclosure, such as at Bodhgaya.[33]

MILINDPANHA OR 'DISCOURSES WITH MENANDER'

After Demetrius, Menander is believed to have embraced Buddhism following his discourse with the Buddhist philosopher Nagasena. The *Milindpanha* or 'Discourses with Menander' is a Pali work, dated around the first century BC, records dialogues between King Milind, identified with the Indo-Greek king Menander and the elder Buddhist monk Nagasena. According to historian W.W. Tarn, the *Milindpanha* is the greatest testimony to Menander's legendary fame.[34]

Apart from celebrating the splendid city of Sagala, the *Milindpanha* immortalizes the Indo-Greek king Menander, his dialogue with the monk Nagasena regarding the Buddhist doctrine and his conversion to the faith of the Buddha. Nagasena's answers 'plunged to the hidden depths of Vinaya and of Abhidhamma' and unravelled the 'meshes of the Suttas' net', thus resolving the doubts of the king.[35]

According to historian Demetrios Th. Vassiliades, 'If the Greek king was not himself actually a member of the Buddhist Order, he was at least so great a benefactor that the community looked upon him as one of their own.'[36]

During the Indo-Greek period in the Northwest Frontier regions in the second century BC, several monasteries came up in Gandhara as residences for monks. Under Menander's rule, we learn of the monastery of Milindvihara[37] in Sagala near Gujranwala, where the monk Nagasena resided with five hundred *bhikshus*. The text *Milindpanha* too was set in the region of Gandhara and it portrays a model of the beautiful second-century BC city of Sagala. This was

---

[33] Puri, *Buddhism in Central Asia*, p.91.
[34] Tarn, *The Greeks in Bactria and India*, p.268.
[35] T.W. Rhys Davids (translated from Pali), *The Questions of King Milinds: The Milindpanha*, Columbia, USA, 2018. pp.9–10.
[36] Vassiliades, *The Greeks in India: A Survey in Philosophical Understanding*, p.60.
[37] Hazra, *The Rise and Decline of Buddhism in India*, p.63.

the time when Hellenistic artists put themselves in the service of Buddhism, a faith that they had chosen to adopt, and produced art that was illustrative of this religion.[38] The large population of Greeks who lived in Gandhara favoured Buddhism and greatly contributed to the spread of the religion. The Indianized names of many Yonaka, or Greek, monks and donor inscriptions attest to this process. The Yonaka Dhammarakkhita Thera, who is remembered as the teacher of Punabba-Sukutumbikaputta-Tissa, preached the *Aggikkandopama Sutta* and is reported to have converted 37,000 people to Buddhism.[39]

Charles Eliot is of the opinion that the Greco-Bactrians who entered Gandhara in the second century BC were believed to have already been familiar with Buddhism, owing to the missionary activities of Asoka during the third century BC. They had no problem in adopting Buddhism as their religion as it had no prejudice of race or class and was a strong creed.[40]

The association of Greeks with Buddhism in the Gandhara region in the two centuries preceding the Christian era is also proved by the Ceylonese chronicle, *Mahavamsa*. When the king Duttagamini founded the great stupa 'Mahathupa' in Anuradhapur in Sri Lanka, sometime in the middle of the second century BC, the Yona Mahadhammarkkhita Thera, along with 30,000 monks, came from Alasanda to the foundation ceremony. From the exaggerated number of monks, we might infer that Buddhism was popular in the city during this time.[41] Alasanda is mentioned in *Mahavamsa* as the city of the Yonas[42] and identified in the notes of Wilhelm Geiger as probably the town founded by the Macedonian king Alexander in

---

[38] Bagchi, *India and Central Asia*, pp.181–93.
[39] Vassiliades, *The Greeks in India: A Survey in Philosophical Understanding*, Munshiram Manoharlal Publishers, Delhi, 2000, pp.58–60.
[40] Eliot Charles, *Hinduism and Buddhism: An Historical Sketch*, Vol II: Bibliotheca Indo-Buddhica No. 54, Sri Satguru Publications, Delhi, 1988, pp.69–70.
[41] Puri, *Buddhism in Central Asia*, p.93.
[42] Wilhelm Geiger, *The Mahavamsa or The Great Chronicle of Ceylon*, Asian Educational Services, Delhi, 2000, p.194.

the country of the Paropamisadae near Kabul. Puri places Alasanda at Charikar between Panjshir and Kabul rivers.[43]

CONCEPT OF VOTIVE OFFERINGS

The concept of votive offerings or *dana* in the name of the Buddha and prayers for the 'well-being of many' and 'relic worship' prevailed among the Greek population of Gandhara as is clear from epigraphic records of the *Corpus Inscriptionum Indicarum* edited by Sten Konow and mentioned in *The Rise and Decline of Buddhism in India* by Buddhologist K.L. Hazra. Inscriptions pertaining to Greek donors throw light on the development of Buddhism under the patronage of Greek rulers. Names of several Greek donors such as Meridarch Theodorus, Yona Sihadhaya and Yona Dhammadhaya, who gifted to monasteries, are known to us today.[44]

A vase, donated by the Greek official Theodorus, has an inscription in Sanskrit: 'The body of the revered god Sakyamuni is installed by Meridarch Theodorus for the prosperity of many people.'[45] It referred to the idea of the Buddha as a god who has the power to bestow prosperity on the donor and mankind. The vase dated from the late second or early first century BC was discovered in the Swat region of Khyber Pakhtunkhwa and contained Buddhist relics.

A relic of the Buddha, deposited by one Vijayamitra, a vassal of the Indo-Greek king Menander, recorded: 'On the 14th day of the month of Kartikka, in the reign of the Maharaja Menedra... A bodily relic of the Buddha, which is endowed with life...is installed.' Another inscription says 'by Theidora or Theodour, the Dataiputra, [this] tank was caused to be made in honour of all beings in the 113 year on 20th day of Sravana.'[46]

---

[43] Puri, *Buddhism in Central Asia*, p.93.
[44] Hazra, *The Rise and Decline of Buddhism in India*, p.4.
[45] Hazra, *The Rise and Decline of Buddhism in India*, p.64.
[46] Hazra, *The Rise and Decline of Buddhism in India*, p.63.

KUSANA ROYAL PATRONS

The Kusana period (first–third century AD) is considered the golden period for the propagation of Buddhism and Buddhist art not only in Gandhara but also in Central Asia and China. It was a period of great literary, missionary and architectural activity. Kujula Kadphises (r. AD 15–65) has been regarded as the founder of the Kusana kingdom. The Kusanas, belonging to a nomadic Turkish tribe, the Yueh-Chi, established a vast empire in Bactria after vanquishing the Parthians and the Greeks by the first century AD. They ruled over large tracts on both sides of the Hindu Kush mountains including the Northwest Frontier regions of India.[47] Kanishka (r. AD 78–101), the successor of Kadphises II, conquered the whole of north India including Kashmir and Magadha, and his power extended up to the borders of Gobi in Central Asia. He is further credited with the conquest of three rich provinces belonging to China, namely Kashgar, Yarkand and Khotan.[48]

Short epigraphs on copper coins discovered in many places, issued by the Kusana king Kujula Kadphises, give us sufficient evidence that he had embraced Buddhism. The Kharosthi legends on the reverse of some coins have the following inscriptions: *Kusanasa Yanasa Kujula Kaphasa sacha-dhramathidasa* and *Kujula Kasasa Kusana Yav(u)gasa dharmathidasa*, meaning the coin of Kujula Kaphasa, chief or king of the Kusanas, is steadfast in faith.[49]

Kanishka is regarded as the greatest of the Kusana rulers and

---

[47] Majumdar, *Ancient India*, p.122. See also, Khan and Lone, *Gandhara Geography, Antiquity, Art and Personalities*, pp.6–7.
[48] Majumdar, *Ancient India*, p.122. See also, B.S. Upadhyaya, *Some Great Buddhists after Asoka*, in P.V. Bapat (ed.) 2500 Years of Buddhism series, Publications Division, Ministry of Information and Broadcasting, Government of India, 2012, p.167.
[49] J. Harmatta with contributions by B.N. Puri, L. Lelekov, S. Humayun and D.C. Sircar, *Religions in the Kushan Empire*, Vol. II: History of Civilisations of Central Asia, Motilal Banarsidass Publishers, Delhi, 1996 and UNESCO, New Delhi, 1999, pp.317–18. See also, Hazra, *The Rise and Decline of Buddhism in India*, pp.68–73.

a staunch supporter of Buddhism. The Fourth Buddhist Council by Kanishka held *c.* AD 100 was a landmark event in the history of the Buddhism. Convened at Jalandhar or in Kashmir, the council finally put an end to the dissensions that had distracted the Buddhist Order for nearly a century. It concluded with the compilation of the doctrines of Buddhism and writing of the *Mahavibhasa*, a vast commentary based on the Sarvastivada School of Buddhism.[50] As a result, Mahayanism, a liberal and progressive school of Buddhism, flourished in Gandhara. This school laid emphasis, among other things, on the transformation of Buddha into an eternal god. In the visual arts, the Buddha was permitted for the first time to be represented in human form.[51] It was also the first time that Pali gave way to Sanskrit.[52]

The council also opened the way for Buddhist missions to China. The first Indian missionaries, Dharmaraksa and Kasyapa Matanga, went to China during the Kanishka period in the third quarter of the first century AD and lived at the White Horse Monastery in the Chinese capital.[53]

Kanishka's reign also witnessed great literary activity by Buddhist scholars. Numerous scholars of high repute lived at the capital city of Peshawar. Some of these erudite men include Parsva, Vasumitra, Asvaghosa, Sangharaksa, Dharmatrata, Ghosaka and Buddhadeva.

Afghanistan too had several centres of Buddhist studies in the Kusana period as is evident from the Kharosthi inscriptions discovered there. A record from the Khosthi region suggests *Sarvastivada* establishments in Afghanistan, West Punjab and Sind.[54] B.N. Puri also discusses the location of the headquarters of the Sarvastivadins at Nagarhara in Jalalabad in Afghanistan, as mentioned in the 'Lion capital inscription' of the time of Sodasa.[55] *Mahasanghikas* too had

---

[50] Upadhyaya, *Some Great Buddhists after Asoka*, p.167.
[51] Eliot, *Hinduism and Buddhism*, pp.5–6. See also, Hazra, *The Rise and Decline of Buddhism in India*, pp.70–71.
[52] Upadhyaya, *Some Great Buddhists after Asoka*, p.167.
[53] Bagchi, *India and China*, p.37.
[54] Puri, *Buddhism in Central Asia*, p.103.
[55] Puri, *Buddhism in Central Asia*, p.103.

their establishment in Afghanistan as is evident from the Wardak Inscription of year 51 of Huviska, referring to the deposit of the relics of Lord Buddha in the Vagramarega Vihara.[56] Hundreds of stupas and monasteries were erected in various places in Gandhara such as Peshawar, Swat, Mardan, Taxila, Buner, Bajour and eastern Afghanistan.[57] The tallest stupa in Gandhara, more than 600 feet in height, was built by Kanishka at Peshawar.[58] The famous Kanishka casket recovered from Kanishka stupa and showcased at the Peshawar Museum has a series of three seated Buddha figures, attendant worshippers and the figure of Kanishka himself. Many monuments were also created to commemorate the Jatakas.

The Gandhara and Mathura schools of Buddhist art that produced fine images and specimen of the Buddha and bodhisattvas also flourished during the reign of Kanishka.[59] Today, the Kabul, Swat and Indus river valleys are littered with ruins of stupas and monasteries adorned with masterpieces of Gandharan art produced during this period.

In conclusion, it can be said that the establishment of Buddhism in Gandhara was a protracted affair beginning from the third century BC during the rule of Mauryan Emperor Asoka. It saw its zenith during the Kusana rule in first–third century AD, especially during Kanishka's reign when the landscape of Gandhara changed dramatically with hundreds of stupas and monasteries coming up along trade routes. These were not only places of worship but also functioned as schools for composing, teaching, translating Buddhist texts and ateliers of the renowned Gandharan art. This was the also the period when acclaimed scholars from Gandhara travelled to Central Asia and China to disseminate Buddhist teachings.

---

[56] Puri, *Buddhism in Central Asia*, p.103.
[57] Upadhyaya, *Some Great Buddhists after Asoka*, p.167. See also, Hazra, *The Rise and Decline of Buddhism in India*, p.69.
[58] Warder, *Indian Buddhism*, p.345.
[59] Hazra, *The Rise and Decline of Buddhism in India*, p.71.

Chapter 3

ON BUDDHA'S TRAIL IN PAKISTAN

BUS TO LAHORE: THE JOURNEY BEGINS

Poet T.S. Eliot had dubbed April as the cruelest when lilacs would struggle to come out of the dead land. But that April of 2014, there were no strokes of lilac in Islamabad. Just hints of red and protests as cricketer-turned-politician Imran Khan barged into the Red Zone of the Pakistan Parliament with a bunch of followers. Protestors demanding a national government hid in tanks and refused to budge. Hundreds of miles away, with a Pakistan itinerary in hand, I was passively watching the goings-on. Around me, sane voices were exhorting me to drop the idea of stepping into a burning Pakistan. I had not yet applied for the visa—well-wishers were discouraging me from even venturing into the Pakistan Embassy in Delhi for a visa where, in all probability, a refusal awaited me. But for Buddha, I was ready to do anything, go anywhere. Discontentment and rage were spreading; yet, there lay my itinerary—a Silk Road tour to the Buddhist sites along the old Grand Trunk Road. But I had to go.

I did not wait for my book *Buddha in Central Asia* to be released. I picked 10 advance copies from the publisher and left a day later before at dawn and headed to the Ambedkar Terminal in Old Delhi where a new festooned bus waited. Holding a small piece of stamped paper, my ticket, a bottle of water and a cross body bag, I took a seat with great trepidation. Around me were whispers of the fury in Islamabad. In the midst of the pandemonium, there was a calm man. Mr Sharma, the bus in-charge, who shattered the uneasiness with a joke and a stop for quick breakfast at Pipli. As the bus covered miles, fear was forgotten and a sense of bonhomie filled the air-conditioned bus.

It was not my first trip to Pakistan and I sank into the past as the Delhi–Lahore bus rolled leisurely through the cities of Haryana and Punjab along the Grand Trunk Road. The police escort diligently cleared traffic on the busy national highway, and I took a walk back in time when possibly the same road—for decades, generations, nay, for centuries—quietly snaked through India and Pakistan as if mocking at the turn of history of the 1947 Partition. History drew a line, divided the land and turned brothers into enemies. But, for me, nothing had changed. To me, it was still the beautiful and pure land of the Buddha. The Buddha I had come seeking once again.

With no checked-in luggage, I breezed through the mandatory Customs check at Wagah Border. Other fat bags were being rummaged and belongings strewn around. The scanner spit out my small bag in a split second, not noticing the few gold coins that I had brought to offer at the feet of the Great Jaulian Buddha of Taxila. I am not sure whether the scanner was faulty or it was 'kindly' left undetected.

A few more metres, and I was in Pakistan. In Lahore, I wanted to savour the beauty of medieval monuments for a few days before venturing on the road to Taxila and Peshawar, and opted for Ambassador Hotel in Gulberg which was close to the Lahore bus station. Every morning after a staple breakfast of puri, halwa and chole bhature, I took a taxi to the inner areas of the city which looked like a long-lost cousin of Delhi, my hometown. There was remarkable similarity in the street food, bazaars, the Mughal monuments and even the Sufi mausoleums.

The Badshahi Mosque, just a few hundred metres to the west of Lahore Fort and adjacent to Guru Arjan Singh Gurudwara at the Gurudwara Dera Sahib tri-junction, appeared to replicate the tri-junction of Old Delhi where the Jama Masjid, the Red Fort and the gurudwara remain as happy neighbours. The same beauty, the same ugliness, the same rush and the same sense of Mughal history as in Delhi.

Lahore was the favourite city of the Mughals. Emperor Jehangir planted large trees that still lend shade to travellers. The Lahore–Agra road still has shady Banyan and Peepal trees, perhaps offshoots of the ones planted by Jehangir.[1] The serais, or inns, that he built every 19 km along the road still provide fresh water for ablutions to the weary traveller.

Lahore had witnessed scenes of royal battles for the throne of Hindustan. From Turks and Afghans to the Mughals and the Sikhs, Lahore was the gateway to the throne of Delhi. Harold Lamb writes:

> Every invader, marauder, wanted to capture this chief city of Punjab that lay on the pleasant Ravi river and which was guarded by the Thar desert to the south and the Himalayas–Hindukush to the north. Thus, Babur wanted to make Lahore a second Kabul.[2]

Lahore boasts about its rich history, but there are no traces of Buddha or Buddhism here. The city may have only gained prominence during the medieval era. It is said that during the campaign of Mahmud of Ghazni, the Hindu Shahi kings of the Kabul Valley, being driven from Peshawar and Ohind, established their new capital at Bhira on the Jhelum and later at Lahore. Thus, the historian Farishta claimed that both Jayapal and his son Anandpal, the successive antagonists of Mahmud, are called Rajas of Lahore. This Hindu Shahi dynasty was subverted in AD 1031 when Lahore became the residence of Malik Ayaz, a Mohammaden governor under the king of Ghazni. After almost a century, in AD 1152, when Bahram Shah was the sultan of the Ghaznavid Empire, he was driven from Ghazni by the Afghans of Ghor and Bahram's Shah's son Khusrau established himself at Lahore.[3]

Al-Beruni, a scholar from Khiva, was commissioned by Mahmud of Ghazni to produce a monumental work on Indian philosophy and culture in AD 1030. In *Alberuni's India*, he mentions:

> ...the marching distance from Kannauj to Sunnam and thence towards the north-west to Mandahukur, the capital of Lauhawur

---

[1] Major David Price (trans.), *From Persian Memoirs of the Emperor Jahangueir*, Mittal Publications, Delhi, 1829 (rev. eds 1904 and 1995), p.157.
[2] Harold Lamb, *First of the Mughals*, Natraj Publishers, Dehradun, 2003 (1st ed. 1961), p.149.
[3] Alexander Cunningham, *Ancient Geography of India*, Low Price Publications, Delhi, 1990 (1st ed. 1871), p.167.

[Lahore] lying east of the river Irava or Ravi as 8 farsakh; Purushawar, 14 farsakh; Kabul 12 farsakh; Ghazna 17 farsakh; Waihind, west of river Sindh, 20 farsakh [one farsakh equals 5–5.5 km].[4]

ALONG THE CANAL ROAD

Within a few days, Lahore was bidding farewell to spring and the sun was getting harsher by the day. The first flush of spring on the banks of Ravi was beginning to fade as the last rush of winter flowers were wilting and withering away. But the reds, oranges and pinks of Semal and Kachnar and the bright yellow of laburnums were lending colour to Lahore. The Gulmohar was in full bloom over Canal Road and the tidily arranged tiny lights all around gave the place a fairy-tale look.

The 30-km, six-lane Canal Road running along the Lahore Canal covers many important areas of Lahore such as Gulberg, University of Punjab and Mughalpura concluding at the village of Khera bordering India. The 60-km canal, built by the Mughals begins at Bambawali–Ravi–Bedian and is an important part of Lahori culture. During summers, hundreds of people come here to swim; in the evenings, families bring along picnic baskets and soak in the pleasant atmosphere. Whoever thought of digging a canal through the heart of Lahore must have been a genius.

I spent the rest of my Lahore days at the University of Punjab guest house, which is set within a series of gardens. My evenings were reserved for the open-air restaurant from where I could watch the Gulmohars bloom and the moon hanging low in the sky, and dig into mouth-watering chapli kebabs and chicken kofta.

One day I walked to the History Department to meet Prof. Mohammad Iqbal Chawla, who had invited me to present a paper on Taxila at the History Conference. It was here that I met Dr Kyo Soon Park Esther (Secretary) and Zulfiqar Rahim (Director)

---

[4] Edward C. Sachau, *Alberuni's India*, Rupa Publications, Delhi, 2002, p.193.

of the Gandhara Art and Cultural Association, formed under the chairmanship of Mian Imran Masood for the promotion and preservation of Gandharan art. Zulfiqar and Esther were to be my companions on the Silk Road through Pakistan.

Chapter 4

BUDDHIST CITIES ON DELHI-LAHORE ROUTE*

At the time when the army of Muhammad ibn Qasim, the Umayyad general, attacked Sindh and Lower Punjab in AD 713, the Sindhis and Punjabis including the Lahoris, like the rest of Gandhara, were predominantly Buddhists. Today, after Peshawar, Lahore is among the few cities in the world that possesses a vast repertoire of Buddhist antiquities.

In many respects, the immense wealth coming chiefly from trade in horses, ivory, salt, spices and textiles along the Uttarapath or the Northern Highway, changed the geographical landscape not only of Punjab but also of other provinces on the Delhi–Lahore–Peshawar–Kabul route. Ruins of extensive Buddhist establishments lining the Grand Trunk Road stand testimony to Punjab's rich tradition in art and scholarship. It was commerce that sustained the grand university of Taxila, which contributed to the making of the giant stupas of Manikyala and Dharamrajika and the splendid monastic adornments by itinerant artists, and provided patronage to tens of thousands of monks who resided there.

This Buddhist connect stemmed not only from trade and agriculture but also from rich endowments provided for setting up Buddhist centres from the time of Asoka through the reigns of the Indo-Greeks, Kushans and Harshavardhana. What history does not often elaborate upon is the importance of the mixed ethnicity of the land as one of the major contributors to the propagation of Buddhism. Since the time of the Persian sovereignty, people from different ethnicities were more receptive to the tenets of Buddhism that was non-casteist and preached equality, non-violence and tolerance of

---

*For a detailed reading, refer to Alexander Cunningham's *Ancient Geography of India*, 1990; D. Devahuti's *Harsha: A Political Study*, 1998 and D.C. Ahir's *Buddhist Sites and Shrines: History, Art and Architecture*, 2003.

other sects and faith. They had no problem in adopting Buddhism as their religion as it had no prejudice of race or class and was a strong creed.¹ Not surprisingly, if we trace the river valleys of Punjab, we find mention of numerous monastic establishments in the Doabs of Punjab and Haryana. Sadly, most of these sites are lost and forgotten.

Renowned Buddhist scholar D.C. Ahir states that Buddhists came to Punjab through the Buddha himself and gained a good hold in the Punjab–Gandhara region after the *Mahaparinirvana* of the Buddha in 483 BC. Thereafter, for more than 1,000 years, Buddhism was the predominant religion of the region.²

Notwithstanding the period of Mohammedan invasion in the seventh century AD, the northern Bengal–Balkh highway was brimming with trade and pilgrimage activities since the period of Asoka from the third century BC to the tenth century AD. A slew of Buddhist saints, scholars, artists, poets and philosophers were not only travelling from the eastern to the western extremities of the Indian subcontinent, but also along the river valleys of the Indus and its tributaries, setting up Buddhist shrines and monastic institutions for the study and propagation of the Buddha's faith.

Three of the illustrious Buddhist kings ruling from Gandhara: Milinda, Kanishka and Harsha flourished in Punjab. The earliest and the most renowned emperor following the Buddhist faith, Asoka, also started his career as viceroy at Taxila.

The route to Lahore goes via Delhi, Haryana and Punjab. The state of Punjab (split between India and Pakistan in 1947) and Haryana, which till 1966 was a part of Punjab, boast of numerous Buddhist sites along the Royal Road. This road was later developed into the Sher Shah Suri Road and the Grand Trunk Road from Delhi up to Taxila.

On an ancient map of undivided Punjab, several Buddhist sites en route from Delhi to Lahore and Taxila can be located along the

---

[1] Charles Eliot, *Hinduism and Buddhism: An Historical Sketch*, Vol II: Bibliotheca Indo-Buddhica No.54, Sri Satguru Publications, Delhi, 1921 (reprint 1988), pp.69–70.
[2] D.C. Ahir, *Buddhist Sites and Shrines: History, Art and Architecture*, Satguru Publications, Delhi, 2003, p.223.

river valleys of Haryana and Punjab across which runs the Grand Trunk Road.

Some important sites in Haryana are the monastery of Agroha in Hissar, the stupa of Asandh at Karnal, the stupa of Kurukshetra and the Buddhist site of Chaneti at Yamunanagar.

In Buddhist scriptures, Kuru (located in Punjab before 1966, now in Haryana and contiguous with Punjab) is mentioned as one of the *Janpadas* where Lord Buddha delivered a number of discourses. The ancient *Janpada* is said to have comprised Kurukshetra, Thanesar, Karnal, Panipat, Sonipat and some other areas. During his visits to Kuru, the Buddha is said to have invariably stayed at Kammasadhamma, a market town in the Kuru.[3] According to Ahir, it was in Thullakotthita—identified with Sthaneswara (Thanesar) in Karnal district—another important town of Kuru-Desa, that Ratthapala, a Kuru noble, after hearing a discourse of the Buddha joined the *bhikshu* Sangha.[4]

Xuanzang, the celebrated Chinese pilgrim, who passed through present-day Haryana in AD 636 saw Asokan pillars and stupas at Sthanesvara and Srughana (modern-day Sugh, near Jagadhari). An inscribed pillar put up by Asoka at Topra, a village near Sugh, was shifted to Delhi by Sultan Ferozshah Tughlaq in AD 1356, and now stands at Ferozshah Kotla in Delhi.

According to historian D. Devahuti, many monasteries in Punjab were likely built by Harsha, king of Thaneswar and Kannauj, who reigned in AD 606–647. By AD 612, Harshavardhana's empire stretched from Pundravardhana (in north-west Bengal) in the east to roughly the river Beas in the west.[5]

The kingdom of Sindh extended well up to the point of confluence of the Punjab rivers not far from the boundaries of Harshavardhana's empire. According to Xuanzang, Harsha became a devout Buddhist and built monasteries and gigantic stupas and perpetuated the

---

[3] Ahir, *Buddhist Sites and Shrines*, p.115.
[4] Ahir, *Buddhist Sites and Shrines*, p.115.
[5] D. Devahuti, *Harsha: A Political Study*, Oxford University Press, Delhi, 1970 (rev. eds, 1983, 1998), pp.104–05.

tradition of Buddhist *pancha parishad* held every five years.[6]

Significantly, Harshavardhana, the last king of the Vardhana dynasty of Thanesar, who was also the last Buddhist emperor of India, hailed from Punjab–Haryana. The flourishing condition of Buddhism in India during his long reign has been well-documented by Xuanzang. In Haryana, the pilgrim saw three *sangharamas* or monasteries with about 700 Buddhist monks at Thanesar; at Sugh, he saw five Buddhist monasteries with over 1,000 monks.[7]

Ahir delineates the Buddhist cities of Punjab and Haryana where, a number of Buddhist stupas, railings, sculptures and Buddha images have been discovered at many places. Among these, he mentions a railing post of a Buddhist stupa from the second century BC from Hathin in southern Haryana and another from Bhadas (19 km northeast of Firozepur Jhirka on the road to Nuh).[8]

Recovered from Jhajjar, the Buddha sculpted in mottled Mathura sandstone is the best preserved image of the Buddha to be found in Haryana. Depicting only the folded legs, the Buddha is identifiable only because of the Brahmi inscription in Kushana characters which reads, *Buddha Kanaka-muni*. Another Buddha image discovered from Rohtak district and preserved in the Gurukul Museum at Jhajjar, is only a torso, with legs and arms missing. A bodhisattva head in spotted red sandstone was found from Mahmudpur in the same district.

Some other images of the Buddha brought to our notice by Ahir from Haryana include an eighth-century bronze Buddha in *bhumisparsa mudra* from Hansi; a sandstone image of the Buddha from the same period from Sanghi; a broken Buddha head from Rohtak and another one from Ad Badri in Ambala district, datable to the ninth–tenth century AD; and a fourteenth-century Buddha image from Sri Ram Temple in Taraori (district Karnal) showing the Buddha seated on a lotus pedestal in *bhumisparsa mudra*.

An inscribed Buddha image dated from the fourth–fifth century

---

[6] Devahuti, *Harsha*, pp.104–05.
[7] Samuel Beal, *Si-Yu-Ki: Buddhist Records of the Western World*, Book IV, Low Price Publications, Delhi, 1884, pp.183–85.
[8] Ahir, *Buddhist Sites and Shrines*, pp.115–17 and pp.223–27.

AD discovered from Gharaura village (Gurgaon district, Haryana) proves that a Buddhist monastery existed on Tosham Hill. Some Buddhist remains found in Ludhiana district are at Tihara (Jagraon tehsil). Another important Buddhist site has been found at Arura, 16 km south of Jagraon.[9]

Xuanzang who was in India for 14 years from AD 630 to AD 644 mentions important Buddhist cities along the Royal Road to Taxila. He took note of Satadru or Sanghol near Ludhiana (Jalandhar), which had 50 viharas and in one of them dwelt the renowned monk Chandravarma; in Chinapatti or Patti in Amritsar district lived the monk Vinitaprabha. The Tamsavana monastery at Jalandhar is also mentioned by the pilgrim.

On the other side of the border in Punjab, the important sites of Sui Vihar can be found, located along the Sutlej before its confluence with the Indus, 26 km south-west of Bahawalpur in the Lower Indus region; a little to the east of the Indus lies the celebrated sites of Attock/Hund, near Hasan Abdal Baoli.

The ruins of Pattan Minara, located at a distance of about 8 km south-east of Rahim Yar Khan city, has been described as belonging to the Mauryan period when a Buddhist monastery came up at the site in 250 BC.[10]

The Buddhist site of Rokri (128 km from Mianwali in Pakistan) was swept away by the flooded Indus in 1968. When the river turned placid again, several plastic figures and concrete mouldings were found at the foot of two circular walls that had been laid bare. According to Alexander Cunningham, the archaeological surveyor to the Government of India, the inner wall was the base of a stupa and the outer wall, that is the surrounding circular enclosure, was perhaps the *pradikshana path*. The remains were brought to the Lahore Museum.

Rokri appeared to be a vast site. Excavations at the site pointed to the presence of several brick buildings, a fact corroborated by Cunningham's mention of 'a series of paved rooms of some ancient

---

[9] Ahir, *Buddhist Sites and Shrines*, p.117.
[10] Refer to <https://en.wikipedia.org/wiki/Hindu_and_Buddhist_architectural_heritage_of_Pakistan>(last date of access: 30 January 2020).

dwelling'. In his report of *A Tour in Punjab 1878–79*, Cunningham found no less than 32 sculptural pieces, among which eight were heads of plaster of the Buddha from Rokri belonging to an early period of Buddhism.[11]

On the banks of river Chenab in India, lies the important site of Akhnoor (near Jammu) and the famous city of Sagala across the border. Sagala was the city of Milind, writer of the *Milindpanha*, in the second century BC.

Along the Jhelum, there is mention of the Buddhist cities of Jalalpur, Bhera/Bhira (Pitoo of Xuanzang), Murti and Malot. The sites of Manikyala and Taxila lay in the Doab of the Jhelum and the Upper Indus.

Museums at Chandigarh, Lahore, Taxila, Peshawar and Mardan provide a vital link to the glorious past of Buddhism in Punjab and the north-west regions beyond that were included in or were contiguous with Gandhara. The largest number of Buddhist antiquities found in Punjab on both sides of the border of India and Pakistan and displayed at various museums around the world, speak of the flourishing state of Buddhism and Buddhist art. These include images of the Buddha and bodhisattvas in various postures, scenes from the life of the Buddha and terracotta and stucco heads.

NO MENTION OF LAHORE

The great city of Lahore which has been the capital of Punjab for nearly 900 years is said to have been founded by Lava or Lo, the son of Rama, after whom it was named Lohawar. Another city, Kusawar (present-day Kasur), 51 km south-east of Lahore, was the city of Rama's second son, Kusa. Lohawar was adopted by the Mohammedans under the name of Lahore.[12]

---

[11] Alexander Cunningham, *A Tour in Punjab in 1878–79*, ASI Report of the Buddhist site of Rokri in Mianwali district, p.29. Available at https://archive.org/stream/reportatourinpu00cunngoog/reportatourinpu00cunngoog_djvu.txt (last date of access: 10 February 2020).

[12] Alexander Cunningham, *Ancient Geography of India*, Low Price Publications, Delhi, 1871 (reprint 1990), p.166.

However, it is interesting that none of the travelogues of Faxian, Xuanzang and Hye Ch'o as well as other travellers mention any Buddhist site in Lahore. This may indicate that Lahore on the Ravi river became the premier city of the Uttarapath much later in history. Faxian departed for India in AD 399 and journeyed through the deserts of Central Asia and across the Pamirs and Khotan and proceeded towards Kheecha (believed to be Skardo) and westwards to Gandhara. According to James Legge, Faxian proceeded from the Safed Koh mountains, headed eastwards, and then crossed the Indus before arriving in Petoo (present-day Bhira) from where he left for Mathura. He did not mention Lahore under any other name.[13]

Sung Yun and Hui Sheng were despatched to India by the Empress Dowager Ta-hao in AD 518. They took the southern route via Khotan and reached the region of Gandhara but were unable to proceed beyond the Indus into the region of Punjab due to political unrest in the north-west region and returned to China in AD 521.[14]

I-Ching arrived in India in AD 673 from Canton by the sea route,[15] remained in eastern India at Nalanda Vihar and studied at Sumatra. He however did not visit Gandhara.

There is no mention of Lahore in *Hye Ch'o Diary* either. The Korean pilgrim Hye Ch'o (AD 704–780) arrived in India by the southern sea route like his predecessor I-Ching, and landed in the eastern part of the country, before heading to the 'five regions' of India. From north-central India, he went to south India and then to western India from where he followed the route to the Northwest Frontier regions by way of Jalandhar and visited the kingdoms lying on the banks of the Indus River and then onwards from Sindhukala

---

[13] James Legge (trans.), *A Record of Buddhistic Kingdoms Being an Account of the Chinese Monk Fa-Hein of Travels in India and Ceylon [AD 399–414] in Search of the Buddhist Books of Discipline*, Munshiram Manoharlal Publishers, Delhi, 1998), maps p.xi. and p.41.

[14] Han-Sung Yang, Jan Yun-Hua Yang, Lida Shotaro and Lawrence Preston (eds and trans), *Hye Ch'o Diary: A Memoir of the Pilgrimage to the Five Regions of India*, Asian Humanities Press, Berkeley, CA, 1984, p.9.

[15] Yang et al., *Hye Ch'o Diary*, p.12.

to the Kashmir Valley. After passing through Gandhara and Kapisa, he entered Central Asia on his way back to Anxi where he arrived in AD 727. On his way from Jalandhar across the Indus tributaries towards Kashmir, he probably crossed the region of Lahore, but he makes no mention of the city under any name.[16] It could be that in AD 724 when he was still in the Northwest Frontier region, the city of Lahore had not achieved prominence.

While Xuanzang makes no mention of Lahore, it is almost certain he must have passed through it on his way from Taki to Jalandhar.

---

[16] Yang et al., *Hye Ch'o Diary*, pp.45–46.

Chapter 5

ROAD TO MANIKYALA

ROAD TO MANIKYALA

'The Grand Trunk Road or the Motorway M2?' My friend and Board member of the Gandhara Art and Culture Association, Islamabad, Ayesha Hamid, raised this question. Her hands on the wheel, Ayesha was seeking choice of route for our Lahore to Manikyala trip. We could take one of the two routes—the Grand Trunk Road which is the medieval Sher Shah Suri Marg or the modern Motorway M2.

As raindrops pelted down on the car's windscreen, I took refuge in history and decided to follow the medieval path for its connection with the past. My mind was cluttered with vignettes from the past— the bustle of the caravanserais, the chatter of men and women, the passing caravans, the clip-clop of donkey carts and camel safaris, old banyan trees and ponds that possibly still hid somewhere along the long winding road to Peshawar and even beyond to the hills of Kabul, and the villages that flanked the Grand Trunk Road offering fascinating glimpses of the olden days. Yes, it had to be the ancient road and not the motorway which is yet to collect history in its gravel.

We took off from the Kalma Chowk area of Lahore and went via Canal Road on to the Grand Trunk Road. Soon, we were negotiating the twin villages of Muridke/Sadhoke and Kamoke where huge rice mills and a vast, noisy rice bazaar line the road. Part of the rich rice-growing belt of Punjab, the road side was choked with donkey carts and herds of painted goats ready to be auctioned off for Bakri Eid festivities.

Twenty kilometres from Kamoke, we reached the Gujranwala toll plaza. Just before the plaza, the NH-5 at Eminabad is met by the Sialkot Road. In the second century BC, the ancient Sagala or Sialkot city was the capital of the Graeco-Bactrian king Menander under whose rule Sagala became a major centre of Buddhism. The city was razed by Alexander in 326 BC. When Pusyamitra, the brahmin commander-in-chief of Brihadratha, the last Mauryan king, arrived in Sagala, he proclaimed that he would give 100 *dinara* for the head of a Buddhist monk.[1] The first royal persecutor of the Buddhists, he murdered King Brihadratha, *c.*185 BC. He then usurped the throne of Magadha before letting loose a reign of terror. Pusyamitra is also said to have performed *ashvamedhas*, or horse sacrifices, a proof of his support of Vedic Brahmanism and a disapproval of the heterodox sects of Buddhism.[2]

Another persecutor of Buddhists was Sasanka, the king of Gauda from Bengal. His first treacherous act was the murder of Rajyavardhana in AD 605. Rajyavardhana was the elder brother of Harshavardhana, the last Buddhist emperor. Brahmin by caste and Saiva by faith, Sasanka was such a fanatic that in a fit of rage he almost destroyed the Bodhi Tree.[3]

The immediate heirs of what remained of the Mauryan Empire were the Sungas, a brahmin family, who were officials under the Mauryas. Buddhist sources claim that the Sungas had persecuted the Buddhists and destroyed their monasteries and places of worship.

The *Milindapanha: The Questions of King Milind*, a Buddhist text *c.*100 BC, also provides a vivid picture of the city Sagala, also the capital of the White Huns when Mihirakula, the Indo-Hephthalite was king.

We learn that Sagala, the beautiful city of the Greeks, was a great centre of trade, situated 'in a delightful country, well-watered and hilly, abounding in a paradise of rivers and mountains and woods.'[4] It was richly adorned with hundreds of alms-halls, and full of magnificent mansions, which rose high like the Himalayan peaks. Its streets

---

[1] K.L. Hazra, *The Rise and Decline of Buddhism in India*, Munshiram Manoharlal Publishers, Delhi, 1995 (3rd edition, 2009), p.46.
[2] Romila Thapar, *The Penguin History of Early India*, Penguin India, Delhi, 2002), p.210.
[3] D.C. Ahir, *Asoka the Great*, B.R. Publishing Corporation, Delhi, 1995, p.135.
[4] T.W Rhys Davids (translated from Pali), *The Milindpanha: The Questions of King Milinds*: 1890, Columbia, USA, 2018, pp.9–10.

were filled with elephants, horses, carriages and walkers. There were handsome men and beautiful women, brahmins, nobles, artificers and servants. Teachers of all creeds were welcomed in the city. In the shops were sold Benares muslin, Kotumbara stuff and cloths of various kinds; a sweet odour emanated from the bazaars selling all kinds of flowers and perfumes. There were plenty of jewels and traders' guilds displayed all kinds of goods. 'So full is the city of money, and of gold and silver ware, of copper and stone ware, that it is a very mine of dazzling treasures.' Foods and drinks of every sort, syrups and sweetmeats of every kind could be found here. 'In wealth it rivals *Uttara-kuru*, and in glory it is as *Alakamanda*, the city of gods.'[5]

At the Chandakila bypass, we crossed the bloated Ravi canal. Ayesha was blaming the dam's open sluice gates on the Indian side; I was attributing the overflowing canal to incessant rains and floods. India and Pakistan have always argued about the use of the canal and Ayesha is certain that the construction of a dam over the Ravi is a mistake. She says that when water is needed for paddy there is an acute shortage but during the monsoons there is flooding due to opening of sluice gates. As a voracious rice eater, I was appalled!

As soon as we reached Gujranwala, our conversations completely turned to the famous kebabs of the area. I am told that these are not ordinary kebabs, but kebabs made from the meat of specially reared goats by farmers in this rice-growing belt. Export-quality basmati rice is produced in this belt that extends up to the Jhelum, and the best produce comes from the fields around Lahore and Faisalabad.

Apart from scrumptious cuisine, this area is also well known for manufacturing electrical equipment, motorcycles, PVC pipes, ceramics and sanitary wares. The locally manufactured motorcycle rickshaws known as Qinggi crowd the roads of Gujranwala, but are great for cheap local travel. Trucks, buses, cycles and tractors are also made in Faisalabad and Gujranwala.

We reached Alipur Chowk, a village near Gujranwala that houses

---

[5] Davids, *The Milindpanha*, pp.9–10.

the massive campus of the University of Punjab and is also known for its steel and wrought iron furniture. As the car zips through Gujranwala Cantonment, I notice the walls pasted with Imran Khan's posters. Within the city limits lies one of Punjab's largest sugar mills Rahwali Sugarmills, and an animal market.

Gakkhar, and the neighbouring villages of Wazirabad and Jandiyala, grow good-quality basmati rice. As far as the eyes can see, there are paddy fields and chimneys of rice mills lining the blue sky. I also hear stories about the fierce Gakkhar tribes inhabiting the region. It is said that a charging mob of the wild Gakkhar chased away Mahmud Ghazni's battalion of fierce archers in the eleventh century AD[6] and even had sharp skirmishes with Babur as he passed through Punjab in the sixteenth century.[7]

After Kot Khizr, we reach Dhunkal Mor from where we leave the main Grand Trunk Road going to Islamabad and take the exit for Gujarat. Crossing the Chenab, I gape at the intense greenery of the adjoining areas of the Chenab catchment. This is a green belt and not so much of a built-up city. Once one of the largest rivers of Pakistan, the Chenab has now shrunk.

A road from Gujarat leads into Kashmir. This is the 47-km Gujarat–Bhimber road, the old route into Kashmir through Bhimber that was used by Xuanzang. Once lying on a strategic route of the Mughals on their way to Kashmir Valley, today, Bhimber is one of the important towns of Kashmir lying 48 km from Gujarat and 241 km from Srinagar. The route between Lahore and Kashmir followed the Royal Road up to Gujarat. From here, the route to Kashmir branched out and passing through Bhimbar, Naushera, Rajori, Thana Mandi and Shopian reached Srinagar.

Gujarat was a part of the kingdom of Porus in the fourth century BC, before he was defeated by Alexander in 326 BC in the Battle

---

[6] Stanley Lane-Poole, *Medieval India under Mohammedan Rule (A.D.712–1764)*, Low Price Publications, Delhi, 1903 (reprint 2003), p.20.
[7] Harold Lamb, *Babur First of the Mughals*, Natraj Publishers, Dehradun, 1961 (reprint 2003), p.152. See also, Stanley Lane-Poole, *Rulers of India: Babar*, Low Price Publications, Delhi, 1890 (reprint 2005), p.144 and p.155.

at Karri on the plains close to the Jhelum River. It is said that the ruler of Taxila desired Alexander's help against his enemies in the neighbouring states. Taxila was then at war both with the hill kingdom of Abhisara (Hazara region of present-day Pakistan) and with the more powerful states governed by Porus whose kingdom included the modern districts of Jhelum, Gujarat and Shahpur.[8] Porus, far from paying homage and tribute to Alexander, proudly let it be known that he would indeed meet Alexander at the head of an army ready for battle. The army that opposed Alexander on the opposite banks of the Jhelum comprised 50,000 strong men and 200 elephants.[9] Fearful of a direct combat with Porus, Alexander resolved to 'steal a passage' and his concealed fleet appeared at the open river and disembarked at day break without opposition.[10]

Historian Vincent Smith writes:

> The battle ended at the eighth hour of the day in a scene of murderous confusion... The Indian army was annihilated. Poros himself was taken prisoner in a fainting condition with nine wounds. Yet proudly requested to be 'treated as a king', which Alexander had the magnanimity to respect.[11]

For his fearlessness in the face of the invincible invader, Porus's name has been written in letters of gold in the annals of world history. Alexander had a tomb of stone constructed and founded a city called Alexandria Bucephala at the place where Alexander started to cross the Jhelum. Near the battlefield where he defeated Porus, he founded another city Alexandria Nicaea, in commemoration of the victory.[12]

From there, Alexander went eastwards and reached Acesines or

---

[8] Vincent Smith, *History of India*, Vol. II, Cosimo Classics, New York, 2008, p.55.
[9] Smith, *History of India*, p.62.
[10] Smith, *History of India*, p.61.
[11] Smith, *History of India*, p.63.
[12] Valerio Massimo Manfredi, *Alexander*, Vol. 3: The End of the Earth (Translated from the Italian by Iain Halliday), Macmillan 2001,Pan Books, London, 2002, p.452.

the Chenab, the second-largest tributary of the Indus. All along the eastwards march, he captured 70 cities coming to a halt near Sagala on the banks of the Ravi (the ancient Hydraotes River), where 17,000 died braving the army of Alexander in defence of Sagala.[13] It was here that Alexander met a *sramana* called Kalanos who spoke of eternal peace and nirvana.[14]

The next day, he set off for the two cities between the Ravi and the Beas (the ancient Hyphasis River). At the Beas, Alexander's troop revolted and refused to cross the Beas which then became the eastern frontier of Alexander's campaign.[15]

EVENING IN GUJARAT

Mian Imran Masood, chairman of the Gandhara Art and Cultural Association, invited us for tea at his haveli in Gujarat. It was a sprawling haveli with ancient crafted doors created by Kashmiri craftsmen. There were separate *janankhanas* (quarters for women) and numerous drawing rooms with large chandeliers, paintings and trophies of antelopes, snow leopards and markhors decorating the floors and walls of the splendid residence. Old photos and portraitures of his ancestors hung from the walls. In the huge drawing room, senior Begum Sahiba regaled us with stories of Masood's childhood and anecdotes from her personal life as she came to the Masood's family when she was barely 16 years of age. Indeed, the house was seeped in the past.

The next day, we were to leave for Islamabad, but Masood exhorted us not to head in that direction as the city was seething with protests called by Imran Khan's Teherik-i-Insaf. We paid heed and enjoyed a lavish meal laid on a huge mahogany table instead. In the evening, we sat in the verandah of the haveli to discuss the activities of the Gandhara Art and Culture Organization over several

---

[13] Manfredi, *Alexander*, p.452 and p.456.
[14] Manfredi, *Alexander*, p.475.
[15] Allen Fildes and Joann Fletcher, *Alexander: The Great Son of Gods*, Duncan Baird Publishers, Ireland, 2004, p.131.

cups of tea. It was quite late in the night when we got to bed. The weather was magical as the copious rain had cooled the city and a refreshing breeze swept through the haveli. It rained through the night and I worried about the condition of the Grand Trunk Road and our drive through heavy traffic.

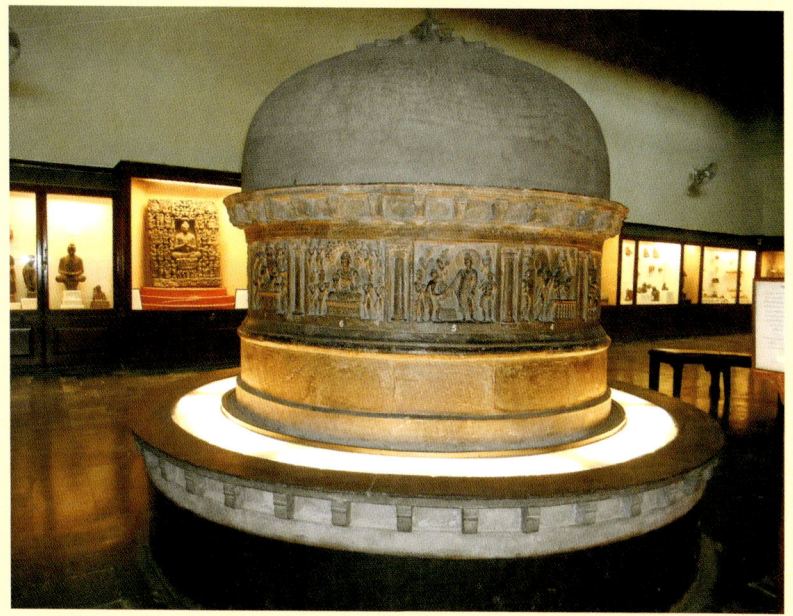

The Stupa of Sikri, dated to the third–fourth century AD, forms the central exhibit at Lahore Museum
Photo courtesy: Lahore Museum

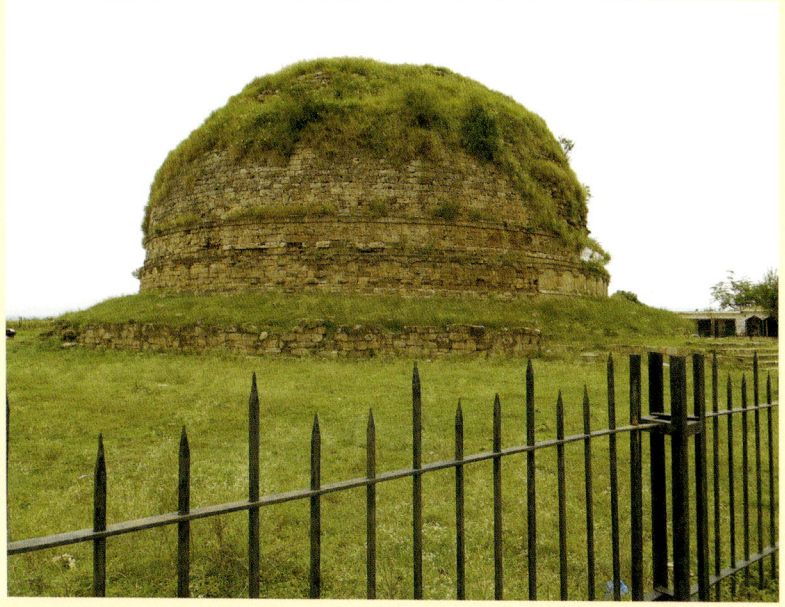

Stupa of Manikyala, second century AD, near village Mandara, Punjab Pakistan

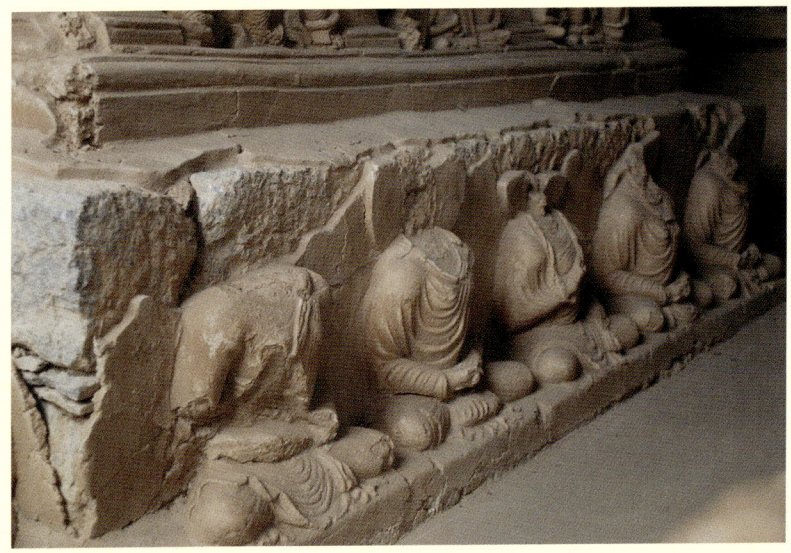

A row of Buddhas decorate a votive stupa at the Jaulian Monastery (second century AD), Taxila

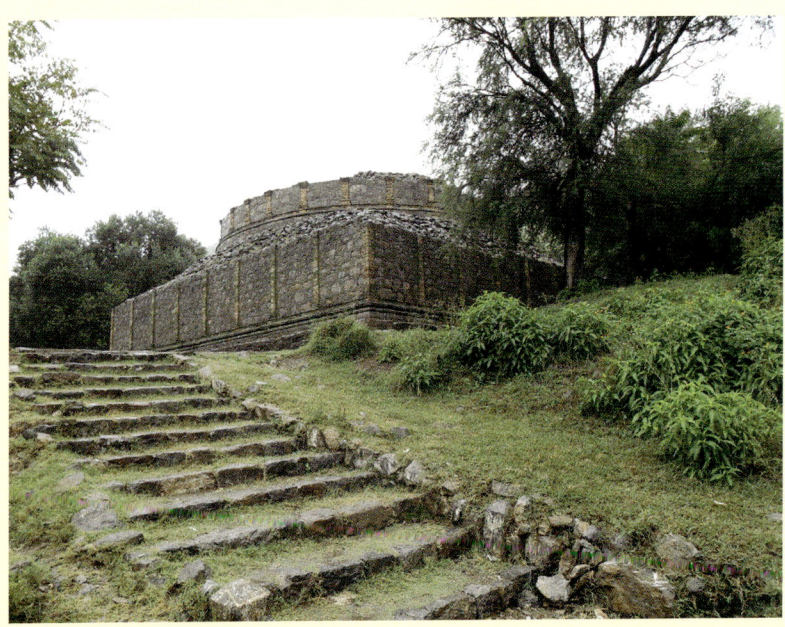

Steps lead to the monastery of Mohra Moradu (second century AD), Taxila

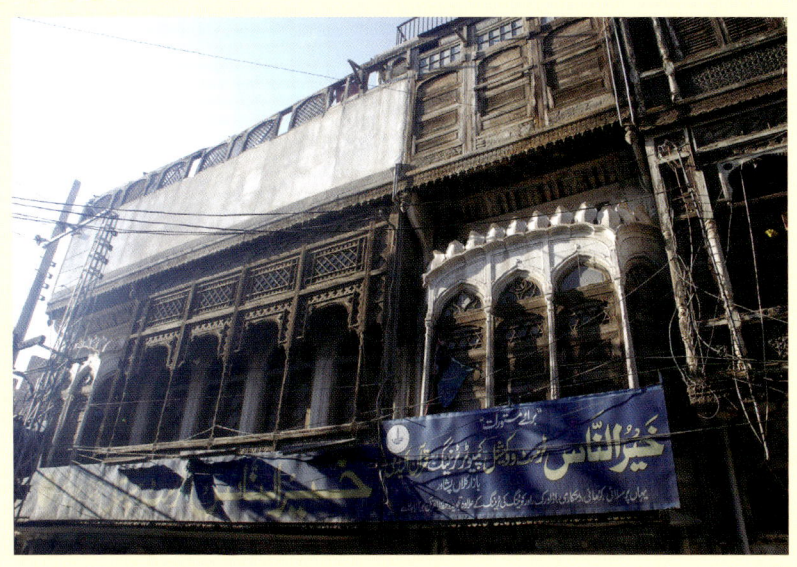

A once-grand *balakhana* in the bazaar of Peshawar

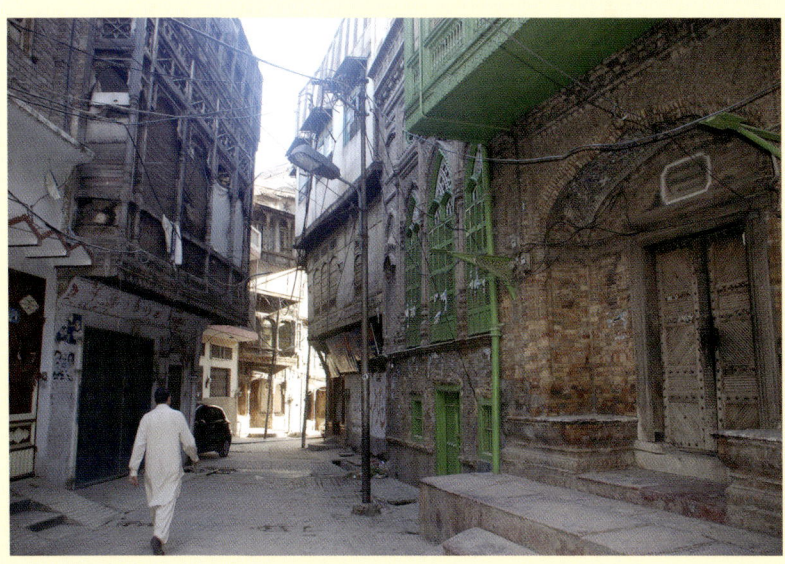

The heritage Mohalla Sethian at Peshawar

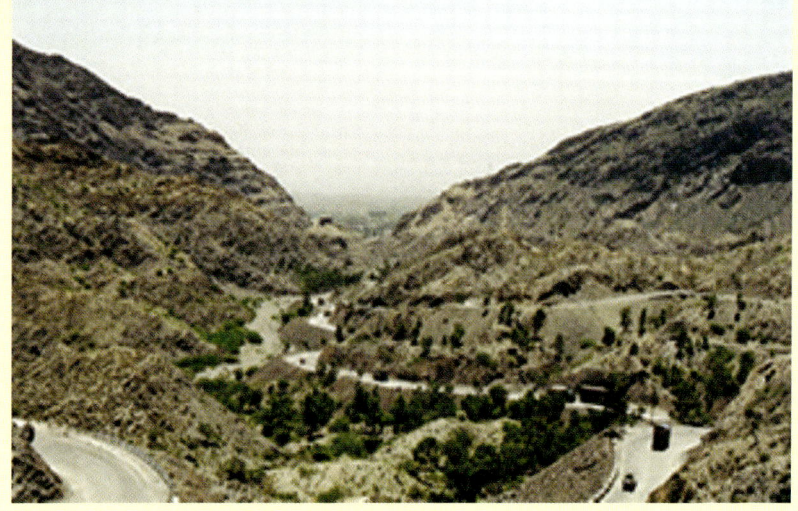

The winding road through Khyber Pass (photograph by Mohd. Usman Mardanvi)

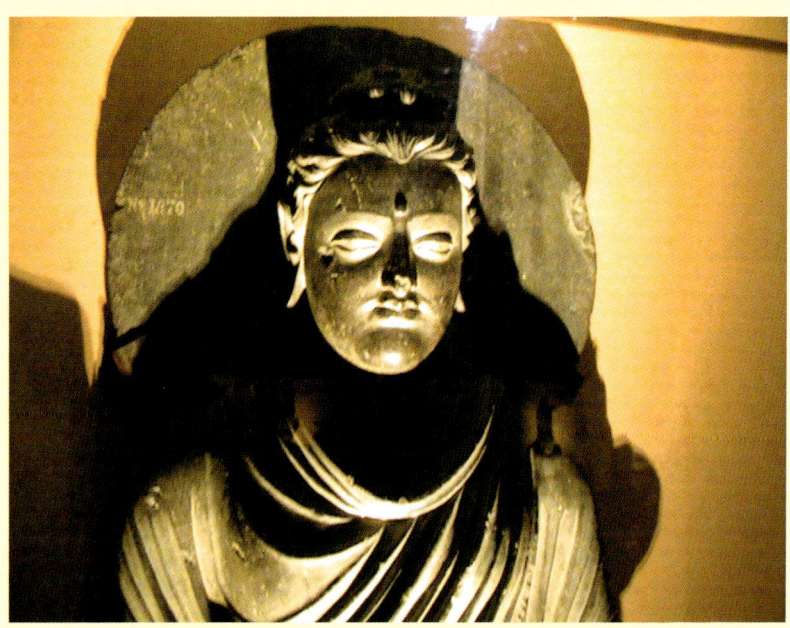

Buddha image in schist from Mamanadheri, Charsadda
Photo courtesy: Peshawar Museum

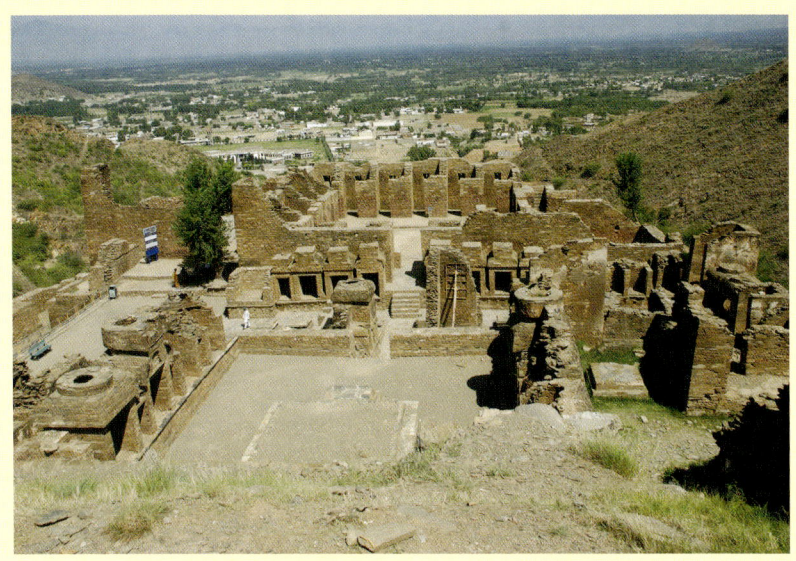

Monastery of Takht-i-Bahi, dated to the first century AD, near Mardan, Pakistan

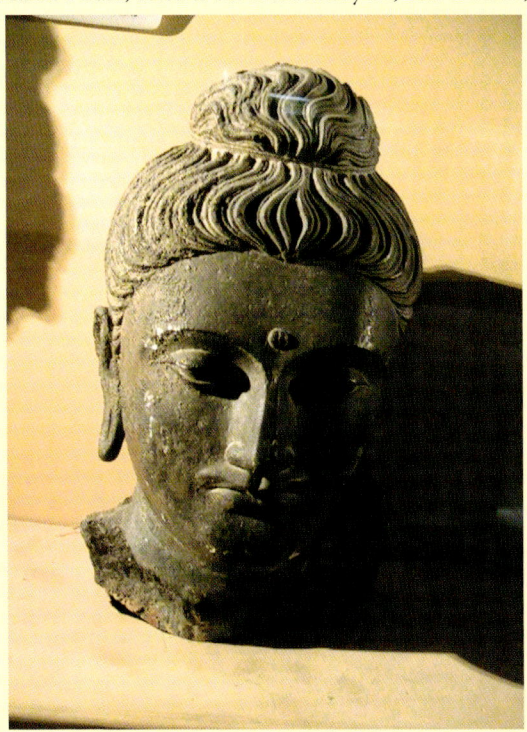

Buddha head in schist from Takht-i-Bahi, second–third century AD
Photo courtesy: Peshawar Museum

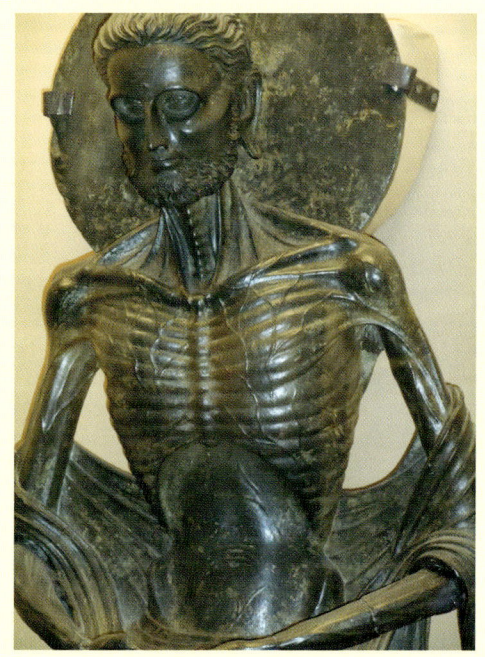

Fasting Siddhartha in schist, Sikri, Mardan, second century AD
Photo courtesy: Lahore Museum

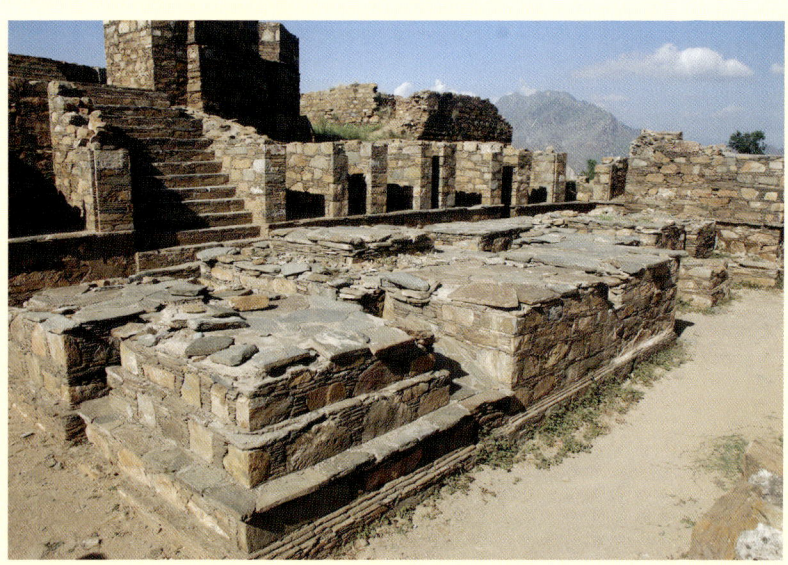

Votive stupa court at Jamalgarhi Monastery, first century AD

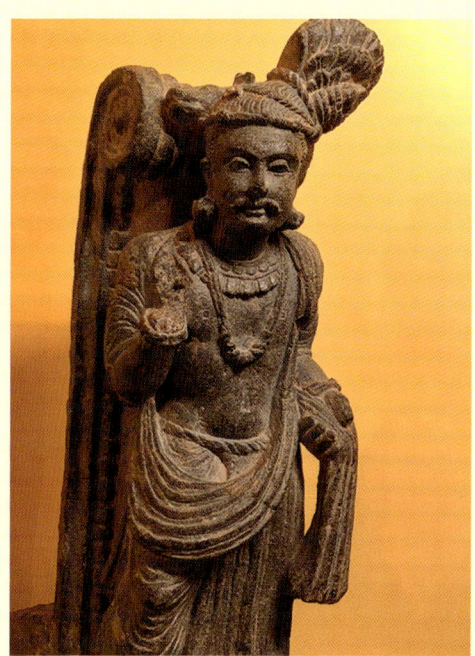

A Naga deity in stone, dated to the second–third century AD, from Gandhara
Photo courtesy: Archaeological Museum, Milan, Italy

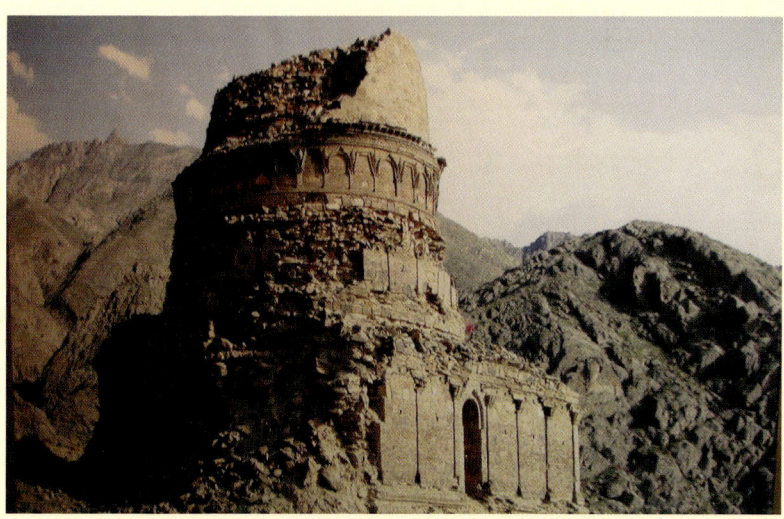

Guldara Stupa near Kabul, second century AD
Photo courtesy: National Museum, Kabul

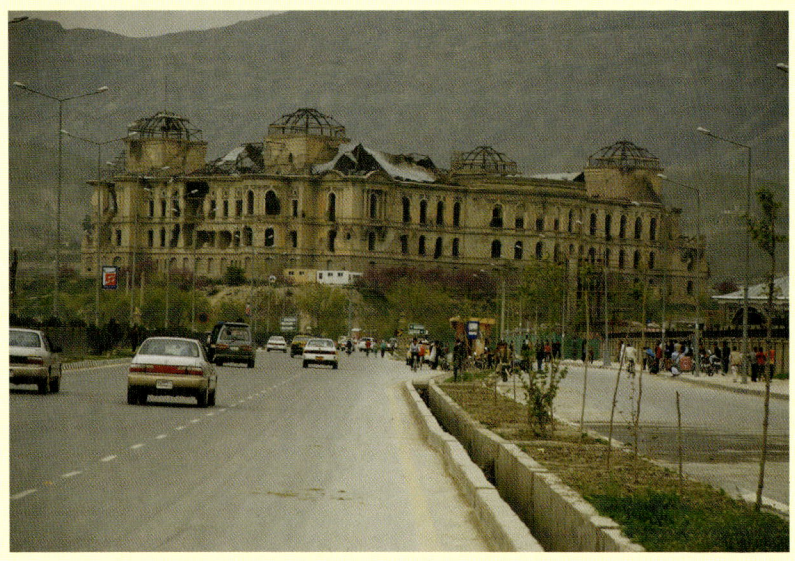

The historic Darulaman Road skirts the Amanullah Khan Palace, the crown jewel of Afghanistan in the heart of Kabul.

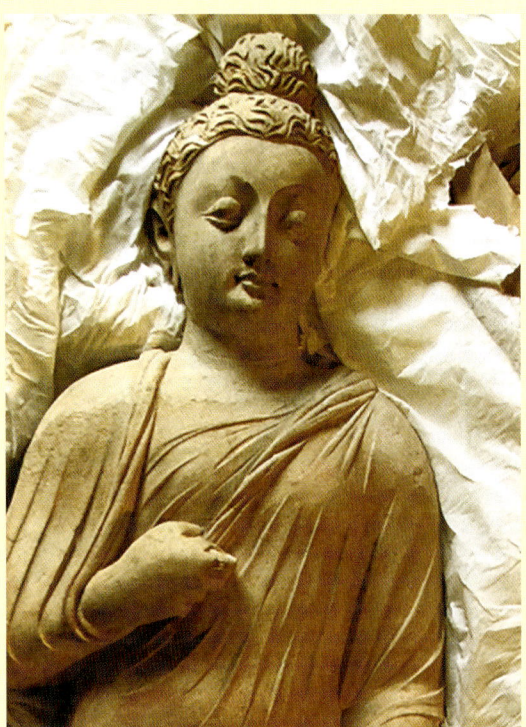

Stucco image of the Smiling Buddha, from the second century AD, from Hadda, near Jalalabad, Afghanistan
Photo courtesy: National Museum of Afghanistan, Kabul

Chapter 6

STUPA OF MANIKYALA

It was 8 a.m. After a light breakfast, we bid farewell to the Masood family, hopped into the car, and after crossing the Chenab, sped on the Grand Trunk Road. As the car accelerated with tyres screeching from time to time, I dabbled in some art. Art facts, that is. About the famous craftsmen of Gujarat who designed and carved wood that came from the northern regions of Kashmir.

At this early hour, there was very little traffic on the Grand Trunk Road. Roasted chapattis were yet to be served and the korma yet to be cooked at the road-side dhabas. Here, tea, parantha and lassi form the staple breakfast for long-distance truck drivers and travellers. Basic ingredients such as paneer, dahi and butter are requisitioned from villages of the Uttarapath. As we passed through the villages of Chak Murtaza and Gakhri, we got caught in heavy rains. Ayesha was pushing the pedal and talking on the phone simultaneously. I was a little scared—not of an accident, but of the police catching her for using the mobile phone while driving! But, as in India, rules here are meant to be flouted too.

From Lala Mussa began the cane belt of Punjab covering the villages of Punjan Kisan, Jandanwala and Kharian. It was a colourful journey through the markets where cartloads of the famous honey-coloured jaggery called 'lal musa gur' vied with high mounds of green leafy vegetables, purple brinjals, white and red radish and orange carrots brought on mules from nearby villages. There was a long queue of white horse carriages for marriage processions as the wedding season was soon approaching. Shortly, we reached Padao Sarai Alamgir on the lower range of the salt ranges where, it is said Porus's army was once stationed on top of the hills while Alexander's waited in the foothills.

From the villages of Sohawa and Domeli, the low hills of Gujjar Khan, the mountain of the herders, is visible. Chak Sikander, a village lying in the foothills, has been named after Alexander, so were its shops. It is quite possible that here there were small Greek settlements from the time of Alexander in the third century BC or the Indo-Greeks in the second century BC. Alexander's route lay along what is now the route of the Uttarapath, and it is not a coincidence that the village at Dina is also the place that according to local tales houses the grave of Alexander's wife, Diana. Another historic site, the Rohtas Fort lies at a driving distance of 45 minutes from Dina from where hails Gulzar, the famous Indian poet. Incidentally, there are many Chak Sikandar villages in India too, such as in Vaishali in Bihar, Allahabad in Uttar Pradesh, and Amritsar and Tarn in Punjab. This prompts us to speculate whether for some reason the people of the Gujjar Khan hills migrated further east along the rivers.

I was curious about the neighbouring village of Chakwal, where men are said to be nearly seven feet tall and houses have rooms that are *naugazi* or nine yards long for these tall men to sleep in! Ayesha and I debated whether these fair-complexioned men with blue eyes are direct descendants of the Greeks. Ayesha was sure about it, I had my doubts.

Finally, we reached Mandara from where we took a U-turn and crossed over to the other side of the Grand Trunk Road. At the Shell gas station, we found Sher Ahmad Jan waiting in his Toyota Land Cruiser to drive us to Manikyala village, which lay between Mandara and Rawat. We bid farewell to Ayesha and climbed into Sher Ahmed Jan's cruiser.

The narrow road to Manikyala splits from the Grand Trunk Road towards the right and passes through an extensive agricultural area before crossing the railway line running from Lahore through Islamabad to Peshawar. The stupa loomed on the skyline even from a distance of several kilometres.

THE GIANT STUPA

Manikyala was beautiful. In the backdrop of the rising stupa, life in the village rolled by. Once bells must have rung from the monasteries, today one hears the call of the muezzin. Herds of cattle lazed about in the fields and carts plied with loads of vegetables and cans of milk. The road leading to the village market was lined with shops; we took the newly built road to the stupa which rose in the sky like a giant green dome of earth covered in wild growth, uncleared for years.

The narrow road ran for several kilometres before coming to a grinding halt near the stupa's main gate. Since the gate was locked, Zulfiqar Rahim, director of GACA, enquired about the site in-charge or ticket counter so that we could enter. But, there was none—no one to guide or open the lock. People sipping tea just opposite the main gate told us they were proud that this was the one of the biggest stupas of Asia.

They prodded us on to go behind the stupa and enter from a side path where the barricade had broken. We tried to do as told, but the path through the broken barricade too was blocked by a herd of buffaloes grazing on the rich pastures of the stupa court. We kept yelling and pushing them till they lazily walked away to the other side of the stupa. In fact, not only buffaloes but also herds of goats had been let inside by their owners through the broken iron grill. One by one we jumped inside and waded through the high grass up to the flight of steps that lead to the plinth of the stupa.

The immense courtyard of the stupa was overrun with elephant grass and tall bushes and had become a free grazing ground for animals. Although the high grills embedded in concrete walls surrounding the courtyard were locked, the villagers had found ways to get into the yard to graze their cattle.

Where shops and school sit smug, was once the site of the monastic establishment of Manikyala. The entire village could have been the site of the monastic establishment. The importance of the stupa can be gauged from its size and carved stone decorations that covered its hemisphere and the flight of steps that lead to the *pradikshana path* at the base of the drum.

The remains of the surrounding monastic institution, however, cannot be seen today, as the village population has multiplied over the centuries and the surrounding land taken up for cultivation.

The location of the stupa, so near the main Grand Trunk Road reveals that the Buddhist missionaries took this same route, and that the modern road indeed covers the ancient route of the Uttarapath. It is said that the Mauryan Emperor Asoka, after his Second Buddhist Council, sent missionary monks to Gandhara where the monks built stupas, such as the Dhamarajika in Taxila Valley and Manikyala in Punjab. The colossal solid brick stupas were mostly replicas of the great stupas at Deo Kothar, Bharhut and Sanchi.

In later periods of the Indo-Greek (second century BC) and Kushan (first–third century AD) rule, new monasteries and stupas were erected. Several stupas from the Mauryan period were also repaired and enlarged. It was common practice to add new domes and architectural decorations like niches and vertical columns. Likewise, during the reign of Kanishka, the gigantic stupa of Manikyala dated year 20 (AD 98) according to its inscription, is believed by many to conceal within an earlier smaller stupa with relics.[1] Alexander Cunningham identified the stupa of Manikyala with the 'great stupa of Body Offering' to commemorate the sacrifice made by the bodhisattva to feed hungry lions.[2] This was also confirmed when in 1834 General Court excavated 14 different mounds near the main stupa and discovered from one an inscription mentioning *Huta Murta* or 'Body Offering'.[3]

The Manikyala stupa was first excavated in 1830 by General Ventura, then again in 1834 by General Court, before being investigated by Cunningham in 1863–64. Relics unearthed in 1830 at three different depths from inside the stupa of Manikyala were investigated by James Princep, and he makes a detailed mention of it in his work published in the *Asiatic Records*. The most startling disclosure around a depth of 64 feet included:

> A copper box enclosing a brass cylindrical box inside which lay another gold cylinder and 49 copper coins and one gold coin belonging to Kushan kings Huviska and Kaniska. In the

---

[1] Alexander Cunningham, *The Ancient Geography of India*, Low Price Publications, Delhi, 1991 (first published 1871), p.103.
[2] Cunningham, *The Ancient Geography of India*, p.103.
[3] Muhammad Ilyas Bhatti, *Taxila: An Ancient Metropolis of Gandhara*, Umar Zirgham Publishing, Lahore, 2006, p.100.

gold cylinder on a small piece of silver were engraved two lines in Kharosthi *Gomangasa* [of the emancipated/one who has abandoned the body] *Kanarakasa* [Kanerki or Kaniska].[4]

According to Prinsep, the two lines *Gomangasa Kanarakas* indicated 'the Great Tope of Manikyala was the mausoleum of Kaniska, the prominent ruler of Kabul, Kashmir and Punjab'.

On further digging was found an immense stone slab under which lay a small chamber, a foot in breadth and depth having a number of relics. Strangely in it was a copper box with brown liquid within which was another brass cylindrical box, again filled with a brown liquid. The brown liquid is thought to have contained the mortal remains of Kanishka mixed with sandalwood and some ash dissolved in liquid.

The lid had an inscription, which is known as Ventura's 'Manikyala Cylinder Inscription'. According to Princep's decipherment the Kharosthi inscription, Manikyala was the place of receptacle of a gem or a relic of a holy personage. It read:

> *Swati Siri* [auspicious invocation] *Munipasa* [holy personage] *Gangaphuka* [bird of the Ganges] *Munipa Putrasa* [son of the holy personage] *danatrayam* [three gifts]

In 1968, the Department of Archaeology and Museums, Government of Pakistan, carried out excavations under the supervision of Saifur Rahman Dar (ex-director general, Department of Archaeology and Museums and ex-director, Lahore Museum). According to Dar, the remains at Manikyala may be dated to the beginning of the Christian era. It was consumed in flames sometime in the fifth century AD. The site was then occupied by people having different cultural traits and finally abandoned in the eighth century AD. The structures exposed by Dar showed high buildings having roof of wooden beams, gilded and decorated with mica sheets, which were most probably used as shrines and chapels. 'Intriguing materials such as pottery and antiquities have emphasised the importance of Manikyala in solving

---

[4] James Princep, *Journal of the Asiatic Society*, Vol. 17, 1860.

many cultural and chronological problems.'[5]

Most importantly, Dar's excavations revealed that the style of masonry at Manikyala bear little resemblance with any other found in the Taxila Valley, or elsewhere in Gandhara.[6] In his opinion, the site could shed light on the diversity of cultures in early Punjab.[7] Today, the upper half of the stupa is filled with rubble. It has deep grooves and vegetation has covered the hemispherical top. However, the base of the stupa is still intact and decorated with beautiful dressed stones with a lotus design. Despite the bushy overgrowth, one can see the four flight of steps made of stone leading to the upper processional path of the stupa. A noisy flour mill runs on one side of the stupa boundary, and close to the stupa courtyard is a cattle shed with dozens of cattle and a lot of cow dung.

CHINESE PILGRIMS AT MANIKYALA

Korean pilgrim Hye Ch'o set out for India in AD 723 and came as far as Gandhara and Udyayana. He mentions having seen stupas built at the places of the bodhisattva's sacrifice of his head and eyes to Yakshas and also at the place of King Sibi's sacrifice for a dove. He, however, does not mention the place of where the bodhisattva fed his flesh to the hungry lions, which is generally associated with the stupa of Manikyala. This is because after arriving at Gandhara, Hye Ch'o, instead of crossing the Indus, went northwards to Udyayana—the Swat Valley and further north-east to Chitral before returning to Gandhara. It seems he travelled westwards to Lampaka near Jalalabad and onwards to Kapisa.[8]

---

[5] Ahmad Nabi Khan, 'Excavations at Manikyala by Saifur Rehman Dar', *Pakistan Archaeology*, No. 7, 1972, p.22.
[6] Khan, 'Excavations at Manikyala by Saifur Rehman Dar', p.20.
[7] Daniel Michon, *Archaeology and Religion in Early Northwest India: History, Theory, Practice*, Routledge, India, 2015, p.67.
[8] Han-Sung Yang, Yun-Hua Jan, Shotaro Iida and Lawrence Preston (eds and trans.), *Hye Ch'o Diary: A Memoir of the Pilgrimage to the Five Regions of India*, Asian Humanities Press, Berkeley, CA, 1984, pp.49–50.

Xuanzang arrived at Manikyala at about AD 630 and mentioned the story of the Buddha's sacrifice to feed hungry lion cubs. Xuanzang travelled 200 *li* (100 km) south-east from Taxila and reached Simhapura identified with Katas for an excursion with Jain pilgrims and returned to Taxila. Later, he reached the northern frontiers of Taxila, crossed the Indus River and travelled another 200 *li* (100 km) to reach the great stone gates of Manikyala.

According to Samuel Beal, translator of Xuanzang's records of his journey to India, after his excursion to Katas, the pilgrim went back to Ohind and crossed and re-crossed the Indus. This is accurate as the distance from Hasan Abdal to Manikyala is 200 *li* (100 km).[9]

Mentioning the 'great stone gate', Xuanzang describes a piteous tale of a bodhisattva who sacrificed his body to feed a hungry tigress. He says that this was the place where formerly Mahasattva, as a prince, sacrificed his body to feed a hungry tiger. This is mentioned in the *Vyagrahi Jataka*. Forty to fifty paces from this stone gate, he mentions having seen a stone stupa. This was the place where Mahasattva pitying the dying condition of the beast, after arriving at the spot, pierced his body with a bamboo splinter, so as to nourish the beast with his blood. The tiger licked the blood and was resuscitated.

To the north of the sacrificial spot, he saw another stone stupa about 200-feet high, built by King Asoka. This could be the present stupa of Manikyala. It was tastefully constructed, adorned with sculptures and gleamed with a divine brightness. Whoever circumambulated the stupa was cured of his illness. Around this stupa were about a hundred small votive stupas with stone niches for installing images. There was a monastery to the east of this stupa where lived a hundred priests who studied the 'Great Vehicle' or the Mahayana texts.

About 16 km from this point, there was another monastery in an isolated mountain where lived another 200 priests studying the 'Great Vehicle'. There were fountains and tanks clear as mirror. By the side of this *sangharama* was another stupa about 300 feet in

---

[9] Samuel Beal, *Si-Yu-Ki: Buddhist Records of the Western World*, Book II, Low Price Publications, Delhi, 1884, p.145.

height. This was the place where the Buddha lived in his old age and restrained a wicked flesh-eating *yaksha*.[10]

It is significant to note that from Manikyala, Xuanzang takes a south-easterly mountainous route into Kashmir through the kingdom of Urasa, which was dependent on Kashmir. According to Hungarian–British archaeologist Aurel Stein, the name Hazara is believed to have been derived from Urasa, an ancient Sanskrit name for the region of Hazara.

---

[10] Beal, Si-Yu-Ki, Book II, p.147.

Chapter 7

TAXILA: CELEBRATED CITY OF UTTARAPATH

It is said that the Buddha's ancestor, the Sakyan Okkakamukho, belonged to the region of the Indus and, Taxila was among his 19 capital cities. Edward Pococke in *India in Greece* presents information from the *Tika*, giving a distinct account of Okkako (Icskwaku of Indus) and his descendants, as well as the derivation of the royal patronymic 'Sakya,' of which, according to Pococke, no clue could be obtained in Hindu annals but which is nearly identical with the account extracted by Csoma de Koros from the Tibetan 'Kahgyur', and published in the *Bengal Asiatic Journal* of August, 1833. These capitals were Kusawati, Ayojjhapura, Baranasi, Kapila, Hatthipura, Ecachckkhu, Wajirawutiti, Madhura, Arittbapura, Ikdapatta, Kosambi, Kannagochha, Roja, Champa, Mithila, Rajagaha, Takkasilla, Kusnara and Tamalitti.[1]

Most importantly, Taxila was the cultural lifeline of Gandhara that brought India into the orbit of Persian, Greek and Roman influence. This was owing to the fact that it lay on the network of international trade routes that linked the city through the Kabul Valley with western routes going into Persia in West Asia up to the shores of the eastern Mediterranean. Lying on the western extremities of the Uttarapath, Taxila was also linked with the Bay of Bengal towards the east and with the land of the Oxus in the north-west.

The famous Taxila–Pataliputra route of the fourth–third century BC connected the city with the Mauryan capital at Pataliputra. A line map of this busy route given by archaeologist Basant Bidari shows the connection of Taxila with Vaishali, Pataliputra and Rajgriha (present-day Rajgir). According to Bidari, the Uttarapath originally extended from Sravasti to Taxila and covered the entire northern India from Anga in the east to Gandhara in the north-west, and

---

[1] E. Pococke, *India in Greece*, John J. Griffin and Co. London, 1852, pp.91–96.

from the Himalayas in the north to Vindhyas in the south.² The eastern sections of this Taxila–Pataliputra route passed through the main Sakyan centres of Kapilavastu and Setavya, the Malla kingdoms of Kushnara and Pava, Bhognagar and the Lichchavi kingdom of Vaishali and Rajgir.³ This was a busy and famous route even during the Buddha's time in the sixth century BC, and it should not come as a surprise that following a bitter feud in Kapilavastu between the Sakyans and the armies of Virudhaka, many excommunicated Sakyans escaped to Gandhara. We also hear the Buddha visiting his kin in Gandhara.

It was along this route that trading caravans from Bactria (present-day Balkh) and Kabul were travelling to Varanasi and Bodhgaya with thousands of carts laden with goods for sale. Horses from the Trans-Caspian Region were also driven along this same route to the eastern kingdoms of India. Two merchants from Bactria—Trapussa and Bhallika—who were travelling along this route from Balkh, met with the Buddha at Sarnath after his Enlightenment at Bodhgaya.

TAXILA PILLAR EDICT OF ASOKA

A map by Bidari shows that in the third century BC, the Mauryan Emperor Asoka laid his pillars along this same route leading towards Taxila. His Aramaic Pillar Edict in Taxila was discovered by John Marshall in 1915.⁴ The inscription on a piece of marble, originally belonging to an octagonal column is written in Aramaic, probably by the Mauryan Emperor Asoka around 260 BC, and categorized as one of the Minor Rock Edicts. The text of the inscription is very fragmentary, but it has been established that it contains twice, line 9 and line 12 and mentions MR'N PRYDRS (our Lord Priyadarsi), the characteristic title used by Asoka. The inscription seems to be addressed directly to the population of the north-west region, the

---

² Basanta Bidari, *Lumbini: A Haven of Sacred Refuge*, Hill Side Press, Lumbini, 2004, p.6.
³ Bidari, *Lumbini*, p.7.
⁴ Bidari, *Lumbini*, p.137.

borderlands where Aramaic was the language of communication. According to Indologist Radhakumud Mookerji, the foreign population of Gandhara, namely the Yonas and Kambojas, had won their status as autonomous communities within the Mauryan Empire and their cultural needs were duly recognized by Asoka. He issued the inscription with Buddhist content in Aramaic language and script at Taxila, the most important centre of foreign population.[5]

Eratosthenes, a Greek geographer who was contemporary of Asoka, informs of a royal highway connecting the Mauryan capital Palibothra (or Pataliputra) with Susa in Iran. This could have been a continuation of the Taxila route. The two Lamghan Edicts of Asoka mentioning distances and directions of several places could be pointing to the same Susa–Taxila–Pataliputra route. This was probably the route that Asoka's emissaries took on their *Dhamma* missions to the kingdom of five Yavana rulers in West Asia, and also brought back fine wine and delicious figs from the Syrian king Antiochus I to their Mauryan counterpart, Bindusara.[6]

As mentioned earlier, Greeks and Persians formed a substantial population of Taxila as early as the sixth century BC, when the north-west regions of India were included in the list of the 20 satrapies of Darius and many pre-Alexandrian Greek settlements had come up. There was close interaction between Greeks and Indians even during the time of Alexander in the fourth century BC—a time much before the establishment the Indo-Greek kingdom in India of the second century BC.[7]

Greek ambassadors to the Mauryan courts were regularly travelling on the Taxila–Pataliputra route. One envoy, Megasthanes, even wrote

---

[5] J. Harmatta, *Languages and Scripts in Graeco-Bactria and the Saka Kingdoms*, Vol II: History of Civilizations of Central Asia, UNESCO, New Delhi, 1994 and Motilal Banarsidass Publishers, Delhi, 1999, Delhi, p.398. Also see, Radhakumud Mookerji, Asoka, Motilal Banarsidass Publishers, Delhi, 2007, pp.275–76. For a general read, see Aramaic Inscription of Taxila on Wikipedia.org.
[6] Ranabir Chakravarti, *Exploring Early India up to c. AD 1300*, Primus Books, Delhi, 2016, p.166.
[7] Mookerji, *Asoka*, p.275.

in his celebrated book *Indica*, about the presence of foreigners in India and about the existence of a separate department in Chandragupta's government that looked after foreigners.[8] It is therefore no surprise that Taxilians were conversant with the Greek language. The *Life of Apollonius Tyana* written by Philostratus c.AD 46 mentions Phraotes, the Indo-Parthian king of Taxila, speaking to the Greek philosopher Apollonios of Tyana in Greek.

The Indian king said that he had been brought up by his father in the Greek fashion till the age of twelve. He was then sent to the Brahmanas who treated him as a son, because they especially loved people who knew and spoke Greek.[9]

Thus, control over Gandhara was crucial for any ruler of India and the Mauryans had placed it under a viceroy—the viceroyalty being generally reserved for Mauryan princes.[10]

Often, the Taxilians became hostile to the governor and discontent had to be quelled as Taxila was an important entrepôt of trade bringing in wealth. During the period of Bindusara (Asoka's father), his two sons—Susima (or Sumana) and Asoka—were appointed as his viceroys at Taxila and Ujjayini, respectively. Later, when Taxila was in revolt—and Susima was not able to supress it—Asoka was transferred to the city, as he was considered more competent for the purpose. Prince Kunala was Asoka's viceroy at Taxila. The emperor on his consecration is also said to have appointed his younger brother, Tisya, as his deputy, or viceregent (*uparaja*), who, on his retirement as a religious devotee, was succeeded by Prince Mahendra.[11]

---

[8] John McCrindle, *Ancient India as Described by Megasthanese and Arrian*, Fragment XXXIV, Munshiram Manoharlal Publishers, Delhi, 2008, p.87.
[9] B.N. Puri, *The Sakas and Indo-Parthians*, Vol. II: History of Civilizations of Central Asia, UNESCO, New Delhi, 1994 and Motilal Banarsidass Publishers, Delhi, 1999, p.197. See also, Demetrios Th. Vassiliades, *The Greeks in India: A Survey in Philosophical Understanding*, Munshiram Manoharlal Publishers, Delhi, 2000, p.74.
[10] Mookerji, *Asoka*, p.51.
[11] Mookerji, *Asoka*, p.51.

TAXILA: A CITY OF WEALTH

The gifts offered to Alexander by the governor of Taxila (Taxiles), are evidence of Taxila's great wealth. Omphis (or Ambhi) was called Taxiles by his people for 'such was the name that accompanied the sovereignty on whomsoever it devolved.' After Taxiles had entertained Alexander with profuse generosity for three days, he presented him and all his friends with golden crowns, 80 *talents* (measure of weight) of silver coins and 25 elephants.[12]

Historian Upinder Singh points out that the wealth of Taxila can also be gauged from the coins issued by its traders' guilds.[13] According to him, the rich city also showed its generosity in the form of a donative pillar established by Antialcidas, the king of Taxila, who was the Greek ruler of Besnagar at Vidisha. With six lines in Brahmi script, the pillar—also known as the Garuda Pillar—of Vasudeva, the god of gods, was constructed by Heliodorus, son of Dion of Taxila, the Greek ambassador to King Antialcidas.[14] Today, the pillar of Heliodorus can be seen at the ancient site of Vidisha, close to the railway station of Bina.

As Litvinsky notes, during the Kushan period, the streets of Taxila were lined with rows of buildings whose lower floors contained ateliers or shops facing the street.[15] Taxila's location on the trade routes ensured its great wealth. There was extensive interaction with regions of Central Asia because of the passes in the north-western mountains of the frontier regions—the Sulaiman Ranges collected less snow than those of the higher Himalayas and their passes were therefore more frequently used. These included the Bolan, Gomal and

---

[12] A.H. Dani and P. Bernard, *Alexander and His Successors in Central Asia*, Vol. III: History of Civilizations of Central Asia, Motilal Banarsidass Publishers, Delhi, 1996 and UNESCO, New Delhi, 1999), pp.79–80.

[13] Upinder Singh, *A History of Ancient and Early Medieval India: From Stone Age to the 12th Century*, Pearson Longman, Delhi, 2008, p.407.

[14] Singh, *A History of Ancient and Early Medieval India*, p.372.

[15] B.A. Litvinsky, *Cities and Urban Life in the Kushan Kingdom*, Vol. III: The History of Civilizations of Central Asia, Motilal Banarsidass Publishers, Delhi, 1996 and UNESCO, New Delhi, 1999, p.309.

Khyber passes, which were used by traders from Central Asia, Iran and Afghanistan and became corridors of communication.[16] Contact with these regions is believed to be as old as the period of the Indus cities in the third century BC.[17]

The fertile Swat Valley connected Taxila to the northern route to the Tarim Basin. This route lay in the Karakoram ranges via Gilgit, Chitral and Hunza which came to be called the Central Asian Silk Route.[18] Engravings of human figures, and depiction on masks of animals like ibexes and those with stylized horns were found during explorations in the Gilgit and Baltistan regions in the far north of Pakistan,[19] which is evidence that these routes were used by early travellers.

Both land and sea routes could be approached through Taxila, and goods from the Tibetan plateau and China flowed down the Indus. The modern Karakoram Highway from Kashgar to Islamabad which covers the ancient route between Pakistan and China, is today the highest international road in the world running through the Khunjerab Pass at an altitude of about 5,000 metre, connecting the Xinjiang province with the Gilgit–Baltistan region and the Khyber region of Pakistan.

Thus the position of Taxila on the Silk Route played a catalytic role in the trade and commerce of Asia. It was connected not only by overland routes to Kashgar and the Tarim Basin through the Karakoram ranges but also by maritime routes of the Arabian Sea via the Indus to West Asia and also Southeast Asia and via the Uttarapath to the Bay of Bengal.

Taxila could thus control trade on the Indus coming from the Tibetan plateau and the sea trade between Alexandria and Barbaricon at the mouth of the Indus, particularly when the east–west route

---

[16] Romila Thapar, *The Penguin History of Early India: From Origins to AD 1300*, Penguin India, Delhi, 2002, p.140.
[17] Thapar, *The Penguin History of Early India*, p.40 and p.58.
[18] Thapar, *The Penguin History of Early India*, p.41.
[19] Thapar, *The Penguin History of Early India*, p.74.

between Rome and Parthia was closed due to trade hostilities.[20]

We also read of rich trade being plied along the Uttarapath, which connected Taxila with Tamralipti in the Gangetic delta.[21] The crucial Taxila to Balkh routes started from Taxila via Peshawar along the Khyber Pass through Hadda and Nagarhara (present-day Jalalabad) and reached Bamiyan and onwards to Bactria (present-day Balkh). From Balkh, a northern road passed into Termez and went along the Oxus to the Khorezm region around the Aral Sea or crossed the Jaxartes, reaching Tashkent and the north-east (along the Chuy River and Ili River) into the Semirechye region to the borders of China and joined the northern route to Hami. Another route passed from Balkh to the Stone tower in Tashkurgan through Badakhshan into the Pamirs towards the Wakhan Corridor.

NAGA KINGS AT TAXILA

From the works of historian Ahmad H. Dani, we learn that the oldest rulers of Taxila were the Takshakas who were the rulers of the hill capital of the Takshakas—their modern descendants are the people of the Taka tribe, whose name originated from their worship of Takila, or serpents. The name of the city too, Taxila (correctly pronounced Taksha-sila) is a derivation of the same. It was also the place where King Janamejaya performed the great *naga yajna*, or snake sacrifice.[22] This Naga or the serpent king is believed to have kin in India, China and Central Asia, Egypt, Greece and Thailand. Dani points to a clash of two cultural trends at Taxila—the Naga culture and the Aryan culture.[23]

Who were these Naga kings? Were they mythical serpents or

---

[20] Joseph Needham, *Science and Civilisation in China*, Cambridge University Press, London, 1954 (reprint 1979), p.182. See also, Jonathan Tucker, *Silk Road Art and History*, Timeless Books, Delhi, 2003, p.41.
[21] Singh, *A History of Ancient and Early Medieval India*, p.407.
[22] Singh, *A History of Ancient and Early Medieval India*, p.281.
[23] Ahmad H. Dani, *Historic City of Taxila*, UNESCO and Centre for East Asian Cultural Studies, 1986, p.39.

members of a tribe? According to renowned social reformer B.R. Ambedkar, the Nagas lived in the Punjab region. They are also a historical people, a clan or dynasty of kings who once ruled the Naga Dwipa or the Island of serpents. The Naga tribe, semi-divine in character, with their totem as the serpent, spread throughout India, from Taxila in the Northwest to Assam in the north-east, and further down to south India and erstwhile Ceylon. There is a Naga tribe still living in eastern India.[24]

In the *Rig Veda*, we are first introduced to the snake-god in the form of Ahivitra, the enemy of the Aryan god, Indra. This shows that the Nagas are a very ancient people who not only occupied a high cultural space, but history shows that they ruled a good part of India as well.

From the Buddhist tradition of Ceylon and Siam, we also know that there was a Naga country called Majerika near the Diamond Sands, in Karachi,[25] and could have been a sea-faring tribe. These Nagas must have been ruling over different portions of Uttarapath until they were vanquished before the conquering armies of Samudragupta.[26]

Not surprisingly, the story of the Takshak Naga of Taxila and its emblem has strange parallels in art found on temples and mosques. The serpent symbol of religious deities in both Hinduism and Buddhism, not only in India but as far east as China and Tibet and as far west as Spain, can be seen today. The great cobra (Takshak) guarded the treasures of the Debod Temple; it carried the message of peace on the portals of the mosque at Bagabat in Turkmenistan; and guarded the holy soma or *haoma* of ancient Margiana.

---

[24] Jan Knappert, *Indian Mythology: An Encyclopaedia of Myth and Legend*, Diamond Books, London, 1995, p.176. See also, B.R. Ambedkar, *The Untouchables Who Were They and Why They Became Untouchables*, Kalpaz Publications; Delhi, 1948 (reprint 2017), pp.47–50.
[25] Ambedkar, *The Untouchables Who Were They and Why They Became Untouchables*, pp.47–50.
[26] Ambedkar, *The Untouchables Who Were They and Why They Became Untouchables*, pp.47–50.

At the Bagabat Mosque, a model of which is displayed at the National Museum of Turkmenistan at Ashgabat, what catches the eye is a pair of wriggling snakes with dragon-like heads, thick stubby claws and holding stalks or branches of blooming flowers in their mouth. They do not appear to be ominous creatures, dreadful or evil. Since they are holding flowering branches in their mouth, they are harbingers of good omen, luck, prosperity, bountiful harvest and good rains in the arid desert region.

A parallel may also be drawn to the Egyptian Temple of Debod (rebuilt in Madrid, Spain) where two king cobras flanking the winged solar deity can be seen. Dedicated to God Amun and Goddess Isis, this temple is from the second century BC. The gateway cornice made of sandstone is dated to 172–170 BC. It is said that in the microcosm of all Egyptian temples, the doorway, cornice and lintels were frequently adorned with a winged solar deity flanked by two cobras.

In Indian mythology,[27] the Naga is represented as mythical beings with a human face and a long tail like a reptile. They reside in the region of Patala under the earth where they live luxuriously in splendid palaces.

Buddhist stories also mention Naga rajas. In some Buddhist caves such as the Kanheri Caves and the caves in Junnar located in Maharashtra, the Naga deity appears at the entrance to the courtyard of the main *chaitya* cave. At Ajanta too, serpents appear on the doorjamb of the vihara, and the *garbha griha* has the image of the Buddha. In all cases, they are depicted as performing the function of guardian deities. Nagas with their five-hooded canopy are also shown as worshipping the stupa on the facade of Cave 19 at Ajanta. At Sanchi, the carved stone panels have the Muchalinda serpent deity worshipping the Buddhist stupa.

Margush (also known by the name of Margiana) in Turkmenistan was known well beyond its borders and had relations with the Indus Valley as shown by Soviet archaeologist Viktor Sarianidi. Copper seals found during excavations at Margush bear images of snakes

---

[27] Knappert, *Indian Mythology*, p.176.

or scorpions. Some picture compositions show struggles between snake and dragon for possession of vital power. One amulet depicted a male tiger with a snake writhing round his hind legs, portraying the abduction of the 'semen of life' of a dangerous beast. Another depicted a swiftly running antelope attacked by a snake-like dragon. Another two-tailed dragon tries to reach its hind legs from below. It is said that the Margushians regarded the snake as a guardian of the people, which protected them from the evil power of the hostile dragon. They portrayed the dramatic episodes of Margushian mythology by highlighting the basic theme of struggle between good and evil.[28]

Some cult vessels intended for drinking *haoma* had wriggling snakes crawling out of the bottom of the vessel and reaching up to the bellies of animals walking along the upper edge of the vessel.

TAXILA: A PREMIER EDUCATIONAL CITY

The University of Ancient Taxila attracted scholars from far and wide. A renowned centre for sciences and the arts, it is said to have existed even before the time of the Buddha and before the occupation of the Taxila Valley by the Achaemenid rulers in the sixth–fifth century BC. Philosophers gathered here to have their own schools of thought and imparted instructions to propound their school of thought, to call for debates and vanquish their rivals, probably from as early as the seventh century BC.

We learn from the stories of the Jatakas that kings from former times often used to send their sons to foreign countries afar to complete their education. This way they could learn to quell their pride and highmindedness, learn to endure heat and cold, and be made acquainted with the ways of the world.

As a result, many royal princes were sent to Taxila. For example, several Jatakas, such as *Tilamutthi Jataka*, *Sujata Jataka*, *Nana-*

---

[28] Wiktor Sarianidi, Margush: Turkmenistan (Ancient Oriental kingdom in the Old Delta of the Murghab River), Turkmendowlethabarlary, Ashgabat 2002, pp.308–09.

cchanda Jataka, *Susima Jataka*, *Parantapa Jataka* and *Atthasadda Jataka* discuss royalty studying in Taxila. The *Darimukha Jataka*[29] tells the story of Prince Darimukha who finished his education in Taxila and then set out on a series of travels to study the manners and customs of people in various parts of the country. He took a friend, the son of a royal priest, along for company.[30] In the *Tale of the Monkey Brothers*, we learn about the wise Taxila guru. The Buddhist text *Uddalaka Jataka* (No. 487) mentions that Uddalaka journeyed to Takshashila (Taxila to the north-west of Rawalpindi) and acquired knowledge from a renowned teacher.

Among the famous scholars from Taxila was Jivaka, later a physician of the Magadhan ruler Bimbisara and physician of the Buddha himself.[31] The great scholar was sent to Jivakarama Monastery at Rajgir in Bihar, the ruins of which can still be found in the city. He also ran a hospital known as the Mardikakkshi at the base of the Gridhakuta Hills. It is here that Buddha was brought after he was injured by a rock hurled by Devadutta in an attempt to kill him and take over the Sangha.

The well-known king Prasenajita of Kosala (located around modern-day Ayodhya) also studied at Taxila.[32] Among the teachers, there was Panini, the great grammarian of the sixth century BC; Kautilya, the author of *Arthsashtra*—a book on political science; and the great physician, Charaka. Today, copies of the *Charak Samhita* in Sanskrit adorn the shelves of the pharmaceutical industry in Tibet. My visit to the Tibetan hospital in Lhasa and a pharmaceutical factory at Nyingchi province brought out this amazing fact. The legacy of

---

[29] *Darimukha Jataka*, Vol. III, No. 376, Book 6, p.156.
[30] E.B. Cowell (ed.), The Jatakas or Stories of the Buddha's Former Births, Vol. 1–6 (Translated from Pali by Robert Chalmers), Low Price Publications, Delhi. See also, Singh, *A History of Ancient and Early Medieval India*, p.407.
[31] Dani, The Historic City of Taxila. See also, Jivaka, Chinese Buddhist Encyclopedia at <www.chinabuddhismencyclopedia.com> (last date of access: 8 February 2020).
[32] T.W. Rhys Davids, *Buddhist India*, D.K. Publishers Distributors, Delhi, 1903 (reprint 2002), p.8. See also, Dani, History in Taxila.

traditional herbal medicines in Tibet owes much of its origin to this great scholar of Taxila.

Indologist B.N. Puri mentions the great scholar Kumaralata from Taxila,[33] who was the founder of the Sautrantika School of Buddhism and a contemporary of Asvaghosa, Nagarjuna and Aryadeva. The king of Khotan is believed to have attacked Taxila and carried him off by force. The ruler of Khotan then built a convent for him.[34] Vasubandhu, the great Buddhist scholar, came from the vicinity of Peshawar, not far from Taxila.[35]

We all know that the great tantric and Buddhist scholar Padmasambhava, one of the greatest exponents of Tantric Buddhism, was known as Guru or Mahacharya in Tibet. He belonged to the Swat Valley and possibly was a student of the Taxila University.

---

[33] B.N. Puri, *Buddhism in Central Asia*, Motilal Banarsidass Publishers, Delhi, 2000, p.105.
[34] Puri, *Buddhism in Central Asia*, p.105n.
[35] Saroj Kumar Chaudhuri, *Lives of Early Buddhist Monks*, Abha Prakashan, Delhi, 2008, p.32.

Chapter 8

ON THE ROAD TO TAXILA

On the way back from the stupa of Manikyala, we crossed the famous Rawat Market where fancy auto-rickshaws and colourful trucks could be seen unloading fruits and vegetables brought from the neighbouring villages. The air was thick with the stench from a distillery near by. Ayesha informed me that the famous sugarcane belt of Punjab ran through Rawat and fed many sugar mills and distilleries. Not just sugar, Rawat was also the hub of polished marble brought from the quarries of Manshera and Mardan.

The famous sixteenth-century Rawat Fort stood 15 km off the main Grand Trunk Road. Founded as a caravanserai built over the remains of an eleventh-century Ghaznavid era fort, the serai was fortified by the Gakkhar rulers to defend the Potohar Plateau from the forces of the Afghan ruler, Sher Shah Suri. The Gakkhar chief Sultan Sarang is said to have died fighting the Afghan king in 1546, and was buried at the fort along with his 16 sons who also died alongside him.[1]

Further on, the Margalla Hills, which are a part of the Himalayan foothills, swung into view. At the town of Bahria, we left the Islamabad road going northwards and took a left turn for Pindi where Saidul Hasan Zaidi, president of the Gandhara Art and Cultural Association, was scheduled to join us for lunch. His wife, born in Peshawar, traces her roots to the city of Lucknow in Uttar Pradesh. She extended a warm embrace on hearing that I came from her ancestral town of Lucknow. My final destination, however, was Zulfiqar's (secretary, Gandhara Art and Cultural Association) residence in Bani Gala, Islamabad, a 30-minute drive from Pindi.

Heavy rains had lashed Islamabad through the night. Banigala was flooded—lanes, by lanes and parks of the city were submerged.

---

[1] For a general read, see https://en.wikipedia.org/wiki/Rawat_Fort

Weather forecasters announced more rains for the next couple of days, but the rain was no deterrent. I woke up with the sun for the 32-km ride to the world heritage site that lay at the foot of the Murree Hills. The drive took barely a couple of hours. Driving along Murree Road, we crossed Avenue 7 and headed towards Taxila. Along this road, one can see the original cobblestoned, medieval-era Grand Trunk Road to the left, cutting through Margalla Hills, which is a heritage site preserved by the tourism authorities of Pakistan. The old road is a pathway to the past when many invaders and missionaries travelled from Kabul to Sonargaon (near Dhaka in Bangladesh) along this road.

The road to Taxila cut away from the main Grand Trunk Road to my right. We took a U-turn and crossed over to the other side and then took a left for Taxila.

ALEXANDER IN TAXILA

When Alexander first landed at Taxila with his army in the fourth century BC, it was one of the largest and richest cities of the Indus situated in a land of flowing streams, fountains and thickly wooded jungles.

A number of streams still flow along the ancient ruins, fountains still rush out of rock crevices and thick jungles still hem the celebrated city. And we drove along the network of roads that approached monastic ruins, we were amazed at the virgin beauty of the low hills covered in immense greenery. The Haro River and numerous other streams water the approximately 10-km-wide and 25-km-long corridor in which the ancient city of Taxila was born and died.

ANCIENT CITIES OF TAXILA

When John Marshall, director general of the Archaeological Survey of India (1902–1928), explored the valley in the early twentieth century, he found ruins of numerous Buddhist monuments comprising vestiges from three different era—Achaemenian, Greek and Kushan—a time when extensive building activities took place here. It has been generally thought that Bhir Mound belonged to the Achaemenian era; Sirkap and Jandial to the Greek era; and Sirsukh, Jaulian, Mohra Moradu, Dharmarajika, Pipplan to the Kushan era.[2] Beside the remains of these three ancient cities, Marshall also found a large number of isolated monuments, mainly Buddhist stupas and monasteries, scattered over the surrounding hilly forests of Taxila.

Driving along the main Taxila road towards the Jaulian Monastery, one will find that the roads run through a long dusty haze of low blue hills that are actually the ruins of the Bhir Mound, believed to be the most ancient of all the sites at Taxila. The sprawling site consists of successive settlements ranging from the Achaemenid period of the sixth century BC to the Mauryan period of the third century BC.

After the city on the Bhir Mound was destroyed, the Bactrian Greek king Demetrius transferred the population to the city of Sirkap on the east side of the Tamra Nala in the second century BC. An inscription found here has reference to 'Priyadarsi', the title used by Mauryan Emperor Asoka who ruled over Taxila in the third century BC. The inscription on a piece of marble, originally belonging to an octagonal column is written in Aramaic—probably by Asoka c.260 BC—and is categorized as one of the Minor Rock Edicts. The inscription is displayed at the Taxila Museum today. The text of the inscription is very fragmented, but it has been established that it contains twice, line 9 and line 12 and mentions MR'N PRYDRS (our Lord Priyadarsi), the characteristic title used by Asoka. According to historian Radhakumud Mookerji, Asoka was the first king in India to have issued inscriptions in the manner of the old Achaemenian kings.[3]

In 1863–64, Alexander Cunningham reports of the famous legend of the Buddha cutting off his head to feed a hungry tiger which is attached to the city of Sirkap (or 'Sirkat', meaning head cutting—*taksha sira*). The copperplate inscription from the beginning of the

---

[2] Sir John Marshall, *A Guide to Taxila*, Royal Book Company, Karachi, 2007, pp.4–6.
[3] Radhakumud Mookerji, *Asoka*, Motilal Banarsidass Publishers, Delhi, 2007, p.275.

Christian era gives the city its name—Taksha Sila.[4] Remains of a stupa were found in the residential area of Sirkap and the most famous structure here is the double-headed eagle stupa, dated second century BC.[5] Towards the extreme south of the Sirkap city excavations have unearthed the possible site of a university or establishment.[6]

The third ancient city of Taxila is Sirsukh of which I could see only a part of the walls. Fragments of the wall spread out in a vast thickly shrubby area. Its stone masonry, rectangular planning and defensive wall indicate that it dates from the first century AD of the Kushan period.[7]

Jaulian, Mohra Moradu and Pippalan, dated to fourth–fifth century AD, are the three well-preserved monasteries on the Hathial spur, and are the main attractions for any visitor to Taxila.

However, the raw beauty of the Zoroastrian temple of Jandiala (dated second century BC to second century AD) built of massive blocks of stone cannot be missed, as it is on the way to the Mohra Moradu and Jaulian monasteries. Here, one will notice that the temple is located on an elevation and reached by stone steps. Whether the elevation was due to a low hill or was artificially created cannot be said. Also, the roof of the entire structure is absent giving an idea that the temple stood in an open courtyard. Ionic columns and pilasters and massive blocks of sandstone are still strewn around giving the appearance that some natural disaster shook the structure and led to its collapse.

The temple once consisted of a square sanctuary, a meeting hall and a courtyard, the remains of which were dug up by archaeologists during the first half of the twentieth century AD. According to historian Ihsan H. Nadiem, the monument closely resembles ancient

---

[4] Alexander Cunningham, *The Ancient Geography of India*, Low Price Publications, Delhi, 1871 (reprint 1990), p.93.
[5] Ihsan H. Nadiem, *Taxila in Buddhist Gandhara*, Sang-e-Meel Publications, Lahore, 2008, pp.79–80.
[6] Nadiem, *Taxila in Buddhist Gandhara*, p.86.
[7] Muhammad Iliyas Bhatti, *Taxila: An Ancient Metropolis of Gandhara*, Umar Zirgham, Lahore, 2006), p.78.

Greek temples and may have been dedicated to a Zoroastrian cult giving evidence of the presence of other religions during the Buddhist period.[8]

North of Taxila, the road reaches Haripur. On this highway N-125 via Khanpur lies the famous monastic site of Bhamala, located in the midst of hills in Haripur district of Khyber Pakhtunkhwa Province, located 45 km from Taxila. The startling discovery of the world's oldest and largest colossal Reclining Buddha statuary was made at Bhamala. The Archaeology Department of Pakistan unveiled the 48-ft-long and 1,700-year-old statuary at the site, lying just beyond the modern village of Khanpur with the Haro River flowing at its foot.

According to Abdul Samad, director of the Department of Archaeology and Museums, the 'Sleeping Buddha' from third century AD is believed to be the world's oldest. In addition to this, over 500 Buddhist antiquities have been discovered at Bhamala.[9] Bhamala is best known for its famous fourth-century cruciform stupa, which is a part of the larger Bhamala Buddhist Complex.

Significantly, the present Karakoram Highway running over an ancient route that connected the Upper Indus Valley with the Tarim Basin in Xinjiang through the Pamir Mountains passed along the celebrated cities of Taxila and Haripur where dense Buddhist settlements came up as early as the first century AD. The Karakoram Highway was the northern extension of the main trade and pilgrim corridor, the Uttarapath connecting the valleys of the Indus and the Oxus.

---

[8] Nadiem, *Taxila in Buddhist Gandhara*, p.91.
[9] Hidayat Khan, 'Smells Like Nirvana: Over 500 New Artefacts Found at Bhamala', *The Express Tribune*, 9 March 2015. See also, Saad Sayeed, 'Pakistan Unveils 1700 Year Old Sleeping Buddha, Evolving Diverse Heritage', 15 November 2017. Available at <https://www.reuters.com/article/us-pakistan-religion/pakistan-unveils-1700-year-old-sleeping-buddha-evoking-diverse-heritage-idUSKBN1DF2RK> (last date of access: 12 February 2020); Liz Leafloor, '500 Ancient Artefacts Uncovered at the Remarkable Bhamala Archaeological Complex in Pakistan', 15 June 2018. Available at <https://www.ancient-origins.net/news-history-archaeology/500-ancient-artifacts-uncovered-remarkable-bhamala-020257> (last date of access: 12 February 2020).

It was noted during the construction of the modern Karakoram Highway that a much earlier route following similar directions existed as early as the first century AD. As mentioned earlier, the Pilgrim Corridor—the location of Asokan Edicts at Mansehra and Shahbazgarhi—marked the start of such a route. According to historian Romila Thapar, inscriptions in Brahmi, Kharosthi and Bactrian, and engravings of Buddhist images and themes along the way date the earlier route to the start of the Christian era.[10] Significantly, at the time of Xuanzang's travels on this road to Tashkurgan in AD 644, the region was populated by Buddhists.[11]

The Karakoram Highway which follows the route of the Indus River right down as far as Thakot descends towards Taxila and Islamabad. To date 30,000 petroglyphs and 5,000 inscriptions in more than 10 different languages have been identified along the highway.[12]

Besides the colossal Reclining Buddha at the Bhamala Buddhist Archaeological Complex near Haripur, another Buddha colossi was found at Kargah, 10 km from Gilgit. A massive figure of the Buddha from the seventh–eighth century AD has been carved on the cliff face. Nearby are the ruins of a monastery with stupas where from a large number of manuscripts from the fifth century AD was found in the 1930s. These documents make up the well-known Gilgit Manuscript. Apart from this, several other Buddha colossi were excavated from the monasteries of Takht-i-Bahi and Sahri Bahlol in Mardan.

TREASURES OF TAXILA

Inaugurated in 1928 by the then minister of Education, Sir Muhammad Habibullah, the Taxila Museum is located along the road to Dharamrajika. The museum's large central hall flanked by two galleries displays exquisite Buddhist statuary art in stone, stucco and terracotta; coins; and inscriptions recovered during excavations at the

---

[10] Romila Thapar, *The Penguin History of Early India*, Penguin India, Delhi, 2002, p.222.
[11] Jonathan Tucker, *Silk Road Art and History*, Timeless Books, Delhi, 2003, p.189.
[12] Tucker, *Silk Road Art and History*, pp.191–93.

various sites at Taxila. There are also numerous stucco images of the Buddha and bodhisattvas, relic caskets obtained from monastic cells and stupas exhibited in showcases, votive stupas, railings of stupas, head of the Buddha and bodhisattvas—some of them found severed from life-size images of the Buddha.

The visitor is welcomed at the entrance by the tall, exquisitely embellished stupa from Mohra Moradu. It is only a copy, the real stupa lies in Cell 9 of the monastery. But the museum provides a closer look and an opportunity to study the stupa in detail. Another object of great antiquity is a fragment of an inscribed marble pillar from Sirkap that mentions Asoka as 'Priyadarshi'. This pillar is one among the many that lined the Uttarapath or the Northern Highroad from Pataliputra to Taxila.

We drove on the Grand Trunk Road to take the Kashmir Highway to Islamabad. It was not an easy ride. Protestors supporting Imran Khan and Tahirul Qadri had blocked the road with containers and were still camping in front of the Parliament despite the heavy rains and an imminent flood. When we reached Bani Gala at 7 p.m., the downpour continued. Inner areas of the city were in knee-deep water and I was worried about the journey to Peshawar the next day.

Chapter 9

MONASTERIES OF TAXILA*

Perched on the top of a hill and home to rare Buddha images and superbly embellished stupas, Jaulian is the most important monastic city at Taxila. A UNESCO World Heritage Site, the original foundation of the monument is dated to the Kushan period between the first and second century AD.

Driving barely 30 minutes on the Taxila road, we found a signpost marking a right-turn for Jaulian. While we were still negotiating the rutted road that passes through a thick forest, rain starts lashing out on Jaulian Hills. At the base of the hill, we took refuge in a small tea shop, but the leaking thatched roof showed no mercy and droplets trickled down exactly where we stood. I was distracted by the carved replicas of the Fasting Buddhas and other Jataka stories in stone at the craft shops nearby. But the Buddha was waiting at Jaulian on the peak of a hill and there was no time for souvenir picking!

The sky was still glum, clouds were gathering and there was no hope for a clear sky. I immediately decided to climb up to the monastery. Before my knees could creak at the steep incline, my umbrella betrayed me. The fierce wind blew it away into a faraway bush and in an effort to retrieve it, I was completely drenched. Though climbing the steep mountain under a heavy rain was an uphill task, it did not dampen my spirit. The hope of seeing the most famous, beautiful and rare heritage site of Gandhara put spring in my steps. The raging wind and downpour did not daunt me. I surged forward even as my clothes and shoes were soaked.

The stepped hilly pathway crossed a wide stream racing from

---

*For details on Taxila, see John Marshall: *A Guide to Taxila*, 2007, p.162; Muhammad Ilyas Bhatti, *Taxila: An ancient Metropolis of Gandhara*, 2006, p.94; Site notices put up by the Archaeological Survey of India.

the mountain top. After a hard climb, I was inside the monastic establishment, a place where I could easily get lost amidst a large cluster of stupas and happily hide behind the closely facing stupa walls and Buddha images that peeped from every crevice.

I paid the admission fee and was thrilled when they charged nothing extra for the camera. But as soon as I pulled out my camera inside the monastery, three staffers from the Khyber Pakhtunkhwa (KPK) Tourism Department warned me about the 'no photography' rule. I was ready to pay the photography fee, but they sternly refused. My plea that I had come a long way from India fell on deaf ears. When I enquired whether a nearby shop sold slides or photos, the answer was a vehement no.

Dr Esther Park, my friend from Korea, came to my rescue. She made a quick phone call to Dr Abdul Samad, director of the KPK Tourism Department and Peshawar Museum, and conveyed my request. When he learnt I was from India, he gave the consent without any extra payment. I thanked Buddha and Dr Samad for their kindness.

I found the stupa court and monastic cells soaked in rain. The weather was changing for the worse; it was getting frosty and my hands were trembling on the camera shutter. According to the plan of the monuments at Jaulian, as illustrated and explained by archaeologist John Marshall who explored the site, it comprises a monastery of moderate dimensions and two stupa-courts by its side on different levels—the upper to the south and the lower to the north, with a third and smaller court adjoining them on the west.[1]

Entering the complex through the lower court, I stepped into the large open quadrangle with highly embellished square stupas having rows upon rows of Buddha images, figures of lions and Atlantes—Greek deity used as architectural adornment; it is a support sculpted in the form of a Herculean figure, which may take the place of pillar. There is a large open hall with numerous small shrines intended for Buddhist images along a staircase leading to the upper storey.

---

[1] Sir John Marshall, *A Guide to Taxila*, Royal Book Company, Karachi, 2007, p.13.

At the entrance, five moderate-sized stupas are arranged in a row. Originally exposed in an open courtyard surrounding the plinth of the enormous main stupa, they are now covered with a protective roof. The moderate-sized stupas have lost their domes and cylindrical drums, but their square bases are still adorned with horizontal tiers of elaborate stucco relief of 'Thousand Buddhas' pertaining to the 'Miracle of Sravasti'. The Buddha and bodhisattva images are held in niches flanked by attendants at their sides, and the rows of elephants, lions or Atlantes supporting the superstructure above them. On D5, one of these stupas, a Kharosthi inscription names the title of the images and the names of the donors.[2]

The main stupa which stands in the middle of the upper court dates from the early Kushan period (first–second century AD). On one of its face (on the northern side), is a seated Buddha figure with a circular hole at the navel intended for a suppliant to place his finger when offering prayers against certain bodily ailments. It also has an inscription in Kharosthi beneath, recording that it was the gift of one Budhamitra, who 'delighted in the Law', or Dharma.

Among the numerous small and richly decorated stupas which are arranged in rows around the main structure, the stupa AII possesses an exceptionally well-preserved bodhisattva figure. At the back of stupa AII, there are colossal images of the Buddha adorning the wall of the main stupa. Dated to the fifth century AD, the heads made of fine stucco and finished with slip and paint were found lying on the floor. They are now safe in the Taxila Museum.[3]

The stupa A15 on the west side of the main stupa has several donative inscriptions in Kharosthi characters. For example, *Saghamitrasa Budhadevasa bhikshusa danamukho*, meaning 'the pious gift of the *bhikshu* Buddhadeva, friend of the holy community.'

The relic-chamber in the main stupa structure was unusually tall and narrow, and in it was a miniature stupa of very remarkable character. Standing 3 feet and 8 inches high and modelled out of

---

[2] Muhammad Iliyas Bhatti, *Taxila: An Ancient Metropolis of Gandhara*, Umar Zirgham, Lahore, 2006, p.92.
[3] Marshall, *A Guide to Taxila*, pp.166–68.

hard lime plaster, it was finished with blue and crimson paint and bejewelled around the dome with gems such as garnet, carnelian, lapis lazuli, aquamarine, ruby, agate, amethyst and crystal. According to Marshall, the workmanship of this 'curious relic casket is undeniably coarse and barbaric, but there is a certain quaint charm in its design as well as in the bright and gaudy colouring of the inlaid gems.'[4] Below the body of the miniature stupa ran a hollow shaft, at the bottom of which were more relics hidden within a smaller copper-gilt receptacle.

Just outside the monastery on the eastern side is a small chapel containing a singularly fine group of stucco figures, one of the best preserved of their kind. Seated in the centre is the meditative Buddha (*dhyana mudra*), with a Standing Buddha to his right and left and two attendant figures behind. Of the two attendants, the one to the left carries the fly-whisk (*chauri*), the other is the Vajrapani holding the thunderbolt in his left hand. The central image still bears traces of the red and black paint and of the gold leaf with which it was once bedecked.

The monastery is quadrangular in structure with ranges of cells on its four sides. At the centre of the court is a depression for harvesting rainwater or a small pond for ablution and a small bathroom in a corner of the court, just as at Mohra Moradu. There is an assembly hall, kitchen, refectory and storeroom grouped on the eastern side of the quadrangular court. There are alcoves for images in front of the cells, niches and windows inside the cells, and a stairway ascending to the upper storey.

Again, on the northern side of the court, there is a small chapel immediately to the left of the stairway in which remains of several burnt clay images adorned with paint and gilding have been found. The entrance of the chapel was relieved by bands of floral designs roughly executed in burnt clay, like the images inside.

From Jaulian, we descend to the base of the hill and walk into the souvenir-making shed for tourists. Here, craftsmen are churning out Fasting Buddha statues, the Meditating Buddha and other stupas.

---

[4] Marshall, *A Guide to Taxila*, p.167.

These are beautiful but in my mind is forever etched the Buddha of Jaulian, the one in *dhyana mudra*.

PIPPLAN MONASTERY

From Jaulian, we swerve back towards Taxila road. A narrow lane to the left soon brings us to the Pipplan monastic site that borrows its name from the huge Pipal trees which once stood over the unexcavated mound. The Pipplan site was included in 1980 in UNESCO's list of World Heritage Sites.

According to an archaeological notice giving details of the site, the ancient remains that were excavated in 1922–23 belong to two overlapping periods. Of these, the earliest monastery belonging to the Kushan era lay towards the east. It functioned for about 500 years before it became dilapidated and outgrew its use. Another monastery was built partly on the ruins and using the rubble of the first. This newer monastery came up on the western side and consisted of a central open courtyard and cells on all its four sides with an assembly hall, kitchen and refectory.

In one of the cells stands a votive stupa decorated with images of the Buddha. Nearly eight-feet high, this stupa rises in three diminishing tiers—the top tier with a dome which was originally crowned by an umbrella; a plain second tier with the sole figure of a Dhyani Buddha; and the lowest tier which was once decorated with a series of Corinthian pilasters alternating with lotus rosettes. At the base of the dome was another series of eight Seated Buddhas, of which two are still partially preserved. This later stucco work dates from the fourth to the fifth century AD.

According to John Marshall, traces of gold, red and black paint were still visible on the stupa at the time of its excavation.[5] Constructed of diaper masonry, this early monastery must have fallen to ruin before the fifth century AD, writes Marshall, for at that time, a second monastery was built on its western side, completely hiding

---

[5] Marshall, *A Guide to Taxila*, p.163.

beneath its foundation all that remained of the old cells and verandah. At the same time, the rest of the early monastery was converted into a stupa-court by dismantling and levelling everything except the stupas in the open quadrangle. The wall of the cells served as an enclosure for the new courtyard. Later on, another stupa was erected near the north-east corner of this court, where it rests on the foundations of the cells of the early monastery.[6]

MOHRA MORADU

Another lane branching from the main Taxila road turns into the next monastic settlement of Mohra Moradu, the grand UNESCO World Heritage Site dated from the second century AD.

History tells us that bounty hunters cut the stupa into half and plundered it. Yet, what remains are well-preserved images in stucco on the stupa and monastery walls. When first discovered by Marshall between 1912 and 1934, both the monastery and stupa were buried beneath debris from the surrounding hills. All that peeped from the debris was a five-feet piece of the stupa's ruined dome which was cut by treasure hunters in search of the relics. Beneath this debris, however, both buildings proved to be well-preserved, standing to a height of 15–20 feet.[7]

The lofty stupa stands on a 15-feet-high plinth with projections on the east for steps. The entire surface of the structure up to the top of the drum was covered with stucco figures that comprised groups of Buddha and bodhisattva figures, many of which were later shifted to the Taxila Museum. The main stupa was constructed over an underground monastery. A path under the main stupa leads into a set of monastic cells that are dark and dingy with streams of water flowing into them. Here, in the glare of the torchlight, I noticed exposed carvings of the Buddha and bodhisattvas on the walls of the underground cells.

The monastery is approached by a flight of steps with a landing

---

[6] Marshall, *A Guide to Taxila*, p.162.
[7] Bhatti, *Taxila*, pp.87–89.

at the top leading into the portico. On the west wall of the portico is an arched niche containing a well-preserved group of figures of the Buddha and his four attendants in high relief.

Passing from the portico into the interior of the monastery, one enters a spacious courtyard surrounded with over two dozen cells arranged on its four sides. Some cells have small niches for lamp. In the middle of the courtyard is a two-feet-deep sunken water tank with descending steps. The projecting eaves of the verandah that ran around the courtyard discharged rainwater into the tank for use by the monks.

A square platform which was once enclosed within walls forms the *jantaghar* (public conveniences for the monks) of the monastery. Around the central depression in the courtyard runs a broad verandah which appears to have been covered at the time. The evidence pointing to this is a series of stone slabs installed at intervals of five feet from each other. These slabs acted as base for the pillars of a broad verandah which was mainly constructed using wood. Besides shading the frontage of the monk cells, the verandah also served to connect with the cells on the upper storey. It also provided a terrace or front space for the upper-storey cells. Perhaps, stairs were provided at intervals to allow passage to the upper floor. A covered drain led waste water into the fields surrounding the monastery. Remains of an assembly hall, a kitchen, refectory and water well are still visible around the central court.

In the monastic cell number 9, one can see an amazing 12-feet-high multi-tiered votive stupa almost touching the roof. Circular in plan, the stupa's plinth is divided into five tiers with elephants and Atlantes alternating in the lower tier and the Buddha seated in niches alternating with pilasters in the tiers above. According to Marshall,[8] a central shaft of iron supported the crowning umbrellas, but in the course of time, this shaft had decayed, and the umbrellas were found lying at the side of the stupa. The edges of the umbrellas are pierced with holes intended, apparently, for streamers or garlands. A copy of the stupa is displayed at the Taxila Museum.

---

[8] Marshall, *A Guide to Taxila*, p.156.

In front of the monastic cells and in the portico there are several niches which held figures in stucco and terracotta, representing the Buddha in different attitudes surrounded by subsidiary gods, heavenly creatures and worshippers. Of these figures, there were six in the courtyard in front of the cells, in addition to the one inside the entrance portico. The best preserved is the one can be seen in front of cell number 4. It portrays the Buddha seated in the *dhyana mudra* (meditation pose) flanked by attendant figures. Of the terracotta, only detached pieces are strewn in the courtyard. Among them, the most notable were a seated image of the Buddha and a very charming head of a *deva* (angel). All these figures from the niches are now housed in Taxila Museum.[9]

DHARMARAJIKA MONASTERY

Constructed around the third century BC, during the reign of Mauryan Emperor Asoka, the Dharmarajika Stupa is considered one of the earliest Buddhist monuments. Also known as 'Dharmaraja', Asoka, the viceroy of Taxila, built the stupa to enshrine the relics of the Buddha. It was continuously enlarged and expanded over the centuries of its existence and was at its glorious best in the second century AD.

The importance and sacredness of Dharmarajika was narrated by no less a person than Xuanzang himself. It can also be gauged from the fact that it became the site of an important Jataka story of the bodhisattva's act of charity. Excavations and inscriptions also attest to the sacredness of the site. A reliquary was found in one of the side chapels containing a silver scroll with a Kharosthi inscription stating that the associated relics were those of Buddha himself. Sacred relics of the Buddha found in stupa S8 were enshrined and worshipped in the world-renowned Temple of the Tooth (Dalada Maligawa) at Kandy (Sri Lanka) by the Buddhists of erstwhile Ceylon. One of the most interesting relics of Gandhara, a gold casket having bone relics

---

[9] Marshall, *A Guide to Taxila*, p.156.

was found in chapel G5. The Kharosthi inscription on a silver scroll dated to the first century AD clearly stated that the relics were those of the Buddha.

During his visit to India, Xuanzang was in Taxila and he mentions that south-east of the Naga tank at a distance of about 30 *li* (15 km), he enters a gorge between two mountains, where there is a stupa built by Asoka-raja.

> It is about 100 feet in height. This is where Sakya Tathagata delivered a prediction, that when Maitreya, Lord of the World, appeared hereafter, there should also appear of themselves four great gem treasures, and that in this excellent land there should be one. According to tradition, we find that whenever there is an earthquake, and the mountains on every side are shaken, all round this sacred spot (treasure) to the distance of 100 paces there is perfect stillness.[10]

He also mentions the story of bodhisattva Chandraprabha:

> This is the spot where Tathagata formerly dwelt when he was practicing the discipline of a Bodhisattva; he was then the king of a great country and was called Chen-ta-lo-po-lo-po (Chandraprabha); he cut off his head, earnestly seeking the acquirement of Bodhi; and this he did during a thousand successive births (for the same object and in the same place).[11]

A road running close to the Taxila Museum leads through a jungle to the base of the Dharmarajika hill on which the great stupa of Dharmarajika is located. It is similar to the Manikyala Stupa. But the big cleft on its hemisphere resembles a scar. Antique diggers must have cut through the solid stone stupa and the cleft gave the stupa a new name, 'Chir Tope', or the stupa that has been cut or torn.

An ambulatory passage paved with stone slabs runs around the stupa and stone sculptures depicting the Buddha and scenes from his

---

[10] Samuel Beal, *Si-Yu-Ki: Buddhist Records of the Western World*, Low Price Publications, Delhi, 1884, p.137.
[11] Beal, *Si-Yu-Ki*, p.138.

life once adorned the great stupa. A large number of votive stupas that once surrounded the main stupa now find a place in the shed constructed in the premises of the Dharmarajika.

According to historian Muhammad Iliyas Bhatti, the courtyard of the main stupa area has several other shrines from different periods and votive stupas erected by pilgrims and visitors.[12]

The great stupa which is circular in plan consists of a 14-metre-tall drum with a raised terrace around its base and four flights of steps, one at each of the cardinal points. According to Marshall,[13] former director general of the Archaeological Survey of India, who carried out extensive excavations at Taxila between 1912 and 1934, a galaxy of small stupas was set in a ring outside the processional path of the central edifice.

A number of monk cells have been dated to the first century BC, of which the most remarkable find is the previously mentioned reliquary. It was found in one of the side chapels G5 containing a silver scroll with a Kharosthi inscription stating that the associated relics were those of Buddha himself. The date of enshrinement and the name of the place 'Takshasila' (Taxila) is also mentioned. The donor describes himself as a Bactrian, resident of the town of Noacha, and records 'the present king, king of kings, the son of Heaven, the Kusana.' The important inscription discovered by Sir John Marshall in 1914–15 states that Urasaka of Noache placed the relics of the Buddha in his chapel at Dharmarajika in AD 78.[14] The inscription also informs that foreign pilgrims could set up their own 'bodhisattva chapel' at Taxila.

In the relic chamber of stupa (S8), Marshall found a vase of grey schist which contained a miniature casket of gold along with three gold safety pins, few small beads of ruby, garnet, amethyst and crystal. Inside the miniature gold casket were few beads of bone and ruby with pieces of silver leaf, coral and stone and a bone relic. In 1917, these relics were presented by the Government of India to the

---

[12] Bhatti, *Taxila*, pp.83–86.
[13] Marshall, *A Guide to Taxila*, p.105.
[14] Marshall, *A Guide to Taxila*, p.113.

Buddhists of Ceylon and were enshrined by them in the Temple of the Tooth at Kandy.[15]

Marshall also found a group of human skeletons in court J, five of which were lying in the open quadrangle. Obviously, there had been a massacre and few heads were severed from the bodies. After the massacre, the building was burnt down, and the bodies were crushed and charred beneath the burning timber and falling masonry. A sixth skeleton was found in room 2 on the west side of the court, hidden among a number of large store-jars, which were also crushed beneath the fallen masonry. On the strength of these finds, Marshall concluded that the massacre in this court was the work of White Hun invaders towards the end of the fifth century AD.[16]

---

[15] Marshall, *A Guide to Taxila*, p.106.
[16] Marshall, *A Guide to Taxila*, p.122.

Chapter 10

DAZZLE OF PESHAWAR

TO PESHAWAR ON MOTORWAY M-1

Peshawar, the capital of the Khyber Pakhtunkhwa, lies at the eastern end of the Khyber Pass. Sitting strategically on the Silk Road between Central and South Asia, it was an important trade entrepôt for import and export of Central Asian goods with roads running eastwards to Hund/Attock, west to Jalalabad, north to Charsadda and through to Chitral to the Wakhan Corridor, and south and south west through Parachinar into southern Afghanistan.

After travelling along the old Grand Trunk Road from Lahore to Islamabad, I decided to spurn the medieval and speed on the modern Motorway M1 for my 200-km ride to Peshawar. Motorway M1 is an east–west Corridor in Pakistan originating at Peshawar on the Ring Road and connecting with Islamabad–Rawalpindi running for about 90 km in north-western Khyber Pakhtunkhwa Province and for about 65 km in the province of Punjab. A vital link with Afghanistan and Central Asia, it was built to ease traffic on the Grand Trunk Road—the NH-5.

En route from Peshawar to Islamabad, the M1 crosses the Kabul River and meanders through the cities of Charsadda, Risalpur, Rashakai and Swabi. Before crossing the Indus, it enters the Punjab Province at Attock and runs along Burhan and Hasan Abdal before merging into Motorway M2 to Lahore.

Zulfiqar, Esther and I hop into our friend and guide Sher Khan's Cruiser parked outside Zulfiqar's house at Bani Gala. Soon, the Cruiser sped along the Rawal Dam, the artificial reservoir that provides water to Rawalpindi and Islamabad. The vehicle was wading through knee-deep water in Bani Gala. It was still dark and too early for us to know about the worsening flood situation and the large crowds that would soon gather on the roads for the blockade called by Imran Khan. Zulfi was fearful of the rising waters levels due to heavy rains and the frightening possibility of a dam burst that would inundate Bani Gala where Zulfi and Imran were neighbours.

FROM BANI GALA VIA RAWAL LAKE

Sitting in the front seat, Zulfi, the master of my travels in Pakistan, was calling up Rehman Durrani to accompany us to the sites in Peshawar and was also enquiring about permission to visit Swat Valley, which is near-impossible for an Indian. But Zulfi was clinging to hope and promised he would take me to Swat even if it meant disguising me in a burqa! I sure was ready for anything!

On the Margalla road, I was savouring the astonishing beauty of low hills covered in thick foliage of trees, flowering shrubs and ribbon-like streams descending into the foothills and rushing towards the lake. The Margalla Hills actually taper off from the Himalayan foothills and are a part of the Margalla National Park. Before getting back on the Motorway M1, Zulfi got off at G11 Bazaar to buy biryani and gosht gravy, the region's staple breakfast. He returned after a few minutes with bags loaded with biryani as well as sandwiches and samosas.

The road took us through the famous Potohar Plateau in north-eastern Pakistan between Rawalpindi and Margalla Hills National Park exactly on the provincial borders of Punjab and Khyber Pakhtunkhwa. At the Brahma Jhand Behtar Interchange, a road cuts away to Taxila through Lohsar Sharfoo joining the NH-5, while another road drops down the Brahma Bahtar-Yarik Motorway south towards Dera Ismail Khan, the famous DI Khan.

Near the Chach Village toll plaza, colourful trucks were queued, beyond which lay vast stretches of vegetable farms that feed the city's capital. Herds of goats and sheep grazed in the grassy low hills. An extremely fertile region of Attock District, it has been identified as Chukhsa of the Taxila copperplate inscription. During medieval times, it was known as Chhachh-Hazara or lying in the plains of Hazara with its chief city, Hazro.

Soon we came to the bridge over the Indus River and crossed the river near Hund. After Swabi, the elevated road ran along flat fields and parallel to the Kabul River which emerged from the Sanglakh Ranges of the Hindu Kush in Afghanistan, passed along Surobi and Jalalabad, flowed into Khyber Pakhtunkhwa Province of Pakistan near Torkham before emptying into the Indus near Attock.

A crowd of tongas, trucks, autocars, mobikes waited at the entrance of Peshawa, which had a very antique feel to it. There were cartloads of jaggery, sugarcane, and so on, in this trading hub of Pakistan. On my left was Hashtnagari where high rises compete with old houses, hospitals and colleges located on both sides of the road. We drove towards Bala Hisar, a historic fortress which was once the royal residence of the Durrani Empire and now serves as the headquarters of the Pakistan Frontier Corps.

Several villages around Bala Hisar in Kabul had monastic centres from where images of the Buddha were retrieved. Incidentally, there were many Buddhist sites around Bala Hisar in Peshawar, too. I wondered if the high ground on which Bala Hisar was built had actually been the site of flourishing Buddhist cities which were usually built on hill tops for safety as the hills of Bala Hisar, Tepe Narenj and Tepe Maranjan, in Kabul.

Peshawar also serves as the administrative centre and economic hub for the Federally Administered Tribal Areas (FATA). The Thal-Parachinar Road connects Peshawar with the Logar Province of Afghanistan through Parachinar and Gawai. The border town of Tari Mangal in the Kurram Valley on the Durand Line at the jutting end of FATA is the shortest route to the famous Buddhist site of Mes Aynak in Logar Province of Afghanistan (40 km south of Kabul). In ancient times, this could have been the direct route of copper trade passing into the Peshawar city on a branch of Uttarapath. This could also have been the route of Buddhist missionaries into the ancient cities of southern Afghanistan like Ghazni and Mes Aynak.

DAZZLING CITY OF PESHAWAR

Peshawar was one of the richest Silk Road cities of Asia from the time of Kushan king Kanishka who made it his capital in first century

AD and, one of the greatest commercial hubs of the Uttarapath due to its strategic position on the frontiers of the Indian subcontinent. Numerous routes from Peshawar went far beyond the confines of Gandhara and practically all commerce of India passed through it.

In Peshawar, Zahoor Ahmad Durrani guided us through the city. We took the Mall Road, bypassed the police station and turned to the Ring Road towards Hayatabad, a modern suburb on the southwestern fringe of Peshawar, the capital of the Khyber Pakhtunkhwa, Pakistan. Here, a new eight-lane road is being laid, probably as a part of the China–Pakistan Economic Corridor (CPEC). Lunch awaited us at the residence of the former tourism minister, Syed Aquil Shah. A long driveway through a lovely rose garden led to his sprawling bungalow. Over lunch, he mentioned the ongoing project that has brought Peshawar's landmark, Mohalla Sethian, on the tourist map of Asia.

Durrani took me back in time to the grand hotels and shopping centres of yore. Established in 1850, the Corporate Shop is the oldest in Saddar Bazaar while the Greens Hotel opened its doors in 1840. When Netaji Subhas Chandra Bose was in Peshawar, he stayed at the Taj Mahal. Now, except for PC Hotel, there are no five-star hotels in the city.

The Oberoi Group's chain of Oberoi Deans and Cecil were the snooze-place for the mighty and the moneyed. Today, at the Cecil, green climbers adorn the courtyard walls around which several dozen hotel rooms have been turned into a tea house. At Cecil, we ordered sandwiches and tea which arrived in shining silver pots and served to us in the finest China.

Later, we passed through the crowded Khyber Bazaar to have a fine view of the Kabuli Gate, one of the city's 16 gates, through which caravans left for Jalalabad and Kabul through the Khyber Pass. Kabuli and Lahori gates were regarded as the city's main entrances. Splendid century-old *balakhanas*—lovely wood-screened guest houses perched atop old shops—were the most sought-after guest houses of Peshawar.

COLOURFUL BAZAARS OF PESHAWAR

Although much mellowed now, the dazzling bazaars of Peshawar that once catered to the markets of Asia and Europe are still a treat to the eyes. Peshawari merchants, along with Sindhis and Multani traders, were the most sought after on the Asian circuit trade routes. They travelled with their goods to the cities of Kabul and Herat in Afghanistan, to Merv, Nisa and Khorezm in the Trans-Caspian Region; to Kashgar, Kuqa and Khotan in Tarim Basin and to Tashkent, Samarkand and Bukhara along the Amu and the Syr Darya valleys. Many settled in cities along the shores of the Caspian Sea.

I imagine the volume of trade from the colourful and myriad bazaars of *chaigaran* (market of tea-sellers), *dalgaran* (grain market), *namakmandi* (salt brought from the Salt Ranges of Punjab), the spice market, the rich craftsmanship of *misgaran*, the leatherwork in the *mochigaran* (leather market) and *batergaran* (bird's market), the woollens of Chitrali Bazaar and jewellery from Sarrafa Mandi. Fruits fresh from the sprawling fruit market at Andar Shahr was sent up to Kolkata by horse carts and later by the long-distance Frontier Mail launched in 1930. Not surprisingly, there is a market of money changers and money lenders too.

The exquisitely crafted copper and brass samovars by Peshawari craftsmen had found takers in the cities of Oxus, Zerafshan and Jaxartes and Multanis, Sindhis, Peshawaris, Shikarpuris, Marwaris could be seen in every city of the Oxus and along the Trans-Caspian Region up to Astrakhan and Moscow.

I stood silent in the bazaar and wondered whether there was any connection between the Bazar-e-Misgaran (the street of copper-sellers) in Old Peshawar where coppersmiths have worked and lived for generations and Mes Aynak/Mis Aynak in the Logar Province of Afghanistan, 40 km south-east of Kabul. The best copper came from Mes Aynak and the Peshawari craftsmen probably obtained the metal from them. An ancient road leading into Mes Aynak through Parachinar along the bed of the Shalozan River was the link between the two regions, and it is possible that the copper was traded along this path for the Peshawari craftsmen for centuries.

After the bazaars, we entered Chowk Yadgare. Here, Peshawari grandeur came alive with its beautiful *balakhanas* and caravanserais that stood near the city gates like sentinels waiting to welcome travellers of the Silk Road and the Qissa Khwani Bazaar where old tales of the Silk Road still buzzed in the air. Here, traders halted to load and offload goods brought from the distant markets of Afghanistan and Central Asia, and those that came along the eastern and southern routes of India, namely Uttarapath and Dakshinapath.

When the tired travellers crossed the Khyber Pass, the first city that welcomed them into its serais was Peshawar in the lower Kabul valley. This was the very 'first city'—known as the old Purushapura (the Premier City)—on their onward march to India. A.H. Dani writes in *Romance of the Khyber*:

> …it was the caravan series of Peshawar that offered the first night of sweet sleep. With the break of dawn and neighing of the animals awake the fatigued men and rush for water, food and fodder. Lo! They all gather in a bazaar, known as Qissa-Khwani Bazaar, the market of story tellers which has been called 'Piccadily of Central Asia'. Over a cup of Kahve they all narrate stories after stories of the adventurous journey of the markets of Central Asia, viz. Bukhara and Samarkand.[1]

It was here in the caravanserais of Peshawar that the art of story narration was finely cultivated as the serais were not only a place where the traveller rested his limbs, gathered and exchanged goods, but also one where he indulged in story-telling—tales about the market, price of commodities, weather and crime situation. These sessions were means to both record experiences of travellers and also prepare others undertaking a journey.

The culture of story-telling over tea was a characteristic of the Peshawaris. It was the city that cultivated, celebrated and kept alive this art. I do not know of any other market in South Asia where the art of story-telling was kept alive as a tradition.

---

[1] Ahmad H. Dani, *Romance of the Khyber*, Sang-e-Meel Publication, Lahore, 1997, pp.10–13.

HERITAGE HAVELIS OF PESHAWAR

In the old city near the Gor Khatri Complex, we walked into a narrow lane that brushes past a modest-sized mosque and entered Mohalla Sethian—the heritage city of Silk Road traders. As is evident from the name, it was once the abode of Sethis or merchants of the Silk Road. The huge multi-storied intricately carved mansions with their hanging balconies and exquisitely decorated inner walls and mosaic and marble floors, hammams, extensive courtyards and skywalk balconies running high above the lane were a reminder of the immense wealth of Peshawari tycoons.

The counterparts of the Mohalla Sethian lived in mansions in the suburbs of Dhaka in East Bengal (now Bangladesh) in the heritage town of Sonargaon—the 'City of Gold'. They are both ghost cities now. No humans live there anymore; even the lone temple at Sonargaon is devoid of worshippers.

From Sethian in Peshawar to Sonargaon in Dhaka, there was a continuous stream of merchants who traded in fine muslin, salt, ivory, silk, tussar silk, fruits, flowers, spices and fish. The caravans arrived and departed along the Uttarapath running through the Gangetic Plains (later the Grand Trunk Road) from Peshawar to Sonargaon, where even today an old Grand Trunk Road bridge can be seen a few metres from the heritage site. Not long ago, the caravan trade was facilitated by the renowned Frontier Mail from Peshawar to Kolkata assisting in the transportation of fruits, nuts, fabrics, fish and metals between Sonargaon and Peshawar.

Today, both the stately mansions of Mohalla Sethian in Peshawar and Sonargaon in Dhaka bear testimony to the extensive trade on the Northern Highway and the immense profits earned by the merchants of the Uttarapath, the lavish lifestyle of the inhabitants and their love for art. Both Peshawar and Sonargaon are a link in the chain of trading cities of Central Asia and China.

Mohalla Sethian, with more than a dozen havelis, was the residence of Hindu merchants who originally hailed from Punjab and migrated to the Northwest Frontier region of Peshawar in the seventh century and, were involved in a highly profitable trade with countries of Central Asia, Russia and China. A parallel can be drawn with the Kabuli Sikh community that settled around the Karte Parwan and neighbouring areas of Kabul and traded in dry fruits. Despite threat to their lives, they have not left Kabul and continue to serve the people with food and shelter. I was fortunate to visit and pray at the Kabul Gurudwara and partake a meal at the langar with my friend, Fauzia Wardak.

The Sethi House at the far end of the Sethi Lane has now been opened to the public as a heritage site to showcase the marvellous architecture and decoration of the eighteenth- and nineteenth-century havelis of the merchants of the Silk Road.

The road passing through the bazaars of Peshawar are interspersed at intervals by narrow lanes running perpendicular to the road and leading into high-walled enclosures with huge wooden gates that are common in the medieval forts of the subcontinent. Durrani led me into one such arched lane and quietly pushed open the wooden darwaza that was embedded with huge iron nails. What lay on the other side of the darwaza was a vast orchard within which stood a massive but dilapidated palace with overhanging balconies and coloured glass doors. Before the crowded shopping centres of Peshawar came into being, the lane must have been the entrance gateway to the grand palace.

Durrani pointed to the lane in which Sir Mehr Chand Khanna, grandfather of film actor Vinod Khanna, had lived. I walked into the lane and saw an ancient haveli, grand even in its old age, surrounded by massive open spaces that were once gardens covered with foliage of fruit trees. It seemed that the massive bungalow had been portioned out and was now rented out or owned by several families. The lane leading into the front was lined with shops selling cloth, basic grocery items and snacks.

The Kapoor Haveli, belonging to Hindi film actor Prithviraj Kapoor, was also a massive palace with dozens of rooms. It is located in Mohallah Dhaki Munawar Shah in the old city, and can be accessed through the narrow, winding streets of the historic Qissa Khwani Bazaar.

Peshawar's connection with the Bukharan Jews was also evident in some houses that still carry the Star of David on their façade. One such house could be seen near the Kabuli Gate.

I stepped out of Mohalla Sethian with a heavy heart, wary of the callousness of time that had snatched the riches of this spectacular city.

BUDDHIST ROUTE THROUGH KHYBER

In Peshawar, I had requested Zulfi for an official permit to visit Khyber Pass, the historic pass that forms the link between Peshawar and Jalalabad through the south-westerly ranges of the Himalayas into the central massif of the Hindu Kush. An integral part of the Silk Road, it connects Landi Kotal at the Afghan border with the Valley of Peshawar at Jamrud by traversing part of the Safed Koh mountains.

The pass begins at Jamrud, the site of the Buddha's footprints marked by the travelling missionaries and Buddhist monks at the village of Qadam. The footprints are no longer traceable, but its history is.

This trade route to Afghanistan and Central Asia was a Pass where marauding armies from the west snaked through to plunder the river valleys of the Indus and the Ganges, and peaceful missionaries from the east marched to the land of the Murghab and the Oxus to spread the *Dhamma* of the Buddha. Caravans of traders and craftsmen also negotiated its ravines and high cliffs in their journey for optimum returns for their goods and skills.

Zulfi brought in bad tidings—the pass was out of bounds for any Indian. Instead of a visit, he suggested some interesting reads on Khyber, among which was the thrilling *Eighteen Years In Khyber* by Sir Robert Warburton and *Romance of the Khyber Pass* by Ahmad Hasan Dani, who captured the thrilling experience of a train journey through the Khyber Pass. Much later, I managed to lay hands on both—the one by Warburton in Sydney at a farmer's market where it lay tattered amidst a pile of old and discarded books, and Dani's book at an exhibition in Jamia Millia in Delhi. While Warburton delineated the Khyber land route that was operational in the early nineteenth century, Dani marked the railway route of the twentieth century in splendid photography.

However, I was in for a big surprise at the Peshawar Railway Station, where the engines of the Khyber Train and the Frontier Mail were on display after being pulled out of service. The Khyber Railway was laid about a century ago by the British for their own use, but the old path between Peshawar and Kabul was always busy for *kafilas*, or caravans, who travelled regularly between the two major cities.

According to Warburton, there was an interesting modus operandi in entering and exiting the Khyber Pass. The caravans from the direction of Kabul were first escorted by the Amir's *khasadars* from Dakka to Landi Khana every Monday and Thursday morning, where they were met by a party of the Amir's Khyber Rifles, who brought them to Landi Kotal by the evening. The *kafilas* proceeding to Kabul left the city of Peshawar every Monday and Thursday, and by sunset collected at Jamrud, paid their tolls and passed the night there. Both caravans then met and exchanged goods at Ali Masjid.

The Khyber Pass too is not without its Buddhist past. Missionaries travelled through it to Central Asia and even today one can see remnants of stupas and monasteries, most lost to Mother Nature and vandals in search of treasures.

According to Dani's route-map, 10.5 km from Jamrud, the road passes Ali Masjid where Buddhists had built a stupa and a monastery near a water spring. In the narrow gorge, there is an upright standing stone with the impression of a palm, which the devout believe to be of the Buddha himself, known to have visited here. Today, on this spot there is a small stone mosque dedicated to Hazarat Ali.

After Ali Masjid, the road passes the highest point at Shahgai. A little ahead of Shahgai lies the Sphola or the Khyber Stupa at the village of Khyber. The only Buddhist monument left in the Khyber Pass, the stupa lies on the summit of the Pass towering 50 feet above the Khyber Road, midway between Ali Masjid and Landi Kotal. Its spherical dome stands on a three-tiered platform decorated with stucco figures. At the foot of the stupa lie the unexcavated remains of a monastery. Gandhara sculptures from the site are now housed in the Peshawar Museum.

The Khyber Stupa, though not described by any of the Chinese pilgrims, reveals that in about the third or fourth century AD, the route was used by Buddhist missionaries, many of whom lived here in close proximity to the Kanishka Vihara. It is possible that the Khyber monastery was a part of the Kanishka Vihara only 25 km away and, provided shelter to the monks on their way to and from the monastery at Hadda near Jalalabad. The stupa marks one of the Buddhist routes through the Sulaiman Mountains. Two other routes went along the Gomal and Bolan passes in the same mountain ranges.

Landi Kotal Bazaar of Khyber is believed to have grown out of an old caravanserai which, in the past, welcomed slow-moving camel caravans that came loaded with merchandise from Kabul and Bokhara. Beyond Landi Kotal lies the fort of the non-believers (in this case, the Buddhists) known as Kafir Kot. It built by the Turki Shahi rulers as a hill fort to guard the pass.

BUDDHA'S BEGGING BOWL AT GOR KATHRI

It is an anecdote that has been oft-repeated that when the Kusana ruler Kaniskha laid siege on Madhya-desa, he demanded only two things from the king—one, the Alms Bowl of the Buddha and, two, the revered monk Asvaghosa, disciple of the great teacher Parsva, the elder. Kaniskha took the two treasures, returned to Peshawar and if history is to be believed, adopted the Buddhist creed under Asvaghosa's influence.[2]

The precious patra or the 'begging bowl' of the Buddha remained at Peshawar and visiting Chinese monks had seen the Buddhist relic at the present Gor Kathri Complex. Faxian, who journeyed through India in AD 399–414, mentions that 700 monks resided at the Monastery of Buddha's Alms Bowl in Peshawar. The monks worshipped the begging bowl twice—once at midday and once in the evening—burnt incense and made offerings of flowers and bushels of grains. He described the bowl as having a bright and glossy lustre

---

[2] Saroj Kumar Chaudhuri, *Lives of Early Buddhist Monks*, Abha Prakashan, Delhi, 2008, pp.16–17.

and its thickness being about a fifth of an inch.³ From inside the Gor Kathri Complex, the patra of the Buddha was whisked away before the monk Xuanzang arrived at Peshawar in the seventh century AD. He found the tower of the patra empty.⁴

In his memoirs, Xuanzang paid glowing tributes to the city and the Great Stupa of Kanishka. He also talked about a site, which many historians argue is the Gor Kathri where the Buddha's giant bowl was kept. A giant bowl that I saw at the entrance of the National Museum at Kabul is believed to be the begging bowl of the Buddha.

> Inside the royal city, towards the north-east, is an old foundation (or a ruinous foundation). Formerly this was the precious tower of the patra of Buddha. After the Nirvana of Buddha, his patra coming to this country was worshipped during many centuries. In traversing different countries it has come now to Persia.⁵

The information provided by Xuanzang that the patra of the Buddha was in Persia could point to the fact that southern Afghanistan (including Kandahar) during Xuanzang's travel in AD 630s was under Persian domination.

According to scholar and expert on Gandhara studies, Alfred Foucher, the search for the *patra chaitya* should be made somewhere near the Panj Tirath. He explains that the site has been a place of continued Hindu worship and rituals over the centuries. He elaborates that at the north-east of the native city between the Grand Trunk Road and the modern railways there still exists a large Hindu establishment known by the name of Panj Tirath, which actually contains five little tanks that are holy bathing places shaded by some sacred Peepal trees. 'It cannot be doubted that the site is ancient...

---

³ James Legge (trans), *A Record of Buddhistic Kingdoms Being an Account by the Chinese Monk Fa-Hein of Travels in India and Ceylon [AD 399–414] in Search of the Buddhist Books of Discipline*, Mushiram Manoharlal Publishers, Delhi, 1998), pp.34–35.
⁴ Samuel Beal, *Si-Yu-Ki: Buddhist Records of the Western World*, Book II, Low Price Publications, Delhi, 1884, p.98.
⁵ Beal, *Si-Yu-Ki*, Book II, p.98.

Unfortunately the place has been too much disturbed.'[6]

Today, the patra of the Buddha stands in the front gallery of the National Museum of Afghanistan at Kabul. It is a massive bowl of black marble that was found in 1925 at the shrine of Mirwais Baba in the city of Kandahar. It is known as the Buddha's begging bowl because of the lotus flowers carved on its underside. Two Islamic inscriptions were etched on it at a later time. The inner inscription, dated to 1490, lists rules and regulations of the Kandahar Madrassa.

Whether or not this is the patra of the Buddha no one can say for certain, because Buddha as a physical being, could not have carried the enormous bowl while on his begging rounds. Made of a single huge piece of limestone or marble, such bowls were generally kept at the gate of monasteries and *khanaqas* (the place for spiritual retreat) of saints. They were meant to symbolize renunciation of life, abrogation of the self, the annihilation of ego and arrogance, and the cultivation of humility of those whose daily food came from begging. I found a similar bowl in Turkestan near Otrar, Kazkhastan, at the mausoleum of the revered Sufi saint, Akhmad Yassavi. Two huge bowls can also be seen at the holy Ajmer Sharif shrine at Ajmer in India.

We also find mention of the Buddha's begging bowl at a monastery in Kashgar, in Xinjiang, China, while reading about the life of monk Kumarjiva who tried to lift the bowl but could not. A similar alms bowl, without decoration and perhaps made of schist, was found at the Buddhist site of Sanchi in India at Monastery 51, which was apparently donated in the third century BC to the Sangha by Queen Devi, the daughter of a merchant of Vidisha and first wife of Asoka.

That the patra of the Buddha was removed to some other place (to Persia, according to Xuanzang) points to two things. First, the precious Buddhist relic of the Buddha or the Sangha could have been traded away in the seventh century AD, possibly for material gain or for its value in gold or in exchange for silk by some greedy abbot of the Kanishka Vihara at Peshawar. However, since it is doubted if

---

[6] Alfred Foucher, *Notes on the Ancient Geography of Gandhara*, Asian Educational Service, Delhi, 2005 (1st ed. 1915), p.5.

it was really the patra of the Buddha, a second probability is that a giant replica of Buddha's small bowl was made by the monastery at Kandahar to attract pilgrims and travellers. Historian Xinru Liu presents interesting details on the trade of Buddhist relics in the region of Gandhara.[7]

Interestingly, Gor Khatri, located in the ancient city of Peshawar, was identified by Sir Alexander Cunningham with Kanishka Vihara (the Great Monastery of King Kanishka).[8]

Notices put up by the Archaeological Department at Gor Khatri state that the complex inside the walled city has been identified as a place of Hindu pilgrimage, where the Hindus performed the *sardukahr* (ritual of shaving off heads). Mughal Emperor Babur too visited the place and mentions its importance in his memoirs *Baburnama* calling it '[a] holy place of Yogis and Hindus' who came from long distances for pilgrimage and shaved their hair and beards as offerings.

Located on one of the highest points of Peshawar, Gor Khatri functioned as a serai during medieval times. Jehan Ara Begum, the daughter of Mughal Emperor Shah Jehan, converted the complex into a caravanserai and named it Serai Jehanabad. She also constructed the Jama Masjid, a sauna bath and two wells inside the serai for the convenience of travellers and traders coming from different corners of the world.

After the Sikh occupation of Peshawar in the early nineteenth century, the complex was turned into the residence and official headquarters of General Paolo de Avitabiles, the governor of Peshawar in AD 1838–42. A Hindu temple, probably the present Siva temple, was constructed in 1834–49. This was in the memory of Gorakhnath, a Hindu religious leader, who came from Kashmir to Sheikhupura and onwards to Peshawar. This worship site remained a centre for Hindu ritual practices until a few decades ago. Original fresco work and paintings of Hindu deities still survive

---

[7] Xinru Liu, *Silk and Religion*, Oxford University Press, Delhi, 1996, pp.34–37.
[8] Alexander Cunningham, *Ancient Geography of India*, Low Price Publications, Delhi, 1990 (1st ed. 1871), p.68.

in the temple's interior. Its main chamber, the *garbha griha*, is also preserved and prayers are offered daily.

Keeping in view the importance of this remarkable monument, the Directorate of Archaeology and Museums, Government of Khyber Pakhtunkhwa, initiated its conservation and restoration. In 1912, the complex became the headquarters of the fire brigade department and also served as tehsil headquarters of Peshawar.

Today, the fortified compound has two prominent gateways—one in the east and the other on the west. The Gorakhanath Temple is situated at the centre, along with a network of cells and buildings in the southern and western side of the complex and a fire brigade building, which was built in 1917.

Currently protected under the Antiquities Act, 1975, archaeological excavations have been initiated to establish the cultural profile of Peshawar city. As per the notice put up at the site, the results of excavations in 1992, 2006–07 and 2009 have pushed back the history of Peshawar to the second century BC.

Ongoing archaeological excavations in old Peshawar in the north-eastern corner of Gor Khatri have further established that Peshawar is one of the oldest living cities of Asia that has been inhabited continuously from the sixth century BC. Farzand Ali Durrani, former archaeology chair of the University of Peshawar, initiated the first vertical excavations at Gor Khatri in 1992–93 and confirmed that the city's foundation went back to at least the third century BC. According to notices put up at the site, the second round of excavations carried on until 2007 in the north-eastern aspect of Gor Khatri pushed back Peshawar's age by another couple of centuries, officially making it the oldest living city in South Asia.[9]

IN SEARCH OF KANISHKA STUPA

Durrani's geographical instructions were a bit sketchy. He had said that the ruins of the great Kanishka Stupa lay near Akhun Ahad No.

---

[9] Site notices by the Department of Archaeology And Museums. For a general read, see <https://en.m.wikipedia.org>Gorkathri>

4, which is the site of the Shah Ji ki Dheri surrounded by a graveyard and the mausoleum of Khwaja Sahib. I took the Ganj Gate and drove down the Challi Market (market of corn-sellers) in search of Shah Ji ki Dheri, the site of the Kanishka Stupa from the second century AD and the place from where the renowned Kanishka casket was found.

We followed Durrani's oral map but instead of Shah Ji ki Dheri, the road culminated in a vast graveyard. So, there I was, standing amidst hundreds of tombstones where there was more than a funereal silence. Some children were flying kites and running among the raw-earth graves. Out of reverence for those who lay buried under, I walked carefully lest I stepped on an unmarked grave. Within the tombstones, I peered for at least a sign of the stupa or its square foundation. A lot of debris of broken mud pieces is all I saw. Nothing else.

Durrani and Zulfi were also diligently scouring the graveyard in search of the historical stupa. After a long wait, they gave up the search to my great dismay. Nothing remains of the stupa, the graves have encroached the land where once stood a monumental stupa.

Locals also reiterated Durrani's conclusion—the stupa no longer existed. But I was not ready to return empty-handed. I *had* to find the stupa. I took a mud track leading to the Khwaja Sahib's Mosque at the far end. Inside the courtyard of the newly constructed mosque lie two large graves of holy men and on the charpoy a saint sat stoically. I paid my respect to the saint who later offered the low charpoy and beckoned a young boy to bring me tea. Tired after a hectic day in Peshawar, the heavily brewed tea was like manna from heaven. It was also an alibi to linger a little longer at the holy site of the great Kanishka Stupa. I touched the ground that Buddha walked on and where he had predicted that 400 years after his death, Kanishka would build a stupa on the site in Peshawar.

Another testimony to the Buddhist origin of the site is that some distance to the north where one should expect to find the Peepal tree of Kanishka, there stands a tiny octagonal shrine of Mughal architecture, which was at one time a Hindu temple.[10]

---

[10] Foucher, *Notes on the Ancient Geography of Gandhara*, p.10.

As pointed out by French scholar Alfred Foucher, with the dominance of Islam, Hindu sites were immediately converted into sacred tombs or mosques. Thus, piety stayed on the site. It still drew pilgrims and offerings as before, although their nature had changed.

By the time Xuanzang visited the stupa, it had already been destroyed by fire three times, but was repaired several times. The stupa was eventually destroyed by lightning. No remains of it exist today. All traces of it have vanished, devoured by an ever-increasing population and uncaring authorities.

FOUCHER'S SHAH JI KI DHERI

Foucher also pointed out the destruction of the vihara and stupa. Both the convent (Kanishka Vihara) and the neighbouring stupa (Kanishka Stupa) had been destroyed by fire. On several occasions, these ruins were the object of excavations by sepoys and collectors of building material and manure who bore tunnels within the structures.[11] However, Foucher is convinced that the excavations have at least resulted in establishing the Buddhist/Greco-Buddhist character of the ruins and have brought to light some statues to prove this. Some vases full of flour found in the large *dheri*, or mound, on the west finally confirm the hypothesis of a convent.[12]

Foucher thoroughly explored the ruins at Shah Ji ki Dheri. He mentions that of the two chief mounds the one to the east is roughly 300 metre in circumference—a size that the Chinese pilgrims assign to the pagoda of 'King Kanishka'. The other *dheri* situated to the west and quite close the former is the exact spot where Xuanzang places the monastery connected with the stupa. It is almost square in form with sides measuring not less than 200 metre. In the middle, there is a pronounced rectangular depression while the raised edges suggest the idea of four blocks of buildings enclosing an inner courtyard.[13]

---

[11] Foucher, *Notes on the Ancient Geography of Gandhara*, p.9.
[12] Foucher, *Notes on the Ancient Geography of Gandhara*, p.9.
[13] Foucher, *Notes on the Ancient Geography of Gandhara*, pp.4–10.

FAXIAN IN PESHAWAR

All pilgrims up to the eighth century AD have described the magnificence of the Kanishka Stupa. According to all accounts up to the time of Faxian's visit to Peshawar in the fourth century AD, the giant stupa of Kanishka was an unrivalled structure and the tallest building in the world. Faxian described the stupa as being over 40 *chang* in height (approximately 400 feet) and adorned with 'all precious substances'. He was so impressed by the grandeur of the stupa that he wrote 'of all the stupas and temples seen by travellers, none can compare with this for beauty of form and strength.'[14]

Going southwards from Gandhara, the pilgrim Faxian arrived in Peshawar in four days' time. He mentions the story of Buddha who while travelling with his disciples in Peshawar had told Anand: 'After my Parinirvana, there will be a king named Kanishka who shall on this spot build a tope. Kanishka was afterwards born into this world and built the king's tope—the Kanishka Stupa.'[15]

But when two other Chinese pilgrims Sung Yun and Hui Sheng arrived in Gandhara around AD 518, they were given a warm welcome by the king of Udyayana.[16] Sung Yun reports that the king of Gandhara was very rough with him and failed to salute him. Sung Yun perceived that these 'remote barbarians were unfit for exercising public duties and that their arrogance refused to be checked.' The pilgrims were unable to proceed beyond the Indus because of the state of turmoil in north-west India as a result of an invasion by the Huns as well as the king's unfriendliness towards them.[17]

---

[14] Legge, *A Record of Buddhistic Kingdoms Being an Account by the Chinese Monk Fa-Hein of Travels in India and Ceylon [AD 399-414] in Search of the Buddhist Books of Discipline*, Book XII, p.33.

[15] Legge, *A Record of Buddhistic Kingdoms Being an Account by the Chinese Monk Fa-Hein of Travels in India and Ceylon [AD 399-414] in Search of the Buddhist Books of Discipline*, Book XII, p.33.

[16] Han-Sung Yang, Yun-Hua Jan, Shotaro Iida and Lawrence Preston (eds and trans), *Hye Ch'o Diary: A Memoir of the Pilgrimage to the Five Regions of India*, Asian Humanities Press, Berkeley, CA, 1984, p.9.

[17] Yang et al., *Hye Ch'o Diary*, p.9.

The stupa existed when Xuanzang visited in AD 634. He tells us that during his visit to Peshawar, the Kanishka Stupa, numerous votive stupas and the Bodhi Tree were visible. The Bodhi Tree was about 100 feet or so in height, its branches thick and the shade beneath sombre and deep. The stupa lay outside the city, about 4–4.5 km to the south-east.

One can imagine the grandeur of the Kanishka Stupa from the narratives of Xuanzang. He mentions at least six images of the Buddha around the Bodhi Tree and the stupa. Narrating the sacredness of the place, he writes:

> The four past Buddhas have sat beneath this tree, and at the present time, there are four sitting figures of the Buddhas to be seen here. During the *Bhadrakalpa*, the 996 other Buddhas will all sit here. Secret spiritual influences guard the precincts of the tree and exert a protecting virtue in its continuance. Sakya Tathagata sat beneath this tree with his face to the south and addressed Ananda thus: 'Four hundred years after my departure from the world, there will be a king who shall rule it called Kan-ishka (Kia-ni-se-kia); not far to the south of this spot he will raise a stupa which will contain various relics of my bones and flesh.'[18]

The pilgrim mentions two more stupas and the light-emitting image of the Buddha at the site.

> On the eastern face of the great stupa, there are two engraved stupas: one, three feet high, the other five feet, both of the same shape and proportion as the great stupa. Again, there are two full-sized figures of the Buddha, one four feet, the other six feet in height sitting cross-legged beneath the Bodhi tree. When the full rays of the sun shine on them, they appear of a brilliant gold colour, and as the light recedes, the hues of the stone seem to assume a reddish-blue colour. On the southern side of the stone steps of the great stupa there is a 16-ft high painted figure of

---

[18] Beal, *Si-Yu-Ki*, Book II, p.99.

Buddha. To the south-west of the great stupa 100 paces or so, there is an 18-ft standing figure of Buddha in white stone which diffuses a brilliant light. To the left and right of the great stupa are a hundred little stupas standing closely together."[19]

THE GREAT UNIVERSITY OF KANISHKA VIHARA

The Kanishka Vihara was the first celebrated university of Peshawar imparting Buddhist education to people spread over Central Asia and beyond. Inscriptions retrieved in India reveal that powerful ancient rulers sent their children to Kanishka Vihara to acquire quality education. The 2,000-km distance between Pataliputra and Peshawar did not deter scholars from coming to the vihara to study under renowned teachers.

The monastery at Peshawar was still flourishing as a place of Buddhist education as late as the ninth–tenth century AD, when Prince Vira Deva of Magadh was sent there to benefit from the instruction by the resident teachers who were famous for their piety.[20]

We learn of Dharmapala, the Pala monarch of Bengal in the eighth century AD, who held a great imperial assembly at Kannauj, which was attended by the vassal kings of all important states of northern India, including Yavana (referring to Muslim rulers of Sindh and Multan) and Gandhara denoting the upper valley of the Sindhu and a part of the Northwest Frontier.[21] After his death in AD 815, his son Devapala ruled as an undisputed master of north India, and his empire extended from the Himalayas to the Vindhyas and from the Bay of Bengal to the Arabian Sea.[22]

Sinologist Saroj Kumar Chaudhari writes:

> Brothers Asanga and Vasubandhu, both exponents of the Mahayana Buddhism belonged to Peshawar. Vasubandhu wrote

---

[19] Beal, *Si-Yu-Ki*, Book II, pp.99–101.
[20] Vincent A. Smith, *History of India*, Vol. II, Cosimo Classics, New York, 2008, p.230.
[21] R.C. Majumdar, *Ancient India*, Motilal Banarsidass Publishers, Delhi, 2013, p.284.
[22] Majumdar, *Ancient India*, p.284.

several treatises on Mahayana as well as commentaries on Mahayana sutras including commentaries on Buddhavtamsaka-sutra, Parinirvana-sutra, Saddharma-pundarika-sutra, Prajnaparamita-sutra, Vimalakirti-nirdesa etc.[23]

According to Prof. Saroj Chaudhari, his language was exquisite and such was his repute that advocates of other sects and heretics feared his name and those who evinced interest in Hinayana and Mahayana studied his texts.

A galaxy of Buddhist scholars such as Asvaghosa (author of the great epic *Buddhacharita* and *Sundaranand Kavya*), Nagarjuna (the Mahayana scholar who composed *Upadesa* consisting of a lakh *gathas*) and Vasumitra (who headed the Fourth Buddhist Council convoked by Kanishka at Kundalavana, Kashmir) adorned the court of Kanishka.[24]

It is said that after receiving two great treasures from the king of Madhyadesa—the alms bowl of the Buddha and the most revered and talented monk Asvaghosa, disciple of the great teacher Parsva—Kanishka returned to Peshawar. Under Asvaghosa's influence, Kanishka is believed to have adopted the Buddhist creed.[25]

AUTHORS OF SASTRAS AT PESHAWAR

Xuanzang in his memoirs describes the great monastery of Kanishka Vihara and mentions that few monks lived there.

> To the west of the great stupa there is an old sangharama which was built by King Kanishka. Its double towers, connected terraces and deep chambers bear testimony to the eminence of the great priests who have lived here and gained distinction. Although now somewhat decayed, it yet gives evidence of its wonderful construction... The priests living in its...are few; they study the Little Vehicle. From the time it was built many

---

[23] Chaudhuri, *Lives of Early Buddhist Monks*, pp.32–46.
[24] Chaudhuri, *Lives of Early Buddhist Monks*, p.21.
[25] Chaudhuri, *Lives of Early Buddhist Monks*, pp.16–17.

authors of Sastras have lived herein and gained the supreme fruit [of Arhatship].[26]

He also mentions the names of the great scholars Parsvika, Vasubandhu and Manorhita who lived in the vihara of Peshawar near the stupa. He tells us that at the vihara, in the third tower (double-storied tower) was the chamber of the honourable Parsvika (Pi-Lo-shi-po), which had long been in ruins and a commemorative tablet to Parsvika had been placed there. To the east of Parsvika's chamber was an old building in which Vasubandhu bodhisattva composed the *O-pi-ta-mo-ku-she-lun* (*Abhidharmakosha Sastra*); here too a commemorative tablet had been placed. To the south of Vasubandhu's house, about 50 paces or so, was a two-storeyed pavilion in which Manorhita, a master of Sastras, composed the *Vibhasha Sastra*. We are informed by the pilgrim that this learned doctor flourished in the midst of the thousand years after the Nirvana of Buddha.

We know that by the time Xuanzang arrived, monasteries were deserted but Hindu temples were flourishing. Speaking about Peshawar, he says that the royal family was extinct and the kingdom was governed by the deputies from Kapisa. The towns and villages were deserted and there were but few inhabitants.

> They [people/inhabitants] love literature; most of them belong to heretical school; and few believe in the true law. From old time till now, this border-land of India has produced many authors of sastras; for example, Narayanadeva, Asanga Bodhisattva, Vasubandhu Bodhisattva, Dharmatrata, Manorhita, Parsva the noble, and so on.

He further makes a note of the decaying state of Buddhism in the seventh century AD. He writes that there were about 1,000 *sangharamas* which were deserted, filled with wild shrubs and in ruins. The stupas were mostly decayed and nearly 100 heretical temples were occupied pell-mell by heretics.[27]

---

[26] Beal, *Si-Yu-Ki*, Book II, pp.103-104.
[27] Beal, *Si-Yu-Ki*, Book II, p.98.

HYE CH'O IN PESHAWAR VALLEY

Kanishka Vihara was still in existence in eighth century AD. The Korean pilgrim Hye Ch'o's visit to Purushapura in AD 726 and his description of the Kanishka Vihara provide ample proof of the continued existence of the Buddhist centre. He mentioned that the Kanishka Stupa 'constantly glows', and also talked of the great residential monastery of Kanishka at Peshawar where the great bodhisattvas Vasubandhu and Asanga resided.[28]

Travelling via Jalandhar and Sindhukala, Hye Ch'o writes in his memoir that the king and military personnel of Gandhara were all Turks.

> Though the king is of Turkish origin he believes in the Three Jewels. The king, the royal consort and the chiefs build monasteries separately and worship the Three Jewels. The king institutes the great assembly of monks twice a year and donates all his belongings to the Sangh and later redeems his wife and elephants at a price fixed by the monks. The rest of his belongings are sold by the monks. The king's children act similarly like building monasteries, offering feasts and giving donations.[29]

Hye Ch'o further informs that south-east from the Peshawar Valley is the country of Sibi, the site where the 'Buddha in his former birth saved the dove for King Sibi'. Here, the pilgrim saw monasteries and monks. The place where the 'Buddha offered his head and eyes to the five yakshas' is also situated in Sibi. Each of these places has monasteries and monks practising both Hinayana and Mahayana.[30]

According to historian Vincent Smith, the final demotion of the celebrated institution of the Kanishka Vihara was undoubtedly due to the invasions by Mahmud of Ghazni and his successors.[31]

However, neither the stupa nor the vihara nor the glories of

---

[28] Yang et al., *Hye Ch'o Diary*, p.49.
[29] Yang et al., *Hye Ch'o Diary*, pp.48–49.
[30] Yang et al., Hye Ch'o Diary, pp.48–49.
[31] Smith, *History of India*, p.230.

Peshawar can ever be forgotten. Proof of the glorious Kanishka Stupa, Kanishka Vihara and the relics of the Buddha that existed in the holy city of Peshawar can be found in the travelogues of numerous ancient pilgrims, as well as at the Peshawar Museum, which is today the custodian of the Kanishka casket that was recovered from the stupa.

Chapter 11

THE MONASTIC CENTRES OF MARDAN

The sun was setting over Peshawar. An orange glow had settled over the ancient caravanserai at the Gor Kathri Complex where I returned to after spending a long day at the graveyard of Akhun Ahad No. 4 searching in vain for the Kanishka Stupa. Children who had come to play cricket at the sprawling maidan of the Gor Kathri were now packing up. I waited to partake in the evening puja at the Siva temple but the priest was not there. Since I did not have the permission to spend the night at any place in and around the Peshawar cantonment, I had to leave the area as soon as possible to prevent any problem with the police. Zulfi took a hurried round of the markets looking for accommodation but could not find any as most hotels and guest houses in this trading hub of the Khyber were overflowing with guests.

Zulfi suggested the *balakhanas* near Chowk Yadgare. One ancient, wood-screened and decrepit *balakhana* had caught my imagination. The thought of spending the night in a forlorn, forsaken place suddenly sounded like a good idea. I was prepped to spend the night like an old trader in a small room with scanty ancient furniture, drinking kahwa—the 'nectar of life'—poured from copper samovars into old tea cups and a steaming wood-fired hammam for a bath. I also conjured up a story-teller from the Qissa Khwani Bazaar narrating fascinating anecdotes of the Silk Road to complete my dream stay at the *balakhana*. My reverie was shattered when Zulfi returned wringing his hands in exasperation. Even the *balakhanas* were full!

We took the motorway to Mardan where Mohammad Usman Mardanvi, an expert on Gandharan sites, joined us. Usman takes his family name from his home town Mardan in Khyber Pakhtunkhwa province. His specialization and interest in Buddhism and keen interest in exploring possible Buddhist sites baffled me. On Usman's suggestion we looked for rooms at a guest house near the Bachcha

Khan Medical College. Thankfully, there were rooms vacant in the big guest house. Perhaps not many had stepped here in a long time—the drains were blocked and elephant grass had encroached every inch of the inner courtyard. Since no food was served here, Usman and Sher Khan went to the bazaar to buy some hot chapattis and vegetable curry for dinner.

After dinner, I stood under the shower to get rid of the thick layer of dust that had settled on me during the day-long tour in Peshawar, especially the lanes and by lanes of the myriad bazaars. But I wasn't prepared for the consequences of a long, lazy bath. The bedroom was flooded with water! The hotel manager allotted another room. But misery was my companion that night. In the new room, instead of cold air, the air conditioner spewed dust. I was too tired to complain again. I switched off the air conditioner and lay on the bed drowned in perspiration. As night progressed, a soothing breeze blew from the hills of the Khyber bringing with it images of buried cities and orange-robed monks chanting a chorus in praise of the Buddha.

It was the time for a call for morning prayers from a nearby mosque as I struggled out of bed to prepare for a long exciting journey to some of Asia's renowned monastic centres in Mardan, the second-largest city of Khyber Pakhtunkhwa region after Peshawar. It formed a part of the ancient Buddhist kingdom of Gandhara and is the district where some of the most important Buddhist heritage sites of Asia were discovered. The reasons for its importance are not too far-fetched. Located in the Doab of the rivers Swat and Kabul, it was a rich agricultural belt of the north-western region. It formed a part of the land between the river valleys of Oxus and Kabul and also benefited from trade on the Indus. The ancient Uttarapath running through Gandhara towards Peshawar passed through the district bringing in high profits from trade along the Himalayan foothills as well as the region of Central Asia.

On this busy crossroad of trade and commerce, Asoka found it convenient to put up his Kharosthi script edicts at the village of Shahbazgarhi in the third century BC. The UNESCO World Heritage

Site of Takht-i-Bahi, the vast monastic complex of Sahri Bahlol and the Kashmir Smast caves dating from the fourth to the ninth century and functioning as the *varshavasa* (rainy season retreat) for *bhikshus* were also found in the district close to the city. Gigantic images of the Buddha and bodhisattvas, unearthed in and around Mardan during excavations are on display at the Peshawar Museum. Mardan is also known for its hundreds of *dheris,* which are mostly unexplored Buddhist mounds waiting for the spade of archaeologists.

Even today, Mardan is in close proximity to the million-dollar CPEC that passes along the Motorway M1 close to the ancient Uttarapath/modern-day Grand Trunk road running along Rashkai.

At Mardan, the Bachcha Khan guest house would be my base and Mohammad Usman Mardanvi, my archaeologist guide. From here I would travel to the monastic sites of Charsadda located to the west, Takht-i-Bahi and Sahri Bahlol to the north, village of Sikri to the north-east and Shahbazgarhi to the south-east. Then, taking the Asian highway I would return to the village of Ranadheri on the Indus near Hund.

My itinerary was packed with the Buddha and I was to begin my travels from Charsadda.

TO HISSARA VILLAGE IN CHARSADDA

The next morning, I was at crossroads. Literally! In Charsadda, a town that borrows its name from *char sadak* or four roads, is one where routes from Peshawar, Balkh, Taxila and Swat are joined. The city identified as the ancient Pushkalavati, or the 'city of flowers', was once the capital of Gandhara and flourished due to trans-Asiatic commerce coming through the Balkh–Bamiyan route along the Kabul Valley.

During the Buddha's time in the sixth–fifth century BC, Buddhism as a religion was patronized by King Pukkusati (Puskarasarin), who ruled over Gandhara in the middle of the sixth century BC, with possibly Pushkalavati or Charsadda as his capital.

History tells us that King Pukkusati's keen interest in Buddhism stemmed from his friendly and cultural relations with Bimbisara, the king of Magadh, who sent ambassadors with valuable gifts including an inscribed golden plate with descriptions of the *triratna* (three jewels) of the Buddha, the *Dhamma* (doctrine) and the Sangha (the Buddhist Order). After reading the inscriptions on the plate sent by Bimbisara, Pukkusati joined the Sangha, became a Buddhist monk and actively propagated Buddhism in his kingdom. He even came to Rajagaha (present-day Rajgir in Bihar) to pay homage to the Buddha who preached to him the *Dhatuvibhanga Sutta*. It should not seem unlikely that Pukkusati invited Buddha to Gandhara and that Buddha actually went there to preach to the Gandharans.[1]

Charsadda was the capital of the province of Gandhara at the time of Alexander's expedition in the fourth century BC. The chief of Pushkalavati was Astes/Hasti who died defending his capital. Upon the death of Astes, the city of Pushkalavati was passed on to Alexander.[2] During the Mauryan period, the capital of the Gandhara province was at Taxila under the viceroyalty of Mauryan princes. After the decline of the Mauryan dynasty, the Indo-Bactrians/Indo-Greeks built a new city just across Jindi River (a tributary of the Swat) at a site later known as Shaikhan Dheri.

The Greeks from Bactria conquered Gandhara and Punjab in 185–180 BC and an independent Indo-Greek kingdom was formed. Demetrius and Menander were the famous Indo-Greek kings who had their capital cities at Pushkalavati (present-day Charsadda), Taxila and later Sagala (present-day Sialkot). Both Demetrius and Menander were interested in Buddhism[3] and contributed to the expansion of Buddhism in the region of Afghanistan that once formed part of the ancient Greco-Bactrian kingdom.[4]

Known as Bala Hissar, the monumental mound of Charsadda in

---

[1] K.L. Hazra, *The Rise and Decline of Buddhism in India*, Munshiram Manoharlal Publishers, Delhi, 1995 (3rd ed., 2009), p.16.
[2] Alexander Cunningham, *Ancient Geography of India*, Low Price Publications, Delhi, 1990 (1st ed. 1871), p.42.
[3] B.N. Puri, *Buddhism in Central Asia*, Motilal Banarsidass Publishers, Delhi, 2000, p.91,
[4] Puri, *Buddhism in Central Asia*, p.91.

village Hissara, is an archaeological site dating from the sixth century BC of the Achaemenid Period, and occupied a strategic position at the confluence of the Swat and the Kabul rivers. Historians call it the eastern-most gates of the Persian Empire. The ruins of the two main cities of Charsadda at Hissara and Sheikhan Dheri across the Jindi were explored and excavated by eminent archaeologists Sir John Marshall in 1902, by Mortimer Wheeler in 1958 and Ahmed H. Dani in 1962.

Today, many *dheris* or mounds of ancient settlements can be seen around Charsadda, the modern area of Hashtnagar in the villages of Rajjar, Ziarat and Shahr-i-Napursan. French antiquarian Alfred Foucher explored the area while tracking the routes of the Chinese pilgrim Xuanzang. Although the name of Hashtnagar refers to the eight towns located close together along the lower course of the Swat river, the name probably goes back to the old name of Hastinagar or 'city of Hasti'.[5]

We took the road to Charsadda Chowk and drove past the engineering university and the then under-construction Mardan Museum. The new Charsadda road that is being widened into a six-lane highway was dusty and in a state of disrepair. The ancient Peshawar–Charsadda road was still visible near the Charsadda Bazaar. Xuanzang could have taken this road while travelling from Peshawar to Pushkalavati.

The confluence of the Swat and Kabul rivers at Charsadda is considered to be sacred and about 25 km from Charsadda Bazaar a vast graveyard has come up along the Charsadda road. This is Asia's third-largest cemetery running up to Nowshera.

After crossing the Jindi River and turning right towards Sheikh Kala, we reached Hissara village, which was once part of the expansive site of Pushkalavati, the sixth-century BC capital of Gandhara. The village was surrounded by a vast treeless area covered by high mounds of yellow earth, standing like low hills extending far beyond the boundaries of the village up to the banks of the Jindi. These

---

[5] Cunningham, *Ancient Geography of India*, p.43.

ruins formed the ramparts of a once grand structure; perhaps, the fortress of the ancient Charsadda. What was once the mud walls of the monumental structure has now turned into layers of glistening yellow earth that rise thick and high. Within the ruins, one can trace the entrance towers, galleries and guard quarters, much like the mud palaces in the Khorezmian desert of Ayaz Kala and Topra Kala in Khorezm, Uzbekistan.

Several mounds surrounded this structure from where marvellous pieces of statuary art were recovered. These are now housed in Peshawar Museum. Many have also reportedly been whisked outside the country by unscrupulous traders who descend on the *dheris* after monsoon to collect antiquities washed to the surface of the earth. From the nearby Mamanadheri (near Charsadda), an exquisite statue of a Buddha colossi was unearthed, and is now on display at the Peshawar Museum.

When Xuanzang visited Charsaddda in the seventh century AD, every stupa crafted on stone by expert stone carvers of Gandhara, but now turned into mounds or *dheris*, must have narrated the story of the Buddha's life as a bodhisattva. Xuanzang mentioned a number of sites connected with previous incarnations of the Buddha and eminent Buddhist institutions, where scholars such as Vasumitra and high priests composed sutras.

The pilgrim recounts, 'about 50 li to the north-east of the Kanishka Vihara in Purushapura [Peshawar] we cross a great river [Kabul River] and arrive at the town of Pushkalavati (Po-shi-kie-lo-fa-ti).'[6]

Xuanxang was disappointed to see the state of religion in Pushkalavati where there were only a few priests and the halls of monasteries were deserted.

To the east of the city is a stupa built by Asoka-raja. This is the place where the four former Buddhas delivered the law. Among former saints and sages many have come from mid-India to

---

[6] Samuel Beal, *Si-Yu-Ki: Buddhist Records of the Western World*, Book II, Low Price Publications, Delhi, 1884, p.109.

this place to instruct all creatures. For example, Vasu Mitra, doctor of Sastras, composed the *Chung-sse-fen-o-pi-ta-mo* (*Abhidharmaprakarana-pada*) Sastra in this place. To the north of the town 4 or 5 li is an old sangharama, of which the halls are deserted and cold. There are very few priests in it, and all composed the *Tsa-pi-ta-ma-lun* (*Samyuktabhidharma Sastra*).[7]

It is significant to note that three important Jataka stories had their settings in Pushkalavati; for example, the story of the Eye Gift, *Hariti Jataka* and *Syama Jataka*. Pilgrims from far and wide arrived to pay homage to the memorial stupas built at the site where the bodhisattva performed acts of charity. According to the *Si-Yu-Ki*, 'By the side of the *sangharama* is a stupa (Stupa of Eye Gift) several hundred feet high, which was built by King Asoka. It is made of carved wood and veined stone, which was the work of various artists.' It further read:

> When Sakya Buddha was the king of this country, he prepared himself as a bodhisattva. He gave up all he had at the request of those who asked, and spared not to sacrifice his own body as a bequeathed gift. Having been born in this country a thousand times as king, he gave during each of those thousands births in this excellent country, his eyes as an offering.[8]

Xuanzang further states that not far east from this place, there are two stone stupas, each about 100 feet in height. The one on the right was built by Brahma Deva and that on the left by the king of devas, Sakra. They were both adorned with jewels and gems. Going northwest about 25 km from these stupas, there is another stupa where Sakya Tathagata converted Hariti Jataka, the mother of demons, and stopped her from hurting men. It is for this reason the common folk of this country offer sacrifices to her for obtaining children.[9]

According to his memoir, 25 km or so to the north, there is

---

[7] Beal, *Si-Yu-Ki*, Book II, pp.109–10.
[8] Beal, *Si-Yu-Ki*, Book II, p.110.
[9] Beal, *Si-Yu-Ki*, Book II, pp.110–11.

another stupa. It was here that the young boy Samaka Bodhisattva (Shang-mu-kia), walking piously, provided nourishment to his blind father and mother. One day while gathering fruit for them, he was wounded by a poisoned arrow by the king who was out hunting. However, he was restored to health by some medicaments, who were moved by his holy conduct and spirituality and applied healing herbs to the wound.[10]

Foucher, who earnestly followed the route taken by Xuanzang from Peshawar to Charsadda and further to Shahbazgarhi in 1895, notes that Xuanzang quit the high road at Charsadda and headed to north-west India for an excursion to visit some stupas. To arrive there, he had to follow the road which ascended from the Swat Valley running towards Udyayana. The road passed through the villages of Hashtnagar and was lined by the debris of Buddhist convents and stupas, that is, the ancient ruins of villages now known as Rajjar, Utmanzai, Turangzai and Umarzai. However, Xuanzang does not mention these in his memoir. There is only a mention the stupa of the 'Mother of Demons'.

Foucher mentions the village of Sare-makhe Dheri as the site of the Hariti Stupa, the second stupa of the site of the *Syama Jataka* (identified by Foucher along with the ruins of Periano *dheri* near the village of Gandheri).[11]

A map illustration by Foucher shows the old road to India that does not run straight eastwards from Charsadda to Shahbazgarhi. Instead, it curves to avoid the stony desert or the *maira* on its south and the mountains of the Yusufzai surrounding the region from the north.[12] According to him, Xuanzang returned southwards from Gandheri to Charsadda by the same road. Rejoining the old high road to India and travelling eastwards for 38 km, the pilgrim would have reached Polusha (near Shahbazgarhi).[13]

---

[10] Beal, *Si-Yu-Ki*, Book II, p.111.
[11] Alfred Foucher, *Notes on the Ancient Geography of Gandhara*, Asian Educational Service, Delhi, 2005 (1st ed. 1915), p.18.
[12] Foucher, *Notes on the Ancient Geography of Gandhara*, p.22.
[13] Foucher, *Notes on the Ancient Geography of Gandhara*, p.21.

Usman gave me the names of several Buddhist villages that were part of Hashtnagar, namely Mohammadzai, Rajjar, Sherpao, Tangi, Turangzai, Umarzai, Utmanzai and Dargai.

BUDDHA IMAGES FROM LORIYAN TANGAI

One important Buddhist settlement near Charsadda is the village of Loriyan Tangai where excavations led to the discovery of not only a stupa but also monastic ruins and numerous Buddha and bodhisattva images and relief scenes from the life of the Buddha. Displayed at the Indian Museum, Kolkata or in Peshawar, these images indicate that Loriyan Tangai was an extensive Buddhist settlement, inhabited by a large number of monks.

The name of Loriyan Tangai is mentioned as part of Peshawar district but later when Charsadda and Mardan districts were carved out of Peshawar, the village became a part of Charsadda. However, it is difficult to find Loriyan Tangai on the satellite map of Khyber Pakhtunkhwa or in the maps of Peshawar or Charsadda. Instead, what we find is the village of Tangi.

Incidentally, the antiquities recovered from Loriyan Tangai are also listed as antiquities from Palatu Dheri and Hashtnagar which creates doubt regarding Palatu Dheri and Loriyan Tangai being one and the same settlements in the Hashtnagar constituency of Charsadda. It must be noted that in one map, Loriyan Tangai has been shown to be part of Buner.

In the neighbouring Shar-i-Napursan archaeological site in Charsadda tehsil near village Rajjar (forming a part of Hashtnagar), excavations have unearthed two distinct settlements from the Buddhist period. Coins issued by Menander, Hermes and Kanishka have also been found here.

At Palatu Dheri (or Loriyan Tangai, perhaps), an archaeological site in Charsadda tehsil located a mile from Shar-i-Napursan, a mound containing the remains of a stupa dated first century AD was unearthed. Three inscribed jars, gifts of lay devotees to the

Community of the Four Quarters,[14] are now in Peshawar Museum. Several statues of the Buddha and bodhisattvas from Loriyan Tangai can be found today at the Indian Museum in Kolkata. Among these is a larger-than-life Meditating Buddha. A pedestal and a headless statue from Loriyan Tangai in Hashtnagar were dug up in the nineteenth century by a tradesman quarrying the mound for stone. The pedestal depicts a bodhisattva flanked by Brahma and Indra and other figures imploring the Buddha to preach his doctrine. Initially, the head from another statue was glued to the headless statue and installed for worship at a pilgrims' resthouse at Rajjar in Charsadda district. In 1883, Sir Lucas White King, former commissioner of Rawalpindi Division, was allowed to cut off the inscribed pedestal and take it away for study.

In *A Guide to the Sculptures in Indian Museum*, N.G. Majumdar describes a Buddha image from Loriyan Tangai dated from an unspecified year, possibly AD 318, flanked by two seated bodhisattva, one of whom is carrying a manuscript identified with Manjusri and the other carrying a bunch of flowers with Padampani or Avalokitesvara.[15]

MONASTERY OF TAKHT-I-BAHI

We drove back on Charsadda road from the village of Hissara, and after a few kilometres turned left for Rajrah on the NH-5. From this point, the Takht-i-Bahi monastery is 25 km away. Charsadda ends and Mardan begins at Khanmai stream. Usman informed that there are many *dheris* or mounds on the way to Takht-i-Bahi. These were once monastic settlements from where numerous Buddhist antiquities were recovered.

Foucher too had found many *dheris* on the road beyond Charsadda up until Gandheri while tracking the route taken by

---

[14] Sten Konow, *Kharoshthi Inscriptions*, Vol 2. Part I, Government of India, 1929, p.120. Available at https://archive.org/details/in.ernet.dli.2015.53483/page/n9/mode/2up (last date of access: 5 February 2020).
[15] N.G. Majumdar, *A Guide to the Sculptures in Indian Museum*, Part II, Archaeological Survey of India, Delhi, 1937, pp.18–19.

Xuanzang. In the entire division of Mardan and Swabi, there are hundreds of such *dheris*.

My next stop was Takht-i-Bahi, a monastery situated atop a 500-feet-high hill, exactly 2 km east of the Takht-i-Bahi Bazaar and 15 km from Mardan, along the NH-7 to Swat. One of the most splendid monasteries yet seen on the Asian Silk Road, the place takes its name from Bahi (stream) and Takht (throne), meaning a throne on a stream or Takht-i-Bahi. Locals believe that the site got its name from two wells on the hill or springs flowing near the site. The location of the site protected it from the numerous invasions in the Gandhara region and the site continued to be occupied up to the seventh century AD when royal patronage ceased.

An inscription here from the time of the Indo-Parthian king Gondophares (r.AD 20–46) suggests that the establishment is pre-Christian.[16] After the rule of the Indo-Parthians, the place fell under the control of the Kusanas.

In use for 700 years, the Takht-i-Bahi monastic centre is the most imposing relic of Buddhism in all of Gandhara. It was listed as a UNESCO World Heritage Site in 1980. The site has many peculiarities and seems to be the main monastic site of Gandhara where a large multitude of scholars and monks resided. The underground chamber with separate meditational cells is evidence that very senior monks and scholars lived here.

Offerings were made by the worshipping laity to the numerous votive stupas with their façade and plinth covered with stucco images of the Buddha. The tall niches in the courtyards surrounding the massive central stupa suggest that colossal Buddha images were once installed at Takht-i-Bahi. These are now displayed at the museums of Lahore and Peshawar.

One wonders how such massive images were transported to the hill monastery. Were they sculpted in the vicinity or were they made to order at the ateliers of Sahri Bahlol from where they were exported? The question remains unanswered.

---

[16] Debala Mitra, *Buddhist Monuments*, Sahitya Samsad, Kolkata, 1971 (reprint 1980), pp.120–21.

Explorations and excavations on this site began in 1864 and a significant number of Buddhist statuary art was recovered and sent to the Peshawar Museum. The site affords an interesting study into the techniques that must have been available to ancient architects for constructing and embellishing a hill monastery and for making excellent use of hill terraces for building different parts of a monastery. It also offers an insight into the rituals of monastic life in the Sangha—from the circumambulation to meditation—activities that were carried out in separate courts or enclosures of the establishment. Excellent use of space and planning went into the construction and location of assembly halls where discourses were held. Equally worthy of appreciation are the system of acoustics in the vaulted underground chambers, the channelled water system, the security system for guarding against animals and invaders, the kind of material used for the construction of stupas, chapels and, above all, the ateliers that were functioning in the surrounding hills which supplied statuaries and finally the means by which they were hauled up the mountains and installed in the chapels of the stupa courts.

A lovely garden spreads out at the base of Takht-i-Bahi hills. The climb to the hilltop is steep and a wide stairway has been cut into the hillside. As the monastery is built at various levels on the hill, it is difficult to say whether this was the sole entrance. Armed guards with loaded rifles stand at the entrance of this Buddhist monument, which is considered one of the most well-preserved in Asia. Not just this, the beauty and variety with regard to the embellishment of bodhisattvas (displayed at Lahore and Peshawar museums), their regal attire as well as choice of jewellery, hair styling and turban designs are a marvel of Gandharan art.

A steep stairway leads into the lower votive stupa court surrounded by narrow high chapels, with the gigantic base of the main stupa being the main attraction. Oblong in structure, the 56.6 x 45.6 feet base stands in the middle of the court. The main stupa rests on a square platform of 20.6 square feet, receding in three stages and with a total height of 8.6 feet. The façade of the upper and lower tiers are relieved with a row of pilasters. The top of the platform which served as a processional path around the drum was approached by a flight of steps, provided in the central projection of the north-side facing the entrance of the stupa court. The dome of the stupa has now completely vanished but broken parts of the umbrella, its pillar and the *triratna* lie in another courtyard called the Three Stupa Court.

On the floor of this court lies a virtual forest of votive stupas arranged in several rows. Some of these are double stupas having niches supported by pilasters and once decorated with figures of Buddhist deities. One can still trace out stucco and stone figures of deities in the niches of some votive stupas.

Interestingly, some of the votive stupas have circular bases with one having a circumference of around 24 feet. Another interesting structure is the octagonal stupa with a circumference of 25 feet. The base has niches that were once decorated with stucco figures of Buddha.

Chapels

On three sides, the votive stupa court is surrounded by lofty chapels in which gigantic Buddha and bodhisattva images were once enshrined. These statues now adorn the Peshawar Museum. Some chapels are small and once held small Buddhas, rows of bodhisattva or Buddha heads; other chapels are double-storeyed. One 18-feet-high chapel held a 12-feet-high Buddha, also on display at the Peshawar Museum. Smaller images of the Buddha—generally sitting images of the Buddha in *dhyan mudra*—ranged from three to five feet. While many chapels are roofless, some still have roofs, though they are in a dilapidated condition.

A few dozen chapels are situated to the south of the votive stupa court. Among these, two lying adjacent to each other are the loftiest, measuring 40 feet in height and once held 20–25-feet-high Buddha images. Believed to have been donative chapels offered by the laity, they were crowned with domed stupa-like structures and built on a plinth that was decorated with carved niches having relief images of Buddhist deities and floral patterns.

Monastery

Steps lead from the votive stupa court to the monastery, the residential area for monks which lay buried until excavations in 1907–08. The monastery appears to have been a double-storeyed structure as one can see steps leading upstairs to the second storey which no longer exists. What remains of the monastery are 14 monk cells with niches for lamps around a central courtyard. In a corner is a water tank which drew water from a spring. A kitchen, a refectory and bathrooms were attached to the monastery.

During excavations, a stone image of an 'emaciated Siddhartha', similar to the one found at Sikri was unearthed, is now on display at the Peshawar Museum.

Meditation Cells

A flight of stairs lead from the stupa court into the dark and cold underground structures at the base of the Takht-i-Bahi hill. These completely isolated underground cells with corbelled ceilings in two rows on either side of a vaulted passage were used by monks for the purpose of meditation.

An open courtyard lies west of the meditation cells and is enclosed by a clay wall which was probably a part of the hill from which it had been carved out. The courtyard opens into the meditation cells or is a continuation of it. This high-walled quadrangular hall that is now roofless is thought to be the place where the monks assembled for meetings or reading scriptures. There are small niches in the walls that once held burning lamps, evidence that monks used to assemble after sunset.

It is possible that a large number of monks who resided at Takht-i-Bahi (as evidenced from the double-storey monastery) used both courtyards for prayers and lectures.

Three Stupa Court

Coming up the stairs from the meditation cells and the open courtyard of the assembly, I took another stairway to descend into the Three Stupa Court. Here lie two small stupas about five feet in width and one big square stupa base about 17 feet in width and 3 feet high. The stupas are covered with stucco carvings and have niches with traces of stucco Buddha images at their base. Some broken images in stucco lie in the covered porch of the stupa court, among which is a beautiful sculpture of Panchika and the goddess of fertility, Hariti.

Monk Cells on Hillside

Several single- and double-storeyed monk cells can be seen covering the hillsides of Takht-i-Bahi. They are in a ruinous condition and only their walls and stairs leading to the upper storey can be seen. The vast number of monk cells covering the hills around the monastery is proof of the huge Buddhist population that lived here and the sacredness and popularity of the site.

The extensive use of stone at Takht-i-Bahi will baffle the visitor. Though the quarry was near by, how were the huge slabs carried up the hill? Perhaps carved pathways led up the hill and wheeled carts carried huge blocks of stone. But what about the monolithic stone sculptures of the giant Buddhas? Were they sculptured inside the monastery itself? It is possible that the meditation hall located deep underground was the quarry itself from where stones were obtained easily. Another huge depression which could have been the quarry lies near the Three Stupa Court where the large *dharmachakra* and canopies are stored.

I walked out of Takht-i-Bahi thinking of the men who laboured for hours together to create these Buddha artefacts with their sweat and blood.

STATUARY ART FROM SAHRI BAHLOL

From Takht-i-Bahi site, we proceeded south-west to Sahri Bahlol, one of the richest sites in stone and stucco sculpture dated to the reign of the Kushanas and the Kidara Kushanas between the second and fifth centuries AD. As our vehicle stopped near Sahri Bahlol, I noticed that the road ran several feet below the village that is perched on a high mound of the monastic village. On seeing us get out of the vehicle, there was a commotion in the village. A big crowd collected on the overhanging hill, curiously looking down as if questioning the purpose of our visit. Walking on the road along the base of the village, I found an ancient wall embedded in the hillside running along the base. Was it the base of a stupa? I wondered. But archaeological reports suggest that this could be the ancient wall of the city built in a 'diaper' style, characteristic of the early centuries of the Christian era.

The path going up the mound, about 50 feet high, was clearly visible despite thick overgrowth. I waded through a mountain of garbage that must have collected over a long period of time by a large population living over the mounds. Shortly, we returned to the road to avoid any problem with the villagers.

Usman informed me that a dozen monastic establishments that surrounded the main site of Sahri Bahlol were all occupied and encroached upon by villages constructed over the high mounds. Renowned archaeologist Debala Mitra who explored the site points out that the expansive Buddhist establishment consisted of numerous separate units of quadrangular monasteries with their stupa courts, stupas and monk cells radiating in a vast campus around a central or the main monastery.[17] Much of the splendid establishment is lost, not only due to human greed and vandalism, but also due to the mud and wood material that withered over time.[18]

Stone Carvers of Sahri Bahlol

The monastery flourished during the reign of the Kushanas and Kidara Kushanas and is counted as the richest in stucco and stone art running into thousands.

Several mounds in Sahri Bahlol excavated in the early twentieth century yielded stupa courts with one or more stupas surrounded by chapels which were adorned with Buddha images, quadrangular monasteries with monk cells, a kitchen and refectory. The base of these stupas was embellished with stucco figures and the stair risers

---

[17] Debala Mitra, *Buddhist Monuments*, pp.121–22.
[18] Mitra, *Buddhist Monuments*, pp.121–22.

narrated stories from the Jatakas and the life of the Buddha. The façade of the stupa plinth was decorated with mouldings, stucco work, friezes of the Buddha between Indo-Corinthian pilasters and scenes from the life of the Buddha.

According to Mitra, Sahri Bahlol was probably exporting statuary of Buddha and Buddhist deities to the monasteries of Gandhara. Since it lay close to the Uttarapath, the trade in Buddhist art flourished. This was the atelier that was providing images to Takht-i-Bahi located 4 km away, Jamalgarhi about 5 km away and possibly to Charsadda and Peshawar and monasteries of the Yusufzai region in the Khyber Pakhtunkhwa.

The splendid array of hundreds of sculptural pieces from the site in the museums of Pakistan, India and Europe, is evidence that the establishment was a monastery-cum-atelier where stones brought from quarries in nearby mountains were worked upon by craftsmen. It is possible that the structures of mud and wood mentioned by Mitra were actually used as habitation by the village craftsmen who came and settled near the main monastery. The stucco and stone carvers were well-conversant with Buddhist tales and the depth of emotions portrayed in the art of Sahri Bahlol shows they might have been monks themselves or artistes hired by the devotees. Beautiful specimens of Gandharan sculptures point to the existence not only of a Buddhist art school, but also workshop for stone carvers.

We learn of Greek, Central Asian, Chinese and Indian monks who left their countries to journey to other lands in order to construct monasteries. It is strange that both Faxian and Xuanzang did not mention any such monastery in the vicinity of Pushkalavati. Xuanzang on his way from Charsadda to Polusha or Shahbazgarhi must have come across important monastic centres of the Yusufzai region. However, Sahri Bahlol must certainly have been among his list of 100 monasteries of Gandhara.

I left behind the statuary, crossed the Kalpani stream and reached the historical village of Sikri.

AT THE VILLAGE OF SIKRI

Located next to Katlang, Sikri is a historical village named after the famous shrine of a Sufi saint Shikray Baba, the mazar at which I was seated for a cup of tea.

I entered the Sikri village after crossing a stream of the Kalpani that rises along the valley of Katti Garhi and flows south, irrigating vast lands of the Kabul Valley and finally emptying into the Kabul River. Usman led me through the village road to a group of brick houses. One particularly large house with high walls had a small door built into its outer wall and a young girl peeped from the slightly ajar door and beckoned me over. As I moved towards her, I got a full view of the large courtyard where a couple of women were sitting on a charpoy while others were busy with their daily chores. A few rooms at the far end with a running verandah opened into the courtyard.

At one end of the village was a high mound covered with shrubs and wild grass. The villagers who followed me pointed out that this was the spot where the famed Sikri Stupa was found in a dilapidated condition hidden under thick shrubs. The severely damaged stupa was reconstructed by experts from the Lahore Museum and put on display at the centre of the Buddha Gallery. The splendid stupa has its drum decorated with stone panels depicting Jataka tales of the Buddha's previous incarnations. It rivals the beauty of the Mahachaitya of Amravati and is unique in its narration of at least 13 Jataka stories and episodes from the life of the Buddha.

Assuming that the entire village might have been founded on a large monastic site, I walked through the village to check on some more mounds. As news spread that an Indian woman was touring their village to trace the ancient roots of a Buddhist establishment, a crowd gathered and followed me everywhere. I climbed an empty mound and tried to clear some garbage and tall elephant grass covering it, and found only rubble covering the mound from where the stupa was removed and taken to the Lahore Museum where it is still the centre of attraction. A mosque in the vicinity of the mound was probably the most sacred place in the village.

During his extensive travels from Peshawar to Charsadda and thence to Shahbazgarhi, Xuanzang missed the cluster of monastic sites including Sikri, by whatever name it was known in the early centuries of the Christian era. I do not know how Xuanzang skipped the monastic sites, but I certainly was crestfallen as no sign of any Buddhist establishment could be detected in the village except for one or two high mounds under tall shrubs and boundary walls of houses built of large ancient bricks and dressed stones.

Once upon a time, the entire population of this village must have been Buddhists, and the village with its magnificent stupa must have attracted pilgrims from all over the Buddhist world. The village must have resonated with the chants of Buddhist sutras; there must have been monks' cells around the perennial Kalpani River. I thought about the saint's mausoleum and the mosque near the mound of the stupa and found piety everywhere. The maulvi exhorted me to catch a breath and ordered ginger tea for me, while the women sent for a tall glass of sherbet that I gulped down eagerly. I walked to their door, held their hands and bid them goodbye. I wish I could have spent some time in their courtyard and chatted with them.

The 'Fasting Siddhartha from Sikri' is a rare piece of sculpture in bluish schist stone presenting a fine narration in stone of the Buddha's renunciation of the world and his physical condition as a result of fasting. Buddhist tales provide details of how the bodhisattva went to a forest near the village Uruvela and chose his abode on the bank of the Nairanjana River. For six years, he refused food and practised austerities, so that his glorious body wasted away to skin and bone. He allowed himself to feed on a single *sesamun* seed or a grain of rice, until one day he was overcome by a severe pain, causing him to faint and fall. Finally, he perceived that mortification was not the road to Enlightenment and resolved to beg for food in towns and villages, so that his health and strength might be restored. The image of the Fasting Siddhartha is displayed at the Lahore Museum.

JAMALGARHI MONASTIC CENTRE

History tells us that a cluster of Buddhist settlements existed around Takht-i-Bahi, a monastic university. Numerous satellite cities were set up around Takht-i-Bahi as branches to accommodate the growing number of monks who came there to study religion between the first and seventh century AD.[19] According to Nawaz-ud-Din, research officer at the Peshawar Museum, archeological sites including Takht-i-Bhai and Jamalgarhi served as universities where monks from across the world arrived to study Buddhist texts.

The Jamalgarhi monastic site was one of such monastic college in the vicinity of Takht-i-Bahi. The Buddhist site comprising numerous chapels and courtyards, stray monastic cells and a large circular stupa, functioned from the first to fifth century AD and was one of the earliest sites built in the region. The ruins of Jamalgarhi were first discovered by British archaeologist Sir Alexander Cunningham in 1848 and further excavations were carried between 1852 and 1873.

Both Sahri Bahlol and Jamalgarhi lay within a few kilometres of Takht-i-Bahi. While Sahri Bahlol has been totally encroached upon, Takht-i-Bahi and Jamalgarhi continue to hint at the grandeur of the monastic establishments of Khyber Pakhtunkhwa province of Pakistan, part of ancient Gandhara. These sites in and around Mardan housed the most beautiful statuaries from their chapels, and are now on display at the Indian Museum, Kolkata, Peshawar and Lahore museums in Pakistan and at the British Museum in London.

AT JAMALGARHI

From Sikri we returned to the Khanmai stream along the main road to Jamalgarhi, a small town located 13 km from Mardan. The elevated site on a high mound had a difficult approach. There were no rock-cut steps along the uneven and high grassy hill on which

---

[19] Refer to <https://gulfnews.com/news/asia/pakistan/bakhshali-manuscript-throws-new-light-on-rich-history-of-gandhara-1.2094741> (last date of access: 5 February 2020).

the monastery was located. We walked around the hill to look for a vantage point to negotiate the steep incline. There was none and we had no option but to crawl up the hillside. The Jamalgarhi hill appeared dwarfed by the surrounding mountain ranges and seemed to lie in a bowl of towering cliffs. The lofty hillock of Karamar takes its name from Lord Siva who generally has a serpent rising behind his matted hair. It is likely that the presence of a carved figure of Lord Siva's serpent gave rise to the modern name of Karamar—literally, standing snake. It is said that the carved figure of Bhima Devi, the wife of Siva, once stood here, high up on the hill where there is a water spring and a reservoir.[20]

The site has been laid out in a circular plan around the circular stupa just as the Dharmarajika at Taxila. It is distinct from the rectangular plans of the nearby Takht-i-Bahi and Mohra Moradu and Jaulian at Taxila. The general planning of the site with its tall chapels surrounding the central stupa, however, bears similarity with Takht-i-Bahi. The focus of the establishment is the circular stupa, of which only the circular base remains.

The façade of the circular base was once embellished by stucco figures of the seated Buddha in niches separated by pilasters. Now, one can barely trace the eroded pilasters, niches and missing figures. The existing circumambulatory passage around the stupa is paved with dark slate slabs. Mitra who explored the site, mentions that the passage was at some places inlaid with coins, one of which was issued by the Kushan king, Vasudeva (r.AD 145–76).

Around the courtyard on the periphery of the *pradikshana path* is a ring of roofless chapels, similar to the ones at Takht-i-Bahi, but much smaller in size. These chapels were erected to hold standing images of the Buddha and bodhisattvas. The chapels lie empty as their images have been pilfered. The façades of the chapels were also embellished with small figures of the Buddha, now missing, but seen by Mitra during her explorations of the site. She found a large number of images and Indo-Corinthian pilaster capitals, votive

---

[20] Ahmad H. Dani, *Shahbaz Garhi*, University of Peshawar, Peshawar, 1964, pp.1–8.

stupas and a shaft lying in front of the chapels on the pavement. The circular stupa court is connected with a lower oblong court by a flight of steps. Various Jatakas stories adorned the stair risers in bas-relief. A number of these decorated stair risers can be seen at the Peshawar Museum. One rare and beautiful stair riser illustrating the Syama Jataka is now on display at the British Museum.

This lower court was reserved for votive offerings and comprises small oblong chapels built so as to form a ring around a group of small votive stupas. This lower court yielded a rich crop of sculptures including images of the Buddha, bodhisattvas and pillar capitals. A flight of steps from the lower court descend into another small court with chapels. The multi-stupa courts are similar in plan to the Takht-i-Bahi site, where one stupa court leads into another, each having a ring of chapels erected to hold images of the Buddha.

However, unlike Takht-i-Bahi, there is no quadrangular monastery. Ruins of monk cells built as isolated units, sometimes double-storeyed with a verandah, can be seen along the slopes of the Jamalgarhi hill and nearby mountains.

Among the landmark sculptures from Jamalgarhi, the most notable include the Atlantes from Jamalgarhi and Ordination of Nanda.

The Atlantes from Jamalgarhi is made of grey schist. The Ordination of Nanda is an upright panel of greyish white schist from Jamalgarhi. It depicts scenes from the story of Nanda, half-brother of the Buddha, who was lured into joining the Sangha by the Buddha. Nanda leaves his lovely wife and starts out with the Buddha's begging bowl in hand, to accompany him to his monastery. His head was shaved and he was ordained into the Order. The scene is depicted in the panel where the barber is in the act of tonsuring Nanda while the Buddha pours out the ceremonial water. From then on, Nanda was kept as an unwilling prisoner in the monastery and the top panel depicts his many attempts to escape. As he made his way stealthily through the wood, the Buddha suddenly appeared, advancing towards him and when Nanda tried to hide behind a tree, the tree rose into the air leaving him face to face with the Buddha. Both these relics are now kept at the Indian Museum in Kolkata.

ASOKA AT SHAHBAZGARHI

Shahbazgarhi's fame rests on the 14 Major Rock Edicts of the Mauryan Emperor Asoka cut into the surface of two large boulders on the side of a low rocky hill in the village. According to scholars, the edicts, written from right to left in the Kharosthi script, are the earliest deciphered epigraphy of the third century BC found in the Indian subcontinent.[21]

Why were the edicts put up in this forlorn and remote town? Why was this place so important to Asoka? It is said that the ancient trade route, the Mauryan highroad or the old east–west Uttarapath, passed through Shahbazgarhi at a point where other ancient routes coming from the north and south also met, to form an important crossing in the third century BC. The old road to Shahbazgarhi was a bustling trade route and the modern motorway or the modified and upgraded Grand Trunk Road had not yet been built.

It is certain that the ancient site where life throbs silently today once witnessed the din and bustle of a flourishing city of Gandhara. Of all the places on the western side of the river Indus, it is only at Shahbazgarhi that the royal edicts of king Asoka are found. These edicts were definitely not engraved in wilderness. They were meant for propaganda among the people—to proclaim to them the great commandments and message that the king desired to convey. Hence, it is obvious that the site was on the frequented route of traders, merchants, soldiers and missionaries.

Historian Ahmad H. Dani explains that this route is hardly understood by modern visitors who travel by the new road south of the Kabul River from Rawalpindi to Peshawar. This new road became popular after the Attock ferry was installed by the Mughal Emperor Akbar (r.AD 1556–1605) and was used even more after the Attock Bridge was built by the British. Prior to this, the main Indus crossing was at Hund (ancient Udbhandapura), 24 km north

---

[21] Irfan Habib and Vivekanand Jha, *Mauryan India*, The People's History of India series (no.5), Tulika Books, Delhi, 2011 (first published 2004), pp.52–54.

of Attock, and the old road ran north of the Kabul River almost parallel to it.[22]

The 14 Major Edicts of Asoka put up at Shahbazgarhi for the inhabitants of the Northwest regions of the subcontinent present the aspects of Asoka's *Dhamma-vijaya* campaign for the 'Conquest by Dhamma' of the Righteous Law. Recognized as the first great royal patron of Buddhism, who translated the gospel of the Buddha into a universal kind of *Dhamma*, Asoka not only adopted the Buddha *Dhamma* as a way of life but also preached it vigorously in India and abroad. Soon after the Kalinga War of 261 BC, he launched a concerted campaign for the dissemination of *Dhamma*. To this end, he defined the concept in simple language, had the instructions engraved on rocks and pillars throughout his empire and appointed a new category of high officials, the *Dhamma Mahamatras* whose primary duty was to preach and propagate the *Dhamma* among people of all faiths and persuasions.[23]

The largest rock contains text of 13 Edicts (RE 1-XIII), with the exception of RE-XII that is engraved on a separate rock near by. An important peculiarity of the Asokan Rock Edicts at Shahbazgarhi is the engraving of this separate RE-XII for the institution of women superintendents.

As per RE-XII, separate officers called *Stri-adhyaksa Mahamatras* (ministers in-charge of the superintendents of women) were appointed for the purpose of supervising 'female morals'. According to Radhakumud Mookerji, engraved as it is on a separate boulder at Shahbazgarhi, the principles of this edict must have been regarded as being of exceptional importance for the people in that region.[24]

---

[22] Dani, *Shahbaz Garhi*, pp.1–8.
[23] D.C. Ahir, *Asoka, the Great*, D.K. Publishers, Delhi, 1995, pp.87–95.
[24] Radhakumud Mookerji, *Asoka*, Motilal Banarasidass Publishers, Delhi, p.39 and pp.160–61.

VALUE OF 'CONCORD'

The Shahbazgarhi Edict lauds the value of 'concord'

> His Sacred and Gracious Majesty the King is honouring all sects, both ascetics and house-holders; by gifts and offerings of various kinds... But His Sacred Majesty does not value such gifts or honours as that how should there be the growth of the essential elements of all religious sects...the root of it is restraint of speech, that is, there should not be honour of one's own sect and condemnation of others' sect without any ground... Hence concord alone is commendable, in the sense that all should listen and be willing to listen to the doctrines professed by others. For this purpose are, indeed, employed the *Dharmamahamatras*, *Stri-adhyaksa-mahamatra*, the officers in charge of pastures and other bodies.[25]

According to Mookerji, it can be simply translated as 'censors of women', ignoring the word *adhyaksa* (superintendents of women). He says it is possible to take the *Dhamma Mahamatras* as being themselves the *adhyaksas*. That the *Mahamatras* were in-charge of women is stated in RE-V, Mookerji further adds that regarding women, 'perhaps it was necessary to preach the dharma of toleration to them as a class.' It is said *Mahamatras* were attached to the royal harem because they had to deal with ladies, their special qualification emphasized sexual purity, and they had to be placed in-charge at places of pleasure, both in the capital and outside.[26]

Who were the people living in the Northwest Frontiers regions of India in the third century BC for whom the emperor Asoka appointed *Stri-adhyaksa Mahamatras*? And why was this done? Or, whose attention did he want to draw? Were the censors or high officers of the Law of Piety appointed specially to look after the morals of the women? These had never existed before.

---

[25] Mookerji, *Asoka*, pp.159–61.
[26] Mookerji, *Asoka*, pp.160–161, notes 3 and 4.

XUANZANG'S POLUSHA

Foucher and Dani trace the ancient name of Polusha by which Shahbazgarhi was known but now has been completely forgotten. It was through the efforts of Cunningham and Foucher that the old name of 'Polusha' has been traced to the ancient accounts of Chinese travellers. Sung Yun, who visited in AD 520, calls it 'Fo-Sha-Fu', and Xuanzang, who passed through the region in about AD 630, records the name as 'Po-Lou-Sha'. These Chinese names are obviously corruptions of some local Sanskrit word; the original is very often considered Varusha or Varushapura.

Although the memory of fifteenth–sixteenth-century saint Shahbaz Qalandar has faded, he still lives on in the present name of the city. It is only in the memoirs of Babar that he is recorded as an 'Impious unbeliever, who, in the course of the last thirty or forty years, had perverted the faith of numbers of the Yusufzais and Dilazaks'. Babar further says:

> At the abrupt termination of the hill of Makam there is a small hillock that overlooks all the plain country; it is extremely beautiful, commanding a prospect as far as the eye can reach, and is conspicuous from the lower grounds. Upon it stood the tomb of Shahbaz-Qalandar. I visited it, and surveyed the whole place. It struck me as improper that so charming and delightful a spot should be occupied by the tomb of an unbeliever. I, therefore, gave orders that the tomb should be pulled down and levelled with the ground. The name of the saint has survived in that of Shahbaz-garhi.[27]

JATAKA STORIES SET IN SHAHBAZGARHI

The city was important not only to Asoka but also to the Buddhist Sangha who set up three monasteries to commemorate events in the

---

[27] Harold Lamb, *Babur: First of the Mughals*, Natraj Publishers, Dehradun, 2003 (1st ed. 1961), p.35.

life of Prince Vesantara of the *Vessantara Jataka*—tales of past life of the Buddha in various incarnations of a bodhisattva. These three convents lying in close proximity were explored and identified as: Chanaka Dheri on the north gate, But Sahri on the east gate and Mekha Sanda on the hill.[28] Another Jataka story of Ekasringa Rishi also found its setting in Shahbazgarhi.

Xuanzang mentions in his memoir that to the north of Polusha is a stupa. It was here that the Prince Sudana, having given the great elephant of his father in charity to some brahmins, was blamed and banished. Leaving his friends behind at the gate, he bid them farewell at this point. Beside this was a *sangharama* with about 50 priests, who studied the 'Little Vehicle'. Formerly Isvara, master of sastras, composed the *O-pi-ta-mo-ming-ching-lun* at this place. Xuanzang also informs about the existence of another monastery outside the eastern gate of the town of Polusha with about 50 priests who studied the 'Great Vehicle'. There was also a stupa built by Asoka at this place.[29]

The site of Polusha also became the site for another Jataka story of Ekasringa Rishi who, after being deceived by a woman for pleasure lost his spiritual faculties. The woman, mounting his shoulders, returned to the city. Xuanzang goes on to add that after travelling north-west about 100 *li* (50 km), he crossed a small hill and came to a large mountain. To the south of the mountain was a *sangharama* with a few priests as inhabitants, who studied the 'Great Vehicle'. By the side was a stupa built by Asoka. This is the place which in old time was occupied by Ekasringa Rishi.[30]

Foucher also points out that Xuanzang did not proceed to Polusha straightaway from Pushkalavati on the old road of India. He quit the high road of India and ascended the road to the Swat Valley on an excursion to the north-west. It was from the village of Gandheri that he returned in a southerly direction back to Pushkalavati and travelled on the road to India, about 38 km to the east to reach

---

[28] Foucher, *Notes on the Ancient Geography of Gandhara*, p.29.
[29] Beal, *Si-Yu-Ki*, Book II, p.112.
[30] Beal, *Si-Yu-Ki*, Book II, p.113.

Polusha (present-day Shahbazgarhi), one of the four great cities along the commercial road of Gandhara.[31] According to Dani, since the site is in the vicinity of the Mukam River the area is also called the Mukam plain.[32] Another name for the area is Sudana plain, an ancient name that has survived from the legend of Prince Sudana, popular under the name of Visvantara Jataka, narrated by the Chinese pilgrim Xuanzang in the *Si-Yu-Ki*. The sacred sites and convents mentioned by the Chinese pilgrims Sung Yun and Xuanzang at Polusha, and researched by historians and archaeologists in the nineteenth and early twentieth centuries, are connected with different scenes from the Jataka story.

From Polusha, Xuanzang headed eastwards on the same old road to the town of Hund in Swabi district on the Indus River. Foucher points out that Xuanzang travelled from Polusha to the north-west about 100 *li* (50 km) and that road led him by the ancient sites of Bakshali and Sawal Dher. He was quite close to the sites of Takht-i-Bahi, Jamalgarhi and Sikri but did not mention these sites at all. His silence could mean that the convents of Takht-i-Bahi, Jamalgarhi and others had been abandoned and taken over by wild overgrowth and forests by mid-seventh century AD. After crossing the Paja chain of hills, the road runs north towards Udyayana and the pilgrims arrived near the 'high grey mountains' of Swat. The second stage led him up to the foot of the southern slope of the Swat mountains which was near a stupa and a monastery of the legendary Rishi Ekasringa.[33]

For returning to Polusha, the pilgrim descended by way of Bhimadevi Parvata and Shiva and then took the road to Udabhanda. The second stage led him to the neighbourhood of Swabi and on the third day by way of the valley of Bhadrai, he reached the bank of the Indus.[34]

---

[31] Foucher, *Notes on the Ancient Geography of Gandhara*, pp.20–22.
[32] Dani, *Shahbaz Garhi*, pp.1–8.
[33] Foucher, *Notes on the Ancient Geography of Gandhara*, p.32.
[34] Foucher, *Notes on the Ancient Geography of Gandhara*, p.37.

'DHERIS' OF KHYBER PAKHTUNKHWA

Since my departure from Charsadda many *dheris* or mounds had crossed my path. Lying along the river valleys of the Khyber Pakhtunkhwa, many were hidden in fields and among low hills. These numerous *dheris* give an idea of the vast number of Buddhist settlements that were buried under mounds of earth over the centuries as a result of abandonment and collapsing structures that were made of mud and boulders or stone walls and reinforced with pebbles and plaster. The *dheris* take their name from the village of their origin and dot the landscape of the Khyber Pakhtunkhwa province that once formed a part of the Buddhist Gandhara kingdom. They have been spewing out objects of Buddhist art including life-sized images of the Buddha, now on display at the Peshawar Museum.

The evidence of a vast number of Buddhist settlements in Khyber Pakhtunkhwa is also provided by several Kharosthi inscriptions which inform us of the flourishing state of Buddhism in the region of Gandhara as well as the wealth and the trade prospects that brought merchants, pilgrims and Buddhist scholars and monks here. A majority of these Kharosthi inscriptions record donation of various articles including statuaries, vessels, wells, water halls, tanks, ponds to religious institutions in order to gain merit. Over the centuries, many establishments collapsed and turned into heaps of debris or *dheris*.

Many *dheris*, on excavation, have been found to be complete Buddhist settlements with stupas, courtyard and monk cells, dated to the Indo-Greek and the Kusana periods. Inscriptions on their stupas and statuary art inform us about the period of their existence and about the monks who made gifts to the monastery. Inscriptions could also be an evidence of the existence of a monastic settlement at the site where the donations were found.

The *dheris* are generally part of an extensive monastery. Sometimes, a large number of monks who came to study at a monastic centre set up separate settlements by the side of the main monastery, and donations were made in the form of wells for providing water to the settlement.

Several donative inscriptions from the Yusufzai region[35] go on to show that it was a favourite destination for monks and pilgrims. Evidence that such a Buddhist settlement existed in Paja near Jamalgarhi comes from the famous Paja inscription from the year 111 (corresponding to AD 53) engraved on a stone that records the digging of a well by Sanghamitra, the son of Anand. The name Sanghamitra denotes their Buddhist affiliation.

Similar settlements could have existed at Kalasang near Cherorao and at Muchai from where inscriptions record donation of wells by Pipalakha 'companions' in AD 42 and by Vashisu 'companions' in AD 23, respectively. Similarly, Buddhist settlements which existed at Marguz village near Peshawar, received a gift of a well by some 'companions', as is ascertained from the Marguz Inscription of AD 59. We also have Peshawar Museum Inscription No. 20 that records the donation of a well to Khudacha Vihara in AD 110 and the Shankardara Inscription of AD 118 found at Shankardara near Campbellpore, recording donation of a well at Sala ferry by Donipadra 'companions'.

The monks also set up their *varshavasa* abodes for three to four months during of the rainy season at whatever place they happened to be at the time. These retreats slowly assumed the shape of an extensive monastic settlement.

Several such settlements came up in the region of Hashtnagar near Peshawar and around the site of Takht-i-Bahi and Jamalgarhi in Mardan.

The *dheris* could also be settlement of craftsmen who set up their ateliers from where they handcrafted images in stone and stucco, just like the artist's shed at the Jaulian Monastery even to this day. We know that Charsadda formed one of the biggest art centres of Gandhara as craftsmen from Pushkalavati went to decorate monasteries in foreign countries. *Sutralamkara* (IV.21) tells the story of a pious artist from Pushkalavati who journeyed to the land of Asmaka, 'land of stone' believed by some scholars to have

---

[35] Prashant Srivastava, 'Aspects of Buddhist Donations in Some Kharoshthi Inscriptions from North-Western India', in Anand Singh, *Dana: Reciprocity and Patronage in Buddhism*, Primus Books, Delhi, 2017, pp.65–67.

been Tashkent, to decorate a monastery.[36] We know of settlements such as Sheikhan Dheri and Mamana Dheri in Charsadda from where Buddha images were recovered and are now on display at the Peshawar Museum.

Dheris that have been excavated display their wealth in the form of ancient coins from the Indo-Greek and Kushan era, stone and stucco Buddhist statuary and votive stupas, monk cells, ablution ponds, manuscripts hidden in jars, and so on.

The adjoining districts of Mardan and Swabi, which were a part of Gandhara, also report of *dheris* in many of their villages. Many inscriptions in and around Mardan provide evidence of the high number of monks visiting the Gandhara region, the wealth of donors and the existence of numerous monastic settlements to which donations were possibly made by these donors in lieu of divine blessings.

Today, apart from archaeological sites such as Hund that have been explored and excavated, there are numerous other sites that still lie buried under mounds of earth. While the archaeology department continues its excavation work to uncover Buddhist antiquities, illegal diggers and antique sellers are also actively trying to get under the mounds by tunnelling and extracting treasures.

There are numerous other famous *dheris* that have been identified in the districts of Swabi and Mardan. Some close to and surrounding Hund include Sheikhdheri, Ranadheri, Dodheri, Tordheri (near Ambaar), Ranagarhi (on Yar Hussain Road), Marghuz (on Zaida Road), Jangidheri (on the Swabi–Jehangira Road), Sudheri (on the Dargai–Ghazikot Road) and Kaludheri (on the Mardan–Swabi Road). *Dheris* near Shahbazgarhi include Kafirdheri, Bagichadheri, Etamdheri, Garhi Kapura, Surkhdheri and Palodheri. Those near the city of Mardan include Sardheri, Dheri (near Jamalgarhi), Shergarhi and Kattigarhi.

Ruins of an extensive Buddhist settlement were discovered in 1976 and 2013 during excavations at Aziz Dheri near the Gango Dheri Village in Swabi. According to the Khyber Pakhtunkhwa Directorate

---

[36] B.A. Litvinsky, *Cities and Urban Life in the Kushan Kingdom*, Vol II: History of Civilizations of Central Asia, Motilal Banarsidass Publishers, Delhi, UNESCO 1996, Delhi, 1999, pp.308–09.

of Archaeology and Museums, a complete votive stupa and other antiquities such as coins, seals and sculptures were found during excavations.[37]

Sawaldheri Village, 10 km south-west of Katlang and 4 km southwest of Jamalgarhi in Mardan district, also boasts of an ancient monastic settlement. Most Buddhist sculptures found here are now in museums in Lahore and Peshawar. It is reported that the grand mosque Masjid-e-Bala of the village was constructed on the ruins of a Buddhist stupa, to maintain the sacredness of the site.[38]

Another excavated site at Mian Khan Village in Katlang, located in Mardan district, has revealed Buddhist antiquities dated from the second century BC, putting the village on the world's archaeological map. Excavations were carried out in the Koi Tangay Kandaray area of the village under the supervision of renowned archaeologist, Ihsan Ali. The relics unearthed so far include over 267 coins, most dating back to the periods of the Indo-Greeks, Kushans and Hindu Shahis; 32 beads; two rings; earrings and 13 sculptures/pieces.[39] Other *dheris* in Mardan include Damano Dheri, Zarkot Dheri and Khazana Dheri—here, the name itself denotes concealed treasures.

THE HERITAGE ROAD TO INDIA

It was almost evening, the sun was no longer cruel and it was time to end my tour of the famous monastic centres on the great highway to India. Usman insisted I visit Ranadheri Village in the neighbouring Swabi district to watch the sun dip into the Indus. On my way from Mardan to Swabi, I noticed several villages named after their *dheris* and surrounded by a large expanse of land that was once probably attached to the monasteries for the upkeep of the Sanghas.

As forests, fields and orchards flitted past, I thought of the warring armies, trade caravans, monks and craftsmen who had taken the same

---

[37] See <https://commons.wikimedia.org/wiki/File:Aziz_Dheri_Stupa.jpg>
[38] See <https://en.wikipedia.org/wiki/Sawal_Dher>
[39] Hidayat Khan, 'Echoes of the Past: Relics Dating Back to 190 BC Unearthed in Archaeological Dig', *Express Tribune*, Pakistan, 2 June 2014.

road between India and Central Asia. This was called the 'Old Road to India.' While the armies long passed away in triumph or defeat and kingdoms changed hands over the centuries, religions arrived and vanished. Though the 'Old Road to India'—as the Peshawar–Swabi Road was called by Foucher—continues to exist, it is not in much use today.

The road with its numerous monuments of the Buddha, unearthed by archaeologists of the nineteenth and twentieth centuries is a heritage road. Hundreds of monuments still remain buried along this road in the form of *dheris*. According to the archaeological department, the desolate sandy track stretching from Salatura to Jaganat near the modern village of Yar Hussain (in the vicinity of Jahangira in Swabi district) was identified by Sir Aurel Stein as the gold mining area of Caspapyros of the Greek historian Herodotus. Today, it is in the same region of Swabi where illegal miners and antiquity traders are active.

We passed through several *dheris* before coming to Ranadheri, only a few kilometres upstream from the Hund. We chose a lovely spot in a garden at Ranadheri to watch the river flow. In the past, many monks, pilgrims and invaders had moved across the Indus, the river which now forms the boundary between the land of Punjab and the Khyber Pakhtunkhwa region. The setting sun gave the river a burnished orange hue. I sat quietly, soaking in the splendid moment.

A publication of the Peshawar Museum by Sehrai Fidaullah titled *The Forgotten City of Gandhara* mentions that the Buddha in his previous birth appeared as a great fish in the river Indus at Hund to feed the hungry with his flesh.[40] Due to its sacredness, Hund was also visited by Sung Yun in the fifth century AD and by Xuanzang in the the seventh century AD.

During the course of his scientific mission to explore the ancient geography of Gandhara between 1895 and 1997, Foucher visited the district of Peshawar and travelled on the old road to Hund, also

---

[40] Fidaullah Sehrai, *Hund: The Forgotten City of Gandhara*, Peshawar Museum Publication, New Series No. 2, 1979, p.3. Available at <https://www.kparchaeology.com/uploads/books/book-1445313689182.pdf>

known as the 'Dvar-e-Hind' or the Gateway of India. He followed inch by inch the itinerary of the Chinese pilgrim Xuanzang more than 1,200 years later, and observed that there were scarcely any remains that were not Buddhists.

Foucher notes that on the right bank of the river rose a rich and busy town, which Xuanzang called Udbhandapura. Here, varied goods of the 'rarest and most esteemed'[41] kind from India could be found. This is the Und of today; also known by the names of Ohind, Wayhand and Udabhanda. The ancient village was not without traces of its former splendour, one of the great markets for Indian trade with Central Asia.

After crossing the river, the pilgrim road enters Chach, the plains of Punjab, the ancient country of Chuksa in the territory of Taxila. Thus, from Khyber Pass to the Indus, the four main stopovers were Purushapura, Pushkaravati, Polusha and Udabhanda.[42] This was the 'highroad of all conquerors'—conquerors since the time of Alexander. Bactrians, Greeks, Parthians, Kushans, the Turks and Mongols, Timurids and Chagtais, all crossed the Indus in the region of Swabi.

Swabi, now also a district and tehsil, has been mentioned in Babur's memoirs as Sawati. During his time, its vicinity was covered in thick forests. Alexander arrived here in 327 BC as he crossed the river at Hund where one of his generals prepared a boat bridge; Xuanzang passed through this area in AD 644; Mongol invader Ghengis Khan passed through here in AD 1221, while chasing the Shah of Khwarezm, and is known to have followed the same route to the Indus. Interestingly, the Khwarezm Shah Jalauddin escaped by jumping into the Indus at Hund. Hund was also the third capital of the Hindu Shahis after Peshawar and Charsadda.

Veteran archaeologist and former director of the Peshawar Museum, Fidaullah Sehrai, puts forward an interesting point that the Indus was crossed at this point in Swabi in a most primitive manner with the help of *bhand* or pots by immersing the rim upside down in water under the chest in order to float. The villagers of

---

[41] Foucher, *Notes on the Ancient Geography of Gandhara*, p.38.
[42] Foucher, *Notes on the Ancient Geography of Gandhara*, p.39.

Swabi still cross the river at the Hund ferry point with the help of bloated goat-skin or cow and buffalo hide.

On the opposite bank of the Indus lie the plains of Chach, in Punjab. The present road running south of Kabul River connected Delhi with Kabul via Peshawar. However, the traveller from Peshawar used the same old route that ran from Shahbazgarhi to Hund to reach Lahore. The old route was finally discarded when the British opened the Attock Bridge over the Indus in 1883 and the railway reached Mardan and Dargai at the foot of the Malakand Pass.[43]

---

[43] Sehrai, *Hund: The Forgotten City of Gandhara*, p.3.

Chapter 12

BUDDHIST HERITAGE OF AFGHANISTAN

FROM KUNDUZ TO KANDAHAR

Writing about India, as early as the eleventh century, Khorezmian scholar of the medieval Islamic era, Al-Biruni threw light on the exalted status of Buddhism in Khorasan, a historical region that included the present territory of Afghanistan.

According to German orientalist Edward C. Sachau:

> In former times Khurasan, Persis, Irak, Mosul, the country up to the frontier of Syria, was Buddhistic, but then Zarathustra went forth from Adharbaijan and preached Magism in Balkh [Baktra]. His doctrine came into favour with King Gushtasp, and his son Isfendiyad spread the new faith both east and west, both by force and by treaties. He founded fire temples through his whole empire, from the frontiers of China to those of the Greek empire... In consequence the Buddhists were banished from those countries, and had to emigrate to the countries east of Balkh.[1]

Buddhism had immense reach, not only in Afghanistan but up to the frontiers of Syria, territories that were once under the Persian Achaemenid Empire of the sixth–fifth century BC. It is significant to note that the first stupas in the region of Balkh came up in the sixth century BC during the lifetime of the Buddha when Trapussa and Bhallika, two traders from Balkh, came to India for trade and met the Buddha at Sarnath after his Enlightenment. As his first lay disciples, they built the first stupas at Balkh with hair and nail relics of the Buddha, a fact mentioned in the memoirs of the Chinese pilgrim Xuanzang who visited Afghanistan in seventh century AD.

---

[1] Edward C. Sachau (trans), *Alberuni's India*, Rupa Publications, Delhi, 2002, p.4.

The route that the traders followed from Balkh to Bodhgaya in the sixth century BC was the precursor to the Uttarapath built later. It was along this and other highways and caravan routes along the Bolan and Gomal passes to Kandahar and Ghazni that the message of the Buddha reached the territory of Afghanistan, where it flourished in huge monastic establishments.

If monk Xuanzang is to be believed, there was close association between the Sakyans of Kapilavastu and Afghanistan. In fact, the rulers of the country of Himatala to the east of Kism in Badakshan province, were of the Sakya race who claimed descent from one of the four Sakyan princes driven out of Kapilavastu for having fought against Virudhaka against the advice of the Budhha. According to P.C. Bagchi, the name has been restored as Hephthal (from Hema-Hevatala).[2] The banished Sakyans went to the north to the 'Snowy Mountains'—one became king of Bamiyan, one of Udyayana, one of Himatala, one of Sambi. These kings 'transmitted their kingly authority from generation to generation without any interruption.'[3]

Xuanzang also talks of the invasion of Kashmir and the assassination of the Kritiya sovereign, by Himatala, the Sakyan king of the Tokhara country, in the 600th year after the Buddha's death. Legend has it that after Kanishka's death, a native dynasty had arisen in Kashmir and its sovereign had become a persecutor of Buddhism. Hereupon, the king of Himatala, who was a Sakya by descent and a zealous Buddhist, was determined to drive the cruel Kritiya king from his throne and restore Buddhism. By a stratagem, cunningly devised and skilfully carried out, he succeeded in killing the king of Kashmir. He banished the chief ministers of the court, reinstated Buddhism as the religion of the country, and then returned to his own kingdom. But Xuanzang adds that in the course of time, the Kritiyas, who still hated the Buddhists and bore them grudges, regained the

---

[2] P.C. Bagchi, *India and Central Asia*, National Council of Education, Kolkata, 1955, p.27. See also, Samuel Beal, *Si-Yu-Ki: Buddhist Records of the Western World*, Low Price Publications, Delhi, 1884, Book I, p.40 and Book XII, p.290.
[3] Basanta Bidari, *Lumbini: A Haven of Sacred Refuge*, Hill Side Press, Lumbini, 2004, p.116.

sovereignty and during the period of his visit, the country had no faith in Buddhism and had embraced other sects.[4]

Another Sakyan connection was found at Bamiyan where Xuanzang mentions having seen the robes of the Sakyan Sankavassa, disciple of Anand, who it is believed, lived for a considerable time in Bamiyan.[5] The famous Jataka story of Dipankar Buddha is set in another Afghan city of Nagarhara.[6]

State Propagation

The official propagation of Buddhism in Afghanistan began with the establishment of the Mauryan Empire in India in about the third century BC during the reign of Asoka. The empire controlled areas south of the Hindu Kush up to about 185 BC. This happened as a result of a treaty signed in 305 BC by which Seleucus Nikator, the successor to Alexander, ceded three territories to Chandragupta Maurya I (Asoka's grandfather). These territories were Paropamisadai (areas to the south-east of Hindu Kush ranges), Arachosia (present-day Kandahar) and Gedrosia (present-day Baluchistan).[7] With this, the trade routes passing through Baluchistan, Makran and Afghanistan came under Mauryan control. At the time of death of Chandragupta's son, Bindusara, in 272 BC, a large part of the Indian subcontinent was under Mauryan suzerainty.

Asokan Missionaries and Inscriptions

During the period of Mauryan Emperor Asoka, who had converted to Buddhism following the Kalinga War, the Third Buddhist Council of Pataliputra in 250 BC decided to send missionaries to various parts of the subcontinent to propagate Buddhism. All routes to the Greek kingdoms passed through Afghanistan and several Asokan

---

[4] Thomas Watters, *On Yuan Chwang's Travels in India AD 629–645*, Munshiram Manoharlal Publishers, New Delhi, 2012, pp.278–79.
[5] Beal, *Si-Yu-Ki*, Book I, Low Price Publications, Delhi, 1884, p.53.
[6] Beal, *Si-Yu-Ki*, Book II, p.92.
[7] Ranabir Chakravarti, *Exploring Early India up to c.AD 1300*, Primus Books, Delhi, 2016, p.132.

inscriptions were set up on busy thoroughfares. Historians Irfan Habib and Vivekanad Jha list Aramaic and Greek inscriptions at four different sites in Afghanistan,[8] which were inhabited by a large Greek-speaking population: a bilingual inscription from Shahr-i-Kuhna near Kandahar (*c.*260 BC); a slab from Kandahar having a Greek version of Rock Edict XII; a fragmentary Aramaic inscription on limestone obtained from Kandahar Bazaar; three Aramaic inscriptions from the Lamghan Province, which includes a broken stone slab from Pul-i-Duranta; and two highway inscriptions (*c.*254 BC) with prohibition on hunting and fishing.[9] The Lamghan road inscriptions in Aramaic attests to the presence of a long-distance highway, or the Uttarapath, which Habib and Jha call the *karapathi* or army road connecting the Mauryan capital of Pataliputra with the empire's western frontier.[10]

The edicts based on the essential principles of Buddhist teachings are evidence that the tenets of *Dhamma* had been introduced in Afghanistan as early as the third century BC. The edicts installed along important highways targeted a vast population, not only in Afghanistan, but as far as the shore of the Mediterranean. This included all travellers on the east–west Uttarapath to and from the Khyber Pass and the north–south Kandahar–Ghazni–Kabul highway that connected with northern and western India through the Bolan and Gomal passes. The north–south route linked Kandahar via Herat into eastern Persia and the Trans-Caspian Region of Margiana where huge monastic establishments came up at Gyaur Kala and Erk Kala. Both the highways joined at Kabul and ran westwards to Herat and northwards to Balkh and Kunduz, thus covering a large part of Afghanistan through the Kunduz–Kandahar route and its diversions.

The faith gradually spread from the regions of Afghanistan to eastern Iran and northwards into Bactria and the Sogdiana regions of Central Asia and onwards to China. The Oxus, Chuy and Ili river valleys of Central Asia and the Tarim Basin became the routes for

---

[8] Irfan Habib and Vivekanand Jha, *Mauryan India*, The People's History of India series (no.5), Tulika Books, Delhi, 2013, pp.61–62.
[9] Habib and Jha, *Mauryan India*, pp.61–62.
[10] Habib and Jha, *Mauryan India*, p.127.

itinerant Buddhist missionaries and locations for Buddhist structures endowed with exquisite statuary and pictorial art.

After Asoka, there were other kings who patronized Buddhism in Afghanistan, of which were the Indo-Greek kings, Demetrius and Menander in the second century BC, and Kushan king Kanishka in the first century AD.

Hundreds of monasteries with shrines and stupas were established under the patronage of Buddhist kings along the trade routes from Kunduz to Kandahar and from Herat to Jalalabad. These were embellished with beautiful statuary and mural art that became famously known as Gandharan art. The remnants of this art were found in the monastic ruins of Kunduz, Kabul, Kapisa, Bamiyan, Kakrak, Mes Aynak, Ghazni, Hadda, Tepe Naranj and Tepe Maranjan. Many specimens of this art are showcased at the National Museum, Kabul, and other museums around the world.

Manuscripts

Consisting of birch bark, palm leaf and vellum manuscripts found in the caves of Bamiyan, the Buddhist works with the Schoyen Collection preserved in the library of the National Museum, Kabul, are a scholar's delight. Dating from about the first century AD, they are believed to be the oldest Buddhist manuscripts yet discovered. Most of these manuscripts were written in Brahmi script with a small portion in Kharosthi script and were bought by Norwegian collector, Martin Schoyen.[11] In addition to texts in Gandhari, the Schoyen Collection also contains important texts in Sanskrit and fragments of canonical sutras, *Abhidharma*, Vinay and Mahayana texts.

Fragments of manuscripts are still found in Bamiyan and I found a few for sale at an antique shop in a bazaar in Bamiyan.

Buddhist Headquarters in Afghanistan

Afghanistan had several monastic centres dating from the Kusana period, which is evident from the Brahmi and Kharosthi records

---

[11] *Schoyen Collection of Mahayana Palm Leaf Manuscripts* at National Museum, Kabul Library.

of the time.¹² The headquarters of the Sarvastivadins was at Nagarhara near present-day Jalalabad.¹³ The Mahasanghikas too had their establishment in Afghanistan as is evident from the Wardak Inscription (year 51) of Huviska, referring to the deposit of the relics of Lord Buddha in the Vagramarega Vihara,¹⁴ where Mahasanghika teachers are known to have been present.

Buddhist scholars from Afghanistan

During the reign of Kusanas, Kabul was an intellectual hub. The credit of translating complicated Buddhist texts into Chinese language goes to some great scholar monks from Afghanistan. Historians B.N. Puri and P.C. Bagchi have listed names of several monks from Kabul who went to China and translated Buddhist canonical works into Chinese around the fourth century AD. Some of them are Gautam Sanghdeva in AD 383, Vimalaksha in AD 406, Sanghabhuti in AD 381–385, Punyatrata in AD 399–415 and Dharmayasa in AD 407–415.¹⁵ According to Puri, among the 72 translators who worked between AD 67 and AD 420, seven were Kubhans (people from Kabul) and among the 43 translators who worked between AD 420 and AD 550, 10 were from Kubha.¹⁶

Bagchi mentions names of scholar monks from the Nagarhara and Kapisa monasteries in eastern Afghanistan, which were both centres of Buddhist learning. In the fourth century AD, Buddhabhadra claimed descent from the Sakya family of Kapilavastu and reached South China at the beginning of the fifth century. Buddhatrata was a Buddhist monk of Kapisa, who went to China towards the end of the seventh century and resided in the monastery of Po-ma-sse at Lo-yang. Buddhapala, also from Kapisa, went to Lo-yang in AD

---

[12] B.N. Puri, *Buddhism in Central Asia*, Motilal Banarsidass Publishers, Delhi, 2000, p.103.
[13] Puri, *Buddhism in Central Asia*, p.103.
[14] Puri, *Buddhism in Central Asia*, p.103.
[15] Puri, *Buddhism in Central Asia*, p.104. See also, P.C. Bagchi, *India and China*, Saraswat Library, Kolkata, 1981, p.258.
[16] Puri, *Buddhism in Central Asia*, p.94. See also, Bagchi, *India and China*, p.258.

676, resided in the monastery of Si-ming sse at Chang'an, Xian, and translated Buddhist texts into Chinese.[17] In AD 630, just a few years before the Arab armies arrived in Afghanistan, Chinese pilgrim Xuanzang first stepped into Kunduz. He had already offered prayers at several monasteries of the Oxus valley before crossing the river into Kunduz. Incidentally, he did not cross the Oxus at the traditional crossing at Arytam at Tarmita (present-day Termez) where the river flowed just behind the caves of the Karatepa monasteries. He turned eastwards from Termez and later commented upon the spate of establishments in the Oxus valley and the scholars of high repute who resided there. We also infer that the Western Turk rulers of Afghanistan were favourably inclined towards Buddhism and patronized monastic establishments.

Antiquities

The National Museum at Kabul brings to life the glories of ancient Afghanistan as the prime land where the faith of the Buddha flourished for over a millennium, where rare images of the Buddha were cast in stone and stucco, and where eminent scholars studied, preached and practised the *Dhamma* of the Buddha. The museum was once the proud custodian of about one lakh pre-Islamic and ethnographic objects, including paintings and statuary art from several sites.[18] Newly excavated artefacts from Tepe Naranj and Mes Aynak are also being added to the museum's collection.

Even today, a traveller will find traces of Buddhism in the ruins of monastic establishments dotting the landscape and mountain caves. These once held colossal images of the Buddha in rock-cut niches and had their walls painted with beautiful murals depicting scenes from the life of the Buddha.

Unfortunately, many Buddhist antiquities were stolen, destroyed

---

[17] Bagchi, *India and China*, p.258.
[18] Omara Khan Massoudi, 'The National Museum of Afghanistan', in Fredrik Hiebert and Pierre Cambon (eds), *Afghanistan Crossroads of the Ancient World*, The British Museum Press, London, 2011, pp.35–36.

or lost during the political turmoil of the 1970s.[19] However, several looted or stolen objects have been relocated to the museum with the help from the United Kingdom that has been instrumental in returning the artefacts.

---

[19] Massoudi, 'The National Museum of Afghanistan', pp.35–36.

Chapter 13

MONASTERIES OF NAGARHARA

Nagarhara, Lamghan, Kabul and Parwan provinces in eastern Afghanistan were important stops for pilgrims on the Indo-Afghan Northern Highroad, the Uttarapath. The Silk Road dropping southwards from Tarmita or Termez in Uzbekistan passing into Balkh via Kabul entered the Khyber Pass onwards into Peshawar and Taxila. Running through the Ganges river valley, it reached the Bay of Bengal. This was the route that connected the Oxus valley with the plains of the Ganges. Since goods from all parts of India passed along the highway through Jalalabad, Kabul, Bamiyan and Balkh (the eastern and northern provinces of Afghanistan), it was a busy highway and a trade corridor with Central Asia and Persia up to Syria (eastern Mediterranean).

Travelling monks took about three to four days to cover 130 km between Kanishka Vihara at Peshawar and the viharas at Hadda in Nagarhara (present-day Jalalabad). On the way, there were halting places at village Qadam near Jamrud about 24 km from Peshawar and a monastic centre near present-day Ali Masjid. A third monastic centre lay 16 km away at the village of Khyber/Sphola, where the stupa still exists near present-day Landi Kotal about 70 km from Hadda. Thus, three well-placed monk shelters existed between Kanishka Vihara and the Hadda Monastery, and monks could break their journey after every 15 to 20 km at the most. In present times, the route follows Peshawar to Jamrud (20 km), Jamrud to Ali Masjid (12–15 km) and Ali Masjid to Landi Kotal (16 km). The last leg is the longest distance from Torkham to Hadda covering a distance of 70 km.

Presently the NH-5 runs from Peshawar through Khyber Pass, and then passes into eastern Afghanistan at Jalalabad, the first major city on the Silk Road through eastern Afghanistan, located at the junction of the Kabul and the Kunar rivers. This capital of Nagarhara

Province was linked by a 150-km highway with Kabul in the west (the Kabul–Jalalabad Road) and 130 km by the NH-5 to Peshawar in the east. It was one of the busiest cities of the Grand Trunk Road and a rich agricultural region due to a wide network of natural waterways from the streams of the Kabul and the Kunar rivers.

From the Pamirs, a route follows southwards through the Chitral and the Kunar valleys into the Kabul Valley, just east of Jalalabad. For this reason, the Mauryan Emperor Asoka found the eastern Afghan region a strategic place for his edicts. One written in Aramaic was recovered from Jalalabad district.[1] Three Aramaic inscriptions from Lamghan (11 km west of Jalalabad in the Darunta Plains) includes one from Pul-i-Duranta and two highway inscriptions from *c.*254 BC mentioning distances and prefaced with a prohibition on hunting and fishing.[2] The *Archaeological Gazetteer of Afghanistan* mentions that on the east bank of the Lamghan River, midway between the villages of Shalatak and Qargha, an Asokan Edict was discovered in 1968. Written on the rock face above the river, the edict has four texts—three in Sanskrit and one in Aramaic. A second Asokan Inscription, in Aramaic, was discovered in 1973.[3]

The Lamghan Edicts of Asoka mentioned a *karapathi*, or a highway, and recorded several places mentioning distances and directions. This royal highway connecting the Mauryan capital Palibothra (or Pataliputra) with Susa in Iran is believed to have been the same road to Susa mentioned by Eratosthenes, a Greek geographer contemporary to Asoka. According to historian Ranabir Chakravarti, the edict may have been a typical instance of a signpost or road register of the time.[4] Through this western highway, the

---

[1] R.C Majumdar, *Ancient India*, Motilal Banarsidass Publishers, Delhi, 2013 (1st ed. 1952), p.109.
[2] Irfan Habib and Vivekanand Jha, *Mauryan India*, The People's History of India series (no.5), Tulika Books, Delhi, 2013, pp.61–62. See also, Majumdar, *Ancient India*, p.109.
[3] Warwick Ball, *Archaeological Gazetteer of Afghanistan*, 1982, No. 1067.
[4] Ranabir Chakravarti, *Exploring Early India up to c. AD 1300*, Primus Books, Delhi, 2016, p.166.

Mauryan rulers had built close linkages with Greek rulers of West Asia during the reigns of Bindusara and Asoka. We find that five Yavana kings are explicitly mentioned in RE XIII as rulers over areas beyond Asoka's realm. They were clearly his contemporaries, kings to whom he sent *Dhamma* missions.[5]

Nagarhara was famous throughout the Buddhist world as it harboured important relics of the Buddha. The parietal bone of the Buddha in Hadda and his tooth in Nagarhara were among the famous objects of worship. The Buddha's robe and staff were also sacred remains in Hadda.[6] Besides these, some of the most important Buddhist establishments were also located here. Travelling monks along this caravan route often spent their rainy season retreats at one of the numerous monasteries that were erected along the highway where scholar monks composed, studied, translated and copied Buddhist texts.

BUDDHIST HEADQUARTERS AT NAGARHARA

According to an inscription mentioned by B.N. Puri, the headquarters of the Sarvastivadins was located at Nagarhara. This was the 'Lion capital inscription of the time of Sodasa'. In the backdrop of the rivalry between the two Buddhist schools of Sarvastivadins and Mahasanghikas, the inscription refers the Sarvastivadin monk Budhila from Nagarhara, who was called to debate with his rival *mahasanghikas* in Mathura.[7]

It is said that the Sarvastivadins in Mathura were facing stiff opposition from their rivals, the Mahasanghikas, and therefore had to seek help from their fellow brother dialectician at the other end of the Kusana Empire in the Gandhara region at Nagarhara. Mahasanghikas too had their establishment in Afghanistan as is evident from the

---

[5] Chakravarti, *Exploring Early India up to c. AD 1300*, pp.134–39.

[6] Samuel Beal, *Si-Yu-Ki: Buddhist Records of the Western World*, Book II, Low Price Publications, Delhi, 1884, pp.95–96.

[7] B.N. Puri, *Buddhism in Central Asia*, Motilal Banarsidass Publishers, Delhi, 2000, p.103.

Wardak Inscription from year 51 of Huviska (c.AD 129), referring to the deposit of the relics of Lord Buddha in the Vagramarega Vihara.[8]

SAKYANS SETTLED IN NAGARHARA

Among the eminent scholars from Nagarhara mentioned by P.C. Bagchi was the Sakyan Buddhabhadra who claimed descent from the Sakya family of Kapilavastu. He was possibly one of the Sakyan family, who had fled from Kapilavastu following an attack by Vidudhaba during the Buddha's time. He studied Buddhist literature in Kashmir and accompanied Che-yen, who had come to India with Faxian, to China and reached South China in the beginning of the fifth century. He stayed most of the time at Nanking and had been to Lushan for some time at the invitation of Hui-yuan. He died in China in AD 429.[9]

During excavations, several Buddhist establishments, dated from the second to the seventh centuries AD have been found in the Jalalabad valley. These stretch from Basawal, south-east of Jalalabad to the gorge at Darunta in the west of Jalalabad city. The extensive complex consists of several groups of caves numbering over a hundred and stretching for over three kilometres of schist cliffs on the north side of the Kabul River. The complex has been dated to the fourth–fifth centuries AD.[10] The major sites of Tepe Kalan, Tepe Kafiriha and Tepe Shotor were located in this complex at Hadda, 13 km south of Jalalabad. Precious antiquities from the sites can be seen today at the Musée Guimet, Paris.

During Xuanzang's journey from Lamghan through Nagarhara and Hadda, the pilgrim mentions a number of important monastic centres.[11] In Lamghan, there were 10 monasteries, and their priests were all followers of the 'Great Vehicle'. Xuanzang called it 'Lanpo' and considered it a part of India. He also informs about the presence of

---

[8] Puri, *Buddhism in Central Asia*, p.103.
[9] P.C. Bagchi, *India and China*, Saraswat Library, Kolkata, 1981, p.258.
[10] Nancy Hatch Dupree, *An Historical Guide to Afghanistan*, Afghan Air Authority Afghan Tourist Organization, Kabul, 1977, p.204.
[11] Beal, *Si-Yu-Ki*, pp.90–97.

Mahayana Buddhists and numerous Hindus pointing to the declining status of Buddhism in seventh century AD. 'For several centuries the native dynasty had ceased to exist… and the state had become a dependency of Kapisa.' Although there were 10 Buddhist monasteries, the monks were few, and most of them were Mahayanists. The pilgrim however notes that Hindus were numerous and they had scores of temples.[12]

Setting of Dipankar Jataka

The Jataka story of Dipankar Buddha and his prophecy is an important one that had its setting in Nagarhara. Here, Asoka built a 300-feet high stupa to mark the place where Sakya bodhisattva met Dipankar Buddha. Xuanzang points out that to the west of the stupa is the Kialan *sangharama* (could this be Tepe Kalan?) with only a few priests. South of this lay another stupa built by Asoka to commemorate the place where bodhisattva covered the mud with his hair.[13] He further adds that within the city, there was the ruined foundation of a great stupa which once contained the tooth relic of the Buddha but which was no longer there.[14]

FESTIVAL OF BUDDHA

A stucco panel found at a monastery in Nagarhara depicts the flourishing state of religion in the city, which celebrated the 'Festival of Buddha'. The royal procession led by the Buddhist king of the city was accompanied by monks carrying the relics of the Buddha on an elephant. The panel displayed at the National Museum recreates the scene of the Buddhist period of Afghanistan when royal processions were organized, much like the Buddhist festival and procession seen in the images in Khotan, as mentioned by Faxian in his memoir during his stay at the Gomati Monastery.

The panel shows a royal personage, over whose head an attendant

---

[12] Beal, *Si-Yu-Ki*, pp.90–97.
[13] Beal, *Si-Yu-Ki*, p.92.
[14] Beal, *Si-Yu-Ki*, p.92.

holds an umbrella. Accompanied by monks, he leads an elephant carrying on his back a huge square-shaped carved box, perhaps holding the relics of the Buddha. The precious relics were publicly exhibited to the worshippers and common city dwellers on auspicious days.

In the narratives of Faxian, we find mention of a similar festival of the Buddha. It involved the worship of the Buddha's relics including the skull bone and others at Nagarhara.[15] Eight men who were entrusted with safeguarding the relics washed their hands with scented water and brought out the holy skull bone 'adorned all over with gold leaf and seven sacred substances.' The relic was placed outside the vihara 'on a lofty platform where it is supported on a round pedestal of seven precious substances and covered with a bell of lapis lazuli, both adorned with a row of pearls.'[16] The pilgrim informed that after the bone had been brought forth, the keepers of the vihara ascended a high gallery, where they beat big drums, blew conches and banged copper cymbals. When the king heard them, he went to the vihara and entered it by the door on the east and made his offerings of flowers and incense. Following this, he and his attendants, one after the other, raised the bone and placed it on top of their heads for a moment and then departed by going out the door on the west. This way the king made his offerings and performed his worship and afterwards attended to his business of governance. After the offerings were over, the skull bone was placed inside the vihara. At this vihara, kings of various countries constantly sent messengers with their offerings.

---

[15] James Legge, *A Record of Buddhistic Kingdoms Being an Account by the Chinese Monk Fa-Hein of Travels in India and Ceylon [AD 399–414] in Search of the Buddhist Books of Discipline*, Mushiram Manoharlal Publishers, Delhi, 1998, pp.36–37.

[16] Legge, *A Record of Buddhistic Kingdoms Being an Account by the Chinese Monk Fa-Hein of Travels in India and Ceylon [AD 399–414] in Search of the Buddhist Books of Discipline*, p.37.

BUDDHA'S RELICS IN DANGER

Haḍḍa, near modern Jalalabad, was the site of one of the largest Buddhist centres in Nagarhara, and was visited and described by Chinese pilgrims.

Faxian writes that at the mouth of a valley near Hadda (according to James Legge, it could be the Safed Koh),[17] he found a huge relic of a Buddhist stupa and a monastery with more than 700 monks in the fourth century AD. 'At this place there are as many as thousand *topes* [stupas] of *Arhans* [arhats] and Pratyeka Buddhas.'[18] However, by the time of Xuanzang in the seventh century AD, 'sangharamas in Nagarhara were many, yet the priests were few; the stupas were desolate and ruined.'[19]

At Hadda, the Buddha's skull bone was preserved in a jewelled box inside a stupa made of seven precious substances. There was also a tower of the skull bone shaped like a lotus leaf. The eyeball of the Buddha and also his Sanghati robe and staff were also preserved here.[20]

No one knows what happened to these relics, but even back in the fourth century AD Faxian wrote about the king of Nagarhara who was anxious about the safety of the Buddha's skull bone deposited in a vihara and covered in gold and sacred substances. He feared the Buddhist relics could be stolen. In order to safeguard the precious relics, the king,

> selected eight individuals representing the great families in the kingdom, and committed to each a seal, with which he should seal [the shrine] and guard [its relic]. At early dawn, these eight

---

[17] Legge, *A Record of Buddhistic Kingdoms Being an Account by the Chinese Monk Fa-Hein of Travels in India and Ceylon* [AD 399–414] *in Search of the Buddhist Books of Discipline*, p.40, note 2.
[18] Legge, *A Record of Buddhistic Kingdoms Being an Account by the Chinese Monk Fa-Hein of Travels in India and Ceylon* [AD 399–414] *in Search of the Buddhist Books of Discipline*, p.40.
[19] Beal, *Si-Yu-Ki*, p.91.
[20] Beal, *Si-Yu-Ki*, p.96.

men come, and after each has inspected his seal, they open the door...²¹

The relics of the Buddha were sometimes forcibly taken away by powerful kings. Asoka had himself opened several stupas to obtain relics of the Buddha. The relics were so much in demand that the Nagas of Ramagrama had to keep vigil, day and night, at the Ramagrama Stupa. In the first century AD, Kanishka, the Kusana ruler, had the Buddha's *patra* (or begging bowl) removed from Vaishali, and installed at the Kanishka Chaitya in Purushapura (present-day Peshawar). The relic was again transferred to Kandahar and was at last found at the khanaqa of Mir Wais Baba from where it was brought to the National Museum of Afghanistan at Kabul.

Xuanzang too informs of a king who used force to take away relics from stupas in Hadda. He mentions two precious stupas in Hadda containing the skull bones (including the bone of the *ushnisa* that was lotus shaped) of the Buddha and other relics. In total, five relics which worked miracles were taken away. He writes: '[A] king hearing of these various articles [namely the eyeball of the Tathagata, the Sanghati robe, the sandalwood staff of the Tathagata] [considered them] his own private property [and] took them away by force to his own country and placed them in his palace.' But after a short time, when he went to look at the relics, they were missing and on further enquiries he found they had been moved to their original place.²²

The relics are said to have been commercialized by the time of Xuanzang. Even to look at the skull bone, entailed an expenditure of a gold coin. Pilgrims who wished to take an impression had to pay five pieces. Even the other relics of the Buddha had a fixed price. 'And yet, though the charges are heavy, the worshippers are numerous.'²³

Interestingly, historian Xinru Liu mentions a Chinese pilgrim

---

²¹ Legge, *A Record of Buddhistic Kingdoms Being an Account by the Chinese Monk Fa-Hein of Travels in India and Ceylon [AD 399–414] in Search of the Buddhist Books of Discipline*, p.37.

²² Beal, *Si-Yu-Ki*, p.97.

²³ Hwui Li, *The Life of Hieun-Tsiang* (translated by Samuel Beal), D.K. Publishers, Delhi, 2001 (1st ed. 1911), p.60.

Wu'kung who carried away the Buddha's tooth relic to China where he was granted official position and honours. In the seventh century AD, the rulers of Kapisa happily parted with the 'small parietal bone [presumably of the Buddha] in exchange for 4,000 bolts of silk'.[24] We learn that the people of Kapisa were so eager to acquire Chinese silk that they even traded their precious Buddhist relics, the parietal bone and some minor relics, for silk.[25] Silk was in turn used for the purpose of acquiring relics, or just to see and worship relics. Therefore, pilgrims carried with them large quantities of silk—banners, pieces of brocade or tapestry, ritual robes or bolts of plain silk. Buying precious relics with silk as envoy Wang Hsuan-ts'e did, or rewarding a tribute of relics with silk, as in the Kapisa case, are the most direct instances of the affiliation between silk and relics.[26] This is how the precious parietal bone was shifted from Nagarhara to Kapisa.[27]

The significance of relics in Tang China motivated worshippers to undertake pilgrimages to obtain them. Liu points out that by this time, Buddhist relics had become commodities for sale and were given up for profit. Transaction in relics had been going on for centuries. Wu-kung carried away the Buddha's tooth that he had 'received as a gift'.[28] In the case of Wu-kung, as in the case of other pilgrims who brought relics to China, the Chinese emperor granted them official positions ad honours.

The small parietal bone that Wang Hsuan-t'se brought from Kapisa in AD 661 was worth 4,000 bolts of silk. According to Liu, the rulers of Kapisa determined this price on the basis of their previous trading experience.[29] Thus, we see that the holy relics of the Buddha were gradually lost from the sites by way of transaction with foreign rulers or taken away by force.

---

[24] Xinru Liu, *Silk and Religion*, Oxford University Press, Delhi, 1996, p.47.
[25] Liu, *Silk and Religion*, p.56.
[26] Liu, *Silk and Religion*, p.69.
[27] Liu, *Silk and Religion*, p.34.
[28] Liu, *Silk and Religion*, p.47.
[29] Liu, *Silk and Religion*, p.47.

This is why stupas in monastic complexes stood ravaged and denuded since they were expected to contain enormous quantities of relics and treasures.[30] Hadda was no exception.

ANTIQUITIES FROM HADDA

The richest concentration of stupas was seen in the river valley near Jalalabad. Many of these stupas, dated between the second and eighth century AD, have been identified at the large complexes of Tepe Kalan, Tepe Kafirha and Tepe Shotor.

While collecting antiquities for the East India Company from 1834 to 1837, archaelogist Charles Masson recovered numerous relics from Buddhist complexes in the Jalalabad valley. Among these, the most precious was a relic casket of gold inlaid with precious rubies and carved with the figures of the Buddha and bodhisattvas, which was recovered from a stupa in Bimaran, near Jalalabad.[31] This casket, known as the Bimaran Casket, is today showcased at the British Museum. According to a detailed description by the British Museum, the casket, considered as a masterpiece of Greco-Buddhist Art of Gandhara, was found inside Stupa No. 2 at Bimaran and dated from the first century AD. There are altogether eight figures in high-relief on the casket, including two identical groups of Brahman–Buddha–Indra and two bodhisattvas in between and two rows of rubies from Badakshan. The casket is made in gold repousse and is 7 cm in height. According to the museum, the advanced iconography of the casket implies that 'earlier forms of Buddha image had probably existed for quite some time before.'[32]

---

[30] Liu, *Silk and Religion*, p.34.
[31] Dupree, *An Historical Guide To Afghanistan*, p.205. See <http://www.britishmuseum.org/research/collection_online/collection_object_de tails.aspx?objectId=182959&partId=1&images=true> See also, Ball, *Archaeological Gazetteer of Afghanistan*, No. 404; For additional information on the Hadda Monastic Cluster, see <monastic-asia.wikidot.com/hadda>
[32] Ball, *Archaeological Gazetteer of Afghanistan*, No. 404. For additional information on the Hadda Monastic Cluster, see <monastic-asia.wikidot.com/hadda>

Valuable Buddhist scrolls on birch bark packed into earthen pots were also found in the library of a monastery in Hadda.[33] The text composed in 'Gandhari Prakrit in Kharoshthi script' have been dated to about the first century AD, and is believed to be parts of the Buddhist Canon and associated with the Dharamguptaka sect of Buddhism.[34]

Immense artistic wealth from Hadda include mud and stucco sculpture; gold, silver and steatite reliquaries; a large numbers of coins (many of them Roman); several Kharosthi inscriptions; and many other articles of gold, silver and precious stone. The most spectacular finds came from Tepe Kalan, which produced a gold reliquary studded with emeralds and sapphires. A series of domed caves near Tepe Zargaran have stucco decoration and frescos, and Tepe Shotor remains an open-air museum.[35]

Beautiful artwork from Hadda monasteries such as Tepe Kalan, Tepe Kafiriha and Bagh-Gai can be seen today at the Buddha galleries at the National Museum at Kabul and Musée Guimet in Paris.

NAGA DEITIES OF TEPE SHOTOR

The theme of the Naga kings seemed to be a favourite with the artistes of Gandhara, a region believed to be populated by the Naga tribe. This also brings us to the theme of Naga deities in Buddhism, so often seen in the statuary and mural art of South Asia, Central Asia and China. Historian–archaelogist Nancy H. Dupree draws our attention to some unique statuary and decorative scenes revealed during excavations at the Tepe Shotor Monastic Complex. One is a 'Seated Buddha' image at the entrance of the site with snakes entwined around Buddha's throne. Another is a unique scene of a 'Fish Porch' revealed in niche XIII at Tepe Shotor which depicts a number of fish and other marine and semi-divine creatures carved on the floor

---

[33] Romila Thapar, *The Penguin History of Early India*, Penguin Books, Delhi, 2002, p.255.
[34] Thapar, *The Penguin History of Early India*, pp.255–56.
[35] Ball, *Archaeological Gazetteer of Afghanistan*, No. 404.

of the niche. The aquatic scene covers the walls with a depiction of waves in which water plants bloom and Buddhist deities emerge from the pool. We get a glimpse of this underwater world in the *Champeyya Jataka*. In the opinion of Dupree, the scene could depict Buddha's meeting with the king of the Nagas.[36] At the monastery of Tepe Shotor at Hadda as also at Tepe Sardar in Ghazni, the world of the Nagas was an important representation in the monastic art.

Unfortunately, much of the antiquities were destroyed when the museum at Hadda was plundered and burned in 1981. The treasures excavated by archaeologists from various sites at Hadda and kept at Jalalabad were also looted and lost forever.[37] Among the salvaged antiquities from Hadda is a superb terracotta image of the 'Smiling Buddha' published by the National Museum. The image was photographed at the moment of its unwrapping at the presidential palace, Kabul in 2004, and appeared in a museum publication.[38] Large-scale pilfering of the Buddhist objects recovered from the sites has also been reported both by museum authorities and Dupree.

Buddha and bodhisattva images, Buddha head, diverse personages like female deities and demons, votive stupas depicting Buddha figures; Atlantes in stucco and women in elaborate hairstyles, dated third–fourth century AD, from Hadda, form a diverse collection of objects from Hadda displayed at Musée Guimet, Paris. Some objects in schist include depiction of events from the life of the Buddha, images of bodhisattvas, *gandharvas*, *shalabhanjikas* and votive stupas from Tepe Kafariha. A row of four headless meditating Buddhas on a decorated multilayered plinth dated third–fourth century AD form the collection from Bagh Gai.

---

[36] Dupree, *An Historical Guide to Afghanistan*, p.222.
[37] Fredrik Hiebert and Pierre Cambon (eds), *Afghanistan Crossroads of the Ancient World*, The British Museum Press, London, 2011, p.36.
[38] Hiebert and Cambon, *Afghanistan Crossroads of the Ancient World*, p.45.

Chapter 14

KABUL AND ITS SURROUNDINGS

The wealth of Buddhist antiquities recovered from Kabul and its surroundings and displayed in the museums around the world, gives ample evidence of the flourishing state of Buddhism in the region during the early centuries of our era. Monastic establishments have been dug out by collaborative teams of Afghan and foreign archaeologists within a radius of 40 km around Kabul. This vast Buddhist region of central Afghanistan was reached by the Khyber–Hadda–Nangarhara route in the east; the Balkh–Samangan–Bamiyan route in the north and the Kandahar–Ghazni route in the south. All three trade routes are dotted with a chain of Buddhist sites, some explored, others still buried.

Buddhist cities lying within a radius of 40–50 km of Kabul include the monastic site of Sarai Khuja (33 km north of Kabul), Paitava (40 km north of Kabul), Shotorak (40 km north of Kabul), Goldarrah (22 km south of Kabul), Gol Hamid and Tepe Kafiriah at Mes Aynak (40 km south-east of Kabul), Tepe Maranjan (4 km east of Kabul), Tepe Narenj (on the slopes of Kabul hills, a few kilometres south of city), Shewaki stupa and monastery (11 km south near Yakhdara), Tope Darra or the Valley of Stupas near Istalif (29 km from Kabul) and the Stupa at Tapa Iskandar (31 km north of Kabul). The Koh-i-Daman Valley, which was the route for trade and religious missionaries going to Kapisa, is also littered with Buddhist remains.[1]

Ruins of several monastic establishments along caravan routes in and around Kabul were brought to light during excavations in the nineteenth and twentieth centuries. Images of the Buddha and bodhisattvas recovered from the sites speak of the artistic eminence prevailing in the region of Afghanistan.

---

[1] Nancy H. Dupree, *An Historical Guide to Afghanistan*, Afghan Air Authority Afghan Tourist Organization, Kabul, 1977.

As early as the first century AD, the status of Buddhism in the region of the Paropamisadae or the Hindukush can be gauged by the fact that from this region alone, 30,000 monks had arrived in the city of Anuradhapur, taking the southern route along the Dakshinapatha through south India into Sri Lanka. These monks were concentrated in the Kapisa–Begram and Kabul regions and were sufficiently motivated to undertake the long and arduous journey to down south.

The *Mahavamsa* reads: '...from Alasanda the city of the Yonas came the thera Yonamahadhammarakkhita with thirty thousand bhikkhus.'[2] The notes tell us that Alasanda was Alexandria in the land of the Yonas (or the Greeks). It is probable that the town was founded by the Macedonian king in the country of the Paropamisadae near Kabul. The king Duttagamini began work on the Great Stupa around the first century AD and invited monks from several foreign countries for consecration ceremony of the Great Stupa at Anuradhapur in Sri Lanka.

The flourishing state of Buddhism in Kabul had much to do with the patronage of rulers and the rich traders' guild. Enormous trade and consequent wealth came along these routes to Kubha (region of ancient Kabul) from as far as the Bay of Bengal, Central Asia, China, Persia and the Mediterranean cities. Buddhist missionaries too followed the trading caravans and a host of monastic establishments sprang up along the halting stations en route from Hadda to Hairatan. With its fine weather, wealth and patronage, the region became home to many Buddhists.

The transport of goods along the overland north–south route across the Oxus and through the Kabul Valley to India was an important feature in the regional economy of both Central Asia and Afghanistan. Excavations at the famous Kushan city of Begram, 60 km north of Kabul, have revealed valuable information on the kind of goods traded on the Silk Road in the Kabul Valley. Several excavated store rooms in the palace situated in the southern part of the city contained hundreds of articles of carved ivory brought from India

---

[2] Wilhelm Geiger, *Mahavamsa or the Great Chronicle of Ceylon*, Asian Educational Services, Delhi, 2000 (1st ed. 1912), p.194, canto 39.

and objects from the Mediterranean via West Asian trade routes.³ Trade along the Kabul Valley was fed chiefly by India's continuous demand for Central Asian horses and in turn Central Asia's demand for Indian elephants from Orissa and the southern states, cotton from Punjab, non-mulberry silk from Assam, textiles, dyes like indigo from as far as Bengal and other goods such as nard oil, costus, musk, ivory, yaka wood, salt and spices. The horse traders formed a regular traffic on the Uttarapath, the royal road linking Kabul with Pataliputra. While trade flourished and rulers patronized the popular religions of the day, religious establishments came up along the routes from the Indus to the Oxus valley. Monks found patronage and means of subsistence in the wealthy city in and around Kabul. The flourishing trade in horses continued through the eighteenth and nineteenth centuries AD.

As late as the sixteenth century AD, Babur sketched a rosy picture of the caravan trade of Kabul, which he admitted was chiefly of horses. Kabul was an excellent market because even 'if the merchants journeyed as far as *Roum* [Turkey] or *Khita* [China] they could make no greater profits than the three hundred or four hundred percent they make here.' Describing the excellent trade, Babur commented that by way of India came 'slaves, good white cloth sugar candy, refined and plain sugar, with spice-yielding roots.' Among the fruits, oranges, lotus bloom and sugar came from the Indus region.⁴

Speaking about Indo-Central Asian commercial activity, historian Scott C. Levi also mentions that India was dependent upon external sources for a regular supply of horses, as efforts to breed horses in India had been largely unsuccessful. He further goes on to say that a great part of this supply came from Central Asia, and therefore must have passed through Kabul. 'The bulk of the supply was produced

---

³ B.A. Litvinsky, *Cities and Urban Life in the Kushan Kingdom*, Vol. II: The History of Civilizations of Central Asia, Motilal Banarsidass Publishers, Delhi, 1996 and UNESCO, New Delhi, 1999, p.296. See also, B.N. Puri, *Buddhism in Central Asia*, Motilal Banarsidass Publishers, Delhi, 2000, p.39.
⁴ Harold Lamb, *Babur the Tiger: First of the Mughals*, Natraj Publishers, Dehradun, 2003, p.83.

by pastoral nomads in the Kalmuk and Qazaq steppes of southern Russia, the Turkoman wastes east of the Caspian Sea, and further to the south-east, Afghan Turkistan.'[5]

The Kabul Valley also provided the crucial river route to the port on the Indus. Caravan routes ran southwards along the Kabul River to the Indus Delta for export of commercial goods by sea.

MAHAVIHARAS OF KABUL

Eminent scholars and language experts emerged from the *mahaviharas* of Kabul, who were masters of scholastic debate, translators and propagators of the Buddhist faith. The *mahaviharas* functioned like modern universities where lessons in art and the sciences were given. Even in the ninth century BC, Kubha was famous as a centre of Vedic studies. Scholar Uddalaka, who is believed to have lived around the ninth century BC,[6] worked on his philosophy of 'evolution' in Kubha,[7] that is his theory of the 'original being' and that 'everything evolved from it'. The 'original being', according to Uddalaka, was that which underlies everything in the universe. He expounded the theory as follows: '[T]here is no supernatural, external, agency but only "being itself", the original matter of the universe, out of which everything comes and back into which everything goes.' Thus the 'law of the gods' give way to 'natural law', a concept which according to Warder becomes 'all powerful later when Buddhism and other extra-Vedic philosophies develop.'[8]

Like Asoka's *Dhamma Mahamatras*, monks and scholars travelled along the Central Asian and Chinese trade routes for the propagation of the faith. Some of their names have come down to us through Chinese

---

[5] Scott C. Levi, *India, Russia and the Eighteenth Century Transformation of the Central Asian Caravan Trade: India and Central Asia Commerce and Culture*, 1500–1800, Oxford University Press, Delhi, 2007, pp.100–02.

[6] A.K. Warder, *Indian Buddhism*, Motilal Banarsidass Publishers, Delhi, 1991, p.32.

[7] Warder, *Indian Buddhism*, p.239.

[8] Warder, *Indian Buddhism*, p.33 and p.275.

records. A number of Kharosthi inscription also point to centres of scholarly excellence during the Kusana period in Afghanistan.[9] From the centres of Kabul, a number of scholar monks went to China to translate Buddhist canonical texts into Chinese in the fourth century AD.[10] Eminent Indologist B.N. Puri refers to several translators of the period: Gautam Sanghdeva, who translated seven Buddhist works into Chinese in AD 383; Vimalaksha, a great teacher of Vinay (with Kumarajiva as one of his disciples), who translated two works in AD 406; Sanghabhuti, who translated three works between AD 381 and AD 385; Punyatrata, who collaborated with Kumarajiva in translations between AD 399 and AD 415 and Dharmayasa, who translated two or three works in AD 407–15.[11]

According to Puri, a close study and scrutiny of the list of the catalogue of the Chinese Buddhist Tripataka reveals the names of 72 translators who worked between AD 67 and AD 420. Among these were 7 Kubhans (people from Kabul), 15 Indians and 7 Yueh-chi. Among the 43 translators who worked between AD 420 and AD 550, 10 were from Kubha and 14 were Indians.[12]

TEPE NARENJ AND TEPE MARANJAN

Inside Kabul, itinerant monks had occupied the slopes of Kabul hills in the vicinity of the present citadel of Bala Hissar that stands south of the city. Excavations here have unearthed the monastic sites of Tepe Naranj (meaning 'the orange hill') to the south and Tepe Maranjan to the east of the hills, which form the eastern ranges of the Hindu Kush. Beautiful life-size Buddha and bodhisattva images as well as Buddha heads excavated from two sites prove the existence of large monastic establishments within the limits of Kabul.

Excavations by the Italian Archaeological Mission led by Anna Filigenzi and the Afghan National Institute of Archaeology

---

[9] Puri, *Buddhism in Central Asia*, p.103.
[10] Puri, *Buddhism in Central Asia*, p.96.
[11] Puri, *Buddhism in Central Asia*, p.104, notes 51–54.
[12] Puri, *Buddhism in Central Asia*, p.87.

under the directorship of Zafar Paiman have continued since 2014. The earliest constructed chapels at the site are dated to the second or third century AD, continuing up to the ninth or tenth century AD. During the excavation, the main stupa was found in the middle of the site along with a series of 'cult chapels' that contained ruined polychrome images in unbaked clay, executed in high relief.[13]

The excavations unveiled a complex system that utilized the gradation of hill slopes for a terraced monastery built at different interconnected levels. This architectural style compares with the monastic construction at Takht-i-Bahi, near Mardan in Khyber Pakhtunkhwa province of north-west Pakistan. At Takht-i-Bahi, hill slopes have been similarly utilized for building several courtyards at different levels. The quarry from where the stone slabs were obtained was also converted into a courtyard.

Buddhist antiquities recovered from Tepe Narenj and now displayed at the National Museum, Kabul, show abundant use of clay and stucco, especially unbaked yellow clay in statuaries decorating the chapels at the site. Unbaked clay was used in the moulding of Buddha colossi as well as smaller images. One image displayed at the museum is that of a beautiful, smiling, long and wavy-haired bodhisattva or a prince with sharp features. The deity or prince wears an ornamental crown, at the centre of which is embedded a large gem, which could also be the image of the Buddha. A large slanting eye or an incision mark in the forehead of the bodhisattva bears similarity with the mark of 'third eye' on the forehead of the Buddha colossi found at Kuva dated seventh–eighth century AD and displayed at the State Museum of Fine Arts, Tashkent.

---

[13] For more on work done by the World Monument Fund on Tepe Narenj, see <https://www.wmf.org/project/tepe-narenj> (last date of access: 7 February 2020); See also, WMF Evaluation Summary review by Marika Sardar and WMF Staff (Angela Schuster and Gaetano Palumbo), 10 July 2007. Available at <https://www.kabulpress.org/article766.html> (last date of access: 7 February 2020); See also, Forgione Giulia, 'Tapa Sardar and Tepe Narenj: Widening the focus on the Buddhist art of Afghanistan'. Available at <http://ghazni.bradypus.net/tapa_sardar_and_tepe_narenj> (last date of access: 7 February 2020).

Bodhisattva Siddhartha from Tepe Maranjan

On Maranjan Hill, north of Bala Hissar, once lay the large Buddhist monastery complex of Tepe Maranjan. Among the many sculptures excavated from the monastery in 1933 by the French archaeologists Jean Carl and Joseph Hackin was a life-size image of the 'Sitting Bodhisattva' found in the niches in the western wall of the fort, which was restored after having been seriously damaged. The famous bodhisattva with its 'strong Gandharan features' is the prized possession of the museum and displayed in its upper gallery.[14]

The painted clay statue titled 'Bodhisattva Siddhartha' has been dated to the second–third century AD. The peculiar headdress like a wreath of flowers once held a large precious stone hanging on the forehead. The neck is adorned by two layers of necklaces, one clasping the neck while the second hanging low on the chest. The posture is that of meditation and traces of polychrome are visible on the surface.

According to the notice put up by the museum, excavation at the site was carried out in 1933 by Carl and Hackin of the Délégation Archéologique Française en Afghanistan (DAFA), and from 1981 to 1987 by the Afghan Institute of Archaeology that brought to light a large stupa—said to be one of the largest in Afghanistan—surrounded by other small stupas. Four coins collected from the courtyard span from the era of Kanishka I (AD 127/128–AD 150/151) to the Kushano-Sasanian and Hunnic period.

Significantly, a trench dug into the core of the stupa revealed a recess containing four reliquaries pointing to the sacredness of the stupa. Frescoes, refined pottery and a horde of Sassanian silver drachmas were also recovered from the site. According to the *Archaeological Gazetteer of Afghanistan*, a second monastic complex with a stupa was discovered in 1981. The site could have been

---

[14] Dupree, *An Historical Guide to Afghanistan*, p.83. For more on Tepe Maranjan, refer to <http://monastic-asia.wikidot.com/tepe-maranjan> and <Ausstellungskatalog/http://pro.geo.univie.ac.at/projects/khm/showcases/story229?language=en>

extensive as 12 caves were found to the south of the site, presumably used as residence by the monks. Numerous mounds near the site indicate that parts of the extensive site still lie buried underground.[15]

Shewaki Stupa and a ruined monastery is located 11 km south of Kabul at the foot of mountains near village Yakhdarra, 5 km south-east of village Shewaki. About 15-metre high and 15 metre in diameter, the stupa has a decorative band of semi-circular arches which once held Buddhist images. The main image was installed in a large arched niche of the stupa, and the remains of a monastery enclosure were also found in the vicinity. The site is dated first–third century AD from the Kusana period continuing up to the Hindu Shahi period. Historian–archaeologist Nancy H. Dupree describes it in great details in her work.[16]

MONASTERIES OF MES AYNAK

It is believed that two millennia ago, the city of Mes Aynak, spreading over more than a thousand hectares around the Baba Wali Mountain, was strategically located near the east–west highway linking India with Persia, and was part of the flourishing kingdom of Gandhara.[17]

Large-scale construction of monasteries and shrines at Mes Aynak began as early as the first century AD when the site was ruled by the Kusanas. The Afghan Institute of Archaeology has identified the remains of the Buddhist city that functioned from the Kusana to the late Hindu Shahi period from the first to the ninth century AD. The site lay on the main trade route to India and the great wealth derived

---

[15] Dupree, *An Historical Guide to Afghanistan*, p.83. See also, Warwick Ball, *Archaeological Gazetteer of Afghanistan Cultural Properties Training Resource*, CENTCOM Historical Cultural Advisory Group, 1982, No. 1173. See also, Tepe Maranjan at *Digitaler Ausstellungskatalog*. Availalable at <http://pro.geo.univie.ac.at/projects/khm/showcases/story229?language=en> (last date of access: 8 February 2020).
[16] Dupree, *An Historical Guide to Afghanistan*, p.141 and p.143. See also, Ball, *Archaeological Gazetteer of Afghanistan*, No. 1087.
[17] Information based on the exhibition publication of the National Museum of Afghanistan, Kabul, *Mes Aynak: New Excavations in Afghanistan*, 2011.

from its silver and copper mines financed the exquisite decorations of the monastery.

The huge number of artefacts excavated from the site and displayed in a special hall of the national museum shed light on the Buddhist art of the Kabul region. Unfortunately, the Chinese mining company MCC has a contract to extract the world's largest copper reserves in large open-cast mines, and this poses a great danger to the historical and religious treasures buried in these hills.

GOL HAMID AND KAFIRIAT TEPE

Archaeologists have discovered two large monastic centres—the Gol Hamid and Kafiriat Tepe. Excavators expect to find the remains of two more Buddhist complexes on top of the Shah Tepe and along the main riverbed. Within the centres are monk cells with domed ceilings and richly ornamented shrines in courtyards. Hundreds of painted clay statues of the Buddha, bodhisattvas and donors have been discovered. Painted representations of the Buddha and bodhisattvas have also been found on the walls. Statuaries, paintings and photographs from the site are on display at the National Museum, Kabul.

Several clay images of the Buddha seated on a rectangular podium were discovered in the courtyard of Kafiriat Tepe. There are also stone reliefs portraying scenes from the Buddha's life. One rare and beautiful statuary (dated third–fifth century AD), painted and gilded on schist stone representing the Dipankar Jataka, was recovered from the excavation site and brought to the national museum. The stele represents the meeting of bodhisattva Megha with Dipankar Buddha who grants him an assurance that he will become the Buddha Sakyamuni after many rebirths. The back of the stele, also painted and gilded, depicts a seated Buddha in *dharmachakra mudra*, attended to by apsaras and devas and surrounded by worshippers.

A rare figure in stone is of a heavily bejewelled bodhisattva, wearing the Indian dhoti and a long-winding sash. He is adorned in a gem-laden turban and heavy earrings. He sits under a Bodhi Tree in the posture of *lalitasana* on a round decorated stool. Peeping from the foliage are deities holding what seem like garlands or musical instruments.

Another figure is that of a standing bodhisattva with his right hand raised in the *abhay mudra*. He is bedecked in heavy jewels and wears the Indian dhoti. The stylized aerole at the back of the head is trimmed with geometrical flame-like edge.

There are stucco images of monks in monastic robes and donors in brightly coloured attires and painted faces. The statuaries in stucco have resemblance to those found at Hadda, Tepe Maranjan and Tepe Narenj.

Beautiful wall paintings of the Buddha and donors decorated the monastic complexes at Mes Aynak. One of them, uncovered in the main room of the monastery at Kafiriat Tepe, has the unadorned Buddha, wearing an orange robe covering both his shoulders, standing under a decorated arch and surrounded by devotees. The huge wall painting, in a dilapidated state, yet extraordinarily beautiful, was photographed and displayed at the Buddha Gallery in the National Museum at Kabul.

In one chapel of Kafiriat Tepe was found a three-metre-long Reclining Buddha and a seven-metre-high Standing Buddha. From a second chapel was recovered a five-metre-high Standing Buddha. A wooden sculpture of a seated Buddha was also discovered here.

Today, historians and archaeologists from the Afghan Institute of Archaeology and DAFA are working hard to preserve, catalogue and scan three-dimensional images of hundreds of Buddhas and worshippers, stupas, paintings, coins and ceramics which have been found at Mes Aynak.

Guldara Stupa along the Logar Stream

A huge banner depicting the stupa of Guldara greets the visitor at the National Museum in Kabul. The stupa was found 22 km south of Kabul near the village of Guldara, located near a flowing stream. Safely ensconced in this valley, itinerant monks set up their monastery around the second century AD, not far from the main east–west trade highway running from Jalalabad to Kabul.

The beautifully embellished and painted stupa and Buddhist

statuaries once adorned the central courtyard of the monastery.[18] The stupa, made of rough stone and mud, has a square base with a central niche that once held an image of the Buddha. Motifs of Corinthian columns decorate the base. Niches on the drum were meant to hold images or lamps. A staircase leads to the top of the drum which is elaborately embellished with alternating semi-circular and trapezoidal arches and motifs of umbrella mast.

The walls are of diaper masonry consisting of thin neatly placed layers of schist interspersed with large blocks of stone. The entire stupa was originally painted ochre yellow with red design. The core is a solid mass of rough stone and mud. The small relic chamber of the stupa was opened by Charles Masson who recovered Kusana gold coins and gold ornaments.[19]

BUDDHA IMAGE FROM SARAI KHUJA

The site of Sarai Khuja lies 33 km north of Kabul in the Koh-i-Daman plains. A colossal image of the Standing Buddha in schist, popularly called 'Fire Buddha', dated between the second and the fourth century AD was found here in 1965. The depiction of the Buddha performing the 'Miracle of Sravasti' was a favoured theme in the art of Sarai Khuja. The image depicts the Buddha in *abhay mudra*, with flames of fire arising from his shoulders while streams of water flow from his feet. His garb in low relief is indicated by carved parallel lines on the body. Mythological creatures flank the central image while figures, probably Nagas, arise out of lotuses.

This famous Buddha from Sarai Khuja was among the artefacts looted from the museum in 1990–94. A museum notice informs that a Japanese dealer bought the image and resold it to a dealer in the United Kingdom who bought it with the help of the British Museum. It was returned to the National Museum of Afghanistan in memory of Carla Grissman who had served the museum and worked for the preservation of the cultural heritage of Afghanistan.

---

[18] Dupree, *An Historical Guide to Afghanistan*, p.136.
[19] Dupree, *An Historical Guide to Afghanistan*, pp.136–39.

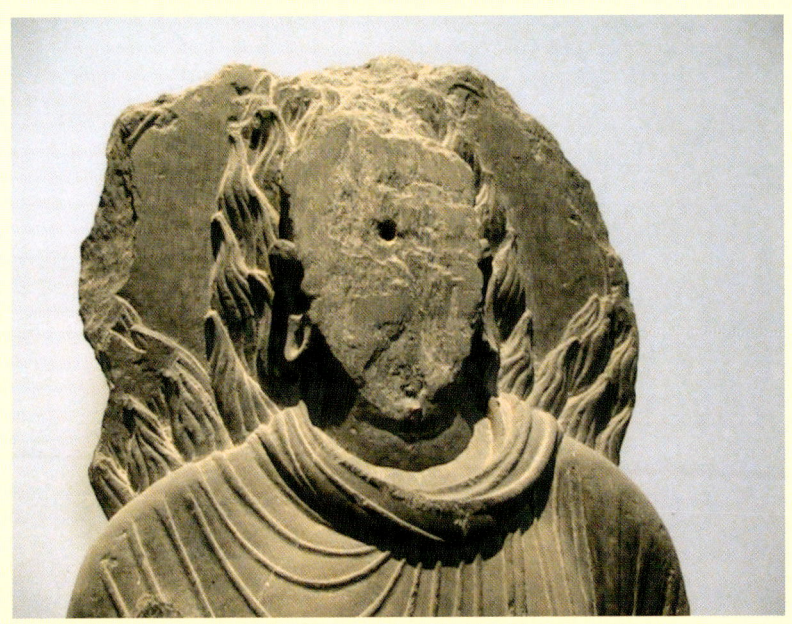

Flames emerging from Buddha's shoulders, Kham-i-Zargar, second–fourth century AD
Photo courtesy: National Museum of Afghanistan, Kabul

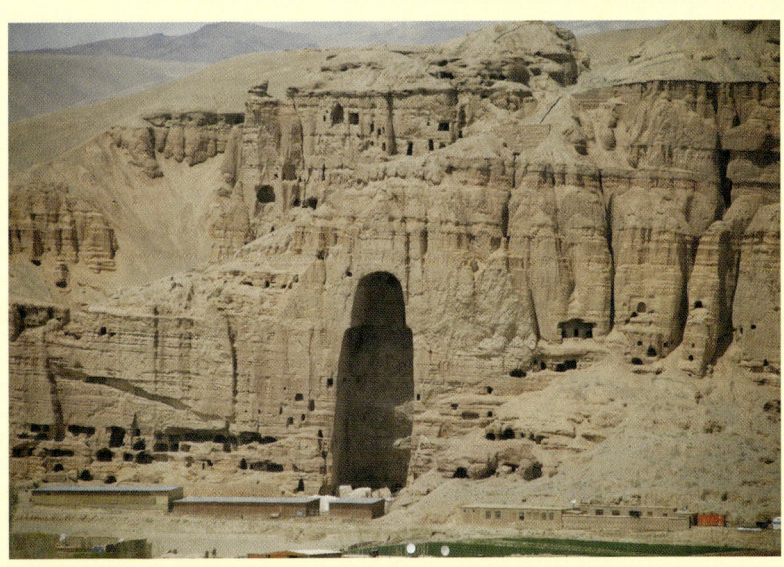

Big Buddha niche at Bamiyan Complex, dated third–seventh century AD, Bamiyan Afghanistan

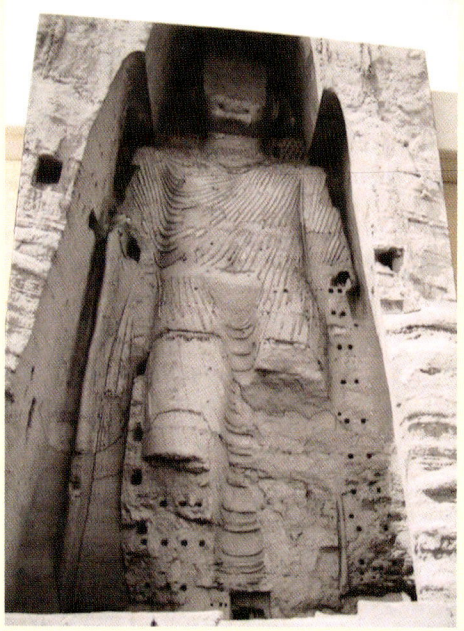

53-metre high Bamiyan Buddha from the fifth century AD, which was destroyed by the Taliban in 2001
Photo courtesy: Tourist Information Bureau, Kabul

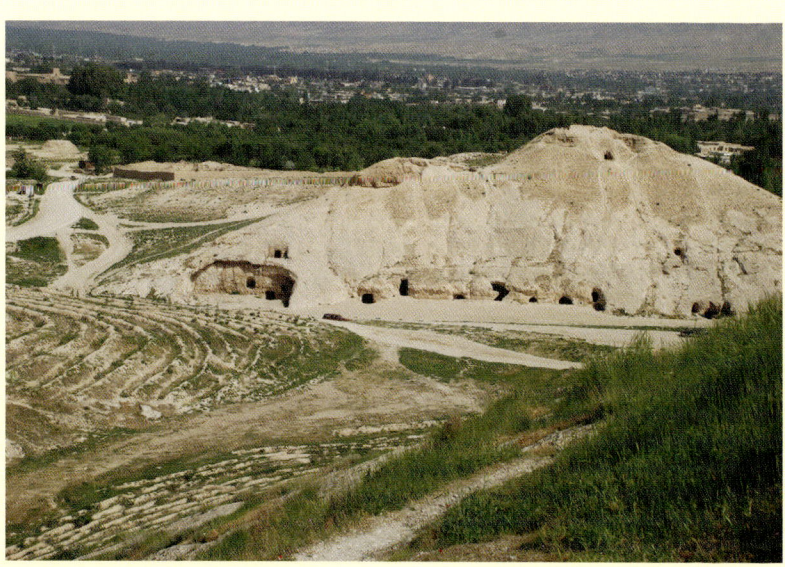

Buddhist site of Takht-i-Rustam at Samangan, second century AD

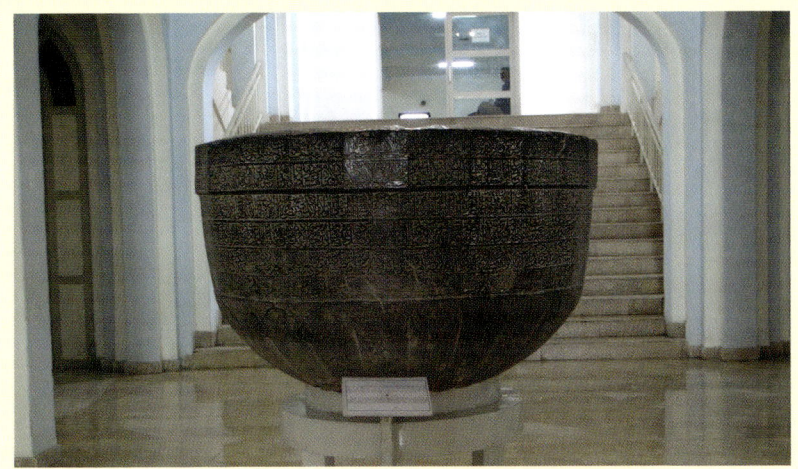

The famous 'Begging Bowl' or *bhiksapatra* of the Buddha, which was found at the *khanaqa* of a Muslim saint at Kandahar and later brought to the National Museum at Kabul
Photo courtesy: National Museum of Afghanistan, Kabul

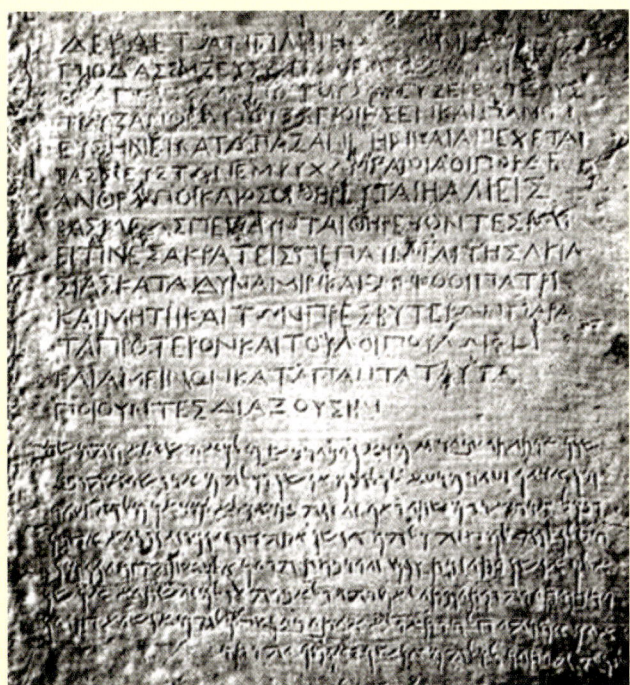

Asoka's bi-lingual inscription (Greek and Aramaic) of the third century BC found at Kandahar
Photo courtesy: National Museum of Afghanistan, Kabul

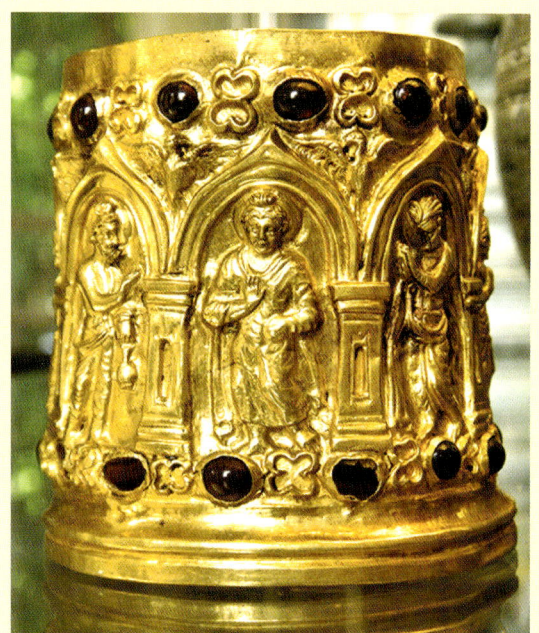

Depiction of the Buddha (centre) on gold encrusted Bimaran Casket, first century AD
Photo courtesy: British Museum, London

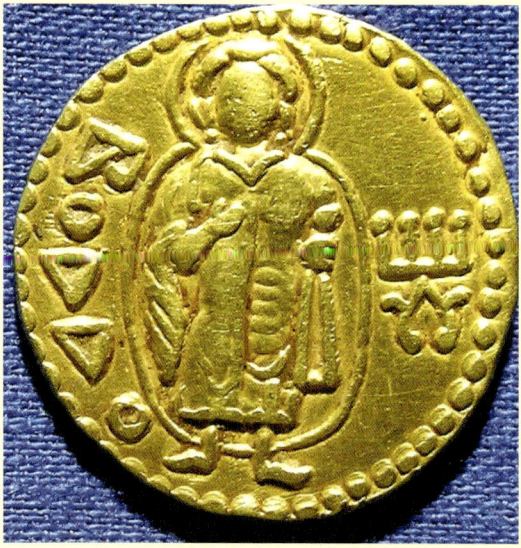

Early image of the Buddha on BODDO coin (127–140 AD)
Photo courtesy: BHU Museum

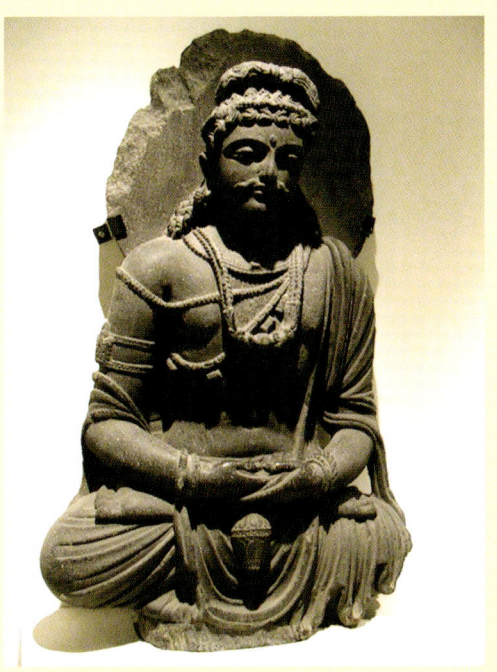

Maitreya from Loriya Tangai, dated to the second century AD, near Mardan, Pakistan
Photo courtesy: Indian Museum, Kolkata

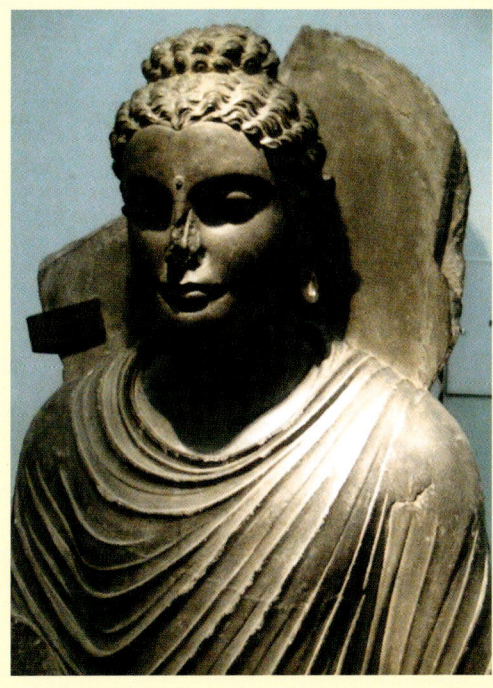

Buddha image in schist from Gandhara, dated from the second century AD
Photo courtesy: Peshawar Museum

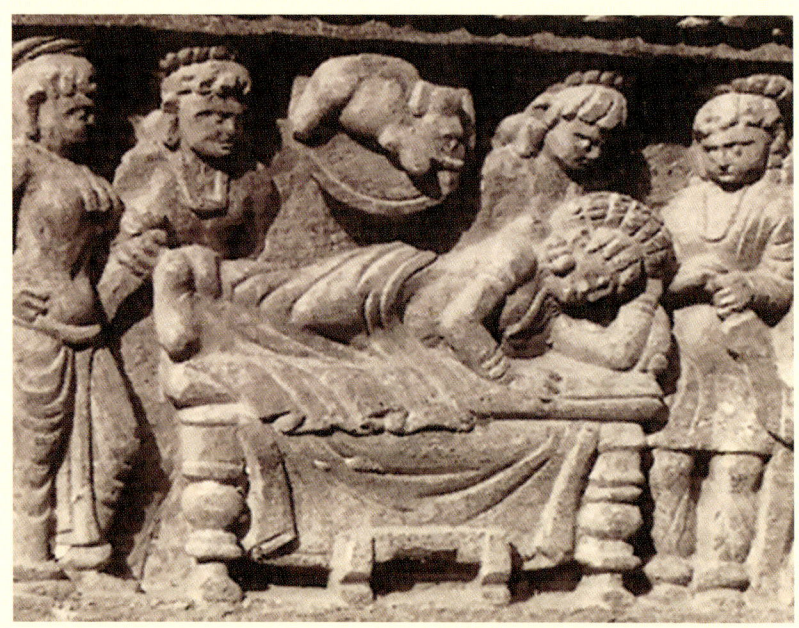

A schist relief dated to the second–third century AD from Gandhara depicts a white elephant entering the womb of Queen Maya Devi
Photo courtesy: Archaeological Museum, Milan

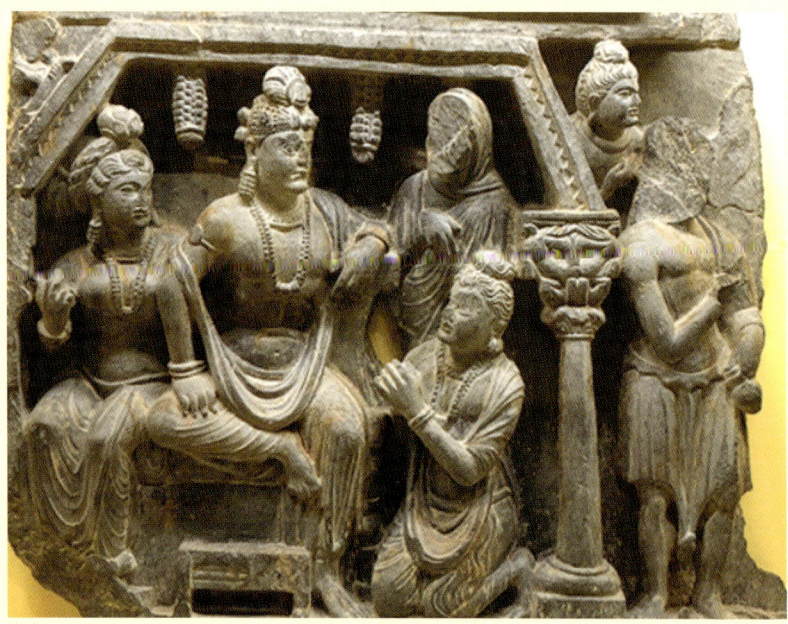

A schist relief from Gandhara depicting the Great Renunciation of Prince Siddhartha, dated to the second–third century AD
Photo courtesy: Archaeological Museum, Milan

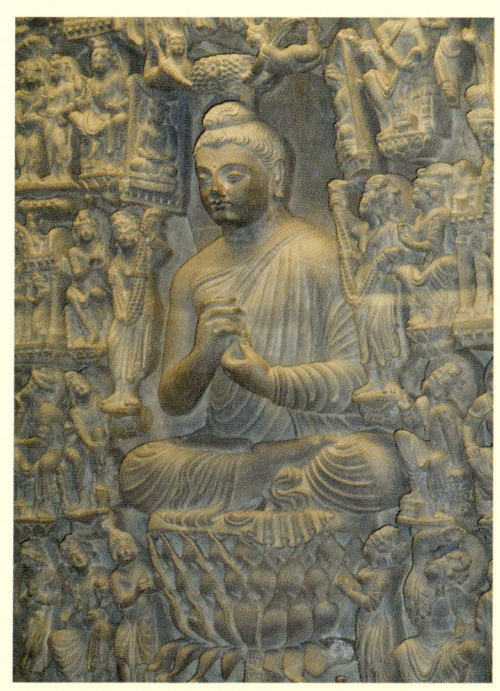

A schist relief depicting the Buddha performing the 'Miracle of Sravasti', dated to the third century AD, from Mohammad Nari, near Charsadda, Pakistan
Photo courtesy: Lahore Museum

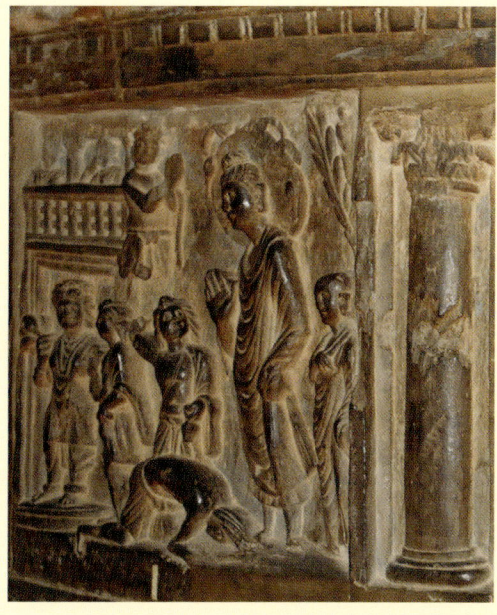

A relief in schist depicting Dipankar Jataka on Sikri Stupa, dated to the third–fourth century AD
Photo courtesy: Lahore Museum

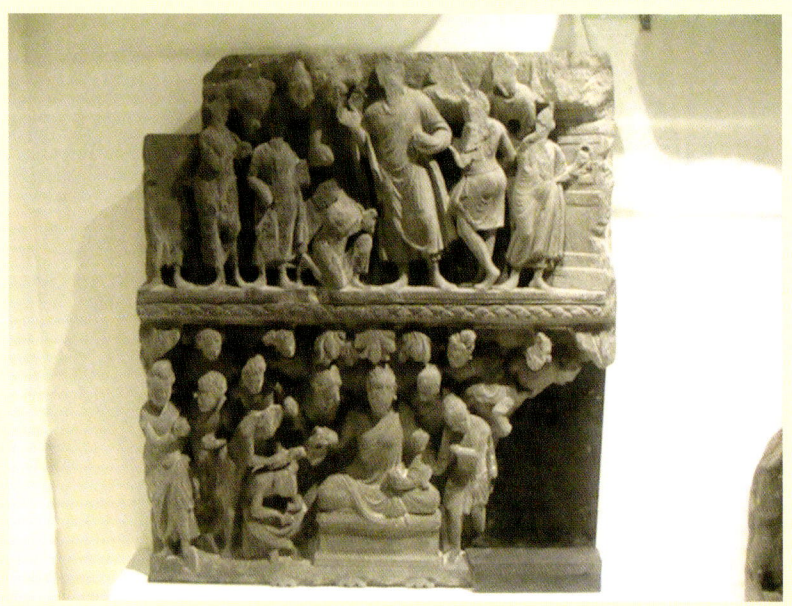

A relief in stone depicts ordination of Nanda, Sari Bahlol, dated to the second century AD
Photo courtesy: Indian Museum, Kolkata

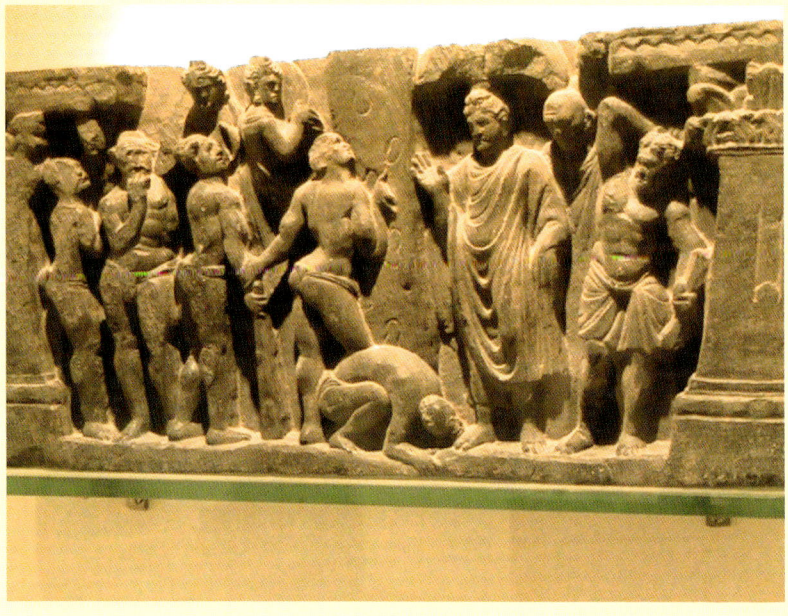

A relief in stone from Jamalgarhi depicts the attack by Devadutta's hireling, dated to the second century AD
Photo courtesy: Indian Museum, Kolkata

Chapter 15

MONASTERIES OF KAPISA

It was the famous Begram Treasure found at Kapisa that established the site as a Greco-Bactrian or Parthian city of 2,000 years ago. Lying 60 km north of Kabul in Begram district and situated at the confluence of the Ghorband and Panjsher rivers, the renowned ancient monastic site of Kapisa was a flourishing trade centre. Strategically positioned on the crossroads of north–south India to Central Asia route and east–west China to Europe route, it was the western capital of the Kushan king Kanishka, and the hub for trade routes from India, the Caspian region, Transoxiana and the Mediterranean region and from the Tarim Basin through Badakhshan.

The strategic location of the city accounts for the 'treasures of Begram', a rich array of objects retrieved during excavations at the Ville de Kapice from chambers 10 and 13. During his stay at Kapisa, Xuanzang mentioned, '[H]ere are also found objects of merchandise from all parts [of the world].'[1] These included an enamelled glass showing scenes of combat and animal hunting from the first century AD; goblets of moulded glass from the first–second century AD and flasks of blown glass, bowls and vases from the first century AD as well as carved ivory plaques and ivory panels with scenes depicting women in various postures. Some of the collections brought from Begram by the Franco-Afghan archaeological excavations of the first half of twentieth century are today displayed at the Musée Guimet, Paris.[2]

---

[1] Pierre Cambon, 'Begram: Alexandria of the Caucasus, Capital of the Kushan Empire', Chapter VI, Section 'Begram' in Fredrik Hiebert and Pierre Cambon (eds), *Afghanistan: Crossroads of the Ancient World*, The British Museum Press, London, 2011, p.160.

[2] Cambon, 'Begram: Alexandria of the Caucasus, Capital of the Kushan Empire', pp.145–61. See also, Museum Collection of Silk Road Art, Musée Guimet, Paris. Information available at <depts.washington.edu/silkroad/

Due to great wealth and patronage of merchants and rulers, a plethora of monasteries were erected on the hills of Begram. Xuanzang informs that there were nearly 100 monasteries with 6,000 priests and renowned scholars of Buddhism living here.[3] The monastic institutions at Kapisa belonged to the 'Little Vehicle' as well as to the 'Great Vehicle'. The king of Kapisa and all the priests went to receive the pilgrim when he arrived here, and each monastery was competing to invite the pilgrim. But Xuanzang and monk Prajnakara stayed in the temple of Sholokia (for the hostage) of the 'Little Vehicle' where they spent their *varshavasa* or the rainy season retreat.[4]

In 1923, archaeologist Alfred Foucher from the the Delegation Archéologique Française en Afghanistan (DAFA) started exploring Begram. According to him, Begram is Kapisi, the ancient capital city of Kapisa region. In 1936, the DAFA began excavations in the 'New Royal City'. Further excavations took place in 1937 and 1939 when the famous Begram Treasure was discovered in two walled rooms (No. 10 and No. 13).[5]

During excavations, several monastic complexes were found on the hills rising east of Begram. These are the Kohi Pahlawan or the Hill of Heroes, a flourishing Buddhist centre having several monasteries from about the second century AD. The list of monasteries included Shotorak, Paitava, Kham-i-Zargar, Sarai Khuja and Karratcha—all dated between the second and fourth centuries AD. It was from these hill monasteries that several images of the Buddha in schist were recovered and which form one of the rare statuary collections of the National Museum at Kabul and at the Musée Guimet in Paris.

Shotorak, lying on the south bank of the Panjshir River at the

---

museums/mg/begram.html>
[3] Samuel Beal, *Si-Yu-Ki: Buddhist Records of the Western World*, Book I, Low Price Publications, Delhi, 1884, p.54. See also, Hwui Li, *The Life of Hieun-Tsiang* (translated by Samuel Beal), Book II, D.K. Publishers, Delhi, 2001 (1st ed. 1911), pp.54–55.
[4] Beal, *Si-Yu-Ki*, pp.54–68. See also, Hwui Li, *The Life of Hieun-Tsiang*, pp.54–55.
[5] Cambon, 'Begram: Alexandria of the Caucasus, Capital of the Kushan Empire', pp.145–61.

foot of the Kuh-i-Pahlawan, 4 km north of Begram, is the location of a small Buddhist monastery complex with some seven or eight stupas. The main stupa was surrounded by a cloistered courtyard and decorated with figures in bas-relief. Finds included many clay stupa models and schist sculptures. Sculptures discovered at the site—carved schist standing figures and bas-relief panel sculptures—during the 1930s are considered some of the most important Buddhist artworks found in Afghanistan. The Dipankara Buddha, from the third century AD, transferred from Shotorak to the Kabul Museum in the late 1930s, was stolen from the museum in February 1993 and remains the single most important item missing from the museum's collection. It was last reported in the hands of a Japanese private collector.[6]

Shotorak could be the same as Sha-lo-kia, which, according to Xuanzang, was built especially for Chinese hostages taken by the Kushan king Kanishka.[7] The story of a Chinese prince taken hostage and kept at Kapisa is narrated by the Xuanzang. He informs that the Temple of Sha-lo-kia belonged to the 'Little Vehicle' and was originally built by a son of a Han Emperor who had been held hostage here. He lived in a vihara near Jalandhar during the winter months. Sha-lo-kia (believed to be Shotorak) had immense treasures buried under the foot of the great image of Vaisravana, near the Hall of the Buddha. The treasures were in the form of countless jewels and gems, stored for later use in the repair of the temple and could have been provided for by the Chinese emperor, perhaps as a ransom for his son. This evidence is provided by Xuanzang who states that in gratitude for such favours, the priests of the temple had painted on the walls the figure of the hostage prince.[8]

Xuanzang's narration about the hostage could well be true as the Kushan king Kanishka was known to have hostages from China in his court. Kanishka conquered the rich Chinese provinces of Kashgar,

---

[6] Warwick Ball, *Archaeological Gazetteer of Afghanistan*, 1982, No. 1088. Available at <https://www.cemml.colostate.edu/cultural/09476/afgh05-193.html>
[7] Beal, *Si-Yu-Ki*, p.54. See also, Hwui Li, *The Life of Hieun-Tsiang*, pp.54–55.
[8] Beal, *Si-Yu-Ki*, pp.54–55. See also, Hwui Li, *The Life of Hieun-Tsiang*, pp.54–55.

Yarkand and Khotan, and hostages from a Chinese principality lived in his court.[9]

Along with Sha-lo-kia, Xuanzang also mentioned the monastery of Pitokia (could this be Paitava?), and writes in detail about these two monasteries of Kapisa—one belonging to the Little Vehicle (where he stayed and was named the Temple of Sha-lo-kia) and the other belonging to the Great Vehicle, where he did not desire to stay. He indicated the location of the monasteries near a large city called Si-pi-to-fa-la-sse, the largest city in Kapisa region. He also found the convents of Rahul (Ho-lo-hu-lo) and the colossal stupa of Pilusara meaning 'elephant strength', which must have been attached to a monastery.[10]

MOKSHA MAHAPARISHAD AT KAPISA

The main monastery of Sholokia at Shotorak had the tradition of holding a five-day religious congregation, *Moksha Mahaparishad*, during which scholarly debates on Buddhist texts and question–answer sessions were held to clarify and expound the doctrines. Mentioning the congregation, Xuanzang states that in this convent lived three great Buddhist priests—Master of three Pitakas, Manojaghosh; Aryaverma of the Sarvastivadin School and another priest Gunabhadra. Xuanzang participated in one of the *mahaparishads* along with the monk Prajnakara. He also addressed the congregation and answered all question regarding the Buddhist doctrine put to him.

In this regard, Indologist P.C. Bagchi mentions a list of renowned Buddhist scholars from Kapisa who were invited to China to translate Buddhist texts into Chinese. Among these were Buddhatrata, who went to China towards the end of the seventh century AD and resided in the monastery of Po-ma-sse at Lo-yang; Buddhapala who went to Lo-yang where he resided in the Si-ming-sse and translated one

---

[9] R.C. Majumdar, *Ancient India*, Motilal Banarsidass Publishers, Delhi, 2013 (1st ed. 1952), p.122.
[10] Beal, *Si-Yu-Ki*, p.68.

work into Chinese; and Dharmagupta who reached Ch'ang-ngan in AD 590. Prajnakara went to China by the sea route reaching there in AD 781 and settled at Ch'ang-ngan in AD 810.[11]

SPLENDID STATUARY ART

The monasteries of Kapisa are known to have adopted a distinct style and representation of some favourite themes taken from the life of the Buddha and Jataka stories. The favoured depiction of the 'Miracle of Sravasti' as stele on schist was recovered from many monasteries, namely Paitava, Shotorak, Karratcha, Kham-i-Zargar and Sarai Khuja. The statuaries in relief and stele are chiselled very finely. The miracle in which Buddha emits fire from his shoulders and a stream of water from his feet was performed seven years after Buddha's Enlightenment before a large audience to meet the challenges of his rivals. These statuaries titled 'Miracle of Sravasti' are the proud possessions of the National Museum at Kabul and the Musée Guimet at Paris. The foyer of the national museum has a row of large Buddhas performing the miracle, including a life-size headless image of Buddha in *abhay mudra* from Shotorak dated from the second to fourth century AD. Others are from the Sarai Khuja and Kham-i-Zargar. One found at Paitava is with the Musée Guimet in Paris.

The Hackin Expedition 1924 recovered another interesting stele in schist depicting the same theme of the Buddha performing the 'Miracle of Sravasti' dated third century AD from the monastery of Paitava, located seven kilometre from Begram. A bodhisattva in schist, also from the monastery of Paitava dated third century AD and another, in schist from the monastery of Karratcha, dated second–third century AD, form the collection from Kapisa at Musée Guimet.[12]

---

[11] P.C. Bagchi, *India and China*, Saraswat Library, Kolkata, 1981, p.258.
[12] Museum Collection of Silk Road Art, Musée Guimet, Paris. Information available at <depts.washington.edu/silkroad/museums/mg/begram.html> [Details: Bodhisattva. Monastery of Paitava, second–third century AD, Schist. Inv. No. MG 21134. Bodhisattva. Monastery of Karratcha, second–third century AD, Schist (Barthoux Expedition, 1925)

Other favoured and distinct themes adopted by the Kapisa monasteries were the depiction of Dipankar Buddha and the idea of a Buddhist paradise created in relief on schist. The former depicts Sakya bodhisattva's meeting with Dipankar Buddha. The bodhisattva spread his deer-skin robe and loosened his hair to protect the Buddha from mud, and in consequence received a predictive assurance that he would become a Buddha.[13] These are now displayed at the Musée Guimet.

The two major works of Buddhist iconography found at Shotorak included a bas-relief depicting the Dipankar Jataka, 83.5 cm tall and dating from the second or third century AD. On the evening of 31 December 1992, the legendary pieces were stolen from the upper storey of the museum.[14] The other carved in slate and dating from the same period depicted the legend of the adoration of the Buddha by the three Kashyap brothers.

The rare depiction of the Paradise of Maitreya dated second–third century AD from Shotorak in schist, and a stone lion 'Support de Marche' in schist also dated from the same period from Shotorak are displayed at the Musée Guimet, Paris.[15] Maitreya, the bodhisattva, who is Ajita, is predicted to succeed Sakyamuni as the future human Buddha. He is born in Tusita heaven where in an inner palace he reveals the Law to the heavenly beings.[16] His paradise is endowed with happiness where the inhabitants are released from all afflictions and enjoy the 'bliss of nirvana.'

At Kham-i-Zargar, the remains of a stupa surrounded by several votive stupas were found on a hill Kuh-i-Kham-i Zargar and an associated monastery below. Significant findings include arms of

---

[13] Hwui Li, *The Life of Hieun-Tsiang*, p.58.
[14] Cambon, 'Begram: Alexandria of the Caucasus, Capital of the Kushan Empire'. See also, Omara Khan Massoudi, *The National Museum of Afghanistan*; Chapter I, p.37.
[15] Paris Paradise of Maitreya and Stone Lion at Musée Guimmet, Museum Collection of Silk Road Art, Musée Guimet, Paris. Information available at <depts.washington.edu/silkroad/museums/mg/begram.html>
[16] Kala Acharya, *Buddhanusmriti: A Glossary of Buddhist Terms*, Somaiya Publications, Mumbai, 2002, p.200.

a throne in the form of lions, four unfinished lion statues and a statue of Buddha.[17] A copper sieve from Kham-i-Zargar from the first century AD, pierced with holes arranged in floral patterns is an important relic of the Buddhist monastic communities that proliferated around Taxila. This sieve is the only object in private collections that mention Taxila and its Buddhist monasteries. Inscription around the rim states:

> In the Buddhist community of every quarter, in the zone of the roe deer, at Taksila, for the acceptance of the monks of the Kasyapiyas Order, this is the gift of the monk Drdha living in the monastery.[18]

Other marvels of art from the monastery of Shotorak at Kapisa include the Bodhisattva of Kapisa in schist dated third–fourth century AD; a fragment of a scene from Dipankar Jataka on schist dated second–third century AD and another fragment of Dipankar Jataka in schist depicting the brahmin Megha, dated second–third century AD. They are the pride possessions of the Musée Guimet, Paris. Treasures in carved ivory from Ville de Kapice dated from the first century AD are also on display.[19]

---

[17] Warwick Ball, 'Kuh-i-Muri in Kapisa', *Archaeological Gazetteer of Afghanistan*, 1982, No. 622.

[18] O. Bopearachchi, C. Landes and C. Sachs, 'De l'Indus à l'Oxus', *Archéologie de l'Asie Centrale*, Bibliothèque Nationale de France, Montpellier, 2003, No. 336; Oliver Hoare Ltd, Every Object Tells a Story (176 Copper Sieve), Kham Zargar, Afghanistan. See <www.everyobjecttellsastory.com/wp-content/uploads/2017/04/176>

[19] Dipankar Jataka, Brahmin Megha/Treasures from Begram, Musée Guimet, Museum Collection of Silk Road Art, Musée Guimet, Paris. Information available at <depts.washington.edu/silkroad/museums/mg/begram.html>

Chapter 16

CAVE MONASTERIES OF BAMIYAN

Bamiyan had close connection with the Sakyans of Kapilavastu. During the lifetime of the Buddha, there was a gruesome attack on the Sakyans by Virudhaka, who was the neighbouring ruler of Kosala during the lifetime of the Buddha. The four rebel Sakyans who were engaged in ploughing their field between the water courses offered resistance to the warring army of Virudhaka and scattered them. However, in return they were punished and banished from Kapilavastu by their clansmen for bringing disgrace on the Sakyan family by acting 'cruelly and impetuously and without patience to kill and slay.'[1] The four banished Sakyans went to the north among the 'Snowy Mountains'; one became king of Bamiyan, one of Udyayana, one of Himatala and one of Sambi. These kings 'transmitted their kingly authority from generation to generation without any interruption.'[2]

We are also informed of a great *arhat*, or an Enlightened Being, Sanakavasa (sometimes identified with Yasa),[3] the disciple of Anand (Si-Yu-Ki) and the fourth patriarch of the Sangha living 100 years after Buddha. His begging bowl and Sanghati were seen by Xuanzang at a monastery near Bamiyan.[4]

Situated about 250 km north-west of Kabul between the mountain passes of the Hindu Kush and the Koh-i-Baba, Bamiyan formed a Silk Road conduit between Kabul and Balkh allowing trade to pass through to the ports on the Oxus. With its fine weather and picturesque landscape, the city became a favourite halting place for caravans travelling between India and Central Asia. Even today, any

---

[1] Basanta Bidari, *Kapilavastu: The World of Siddhartha*, Hill Side Press, Kathmandu, 2004, p.116.
[2] Bidari, *Kapilavastu*, p.116.
[3] Samuel Beal, *Si-Yu-Ki: Buddhist Records of the Western World*, Book I, Low Price Publications, Delhi, 1884, p.53.
[4] Beal, *Si-Yu-Ki*, pp.52–53.

modern traveller to Bamiyan will see a long line of old caravanserais turned into schools, a juvenile jail, depots and shops, facing the Buddhist caves.

If Sakyans ruled at Bamiyan and the Buddha's disciple Sankavasa's robes were worshipped in the Bamiyan's monastic centre, it may be presumed that Bamiyan's connection with Buddhism grew during the time of Buddha as early as the sixth century BC. It is no surprise that the first stupas came up in neighbouring Balkh during the Buddha's time when the Uttarapath, linking the Oxus Valley with the Bay of Bengal, was a busy route and trade caravans moved from one end of the highway to another.

Itinerant monks from the Buddhist centres of India are also believed to have settled in Bamiyan during the time of the Mauryan Emperor Asoka's *Dhamma* missions to the Greek kingdoms of Central Asia. It continued to be a major centre of Buddhism during the subsequent Indo-Greek and Kushan periods. Two immense rock statues of the Buddha, believed to represent *Lokottara* (the Lord of the World),[5] once dominated the Buddhist complex. Thousands of cave shrines, assembly halls and residences for monks were carved out of cliffs between the two giant Buddhas and were decorated with paintings. While the Archaeological Survey of India (ASI) involved in the restoration work at Bamiyan from 1969 to 1976 have dated the colossi between the third and fourth centuries AD,[6] scholar B.A. Litvinsky has dated the entire complex at Bamiyan from the third to seventh century AD, and the Buddhas to the Hephthalite Period.[7]

Today, these are represented by dark empty niches standing like tall shadows in the face of the beautiful Bamiyan mountains.

Sitting 2,500 m above sea level, the long east–west Bamiyan

---

[5] B.N. Puri, *Buddhism in Central Asia*, Motilal Banarsidass Publishers, Delhi, 2000, p.298.

[6] Kasturi Gupta Menon, *A Challenge to World Heritage*, Visual Publication of the Archaeological Survey of India, Delhi, 2002, p.3.

[7] B.A. Litvinsky, *The Hephthalite Empire*, Vol. III: History of Civilizations of Central Asia, UNESCO, New Delhi, 1996 and Motilal Banarsidass Publishers, Delhi, 1999, p.158.

Valley is fed by two rivers, the Kakrak to the east and Foladi to the west, both having their origin in the Koh-i-Baba range. The principal archaeological sites are Bamiyan in the Bamiyan Valley and Kakrak and Foladi sites in their respective river valleys. Today, any visitor to Bamiyan can see the honeycomb of rock-cut shrines and monastic cells around the Big Buddha caves, and in the neighbouring Kakrak and Foladi valleys that speak of the glory of ancient Afghanistan.

FAXIAN, XUANZANG AND HYE CH'O

The Chinese pilgrim, Faxian, who passed through Bamiyan around AD 400, spoke of over a thousand monks in attendance there and an assembly of monks held with great ceremony. Xuanzang visited Bamiyan in AD 630 and found it a thriving Buddhist centre with hundreds of monks living in the honeycomb of caves around the Big Buddhas. Korean monk Hye Ch'o who passed through Hindu Kush around AD 827 found the king of Bamiyan to be a Buddhist, and exercising considerable power.

Xuanzang's travelogue titled *Si-Yu-Ki: Buddhist Records of the Western World*, also mentions 10 religious foundations with several thousand priests belonging to the 'Little Vehicle' and the School of Lokottaravadins.[8] According to the traveller, one statue was 150-feet high while the other was 100-feet high—both standing figures of stone on the declivity of the hill. Xuanzang also spoke of a Reclining Buddha of about 1,000 feet in length within the monastic settlement. While in Bamiyan, the monk made a valuable observation regarding monastic life during the period of the Huns:

> These people are remarkable...for their love of religion...from the highest form of worship to the three jewels down to the worship of the hundred spirits there is not the least absence of earnestness and utmost devotion of heart.[9]

---

[8] Hwui Li, *The Life of Hieun-Tsiang* (translated by Samuel Beal), D.K. Publishers, Delhi, 2001 (1st ed. 1911), pp.52–53.
[9] Beal, *Si-Yu-Ki*, p.50.

In the early eighth century AD, a monk called Hye Ch'o from Silla (present-day Korea) visited Bamiyan, and described it as an area where Buddhism flourished. At the same time, he wrote that the area was not subject to any other country and could not be invaded because of Bamiyan's strong army.[10] Not long after Hye Ch'o left Bamiyan, however, the king of Bamiyan surrendered to the Abbasid Caliphate, after which the religion of Islam gradually spread. Up to this period, Buddhism, Islam and other religions seem to have coexisted in the region, but in the late ninth century, the Saffarid Dynasty (r.861–910) demolished many Buddhist temples and statues. From that time onwards, Buddhist culture in Bamiyan gradually declined.

The giant Buddhas stood guard over the valley for over a millennium and a half before being blown up in March 2001 by the Taliban. Today, the Afghanistan Institute of Archaeology, the Japanese research team from the National Research Institute for Cultural Properties and the Delegation Archaéologique Française en Afghanistan (DAFA) are at the site taking special care of the cave paintings as well as conducting further research and explorations.

Interestingly, the local populace of Bamiyan is proud of the renewed explorations at Bamiyan and the discovery of a 19-metre Reclining Buddha by renowned Afghan–French archaeologist Dr Zemaryalai Tarzi, who along with a team of French archaeologists from DAFA, have been searching for the 1,000-feet-long Reclining Buddha at Bamiyan, mentioned in the memoirs of Xuanzang.

HONEYCOMB SHRINES AT BAMIYAN

In the early twentieth century, DAFA began the first full-scale archaeological exploration of Bamiyan under the supervision of Alfred Foucher, André Godard and Joseph Hackin. In the late twentieth century, Zemaryalai Tarzi started major archaeological research in the area. The ASI also joined hands with the Government of Afghanistan

---

[10] Han-Sung Yang, Yun-Hua Jan, Shotaro Iida and Lawrence Preston (eds and trans.), *Hye Ch'o Diary: A Memoir of the Pilgrimage to the Five Regions of India*, Asian Humanities Press, Berkeley, CA, 1984, pp.51–52.

to preserve this great cultural heritage of the world. The work that started in 1969 was of such magnitude that it continued for the next seven years, and the ASI carried out repairs to the two Bamiyan Buddhas and shrines in the vicinity.[11]

When I visited Bamiyan in 2014, supporting structures of iron railings and wooden roofing had been set up by the Government of Afghanistan with the help of UNESCO and Japanese teams to prevent injury to the restorers and excavators from falling rocks.

A BEEHIVE OF CAVES

Surrounding the massive feet of the Buddha are a number of cave shrines cut into the depths of the mountains in a semi-circle. They do not appear to have been the living areas for the monks, and possibly only served as shrines for Buddhist images installed on pedestals. The base of the pedestals can still be seen rising a foot-and-a-half from the cave floor. Above the pedestals are tall, arched niches that now stand empty, bereft of their deities. Each cave has about five to six such pedestals below tall niches for life-size images.

The caves were once entirely embellished with murals, fading remnants of which linger on the walls. *Sufa*, or raised structures along the cave walls, were perhaps meant as seating arrangements for worshipping monks or for placing images.

The ceilings of most caves are embellished with carvings; at the centre hung a clay chandelier wherein burning lamps were placed to light up the caves during evening prayers. During the day, the caves were lit with natural light. In a few, the architectural decorations are in the form of carved lotuses that hang from the roof like lanterns. The edges are bordered with geometrical and floral motifs. Rows of paintings of the Buddha and Buddhist deities, separated at intervals with floral motifs, peep from beneath layers of dust and grime. Some ruined stucco figures inside the cave shrines appear to represent

---

[11] Menon, *A Challenge to World Heritage*. See also Bamiyan Cultural Centre, 'Bamiyan: Crossroad of Cultures'. Available at <https://bamiyanculturalcentre.org/bamiyan-crossroads-of-cultures> (last date of access: 7 February 2020).

kirtimukhas, which are fierce monsters with glorious faces and large gaping mouths. These creatures are often depicted in Buddhist iconography.

The partially surviving painting in a cave, of a spotted animal, probably a lion, seems to depict the story of a hunter from the Jatakas. A similar portrayal of a spotted beast is found in the paintings on the walls of the Varaksha Palace near Bukhara, now displayed at the Tashkent and Samarkand museums. The Varaksha painting depicts a decorated prince or a bodhisattva sitting on the back of an elephant and being attacked by a winged, spotted lion.

At the cave of the Sitting Buddha in *bhumisparsh mudra*—although the greater part of the Buddha image is missing—one can still trace arms resting on knees. Lying midway between the two giant Buddhas, the massive cave of the Sitting Buddha is surrounded by hundreds of small caves that appear like beehives. Near the foot lies the remains of three stupas; two of these are fairly large sized with cruciform bases. These were found in a wide open space that once may have been a covered courtyard and a surrounding circumambulatory corridor. The third was locked up inside a cave with its window covered by wire meshing. This is to prevent destruction of existing murals on the cave walls.

The ground between the Sitting Buddha and the second giant Buddha is believed to conceal the Great Reclining Buddha. Believed to be about 1,000-feet long, it could be the biggest Buddha ever seen by the world. Even the largest Reclining Buddha at the Kusinagar Mahaparinirvana Temple would fall short by several metres. Or, for that matter even the Buddha from Ajina Tepe or the one found at the Krasnaya Rechka site could never match it in size. The grapevine of Bamiyan suggests that Zemaryalai Tarzi and his team from DAFA have already located the world's biggest Reclining Buddha, but it has been kept a secret.

At several places in the Bamiyan Valley, the rock face has been flattened vertically with tools. These are said to have held several more images of the Buddha colossi making the valley a several kilometre-long open-air Buddha gallery.

Below the mountains, several storehouses have been built to store fragments of the giant Buddhas blasted by the Taliban.

At the cave of the second Buddha colossi, the silhouette of the image can be traced. To the left of the cave is a steep rocky staircase winding up the hill to reach the upper floors of the multi-storeyed shrine. The chiselled stairway becomes steeper, narrower and more slippery with every step. The cave on the first floor has a proper verandah whose ceiling and walls are carved and decorated with paintings which are so faded that they defy identification. Inside the caves are pedestals along the walls for images. While the images are lost, faint black traces of the circular and oval haloes that once decorated the deities' head, are still visible.

The staircase continues to spirals upwards to the second-floor cave. To help visitors and restorers climb the precarious stairway, iron railings have been installed along the walls.

On the second floor, the verandah appears to be fully covered with wall paintings that have peeled and faded over the centuries; only fragments of the paintings are visible. The cave ceiling is designed in stacking lotus or multilayered wheel-like structure from which once hung a lantern for lighting up the cave.

BAMIYAN: A PICTURE OF PARADISE

The splendid decoration of the caves of the Buddha Colossi and the soffit of its vault is unfortunately alive only in photographs presented by the Information Bureau at Bamiyan and in the ASI publication *Bamiyan: Challenge to World Heritage*. It is reminiscent of the Sakyan Palace at Kapilavastu described beautifully by Asvaghosa as resembling a 'heavenly mansion come down to earth...' The paintings created an illusion of a beautiful paradise, tranquil and colourful, where musical angels created a world of joy and beauty and the Buddha looked down from his heaven with love and compassion.

...the palace as glorious as Kailasa, with tambourines whose frames were bound with gold and which sounded softly beneath the strokes of women's fingers, and with dances that rivalled those of the beautiful apsaras.[12]

This paradise was deliberately created to:

> ...provide people with refreshing scenes of heavenly bliss. When people saw the kind and solemn images of the Buddha and bodhisattvas, flying angels, celestial musicians and others, their minds were momentarily occupied by a sense of peace, tranquillity and tenderness.[13]

The Huns were fervent worshippers of the Sun God,[14] and it is no coincidence that in the decoration of the soffit of the niche of the Small Buddha, the Sun God was depicted as flying across the sky in his chariot dispelling the darkness and ignorance of the world.

Such a picture of 'Buddhist Paradise' was trending in the grotto art of the Asian Silk Road from China to Afghanistan and India. Images of a beautiful paradise adorned the cave of most Buddha colossi, and Bamiyan was no exception. We can see the depiction of such a paradise at the Majishan Caves in Gansu Corridor, at Dazu Grottoes at Chongqing and at Yulin Caves at Anxi, where flying deities like apsaras and devas showered flowers and danced in joy. Nature too enjoys the 'bliss of emancipation' as birds fly and silvery clouds sail across the sky. There is heavenly music of the *panchnaad* (five musical sounds) and fragrance from beautiful garlands held by the Gandharvas. There is divine light from the sun and the moon. At Bamiyan, the trend of the 'Buddhist Paradise' was assimilated in the embellishment of the vault above the colossal deity.

A typical paradise scene comparable to Bamiyan can be seen at

---

[12] E.H. Johnston, *Asvaghosa's Buddhacharita or Acts of the Buddha*, Munshiram Manoharlal Publishers, Delhi, 1995 (1st published 1936), p.25.
[13] Tan Chung (ed.), *Dunhuang Art through the Eyes of Duan Wenjie*, Abhinav Publications, Delhi, 1995, pp.34–37.
[14] A.H. Dani, B.A. Litvinsky and M.H. Zamir Safi, *Eastern Kushans in Gandhara and Kashmir, and Later Hephthalites*, Vol. III: History of Civilizations of Central Asia, Motilal Banarsidass Publishers, Delhi, 1996 and UNESCO, New Delhi, 1999, p.173.

the Baodingshan Grottoes near Chongqing in China which depicts a happy world of Buddhist 'Pure Land'—the *Sukhavati*, where there is profound happiness. Darkness and ignorance have been banished by the radiance of Amitabha. Devas bow in obeisance; there is end to suffering and affliction. Here, all beings are equal with the potential of attaining salvation. Three large images painted in cobalt blue and copper green are those of three sages of the 'Pure Land'. The Amitabha dwells in the centre of the paradise and illuminates it with his radiance. He is flanked by the crowned bodhisattvas—Avalokitesvara on the left and Mahasthamaprapta on the right. Other Buddhist deities and apsaras are also present. We see happy joyful children playing the flute or climbing the ladder leading to the paradise.[15] Such a picture of heavenly bliss also adorned the caves of Bamiyan.

ART OF KAKRAK VALLEY

A second centre of Buddhist art in Afghanistan, and also the abode of the Buddha colossi known as Kakrak Buddha, stood in the ravine of Kakrak River, east of the Bamyan cliff. The caves are located about 6 km south-east of the city.

The famous Standing Buddha of Kakrak is said to have been over six metre high. The statue was destroyed by the Taliban along with the two giant Buddhas of Bamiyan in 2001. Unfortunately, nothing is left of it today; only a photo of the Kakrak Buddha can be seen at the Tourist Information Centre in Bamiyan.

The monastic cells were adorned with beautiful murals and three of the most famous ones can be seen in the upper gallery of the National Museum of Afghanistan, in Kabul. Some paintings of 'mystic mandala' found at Kakrak depict a galaxy of small Buddhas around the central image of the Vairochana.

An outstanding painting from the Kakrak Valley is the 'Hunter King', also on display at the National Museum. Having renounced violence, the king took refuge in the Buddha. The painting once

---

[15] Sunita Dwivedi, *In Quest of the Buddha: A Journey on the Silk Road*, Rupa Publications, New Delhi, 2009, p.250.

adorning the drum of a dome at Kakrak portrays a royal personage, presumably the Buddhist king of Bamiyan, worshipping a stupa. The sovereign, bejewelled and adorned in fabulous robes, wears a crown with three crescents, perhaps symbolizing the *triratna* of the Buddha, *Dhamma* and the Sangha. He is seated cross-legged, holding the bow in his hands and the arrows sticking in the ground while the Buddha appears in two different mudras seated on the lotus. Dated to the sixth century AD, it is remarkable for its depiction of *Buddham Sharnam Gachchami*, meaning a sovereign who seeks refuge in the Buddha.

FOLADI VALLEY

A short distance from the western entrance of the Bamiyan caves and the Buddha colossi lie the Foladi Caves, which have been scooped out of high cliffs along the Foladi River. This is the third centre of Buddhist art dated around the sixth century AD in the Bamiyan region. Here lie painted cave shrines and possibly some dwellings of monks in adjacent hills. The steep mountains are difficult to climb; hence a visitor can see the exquisite cave decorations from the foot of the mountains. The exquisitely embellished caves were all dedicated to the Buddha while monks lived in humble dwellings in adjacent hills.

The craftsmen engaged in embellishing the Foladi Caves appear to have been adept in the art of stone carving and mural painting. Tall cliffs have been turned into overhanging balconies, porches and spacious shrines whose exquisite ceiling and wall decorations appear like canopies and painted canvas. The cave ceilings have been carved and moulded in several layers of stucco in geometrical and floral design, some like a large lotus or lantern suspended from the centre. Clay mouldings in the shape of a chess board or a square well-like pattern can be seen in some caves. The edges of cave ceilings are decorated with a chain of lotus blooms from which appears the faded figure of a Buddha. Once upon a time, a thousand Buddhas would have peered down on the chief deity of the shrine. Such ceiling patterns can also be seen at the monastery of Alchi near Leh in Ladakh and in the caves of Dunhuang that boast of ornamental ceilings in the shape of a canopy or royal umbrella.

Some cliffs appear like palace structures with long balconies having embroidered canopies in stone using a variety of mineral colours obtained locally from the mountains. The local belief is that the cliffs of the Foladi were once the home of a Kusana prince who had built a palace inside the hills, the rock being cut to give way to galleries, large halls and residential quarters with verandahs.

Some supporting structures of the verandahs have crumbled, exposing the remains of a richly painted roof with their geometrical patterns and rows of Buddha images. The colours are still bright even though centuries have elapsed since they were created.

Chapter 17

MONASTERY OF KUNDUZ

For travellers entering Afghanistan from Central Asia in the north, there was a choice of routes into northern and eastern Afghanistan; the reason being that northern and western Afghanistan had territorial contiguity with Turkmenistan, Uzbekistan and Tajikistan. Through the Wakhan Corridor, it connected with the Xinjiang region of China and the Northwest Frontier regions of India. Among the numerous routes, there were a few along the Oxus valley and its tributaries, which gained access into Hairatan near Balkh, at Aivaz and Dasti near Kunduz and at Khorog near Iskasim.

Mongol conqueror Ghengis Khan, who stormed Gandhara in the early part of the twelfth century AD, had followed the Termez route into Balkh. Amir Timur too had taken the route from Samarkand to the Oxus crossing at Termez in 1398, somewhere near Arytam to enter Balkh.

There were routes along the Wakhan River that linked Kunduz through Badakshan with Kashgar in the Xinjiang Province of western China. This route went through the long corridor that takes its name from the Wakhan River, and is a narrow Afghan territory that separates Tajikistan and Pakistan. Passing through this corridor, a traveller could enter any of the three countries of Afghanistan, Tajikistan and Khyber Pakhtunkhwa region of present-day Pakistan. This was a vital link running east to west between China and the eastern Mediterranean.

The corridor was used not only as a route of commerce between the regions of Badakhshan and Kashgar, Yarkand and Khotan, but also served as a pilgrim route to Gandhara, which abounded in Buddhist monasteries and shrines.

The vital trade corridor ran along the Wakhan River, which emerges from the Wakhjir Pass and flows west to join the Pamir River near Kala-i-Pyanj to form the Pyanj River flowing out of the

Wakhan Corridor at Ishkasim—the western entrance to the corridor. To the north of the corridor is the Gorno Badakhshan Autonomous Region of Tajikistan and to the south lies the Afghan Badakhshan region comprising the ranges of the Hindu Kush and the Karakoram. The southern part of the corridor is contiguous with the Khyber Pakhtunkhwa region of Pakistan through the Baroghil Pass while the Irshad Pass connects the corridor with the Gilgit–Baltistan region. The eastern-most Wakhjir Pass connects the corridor with China's Tashkurgan region of Xinjiang Province.

XUANZANG FOLLOWS THE TAJIK ROUTE INTO KUNDUZ

The Chinese pilgrim Xuanzang had taken the Kunduz–Balkh–Jalalabad route on his way to India in AD 629–30. He had to present his letter of credentials to the Turk Khagan, who ruled over the region from Kunduz. Instead of crossing the Oxus at Termez, the pilgrim travelled eastwards to Aivaz or Dusti to cross into Kunduz. Tracing his route, we find that he took a very long route eastwards from Termez along the right banks of the Oxus and its tributary and had almost reached the Pamir region of the Gorno-Badakshan.

There were many routes across the Oxus River and its tributary Pyanj that would directly lead into northern Afghanistan. However, for some reason, not revealed by the pilgrim, Xuanzang on arriving at Termez (in present-day Uzbekistan), had avoided the shortest route into Afghan territory through Arytam–Hairatan—two parts of the same village on the Oxus River in the Balkh region. Instead, he took a long detour through the territory that is now southern Tajikistan. He probably did this to see the various monastic centres that fell along the route and offer prayers at each of them. He was in no hurry to cross into Balkh though the most famous monastery of Navavihara (or Naubahar) was located there. There was a river crossing at the Arytam village even during ancient times, where we now have the modern Friendship Bridge going into Mazar-e-Sharif, only 20 km from Balkh.

There were dozens of convents along the Oxus where resided

a large number of monks. We come across names of places such as Chaganian and the eastern towns of Garam, Suman, Kulab and Kobadian. Xuanzang travelled still eastwards through the country of Vakhsh, Khuttal and Kumidha (mentioned as Darwaz and Roshan in his memoirs[1]), which were in the midst of the Pamirs.

After passing through Kumidha, Xuanzang drops any mention of any eastward destination, and in the text informs that he crossed the Oxus. He does not mention crossing the Oxus tributary, Pyanj which bordered on the south-west of Kumidha or the Kokcha along which he must have trekked through a small bunch of kingdoms in order to reach Badakshan and its neighbourhood in Taleqan and Kunduz, which he calls the 'kingdom of Hwo'. The name of the kingdoms on the way from Termez to Kunduz and their order of mentioning is however confusing as similar names are marked on both sides of the Pyanj. And we are left guessing as to the exact place where Xuanzang crossed the Oxus or Pyanj in order to reach Kunduz.

One reckons that it could not have been Aivaz or Dusti as he had travelled far beyond to the east where Darwaz and Roshan were bordered by the Tsung-ling Mountains or the Pamirs. The names of Wakhan and Shignan/Shugnan, mentioned in the notes of Thomas Watters ascribed to Sir H. Yule and Sir Alexander Cunningham[2] and the names of Yamgan, Kuran, Kishm and Ragh, mentioned in the notes of Samuel Beal,[3] leaves us with the conclusion that Xuanzang could have reached Khorog in the Pamirs of the Gorno-Badakshan before he decided to cross the tributary of the Oxus.

Interestingly, one of the kingdoms on the way to the Kunduz was Himatala, at the foot of the 'Snowy Mountains' or the Hindu Kush, where the ruler—just like at Nagarhara—drew his ancestry from the Sakyan race.[4] He was descended from one of the Sakya youths

---

[1] Samuel Beal, *Si-Yu-Ki: Buddhist Records of the Western World*, Book I, Low Price Publications, Delhi, 1884, p.41.
[2] Thomas Watters, *On Yuan Chwang's Travels in India AD 629–645*, Munshiram Manoharlal Publishers, Delhi, 2012, p.280.
[3] Beal, *Si-Yu-Ki*, Book I, pp.41–42.
[4] Beal, *Si-Yu-Ki*, Book III, pp.156–57.

who was driven away from Kapilavastyu for resisting the invasion of Virudhaka. Commenting upon the deteriorating condition of Buddhism in Kashmir, Xuanzang states that the Kritiyas (who may have been brahmins or anti-Buddhists) had more than once been put down by the Buddhists and that is why the they hated the Law of Buddha. In one instance, dated 600 years after the *Parinirvana* of the Buddha, the Sakyan king of Himatala who had great affection for the Law of the Buddha, invaded the Kritiyas of Kashmir with an army of 3,000 Sakyans disguised as merchants and killed the Kritiya king.

This is evidence that even during the hey-day of Buddhism, there was a fight for supremacy between Buddhists and Hindus in the region of Kunduz and Badakshan, and the Sakyan king of Himatala had to invade neighbouring Kashmir and kill the anti-Buddhist king. In the words of Buddhologist Gail Omvedt, there was conflict between the 'Kusanas and the pre-Buddhists of Kashmir, between Shaivites and Buddhists, and between the Huna king Mihirakula and his foe, described as the Tukhura ruler of Himatala who was descended from the Sakya race.'[5] During Xuanzang's journey through these areas in AD 629–44, we learn that Buddhist monastic institutions were already deteriorating, and while there were many Buddhist shrines and monasteries there were also many Deva, or Hindu, shrines in the places that he visited. In this context, he mentions the persistent rivalry between the Buddhists and the Hindus.

Even before Xuanzang crosses into Kunduz, he had stayed and worshipped at scores of monasteries along the Oxus. Interestingly, a crossing over the tributary of Oxus lay near the mouth of the Kafirnihon at the ford of Awwaj or Uzaj (present-day Ayvaj); near the mouth of the Vakhsh was the well-known crossing place of Mela, a three-day journey from Balkh and two *farsakhs* from Termez. In the thirteenth century, this place was called Panjab.[6] Probably, Indians from Punjab had settled at Mela.

---

[5] Gail Omvedt, *Buddhism in India: Challenging Brahmanism and Caste*, Sage Publications, Delhi, 2013 (1st ed., 2003), p.152.

[6] W. Barthold, *Turkestan Down to the Mongol Invasion*, The E.J.W. Gibb Memorial Trust, UK and USA, 1968, p.71.

About a century later, like Xuanzang, Mughal Emperor Babur entered Kunduz from across the Oxus. He too did not choose the river crossing at Termez, but at the confluence of a tributary probably at Aiwaz and moved on to Aibak, near Samangan. He had travelled from Ferghana to the headwaters of the Amudarya (or, Oxus) in the present Gorno-Badakshan region of Tajikistan, and was told by his associates that here lay 'an escape route to the east along a stream past the ice slopes of the Pamir and over to Kashgar.'[7] This shows that not only was there a route from Ferghana to Aivaz—probably along the Kafirnihon River to its confluence—but also that there were routes directly into the Tarim Basin. Babur journeyed down to find a fork in the river and at the confluence of a tributary, which could be Aiwaz or Dusti, he crossed the Amu to reach Kunduz from where he rode further to Kabul.

XUANZANG DETAINED

Xuanzang reached Kunduz and presented his letter of credentials, which he had obtained from the Khagan of the Western Turk to his son, the prince Ta-tu-sheh, ruling over Kunduz and its neighbouring regions. He also wanted to have a religious discourse with the renowned monk scholar Dharmasinha of the Kunduz monastic centre.[8] Ta-tu-sheh had married the sister of the king of Kau-chang (also, Gaochang). Moreover, the king of Kau-chang had sent letters to the Turk Khagan in recommendation of Xuanzang.

A SORDID EPISODE AT KUNDUZ

But in Kunduz, the pilgrim was a witness to a sordid episode of royal succession.[9] On his arrival, Xuanzang learnt that the princess

---

[7] Harold Lamb, *Babur First of Mughals*, Natraj Publishers, Dehradun, 2003 (1st ed., 1961), p.75.

[8] Beal, *Si-Yu-Ki*, Book II, pp.47–48.

[9] J. Harmatta and B.A. Litvinsky, *Tokharistan and Gandhara under Western Turk Rule [630–750]*, Vol. III: History of Civilizations of Central Asia, UNESCO, New Delhi, 1996 and Motilal Banarsidass Publishers, Delhi, 1999, pp.371–72.

Ho-kia-tun (sister of the Western Turk ruler of Kau-chang) was dead, and that Ta-tu-sheh (king of Gochang's brother-in-law) was sick. When he heard that the 'Master of the Law' Xuanzang had come from Kau-chang with letters for himself and his wife, he was overpowered with grief, and calling the pilgrim, said:

> Your humble servant at view of you has received sight. Would that you could remain here a little while, and rest. If I should recover my health, I will personally conduct you to the country of the Brahmans.

Moreover, at this time, there was a brahmin priest who had come to Kunduz to recite certain charms, which gradually had the effect of removing the sickness of prince. Afterwards the prince married the younger sister of Princess Ho-kia-tun. She, at the suggestion of her nephew (the son of her sister who was dead), prepared a poison and killed her husband. After Ta-tu-sheh was dead, his son who had the title of Tele, violently seized the government and became Shah. He then married his stepmother, the princess of Gaochang, the recently widowed queen.

As the funeral ceremony of the late prince was being observed, Xuanzang was detained for more than a month at Kunduz. He notes in his memoir that since he was detained at Kunduz month because of the prince Ta-tu-sheh's sickness and eventual death due to poisoning, he got an opportunity to explore the status of Buddhism there.

MONASTERIES OF KUNDUZ

Xuanzang provides interesting information about the condition of Buddhism in the seventh century AD at Kunduz. He tells us that in Kunduz there were about 10 monasteries with about a hundred monks and, both Mahayana and Hinayana sects prevailed.[10] The main monastery at Kunduz was renowned for its scholastic achievements, its fame having spread far and wide but chiefly in the Turkestan region

---

[10] Beal, *Si-Yu-Ki*, Book II, pp.47–48.

of China in the oasis cities of the Taklamakan Desert. Some of the most renowned scholars of Buddhism resided at the monastery. The most revered scholar monk Dharmasinha, who was well versed in *Vibhasha*, was the head and resided there with his many disciples.

About monk Dharmasinha, Xuanzang writes that Ta-mo-sang-kia (Dharmasinha), had travelled to India for instruction in Buddhist texts. 'Beyond the T'sung-ling Mountains on the western side they called him Fa-tsiang (i.e. Artizan of the Law, or law-maker). The priests of Su-leh [Kashgar] and Yu-tin [Khotan] dare not discuss with him'. Xuanzang, wishing to know his extent of knowledge, sent messengers to Dharmasinha, to ask how many Sutras or Sastras he was able to explain. Dharmasinha answered with a smile: 'I can explain any of them you like.' But Xuanzang, knowing that he did not understand the 'Great Vehicle', turned his questions to the *Vibhasha* and other Sutras belonging to the 'Little Vehicle'. When Dharmasinha could not answer, his disciples were filled with shame. From this time whenever they met, Dharmasinha was full of praise for Xuanzang, 'acknowledging that he was by no means Xuanzang's equal'.[11]

Significantly, at Kunduz the tradition of the Maitreya Buddha appears to have been strong. This was confirmed when a splendid bejewelled image of the Maitreya was found there. The people worshipped the Maitreya (the Future Buddha), who, according to Buddhist traditions, resided in the *Tusita* or the Buddhist heaven waiting to descend into the human realm when the time was right. He was the Universal Buddha and with his unbounded kindness and all-encompassing love, he would deliver mankind from misery. According to historian Romila Thapar, the Dharamguptaka sect, although not conforming to the Mahayana school, accepted some of its teachings, for example anticipating the coming of the Maitreya.[12]

The beautiful Maitreya image from the Kunduz monastic centre—perhaps, the one visited by the Chinese pilgrim—can today be seen at the National Museum, Kabul. The Buddha is seated with both feet

---

[11] Beal, *Si-Yu-Ki*, Book II, pp.47–48.
[12] Romila Thapar, *The Penguin History of Early India*, Penguin Books, Delhi, 2002, p.256.

crossed at the ankles on a pedestal or a throne. He is dressed in the robes of a *bhikshu* and decorated with heavy jewels. The earrings hang up to his shoulders, and a four-layered garland with a beautifully designed pendant reaches down to his chest. There are bracelets around the wrist. The headdress, in the shape of a jewelled crown, holds within its folds what seems to be a conical terraced stupa, believed to be a symbolic reliquary for the holy relics of the Buddha. The stupa appears to emit light or flames marked by carved bands emerging from it. It helps us to identify the image of Maitreya Buddha. A decorated halo with geometrical motifs on the edges adorns the back of the head.

Chapter 18

THE NAUBAHAR OF BALKH

Balkh was called the 'Mother of Towns' because of its antiquity and wealth. It was the oldest and largest town in the basin of the Amu-Darya (present-day Oxus). Balkh lay on an important river route that led up to Khorezm and the delta settlements of the Aral Sea; the lower Jaxartes (present-day Syr Darya) and Arys linked it with Otrar and Sauran and further up to the shores of the Caspian. A prosperous town, Balkh faced Termez, another rich city just across the river. Splendid monasteries were located in these two towns of the Oxus—the famous Fayaztepe and Karatepe in Termez and the renowned Naubahar in Balkh. The sacred city of Arytam across the Oxus and its counterpart Hairatan on the southern bank of the river were parts of the same settlement through which the river flowed. All goods from India to Central Asia and southern Russia passed through Balkh along both land and river routes.

The most important river crossing into Balkh was at Termez, through a large island that facilitated the construction of a floating bridge.[1] However, Arytam was not the only crossing on the Oxus into Balkh; another crossing lay near the mouth of the Kafirnihon at the ford of Awwaj or Uzaj (present-day Aivaj in Tajikistan), while a third crossing was located near the mouth of the Vakhsh River in Tajikistan at a place called Mela. In the thirteenth century AD, this place was called Panjab.[2] The Indian names of places show that these were halts for migrants from India who are known to have worked in the mines of Zerafshan digging for precious ores.

Balkh was the famed city of the Buddhist world as in its neighbourhood lay the Buddhist temple of Naubahar, meaning

---

[1] W. Barthold, *Turkestan Down to the Mongol Invasion*, E.J.W. Gibb Memorial Trust, UK and US, 1968, p.76.

[2] Barthold, *Turkestan Down to the Mongol Invasion*, p.72.

'new monastery', which enjoyed a great reputation even among the Muslims.[3] There were roughly 100 *sangharamas* with 3,000 Hinayana monks. Outside the town was the 'new *sangharama*' which was built by a 'former king of this country'.[4] It covered a vast territory which bordered the Oxus River on the north. With its 12 gates and walls that ran for over 70 km and encircled the town and neighbouring villages, it claimed to be the largest city in Khurasan rivalling Merv, Herat and Bukhara. However, this had ceased to exist in the ninth century as it was destroyed in AD 870 by Ya'qub, the founder of the Saffarid Dynasty.[5] The destruction may have been easy, considering that the walls and all edifices were built of clay.[6]

Interestingly, we are informed by scholar Boris A. Litvinsky that during the time of the Hephthalites in Tokharistan, the principal building materials used for construction were large rectangular, unbaked bricks and large *pakhsa* blocks, which were made of clay mixed with finely chopped straw. Baked bricks were in little use, but wood was often used for columns.[7]

ROAD TO BALKH

Balkh was also linked to remote eastern regions of India as trade caravans from Balkh followed the east to west trade route, through the Uttarapath which was evidently in use during the time of the Buddha in the sixth century BC.

The road to Balkh crossed the Hindu Kush via Salang Pass through the highest tunnel in the world, at 3,363 m. En route about 240 km

---

[3] Barthold, *Turkestan Down to the Mongol Invasion*, p.77.
[4] Samuel Beal, *Si-Yu-Ki: Buddhist Records of the Western World*, Book I, Low Price Publications, Delhi, 1884, p.44.
[5] Barthold, *Turkestan Down to the Mongol Invasion*, pp.77–78. See also, A.H. Dani, B.A. Litvinsky, M.H. Zamir Safi, *Eastern Kushans, Kidarites in Gandhara and Kashmir, and Later Hephthalites*, Vol. III: The History of Civilizations of Central Asia, Motilal Banarsidass Publishers, Delhi, 1999, p.178.
[6] Barthold, *Turkestan Down to the Mongol Invasion*, p.78.
[7] B.A. Litvinsky, *The Hephthalite Empire*, Vol. III: History of Civilizations of Central Asia, Motilal Banarsidass Publishers, Delhi, 1999, p.151.

from Kabul (12 km from Pule Khumiri) lay Surkh Kotal, which was the site for a great religious temple founded in AD 130 by the king of the Kusanas, Kanishka. Nearly 70 km further north lay Aibak, the capital of the Samangan Province. Near Aibak is an important Buddhist cave monastery and stupa, dating back to the fourth century AD, locally known as Takht-i-Rustam (Rustam's Throne) and Top-i-Rustam (the mound or stupa of Rustam), respectively. The stupa crowns the hill in front of the monastery. Almost 60 km north is Khulm, from where the road turns left and reaches Mazar-i-Sharif. From here, Balkh is at a distance of only 18 km.

FIRST STUPAS AT BALKH

In the early centuries under the Kusanas, many Buddhist temples flourished in Balkh. However, the first stupas are believed to have been built by two traders from Balkh—Trapussa and Bhallika—who had travelled all the way to Sarnath and Bodhgaya with cartloads of merchandise and met the Buddha at the Deer Park after his Enlightenment. Two 'sacred towers', or stupas, were built by them at Tiwei and Poli, near Balkh, during the time of Buddha. The first stupas for the Buddha were thus erected outside India by his lay devotees.

Evidence that Buddhism had reached Balkh at an early date also comes from Xuanzang's reports about the existence of a stupa more than two *chang* in height, 70 *li* (35 km) to the west of Balkh that were built 'in the days of Kasyapa Buddha long ago.'[8]

Balkh is also the holy city of Zoroastrianism, as it had been the birthplace of Zoroaster in about 600 BC. Zoroastrianism emphasized on the veneration of fire. Incidentally, many monasteries had wall paintings of the Buddha with auras of flames and inscriptions saying 'Buddha-Mazda', as seen and recorded by scholar Boris J. Stavisky at the Karatepa Caves just across the Oxus.[9]

---

[8] Hwui Li, *The Life of Hieun-Tsiang* (translated by Samuel Beal), Book II, D.K. Publishers, Delhi, 2001 (1st ed. 1911), p.50. See also, Beal, *Si-Yu-Ki*, p.47.

[9] B.J. Stavisky, "'Buddha Mazda" from Karatepe in Old Termez: A Preliminary

A HEPHTHALITE POSSESSION

According to A.H. Dani, B.A. Litvinsky and M.H. Zamir Safi, Balkh was an important Hephthalite possession having an extensive territory. At the Buddhist complex of Naubahar of the late sixth century AD, the Buddhist community was headed by the *Barmak*, a title derived from the Sanskrit word 'parmak' or 'pramukh', meaning superior or chief.[10] The administration of Naubahar was in the hands of the Barmakid family, who governed a large estate. According to Barthold, Balkh and the Naubahar were destroyed by the Arabs during the reign of the Caliph Othman, or, according to other accounts, during the period of Muawiya, and a new town was built in the locality of Barugan, outside Balkh.[11] But in AD 725, the governor Asad B. Abdullah is said to have restored the town to the former site, commissioning the representatives of the same house of the Barmakids to carry out this work. One of the reasons for the reconstruction was that destruction of the renowned monastery resulted in a fall in pilgrim traffic which, in turn, affected trade; the other reason being that the monastery enjoyed a great reputation among the recently converted Muslim population of Balkh.

The famous Barmakid family of Islamic times were apparently descendants of the Hephthalite *pramukhs* of the Naubahar at Balkh. After the Turk conquest, all the principalities of the former Hephthalite kingdom came under the rule of the Turk *Yabghu* of Tokharistan residing in Kunduz.[12]

Writing about the influx of Hindu learning under Harun, German orientalist Edward C. Sachau points out that the ministerial

---

Communication', *The Journal of the International Association of Buddhist Studies*, Vol. 3, No. 2, pp.89–94.
[10] Dani, Litvinsky and Safi, *Eastern Kushans, Kidarites in Gandhara and Kashmir, and Later Hephthalites*, p.178. See also, Barthold, *Turkestan Down to the Mongol Invasion*, p.77.
[11] Barthold, *Turkestan Down to the Mongol Invasion*, p.77.
[12] J. Harmatta and B.A. Litvinsky, *Tokharistan and Gandhara under Western Turk Rule (650–750)*, Vol. III: The History of Civilizations of Central Asia, Motilal Banarsidass Publishers, Delhi, 1999, p.371.

family of Barmak (chiefs of Naubahar), then at the zenith of their power, had converted and migrated to Baghdad. But at Balkh, one of their ancestors was still officiating in the Buddhist temple of Naubahar. Thus, though the Barmak family had been converted, 'their contemporaries never thought much of their profession of Islam, nor regarded it as genuine'. Sachau further states that probably induced by family traditions, they sent scholars to India to study medicine and pharmacology and engaged Hindu scholars to come to Baghdad. Here, the Hindu scholars were made chief physicians of hospitals and they also translated books on medicine, pharmacology, toxicology, philosophy, astrology and other subjects.[13]

Sung Yun who visited Gandhara in AD 520 noted that the Hephthalites had conquered that country and set up their own ruler,[14] and that in Tokharistan 'the majority of them do not believe in Buddhism. Most of them worship foreign gods. The Hephthalites in Gandhara honour *kui-shen* [demons]'.[15] However, Buddhist religious establishments are known to have flourished in Tokharistan especially at Balkh, the premier town of Tokharistan.[16]

CENTRE FOR MONASTIC STUDIES

Naubahar, the main monastery at Balkh, is known to have been the centre of higher Buddhist study for all of Central Asia. Writes in Hwui Li *The Life of Hieun-Tsiang* that three eminent Buddhist scholars resided at the *Navasangharama*, who were all were well-versed in the *Tripitakas* of the 'Little Vehicle', which was an early school of Buddhism. One was Prajnakara whose fame had spread throughout India. He remained at the monastery for a month to study the *Vibhasha Sastra*. Two other priests, Dharmapriya and Dharmakara,

---

[13] Edward C. Sachau, *Alberuni's India*, Rupa Publications, Delhi (4th ed., 2005), p.xxxiii.
[14] Litvinsky, *The Hephthalite Empire*, p.141.
[15] Litvinsky, *The Hephthalite Empire*, p.147.
[16] Dani, Litvinsky and Safi, *Eastern Kushans, Kidarites in Gandhara and Kashmir, and Later Hephthalites*, p.178.

also stayed at the monastery and they too were well-versed in the texts of the 'Little Vehicle'.[17]

After presenting his credentials at Kunduz, Xuanzang travelled with monks to Balkh where he stayed at the Naubahar for a month. He describes it as one of the most splendid monasteries of the Buddhist world. The pilgrim talks of Balkh as the 'little Rajgriha'—the name probably stemmed from the flourishing state of Buddhism with 100 convents and 3,000 monks residing there.[18]

Xuanzang also describes Po-ho (or, Balkh) as the Hephthalite capital with a circumference of approximately 20 *li* (10 km), saying 'This city though well-fortified, is thinly populated.' Xuanzang found Buddhism in Balkh in a flourishing state. Although he noticed the barren character of the city, he called it 'the most excellent land.' Outside the city, on its south-west, there was the imposing *Navasangharama* with unusual adornments. Near this, groups of several hundred stupas had been erected to commemorate priests who had attained the 'four degrees of holiness' and had exhibited miraculous power when they were about to die. While there were thousand other priests who had attained holiness, they had not exhibited 'spiritual changes' or miracles, and so no memorials had been erected for them.[19]

BUDDHIST RELICS AT BALKH

At the *Navasangharama* or the 'new monastery', Xuanzang saw the great statue of the Buddha which shone by virtue of the precious gems studded into it. It stood in a hall which was also embellished with rare precious gems. There was also a statue of Vaisravana Deva, who protected the convent. In the Hall of the Buddha, the pilgrim mentioned a dazzling multicoloured washbasin used by the Buddha. Not far away, lay the inch-long yellowish-white shining tooth of the

---

[17] Hwui Li, *The Life of Hieun-Tsiang*, p.51.
[18] Beal, *Si-Yu-Ki*, p.44. Sally Wriggens, *The Silk Road Journey with Xuan Zang*, West View Press, USA, 2004, pp.41–45.
[19] Hwui Li, *The Life of Hieun-Tsiang*, p.46 and pp.47–48.

Buddha. The sweeping brush of the Buddha, made of the plant 'ka-she' (or kusha grass), with a gem-laden handle was also kept here. To the north of the convent, he saw a stupa about 200-feet high, reflecting a divine splendour and enclosing a sacred relic. The stupa was covered with a plaster 'as hard as diamonds'.[20]

MONASTERY AT AIBAK

It is pertinent to note that the monastery of Naubahar lay outside the town of Balkh whose walls ran for over 70 km. On the other hand, at Aibak, about 100 km from Balkh by the present road, lies the splendid monastery and stupa of Takht-i-Rustam and Top-i-Rustam in the contiguous region of Samangam, one of the most ancient cities of Afghanistan in the valley of the Khulm River. It is in the ruins of these monastic settlements of Aibak that some scholars have traced the existence of the ancient Naubahar monastery which Xuanzang mentioned in his travelogues.

A walk inside the *pradikshana path* around the great polished stone stupa and along the maze of galleries inside the hill monastery is a study in monastic routine of the thriving Buddhist community that lived at Aibak.

TOP-I-RUSTAM

The eight metre high and 28 metre wide stupa of Top-i-Rustam is said to have been built in the second century AD. Cut out from an outcrop of Aibak Hills, the stupa literally shines like the polished Asokan pillars of the third century BC. The base that is embedded in the rocky soil has long grooves leading into underground water tanks. It is said that the grooves were meant to harvest snow melt into underground tanks to be used for drinking and ablution purposes by the monks. One can only imagine the intensive labour involved in the cutting and polishing of a huge cliff of deep grey limestone rocks into a stupa.

---

[20] Beal, *Si-Yu-Ki*, pp.45–46. Wriggens, *The Silk Road Journey with Xuan Zang*, pp.41–45.

Hemmed in between the stupa and the rock wall, a two-metre wide circumambulatory corridor or *pradikshana path* is cut deep into the mountains. It is wide enough for two persons to walk side by side around the stupa. The main entrance to the stupa which leads into the *pradikshana path* is flanked by deep caves with windows for light and air. The natural caves have low roofs but are wide enough to accommodate dozens of meditating monks.

A rectangular structure with a high empty niche stands over the stupa which probably held either the *triratna* or a *chhatri* (umbrella) or an image of the Buddha. Historian, explorer and eminent scholar of Afghan history, Nancy H. Dupree found a relic chamber located in the square *harmika* on the summit of the stupa, which would have originally supported the staff of the *chhatri*.

The massive size of the rock-cut stupa, its grandeur and the hundreds of caves cut alongside the circumambulatory corridor and in the adjacent hill to accommodate the large multitude of worshipping monks are evidence of the importance accorded to this site.

TAKHT-I-RUSTAM

Inside another hill close to the stupa lie massive rectangular and circular halls, courtyards and galleries whose walls have been decorated with floral motifs. There are deep-arched niches and on the floor are water bodies cut into the rocks. The interconnected galleries do not seem to be natural; the galleries, halls and walls were certainly carved by humans.

The expansive multi-roomed establishment with large assembly halls were decorated with carvings and paintings of the Bodhi Tree and a multitude of lotuses adorning the ceilings, walls and floors. The carved and gilded lotuses were meant to convey the impression of a heavenly shower of flowers on the Buddha, who was seated or stood under the carved arches. While the images are no more, the decorations on the cave walls and ceiling provide vivid impressions of the beauty that lay within Aibak Hills.

The corridors leading into the monastery are vaulted. Deep

tunnels cut into the hillside acted as ventilators for drawing fresh air and controlling the temperature inside the monastery. Some halls have a central depression for collecting rainwater that seeped between the hills. These could have been used as a washroom by the residing monks.

After crossing an open courtyard, one comes to an almost circular cave where a *kund* (water body) has been cut into the floor. Perhaps a cool, refreshing stream flowed into the *kund*, and the water there was stored for drinking purposes. On the walls are vestiges of floral carvings and tall niches for holding images.

Above a particularly large arched niche is a carving of a gigantic tree that resembles the Bodhi Tree of wisdom. Under this tree, the niche once held the image of the Buddha in deep meditation. Carvings of lotus flowers on the adjacent walls appear similar to those that grew under the feet of the Buddha at the Chankama at Bodhgaya, symbolizing the seven steps taken by the Buddha after his Enlightenment.

Galleries connect one part of the hill to another and lead into large congregational halls. One of the several halls into which a gallery opens appears to be several hundred feet long and at least 20 feet wide. There are numerous arches and a broad *sufa* (a seat protruding from the lower walls of a monastery) along the walls. Here, several hundred monks could be seated for a congregation, all facing the stupa on the other hill. Along the galleries are deep alcoves for the Buddha images that once decorated the entire monastic settlement. From the size of the hill and the number of large halls and connecting galleries, it can be presumed that several hundred monks lived in the monastic settlement. Incidentally, at the Naubahar of Balkh too, we find that the monastery was extremely large having porticoes and rooms that numbered 360.[21]

The question arises as to which one is the Naubahar, the settlement at Balkh or the Buddhist city at Aibak, only 100 km apart by the present road or perhaps a much shorter distance through

---

[21] Litvinsky, *The Hephthalite Empire*, p.151.

village roads. By any estimate, the kingdom of Balkh must have spread out far and beyond the present boundaries and possibly covered the present Aibak where the colossal stupa of polished rock remains, and the nearby cave monasteries show signs of occupancy by monks and adornments in the shape of lotuses, the Bodhi Tree and arches under which the Buddha image lay reclining or sitting in meditation.

OTHER NAUBAHARS

The monastic settlement of Naubahar was the most important structure of Balkh. It was so renowned that citadel gates of other cities facing in the direction of the Naubahhar drew their name from the monastery. W. Barthold in *Turkestan Down to the Mongol Invasion* mentions that in the tenth century, the residential inner city known, or the *shahristan*, of Samarkand (the area of Afrasiab), had four gates—on the west was the Naubahar gate which was also called the Iron Gate.[22] The gates of Afrasiab belonged to the pre-Islamic times when Buddhist *viharas* were known to exist in Transoxiana.[23]

Today, the chief town of Balkh is Mazar-i-Sharif, 22.5 km to the east of the city of Balkh which was erected around the 'grave of Caliph Ali' (son-in-law of Prophet Mohammad) and discovered in the twelfth century AD near the village of Khayr.[24] Over the tomb of Ali, a magnificent building was erected which became a place of pilgrimage. The present Mazar-i-Sharif with its Blue Mosque is of a much later origin than the old one which was destroyed by Ghengis Khan.

In present times, Mazar-i-Sharif has completely taken over the glory and fame of Balkh, and thousands flock daily to the shrine of Ali to pray, perform charity at the *jhanda* (the flag or the symbol of the saint) and feed white pigeons.

---

[22] Barthold, *Turkestan Down to the Mongol Invasion*, p.85.
[23] Barthold, *Turkestan Down to the Mongol Invasion*, p.85.
[24] Barthold, *Turkestan Down to the Mongol Invasion*, p.79.

Chapter 19

MONASTERIES AND DEVA TEMPLES IN GHAZNI

Xuanzang informs that both Hindus and Buddhists had their shrines in Ghazni. '[T]here are several hundred sangharamas with 1,000 or so priests. They all study the Great Vehicle...' and 10 stupas built by Asoka and several of Deva temples, 'in which sectaries of various denominations dwell together.'[1]

Xuanzang points to the coexistence of Hinduism and Buddhism since those who believed in magic and worshipped spirits also believed in the Buddha.

> [The people] love learning and the arts, and show considerable skill in magical sentences... They daily repeat several myriads of words [possibly magical mantras]... Although they worship a hundred spirits, yet they also greatly reverence the three precious ones.

In the seventh century AD, Xuanzang saw that the river valleys of Ghazni and mountain sides were teeming with herds of sheep and goats that were either meant for sacrifice or 'offering'. He, however, does not clarify for whom the sacrifices were meant. However, during the twentieth century, excavations at the great monastery of Tepe Sardar, also called Tepe-ye-Nagara at Ghazni, idols of Hindu worship were found, that is, of Durga in her avatar as Mahisasur Mardini. This could perhaps have been the site of offering sacrificial animals.

From Xuanzang's record, one can infer that Ghazni was a centre for Vajrayana, as devotion to feminine divinities was one of the features of Vajrayana—a form of Buddhism based on tantras and

---

[1] Samuel Beal, *Si-Yu-Ki: Buddhist Records of the Western World*, Book XII, Low Price Publications, Delhi, 1884, pp.284.

incantation of magical formulae. This reminds us of the feminine deity Sridevi found at the Buddhist temple of Kuva in Ferghana, which had close connections with northern India via the Leh–Yarkand route through the Pamirs and via the Karakoram Highway with Taxila. The famous exhibits lie at the site museum at Kuva and the State Historical Museum, Tashkent.

Xuanzang further elaborates:

…once a year a religious assembly is held in this country when the prince, nobles and people of this country as well as of foreign countries assemble at a season of rejoicing which is not fixed, and offer gold and silver and precious objects of rare value, with sheep and horses and domestic animals.[2]

The religious festival is unnamed, but one can infer that at the festival of the goddess, amidst chanting of mantras and magic formulae, offerings and sacrifices were made by those who converged at the shrine from far and near.

The pilgrim writes that the 'heretics by subduing their minds and mortifying their flesh, get from the spirits of heaven sacred formulae,'[3] using which they were frequently able to control diseases and cure the sick.

XUANZANG'S ROUTE INTO GHAZNI

In order to reach Ghazni and Kandahar, travellers generally took the southern passes of the Sulaiman Mountains instead of taking the northern Khyber route to Kabul. Xuanzang too seems to have taken southern route into Ghazni while returning from his journey to Bannu.

Si-Yu-Ki (Book XII) deals with the pilgrim's southern route to Tsu-ku-cha (or Tsaukuta), which has been identified by archaeologist Alexander Cunningham as Arachosia.[4] The pilgrim adds that the

---

[2] Beal, *Si-Yu-Ki*, pp.284–85.
[3] Beal, *Si-Yu-Ki*, p.285.
[4] Beal, *Si-Yu-Ki*, p.283n. Alexander Cunningham, *The Ancient Geography of India*,

country was 7,000 *li* (3,500 km) in circuit, and its capital was called Ho-si-na (identified with Ghazna or Ghazni). This identification was first made by archaeologist M.V. de St Martin.[5] The country had another capital, Ho-sa-la, about 30 *li* in circuit, and identified as Guzaristan by Cunningham.[6]

The pilgrim's route to Ghazni was through Fa-La-Na, which is identified by the Oriental scholar Thomas Watters as 'Varana' and by the French sinologist S. Julien as 'Varna'. St Martin thinks the country corresponds to the modern Vanen in the middle part of the river Gomal's course while Cunningham identifies Varana with Bannu in the Kurram river district.[7]

The pilgrim could follow the Bannu route through the Gomal Pass and onwards to Ghazni or the Tochi or the Gambila river valley, which also connects Bannu with Gazni.

In 1840, English traveller Godfrey T. Vigne took the route from Multan in the company of Lohani traders and proceeded along the Derabund–Ghazni route and from Ghazni onwards to Kabul. The route ran along river Gomal and through the Gomal Pass.[8]

AMALGAMATION OF LOCAL RELIGION

Even though Buddhism had spread to the region of Ghazni in southwestern Afghanistan, the people continued to profess their local religion and celebrate certain festivals associated with the arrival of the New Year. They also worshipped female deities such as the mother goddess to whom they probably offered sacrificial animals that Xuanzang saw being herded in the valley. They also chanted magic formulae in the hope of controlling diseases, pointing to the

---

Low Price Publications, Delhi, 1990 (1st ed., 1871), p.40.
[5] Beal, *Si-Yu-Ki*, p.283n.
[6] Beal, *Si-Yu-Ki*, p.283n.
[7] Thomas Watters, *On Yuan Chwang's Travels in India AD 629–645*, Munshiram Manoharlal Publishers, Delhi, 2012, p.262.
[8] Godffrey T. Vigne, *Personal Narrative of a Visit to Ghuzni, Kabul, and Afghanistan*, Munshiram Manoharlal Publishers, Delhi, 2004 (1st ed., 1840).

use of spells and magic mantras to gain power.

A similar celebration was held in Sogdiana where the inhabitants 'honour the Buddhist religion' and also 'sacrifice to the god of heaven'. Once a year in Sogdiana, the inhabitants celebrated the coming of the New Year 'which was connected with the ideas about death and revival of nature'. The dead were mourned by their kin by inflicting injury on themselves. They 'lacerated their faces' and 'offered food and drink to those who had died.'[9]

Indian religions, both Buddhism and Hinduism, influenced not only Afghanistan but also Central Asia. The worship of Vishnu and Siva were widespread in the Oxus valley and beyond, in the region of the Zerafshan, especially at Penjikent. Even today, images of Hindu gods Siva and Parvati and of the four-armed goddess riding a lion—both from Penjikent—are objects of much interest and curiosity for local and foreign visitors at the National Museum of Antiquities, Dushanbe. An image on a stele found at the Kuva site is that of a semi-nude god. The figure is described as Kuber, sitting with a jug, perhaps filled with sweet nectar and a large wineskin full of some intoxicating drink.

It must be noted that many Central Asian gods and goddesses show similarities with Hindu deities whose worship was widely prevalent in India. Strange wrathful, divine deities with terribly fierce faces, wearing a garland or a head decoration of skulls found at Kuva in Ferghana are believed to have their antecedents in the divine but wrathful deities worshipped in India, such as the Mahakaal, Kalbhairava and Yamanataka, who were endowed with supreme powers that were invoked by the chanting of incantations. The images of these fierce deities can be seen at the State Historical Museum, Tashkent. An image of the Buddha with the 'Third Eye' of Lord Siva, also recovered from Ferghana, is on display at the Sanat Museum of Fine Arts.

---

[9] B.A. Litvinsky and M.I. Vorobyova-Desyatovskaya, *Religions and Religious Movement–II*, Vol. III: History of Civilizations of Central Asia, Motilal Banarsidass Publishers, Delhi, 1999, p.428.

PRESENCE OF HINDU GODS

The presence of Hindu gods in Central Asia is the evidence of cross-fertilization of local and Indian cultures during the pre-Islamic period. It also points to the migration of Indians to Central Asian cities, not only the Zerafshan Valley at Penjikent but also the valley of the Syr Darya (then known as Jaxartes) at Ferghana and the Amu Darya (then known as Oxus) valley at Arytam.

Any visitor to the Rudaki Museum at Penjikent in Tajikistan and the National Museum at Dushanbe can immediately identify the Hindu gods and goddesses on display. There are images of a goddess riding a lion at the Museum of Antiquities, Dushanbe, as well as others such as Siva and Parvati—Siva with a third eye and Siva with three heads, amongst others. At the Rudaki Museum, Siva is seen sitting in a vast arena that resembles wilderness with his *trisul* or trident next to him.

Among the images of local divinities found in Temple II, one was identified as that of Uma Maheshwar (Siva and Parvati) sitting on the Nandi bull. Incidentally, the Pharro-Ardoxsa image at Ayrtam in the Oxus valley is also believed to be closer to the portrayal of Siva and Parvati.

Renowned Indian scholar and archaeologist S.P. Gupta has noted the presence of Hindu deities, such as Brahma, Indra, Siva, Narayana and Vaisravana in Central Asia, who had their own local counterparts.[10]

It is important to note that nearly 25 marble sculptures and other artefacts of Hindu art dated between the fifth and eighth century AD have been discovered in Afghanistan.[11]

---

[10] S.P. Gupta, 'Hindu Gods in Western Central Asia: A Lesser Known Chapter of Indian History', *Dailogue* (Quarterly Journal of Astha Bharti), New Delhi, pp.1–2. Available at <http://www.asthabharati.org/Dia_April2/Hindu.htm>

[11] Litvinsky and Vorobyova-Desyatovskaya, *Religions and Religious Movements–II*, p.427.

MONASTERY OF TEPE SARDAR AT GHAZNI

When the Islamic armies attacked Afghanistan in seventh century AD, Buddhism was flourishing in the province of Ghazni. One of the monastic centres located on a hill at Tepe Sardar had richly decorated stupas, chapels and monk cells which were excavated by modern archaeologists in the early twentieth century.

The Tepe Sardar Buddhist sanctuary occupying a hill of the Dasht-i-Manara plain was excavated by the Italian Archaeological Mission led by Giovanni Verardi between 1960 and 2003. An inscribed votive pot found at the site attested to the name of the sanctuary as the Kanika Maharaja Vihara, meaning the Temple of the Great King Kanishka. It also said that it was built during the Kusana period in the second century AD. Following the attack by the Islamic armies, it was abandoned in the late eighth–ninth century AD.

The 22-metre square towering central stupa was the focus of the complex and could be the largest yet found in Afghanistan. The chapels surrounding the stupa contain evidence of the colossal statuary art in the form of murals and painted clay images of the Buddha and bodhisattvas. Their fragments have been recovered during excavations. Massive gilded images of the Buddha have also been found at the entrance of the sanctuary. A gigantic Reclining Buddha measuring over 15 metres was found in Chapel 63 of the Tepe Sardar monastic complex.[12] Unfortunately, as per the notice put up by the National Museum, it has been completely destroyed in recent times.

Yet another notice by the National Museum of Afghanistan at Kabul states that although Buddhism had spread in the Ghazni area since the time of Asoka in the third century BC, this particular

---

[12] See details of excavation Ghazni/Tapa Sardar Project, 2014. *Buddhist Site of Tepe Sardar*, Ghazni: Archives of the Italian Archaeological Mission in Afghanistan. Available at <http://ghazni.bradypus.net/buddhist_sites> (last date of access 9 February 2020). See also, Nancy H. Dupree, *An Historical Guide to Afghanistan*, Afghan Air Authority Afghan Tourist Organization, Kabul, 1977, p.191.

complex whose main stupa was the largest in Afghanistan was built in third century AD during the Kusana period, and thrived for nearly six centuries until the arrival of the Arabs.

A large head of the Buddha dated fifth–seventh century AD from Tepe Sardar is an example of the beautiful statuary art from Ghazni, which can be seen at the museum in Kabul. The Buddha head must have adorned a life-size image of the Buddha in *dhyan mudra*. Made of clay, the Buddha's eyes are closed in meditation. The thin, long, curved brows and a high nose appear to be finely chiselled. Small volutes adorn the head and the hairline is sharply drawn.

Another image of grey-blue schist dated from the fifth–seventh century AD is headless, and the throne or the pedestal depicts monks and disciples holding out a large tray of lotus flowers at the Buddha's feet.

GODDESS DURGA AT GHAZNI

Interestingly, the complex also hosted a Hindu Shaivite shrine where an image of Durga Mahisasur Mardini was found during excavations. The size of the original image can be guessed from the colossal head of the goddess preserved in a glass case at the national museum. The image is evidence that female divinities were worshipped in Afghanistan.

In Chapel 23 at Tepe Sardar, excavators also found the decapitated body of Mahisasur, the 'Buffalo Demon', with his severed head lying beside it. This was once part of a composite sculpture depicting the victory of the many-armed Durga over Mahisasur, the demon and enemy of the gods. According to explorer-historian Nancy H. Dupree, Durga defeating Mahisasur was a popular cult theme under the Hindu Shahis—the Hindu dynasty ruling over Kabul Valley and Gandhara after having taken over from the Turki Shahis.[13]

It is possible that the Hindu Shahis installed Durga's image in the Buddhist monastery. It is a good example of the absorption of

---

[13] Dupree, *An Historical Guide to Afghanistan*, p.191.

Hindu deities in the Buddhist pantheon, and also points to the fact that Buddhist shrines were converted into Hindu shrines. This has been discussed by Indologist and art historian P. Banerjee in *New Light on Central Asian Art and Iconography*. In his interesting study, Banerjee explains that though subordinate in position, these Hindu deities made their original importance felt now and then even in the Buddhist framework.[14]

Banerjee presents several examples of the popularity of Shaivism in Central Asia and about Buddhist scholars such as Asanga and Aryadeva who tried to assimilate Hinduism and Buddhism. It is generally believed that Asanga, the well-known Buddhist philosopher from c.AD 400, created an amalgam of Shaivism and Buddhism, as Aryadeva did in bringing Vaishnavism and Buddhism together.[15] Banerjee, says that Asanga tried to reconcile 'two opposing myths by placing a number of Saiva gods, both male and female in the inferior heavens of the prevalent Buddhism as worshippers and supporters of Buddha and Avalokitesvara.'[16]

According to Banerjee, Asanga by reconciling Shaivism and Buddhism made it possible for:

> [T]he half-converted and rude tribes to remain Buddhists while they brought offerings to their more congenial shrines and while their practical religion had no relation at all to the truth of the noble Eightfold path.'[17]

Bannerjee also suggests that the popularity of Shaivism continued in Afghanistan and other parts of Central Asia during the late Gupta and early medieval periods. In Afghanistan, a collection of Shaiva antiquities, attributable to the seventh–eighth century AD, has come to light from the regions of Togao and Gardez. These include a head

---

[14] P. Banerjee, *New Light on Central Asian Art and Iconography*, Abha Prakashan, Delhi, 1992, pp.84–90.
[15] Banerjee, *New Light on Central Asian Art and Iconography*, pp.84–90.
[16] Banerjee, *New Light on Central Asian Art and Iconography*, p.89.
[17] Banerjee citing T.W. Rhys Davids, *Buddhist India*, D.K. Publishers, Delhi, 1903 (reprint), p.208.

of Shiva from Gardez and a smaller head of Durga overcoming Mahisasur. This is an evidence of the spread of Hindu worship during the seventh and eighth centuries when large parts of Afghanistan were under the rule of the Hindu Shahi kings. This list includes the 'inscribed *Mahavinayaka*' or Ganesa with '*Urdhvamedhra*' or erect phallus, clad in a tiger skin from Kotal-i-Khair Khaneh, about 17 km from Kabul and dated to the seventh century AD. Banerjee mentions the inscribed Uma-Mahesvara image, also dated to the seventh century from Tapa Skandar.[18]

NAGAS OF GHAZNI

Another sculpture of extreme beauty found in a chapel called Naga Chapel at the monastery of Tepe Sardar, is that of a Naga, or snake spirit, emerging from a water pond. The Naga holds the stalk of a lotus which served as a throne for a sitting Buddha image of which only fragments remain today. The Buddha was once flanked by bodhisattvas who stood on a pedestal of blooming lotuses emerging from the stalk.[19]

There are several stories of the Buddha's association with serpents and Naga kings such as in the depiction of the submission of Naga Apalala, in the story of the Kasyapa brothers, in *Champeyya Jataka*, in the story of the Nagas of Ramagrama guarding of Buddha's relics, protection of Buddhist sutra by the Nagas, and so on.

Interestingly, the Nagas are believed to have been a very ancient people of India. Writing about the intermingling of religious beliefs and practices, historian Romila Thapar informs, 'another side to the popularity of Buddhism was its readiness to assimilate local cults'. She gives example of a late Kushana monastery in Mathura which carried some donations from those propitiating a fertility deity associated with the popular cult of the area, the Naga cult associated with snake worship. According to her, this raises the question of whether a site originally of Naga worship had been

---

[18] Banerjee, *New Light on Central Asian Art and Iconography*, p.91.
[19] Dupree, *An Historical Guide to Afghanistan*, p.193.

appropriated by the Buddhist monastery through assimilating the cult.[20]

Besides being a fertility cult, the Nagas were also a historical people. In the fourth century AD, we read about the Gupta king, Chandragupta II, having married a Naga princess Kuveranaga.[21] According to B.R. Ambedkar, the Nagas, a tribe believed to be 'semi-divine in character, with their totem as serpent, spread throughout India, from Taksasila in the North-West to Assam in the North-East and to Ceylon and South India. All that can be said about them is that they were a sea-faring tribe.'[22]

In the *Rig Veda* set in the region of *saptasindhu*, or Gandhara, we are first introduced to the snake-god in the form of *Ahi Vitra*, the enemy of the Aryan god Indra.[23]

---

[20] Romila Thapar, *The Penguin History of Early India*, Penguin Books, Delhi, 2002, pp.270–71.

[21] R.C. Majumdar, *Ancient India*, Motilal Banarsidass Publishers, Delhi, 2013, p.235.

[22] B.R. Ambedkar, *The Untouchables, Who Were They and Why They Became Untouchables?* Kalpaz Publications, Delhi (reprint 2017), pp.47–52.

[23] Ambedkar, *The Untouchables, Who Were They and Why They Became Untouchables?* pp.47–52.

Chapter 20

ASOKAN EDICTS AT KANDAHAR

The Kabul–Kandahar–Herat route was already bustling with trade caravans when the Mauryan Emperor Asoka decided to install his rock edicts at Kandahar in the third century BC. He expected to find here a vast floating audience for his *Dhamma* edicts which could easily find propagation in the contiguous regions of Persia, Margiana, the Trans-Caspian and the Lower Indus.

Voluminous trade passed through this southern section of the enormous Ring Road—a Mauryan road from the third century BC that encapsulated the peripheral cities of Afghanistan and connected them with Kabul. The 2,000-km highway wrapping around the major cities of Afghanistan even during the Mauryan times was a busy route. In modern times, Highway-1, which forms part of the Ring Road, is an approximately 500-km road linking the three large cities of Kabul, Ghazni and Kandahar. Forming part of the national road system, it avoids mountain passes and runs along flat land. From Herat, a radial road runs into Mashshad in Iran, and going through Farah, Badghis and Faryab, it reaches Balkh and Samangan and back via Baghlan, it joins Kabul.

Edicts written in both Aramaic and Greek along this important highway targeted a vast local and foreign population not only of Kandahar but the contiguous areas of eastern Persia and the Trans-Caspian regions. These edicts were also meant for the traders and travellers on the east–west Uttarapath to and from the Khyber Pass, as well as all traffic passing through the Bolan and Gomal passes to and from the Lower Indus region. If we consider the location of the three important passes in the Northwest Frontiers regions of the Indian subcontinent that were crucial in Indo-Afghan commerce, we can see why Asoka chose Kandahar, Lamghan and Jalalabad, three of the busiest routes for his edicts.

While the 70-km long Khyber Pass connected Kabul with Peshawar, the Bolan Pass, a 89-km stretch of the Bolan river valley running through the Toba Kakkar Range of Baluchistan connected Kandahar with Quetta and Sibi. Used as a gateway to and from South Asia, it was the nearest route into southern Afghanistan through Jaisalmer, Sibi, Quetta and Kandahar and thence on the Ghazni road to Kabul or via Herat into Persia.

The third pass that is the Gomal Pass in the Sulaiman Mountains, ran midway between Khyber and the Bolan Pass. Taking its name from the Gomal River and located on the Durand Line, which is the border between Afghanistan and Pakistan in the Federally Administered Tribal Areas (FATA) of northwest Pakistan region, it connects Ghazni in Afghanistan with Tank and Dera Ismail Khan in Pakistan.

The north–south Kabul to Kandahar route was also linked with Margiana, and the onward routes along the Caspian to the shores of eastern Mediterranean. Both the east–west Khyber route and north–south Kandahar route joined at Kabul and ran northwards to Bamiyan and Balkh. Thus, Kandahar, like Kabul and Balkh, was a crucial trade entrepôt of Afghanistan receiving goods from as far west as Susa and Syria and as far east as the Bay of Bengal along the Uttarapath, as well as from the western and southern parts of India along the Dakshinapath.

ASOKA'S DEVOTION TO *DHAMMA*

The bilingual Asokan inscription found at Shahr-i-Kuhna near Kandahar was given the Regnal Year 10 (*c.*260 BC).[1] According to historians Irfan Habib and Vivekanand Jha, both its Greek and Aramaic texts appear to be translations of a common Prakrit original, which apparently modified the text of Minor Rock Edict I for an alien audience, and abridged Minor Rock Edict II. Habib also points to a slab from Kandahar containing a Greek version of

---

[1] Irfan Habib and Vivekanand Jha, *Mauryan India*, The People's History of India series (no.5), Tulika Books, Delhi, 2013, pp.60–61.

Rock Edict XII (with some omissions), followed by the initial portion of Rock Edict XIII and another fragmentary Aramaic inscription on limestone recovered from the Kandahar Bazaar. The latter was a close rendering of the corresponding portion of Pillar Edict VII, with some Prakrit clauses directly transcribed in Aramaic.

The Kandahar Edict has been ranked by epigraphist and historian D.C. Sircar as Minor Rock Edict IV of Asoka. According to historian Radhakumud Mookerji, the edicts bring to light some new facts in Asoka's life and reign, including the extent of Asoka's empire which was known as Greater India extending towards the Northwest beyond the natural boundaries of India up to the borders of Persia. Thus, the location of this edict in Arachosia or Kandahar furnishes the epigraphic evidence confirming the extent of India's Northwestern frontiers up to the borders of Persia.

According to Mookerji, the edict also dates Asoka's religious propagandism from the tenth year after his coronation, that is after 260 BC. He states, '[A]fter 262 B.C. his interest in Buddhism became intense (*tivra*) and expressed itself in his practice of the *Dharma of Non-violence* in his own life (*Dharmasilana*), his devotion to *Dharma* (*Dharmakamata*), and its public preaching (*Dharmanusasti*).'[2] The process of this inner change or moral revolution in Asoka, according to the Minor Rock Edict I, took 'more than a year', that is up to 260 BC. According to this new edict, 'Asoka officially organized (*pravarlana*) his work of moral propagandism (*Dharmanusasti*) with utmost (*tivra*) exertion (*Parakrama*).'[3]

Asoka informs that he gave up the slaughter of living creatures for the purpose of his own food and turned a vegetarian. As a result, 'people also abstained from violence towards life, even the royal hunters and fishing folk who derived their living from these violent pursuits.' The general result following Asoka's preaching of *Dhamma* was '[that] people had been rendered more moral and all living things had their good and happiness increased through

---

[2] Radhakumud Mookerji, *Asoka*, Motilal Banarsidass Publishers, Delhi, 2007, p.285.
[3] Mookerji, *Asoka*, p.285.

spread of non-violence.' The practice of morality and non-violence caused a 'decrease of suffering and misfortune'.[4]

BUDDHA'S ALMS BOWL AT A *KHANAQA*

The strategic importance of this southern Afghan city had also prompted later rulers to install holy relics of the Buddha in Kandahar, especially his patra (begging bowl). Following the footsteps of Asoka and considering the importance of this Silk Road city, possibly the Western Turks in the sixth–seventh century AD brought the holy *bhiksha patra* of the Buddha from Peshawar to Kandahar where it was found in the twentieth century in the *khanaqa*, a serai and spiritual retreat of a saint Mir Wais. It was later brought to the National Museum, Kabul. The precious relic was seen by Chinese pilgrim Faxian at Peshawar on the Khyber Pass route to Nagarhara in the early fifth century AD and finds mention in his travelogue.

However, in the seventh century AD, Chinese pilgrim Xuanzang failed to find the patra at Peshawar and mentioned its absence in his records. The bowl had obviously been taken away to Kandahar which was a crucial halting point for trade caravans on the Ghazni–Herat route. It is significant to note that between the sixth and seventh century AD, the Hephthalites and Western Turks and Later Hephthalites (as vassals of the Turks in some areas) were the ruling powers in Gandhara after the weakening of the Sasanian power. While the Huns are said to have been worshippers of Siva and destroyers of Buddhist shrines, the Western Turks favoured Buddhism. It is possible that the precious patra was taken to Kandahar by the Turks who were controlling the Bolan Pass–Kandahar trade route. Or, perhaps it had been installed there to deflect pilgrim traffic from the Khyber Pass to the Bolan route.

Since the Buddha's relics, his nails, hair, parietal bone and tooth attracted pilgrims and offerings by the laity, they became a source of revenue not only for the monasteries and monks but also for

---

[4] Mookerji, *Asoka*, p.285.

rulers. Therefore, there are stories about the relics being traded by greedy monks, stolen or whisked away forcibly by kings in the hope of bringing good fortune.

At the time of Buddha's *parinirvana* at Kushinagar around the fifth century BC, many emperors and tribal chiefs fought for his relics. Even the Sakyans of Swat who were Buddha's kinsmen reached Kushinagar to claim a portion of the relics. In the third century BC, the Mauryan Emperor Asoka himself dug out several stupas and collected relics to build 84,000 stupas around the world, one being as far as Xian at the Famensi in China.

During the Buddha's lifetime, his body relics had been taken away to Balkh and stupas erected over them. His tooth and parietal bone were worshipped at a monastery in Hadda. King Duttagamini of Sri Lanka built the Mahathupa for a relic of the Buddha in the first century AD. Another monastery in Kandy, also in Sri Lanka, contains the Buddha's tooth relic in a shrine where it is worshipped to this day. Besides body relics of the Buddha, items of his daily use such as twigs used for brushing teeth, his broom and his *bhiksha patra* were also installed in monasteries for display and worship.

In 1925, the huge begging bowl of the Buddha was found at Kandahar where, because of its holiness, it had the pride of place at the *khanaqa* of the renowned Sufi saint Mir Wais Baba from where it was brought to Kabul. It now stands in the front gallery of the National Museum facing the entrance, as an object of great piety. The massive black marble bowl is known as the Buddha's 'Begging Bowl' because of the lotus flowers carved on its underside. Two Islamic inscriptions were etched on it later. The inner inscription, dated to 1490, lists rules and regulations of the Kandahar Madrassa. The Archaeological Survey of India (ASI) has procured impressions of the six-line Persian inscriptions on the Buddha's begging bowl claimed to have been used by the Buddha at Vaishali.

We also find a mention of the Buddha's begging bowl at a monastery in Kashgar while reading about the life of monk Kumarjiva, who tried to lift the bowl but could not. A similar alms bowl, without decoration and perhaps made of schist, was found at the Buddhist site of Sanchi in Madhya Pradesh, India, at the Queen's Monastery (No. 51), apparently donated to the Sangha in the third century BC by Queen Devi, the daughter of a merchant of Vidisha and first wife of the Mauryan Emperor Asoka.

Such massive bowls made out of a single piece of limestone or marble were generally kept at the gate of monasteries and *khanaqas* of saints. They symbolized renunciation of life, abrogation of the self, the annihilation of ego and arrogance, and the cultivation of humility by the residents whose daily food came from begging. I found a similar bowl in Turkestan at the mausoleum of the revered Sufi saint Akhmad Yassavi while travelling along the Shymkent–Sauran road in south Kazakhstan. Two huge bowls can also be seen at the holy Ajmer Sharif shrine at Ajmer, Rajasthan, in India.

Phani Kant Misra, regional director, ASI (Kolkata), along with G.S. Khwaja, director in-charge, Epigraphy (Arabic and Persian), ASI (Nagpur) had gone to Kabul to inspect the bowl. Misra revealed that the bowl came 'quite close' to the begging bowl of the Buddha. This was supported not only by circumstantial evidence but also matched well with the description given by the Chinese pilgrims in their memoirs. The bowl is believed to have been carried away in the second century AD by the Kusana ruler, Kanishka, to Peshawar and later transferred to Kandahar during the period of the Western Turks.

Did Buddha ever carry the huge stone bowl on his begging rounds considering its weight and size? It seems improbable that the bowl could ever be taken outside the monastery. In all probability, Buddha on his begging rounds, used a much smaller bowl which he gifted to the Lichchavis of Vaishali on his last visit. The large stone bowl was perhaps installed outside the monastery of Vaishali as is the usual practice of most monasteries for alms collection. The bowl that Kanishka brought to Peshawar and which was later whisked away to Kandahar, could have been a magnified copy of the original bowl at Vaishali. This was done to attract pilgrims and traders' traffic on the north-western routes.

The legend of the begging bowl reflects the connection between trade and Buddhist relics. During the early centuries of the Christian era, when Buddhism flourished under Kusana patronage, and northwest India became the centre of an urban economy, many sacred sites appeared in this region.[5] It became necessary to ensure and augment trade by attracting pilgrims to new sites by linking them with Buddha's relics. Sometimes, copies of rare Buddha statuaries were installed in chapels. Xuanzang on leaving India, had collected several important relics and copies of Buddha images, which were later enshrined in China.

---

[5] Xinru Liu, *Silk and Religion: An Exploration of Material Life and Thought of People AD 600–1200*, Oxford University Press, Delhi, 1998, pp.32–33.

Chapter 21

ART OF GANDHARA

EARLY BUDDHA IMAGES IN GANDHARA

The Great Buddha fasted in Bodhgaya, but the first sculpture of the 'Fasting Buddha' is said to have been carved and etched in stone at Sikri, a small village of Gandhara near Mardan, just as the first stupa for the Buddha's relics was erected in Balkh by merchants from Bactra. The Buddha performed the great miracle at Sravasti, in Bahraich, a remote district in eastern India, but depiction of the miracle became a favourite theme for stone cutter's art in the villages of Kabul and Kapisa. Embellished stupas and colossal images of the Buddha came up at Jaulian, Mohra Moradu, Takht-i-Bahi and Jamalgarhi in Pakistan as well as Mes Aynak, Balkh, Bamiyan, Kakrak, Guldara, Ghazni and Kunduz in Afghanistan. The monasteries of Gandhara had their stairways carved with the stories of bodhisattvas in the act of performing various charities. Many a Jataka tales had their settings in Gandhara while Gandhara itself became the stuff of many Jataka tales.

Travelling through the Buddhist corridor of Pakistan and Afghanistan, one will come across the remains of a vast number of monastic sites and excavated *dheris* or mounds, having stupas, shrines, assembly halls, refectories, stupa courts and bath houses. Images of the Buddha and bodhisattvas from these sites can today be seen in the halls of grand museums of Pakistan (in Lahore, Taxila and Peshawar) and of India (in Delhi, Patna and Kolkata), and far beyond in the museums of St Petersburg, Rome, Milan, Paris and London.

Exposed during excavations, they give evidence of a unique style, that is described by art scholars as a 'hybrid art' drawing influence from Indian, Greek, Roman and Persian styles in the medium of grey or blue schist and later clay, stucco and terracotta.[1] This mixed art style came to be famously known as 'Greco-Buddhist, Greco-Romano Buddhist and Indo-Hellenistic art'.[2]

An extended Foreign Influence Gallery at Peshawar Museum and a separate section on objects of art having foreign influence at the Lahore Museum (found during archaeological excavations in Gandhara), are a befitting commentary on different aspects of this 'hybrid art'.

Many would agree that the 'mixed art' style prevailing in Gandhara was the result of the prevailing Greek, Roman and Persian cultures among the large foreign population living in Gandhara since pre-Alexandrian times. The region saw the churning of different worlds and amalgamation of various faiths, chiefly Zoroastrianism, Paganism, Hinduism and Buddhism, active in Gandhara.

FROM THE ATELIERS OF GANDHARA

Gandhara which included the Northwest Frontier regions of the Indian subcontinent is considered the atelier from where the rare imagery of the Buddha and bodhisattvas arose. This was the land which saw the emergence of the Buddha as a magnificent divine deity whose images in the tall niches of monasteries along the river valleys of Gandhara brought flourishing pilgrim traffic along Asian trade routes, from as far as Central Asia and China. The valleys ran along the course of the rivers Indus, Kabul, Murghab, Oxus and their tributaries in the region of present-day Afghanistan, Pakistan and the neighbouring regions of eastern Turkmenistan, southern Uzbekistan and southern Tajikistan.

This was the result of combined efforts of Buddhist rulers from the Mauryan Emperor Asoka (in the third century BC) to the Kusana

---

[1] Jonathan Tucker, *Silk Road Art and History*, Timeless Books, Delhi, 2003, p.38.
[2] B.N. Puri, Buddhism in Central Asia, Motilal Banarasidass, Delhi, 2000, p. 305. See also, G.A. Pugachankova, S.R. Dar, R.C. Sharma, M.A. Joyenda and H. Siddiqi, *Kushan Art*, Vol. II: History of Civilizations of Central Asia, UNESCO, New Delhi, 1996 and Motilal Banarsidass Publishers, Delhi, 1999, p.359.

king Kanishka (in the first–second century AD) to imbue Gandhara with sacredness. The rulers not only patronized Buddhist institutions, but also set up monasteries and stupas and hired craftsmen to adorn them. Many craftsmen are believed to have been requisitioned from foreign lands since the days of Asoka.

Asoka was instrumental in the movement to reduce the teachings of Buddhism to stories and their artistic presentation in sculpture and painting, along with the use of symbols such as lotus, tree, wheel and pagoda representing the life of the Buddha.[3] He put up pillar and rock inscriptions with *Dhamma* instructions in Kharosthi and Greek. Many Asokan stupas in Gandhara were seen and recorded by the Chinese pilgrim Xuanzang in the seventh century AD while on his way to India through Nagarhara (present-day Jalalabad) and Sagala (present-day Sialkot).

Historian Hans Loeschner is of the view that the pillars of Asoka are the first monumental construction in stone in India. Before transportation, the cylindrical blocks for the pillars were engraved in Brahmi or Kharosthi, which was used only in the Northwest part of his empire. Therefore, the person who was responsible for organizing these Mauryan quarries in the hills of Chunar near Varanasi must have been foreigner to the region. India had no tradition of stone quarrying and chiselling on a large scale prior to the third century BC.[4] According to Loeschner, when Asoka decided to use stone for monumental buildings and for his pillar edicts, he must have invited some expert from the Northwest of his vast domain which earlier belonged to the Achaemenid Iranian Empire where stone monuments had a long tradition.

Greek scholar of Indology Demetrios Th. Vassiliades even points out that stone sculpture, little used in India before the time of Asoka, might be attributed to the Greeks. He draws a striking similarity

---

[3] A.K. Warder, *Indian Buddhism*, Motilal Banarsidass Publishers, Delhi, 1991, p.266.

[4] Hans Loeschner, 'Kanishka in Context with the Historical Buddha and Kushan Chronology', in Vidula Jayaswal (ed.), *Glory of the Kushans: Recent Discoveries and Interpretation*, Aryan Books International, Delhi, 2012, p.140.

between the lions on Asoka's capital (although belonging to the Indian tradition) and the lions erected by the Macedonians in Chaeronia and Amphipolis as victory monuments.[5] He even put forward the supposition that Greek artists, possibly from Gandhara, could have been employed in India from a much earlier date as Greek statues holding lamps were found to be used as decoration by the Sakyans in Kapilavastu.[6]

However, on closer examination, Radhakumud Mookerji finds this supposition to be completely incorrect since archaeological researches have ascribed to Asoka, the great stupa of Bharhut with elaborately carved railings bearing inscriptions,[7] parts of which are today displayed at the Bharhut section of the Indian Museum in Kolkata.

During the Indo-Greek period of the second century BC in Gandhara, a series of square bronze coins were issued by the Euthydemid king Agathocles Dikaios (r.190–180 BC)—believed to be son of Indo-Greek king Demetrius—with Prakrit legend and Buddhist symbolism of a stupa on the reverse and a tree in a rail (Bodhi Tree) on the obverse. B.N. Puri points out that this is evidence not only of the infiltration of Buddhism in the realm of the Indo-Greeks,[8] but also proof of the iconic representation of the Buddha in art of the second century BC. Indo-Greek king Menander's coinage with its display of the 'wheel of Dhamma' on one of his bronze issues can also be seen in this light.[9]

---

[5] Demetrios Th. Vassiliades, *The Greeks in India: A Survey in Philosophical Understanding*, Munshiram Manoharlal Publishers, Delhi, 2000, p.56.
[6] Vassiliades, *The Greeks in India*, p.55.
[7] Radhakumud Mookerji, *Asoka*, Motilal Banarsidass Publishers, Delhi, 2007, pp.79–81 and p.99.
[8] B.N. Puri, *Buddhism in Central Asia*, Motilal Banarsidass Publishers, Delhi, 2000, p.91.
[9] Puri, *Buddhism in Central Asia*, p.92.

FIRST BUDDHA IMAGE

Many scholars believe that the first images of the Buddha started appearing in Gandhara during Kusana times of the first century CE as a result of the 'new thought' that pervaded Buddhism in the form of Mahayana. It saw the emergence of the Buddha as a supernatural deity. During this time, many bodhisattvas and folk deities were added to the Buddhist pantheon. The 'new thought' also involved a belief not only in bodhisattvas but in the power of human beings to become bodhisattvas.[10]

By the first century CE, this new trend was reflected in archaeological evidence with the first depictions of the Buddha on the Kusana coin (BODDO coin) as well as monasteries and reliquaries containing the relics of the Buddha. Depiction of the standing Buddha on the coin from Kanishka's reign with his right hand raised in a gesture of reassurance (*abhay mudra*) is inscribed in Bactrian BODDO. On the obverse is Kanishka himself wearing a Kusana royal bonnet and diadem, holding a spear and elephant goad, inscribed in Bactrian (Greek script), 'King of Kings Kanishka Kusana.'[11]

According to P.C Bagchi, when Buddhism was slowly infiltrating into Central Asia under the patronage of the Kusanas, Buddha images were found in north-west India for the first time and in large numbers too. Bagchi points out, 'They originated in the Indianized Greek milieu shortly before the Kusanas entered India and attained their highest development under the Kushans.'[12] He opines that this art has been styled Indo-Greek or Graeco-Buddhist as its execution was Greek while its inspiration was Buddhistic.

The art made use of Greek architectural motifs such as the Corinthian pillar, it introduced the acanthus leaf for decoration and the toga as apparel. Bodhisattvas were clad in the Indian dhoti and wore ornaments such as the *motilata*, *kamarband*, armlets and

---

[10] Charles Eliot, *Hinduism and Buddhism: An Historical Sketch*, Vol. II, Bibliotheca Indo-Buddhica No.54, Sri Satguru Publications, Delhi, 1988, p.6 and pp.84–85.
[11] Tucker, *Silk Road Art and History*, Timeless Books, Delhi, 2003, p.34.
[12] P.C. Bagchi, *India and China*, Saraswat Library, Kolkata, 1981, pp.181–82.

heavy bangles. With regard to composition, Bagchi points out that it gave representation to the scenes from the life of the Buddha and depicted stories from his former birth.

EARLY IMAGES ON CASKETS

It is believed that the early images of the Buddha were the ones found on the two most famous Kusana reliquaries found in Gandhara and dated from the first–second century CE. The first of these named the 'Kanishka Reliquary' dated from the second century CE, and displayed at the Peshawar Museum, was discovered by D.B. Spooner at Shah Ji ki Dheri in Peshawar in 1908–10. The image of Buddha on the lid with heavy monastic robes and double nimbus resembles the image on BODDO coin. The image on the bronze relic casket is flanked by two Hindu gods, Brahma and Indra.[13]

The second reliquary dated from the first century CE is a gold casket inlaid with rubies. It was found by archaeologist Charles Masson at Bimaran, west of Jalalabad in Afghanistan, in 1833–38. The six figures around the side consist of two Buddhas, each flanked by the Hindu god, Indra, and a devotee or bodhisattva.[14]

GANDHARA OR MATHURA

From the above analysis, we may be tempted to deduce that the earliest images of the Buddha came from Gandhara. However, a great deal of controversy exists regarding the date and place of the appearance of the first images of the Buddha as Gandhara and Mathura both have laid claims to the first Buddha images. These were the two broad schools of Buddhist art that were identified by art historians—a more 'Hellenized' form in north-west Gandhara and a more 'Indianized' style around Mathura.

Refuting the opinion that the first image of the Buddha was created in Gandhara, art historian and archaeologist R.C. Sharma says

---

[13] Tucker, *Silk Road Art and History*, p.34.
[14] Tucker, *Silk Road Art and History*, p.49.

Mathura is a stronger contender as the place where the first Buddha image was created.[15] Sharma further points out that the dating of Gandharan art itself is a highly disputed subject. General consensus favours early first century CE as the starting point while its blooming phase was the Kusana period.[16] According to him, the practice of representing the Buddha in human form had a long background at Mathura. The evidence for this lies in two Buddha images belonging to Mathura School—one, at Kausambi dated AD 80 (second regnal year of Kanishka) and the other at Sarnath AD 81 (third regnal year of Kanishka), as well as other and undated images which are now at the Mathura Museum, such as the Maholi bodhisattva and Katra bodhisattva or Anyori Buddha, also believed to stylistically belonging to the same period.[17]

According to Sharma, the finely executed figures suggest that the practice of representing the Buddha in human form had a long background in Mathura, and the abovementioned statues only show a refined and developed stage by the beginning of the Kushana period in the first century AD.

The fact that the colossal bodhisattva statues were being exported from Mathura to distant places such as Kausambi, Sarnath and Bodhgaya shows that the Mathura School had already earned a good reputation. Images such as the 'Parkham Yaksha' served as a model; hence all standing Buddha or bodhisattva figures are in *Yaksha* style. Sharma also points to the *ayagapattas* (votive tablets) dated to the end of first century BC or early first century AD having *yaksha* and *jina* (nature spirits) figures. Hence, Buddhist icons which are close to *ayagapattas* may safely be dated to the pre-Kanishka period.[18]

Anand K. Coomaraswamy is also inclined to presume on general grounds a priority for the Mathura School,[19] as at the time of Kanishka,

---

[15] R.C. Sharma, *The Splendour of Mathura Art and Museum*, D.K. Printworld, Delhi, p.83 and pp.95–99.
[16] Sharma, *The Splendour of Mathura Art and Museum*, pp.95–99.
[17] Sharma, *The Splendour of Mathura Art and Museum*, p.83.
[18] Sharma, *The Splendour of Mathura Art and Museum*, p.83–84.
[19] Anand K. Coomaraswamy, *The Origin of the Buddha Image*, Munshiram

Mathura had already such a reputation that 'Buddha and Bodhisattva images were being exported among other places even to Punjab and Taxila.'[20]

Coomaraswamy is of the opinion that a definite idea of the Buddha's appearance—a fundamental type like that of the *Mahapurusa Cakravartin*, existed before the time of actual representations. 'This theoretical type, with its thirty-two principal marks (*laksanas*) and other minor marks, is older than the Buddha image, older presumably than the Buddha himself.' According to him, Buddhists had taken over at an early period from non-Buddhist sources a conception of the Buddha as *Mahapurusa*; the *laksanas* were certainly not the invention of Buddhists, but were taken over by them and applied to their 'Master.'[21]

He considers the phrase 'Greek origin of the Buddha image' as representing nothing more than a 'rhetorical misuse of language.'[22] Here, it is pertinent to refer to passages in the *The Mahavamsa* that ascribes to Asoka a desire to behold the likeness of Buddha. He says:

> Let us behold the form of the omniscient Great Sage, of him who hath boundless knowledge, who hath set rolling the Wheel of the True Doctrine. [Then, a Naga king in response to this expressed desire] created a beauteous figure of the Buddha, endowed with the thirty-two greater signs and brilliant with the eighty lesser signs, surrounded by the fathomless rays of glory and adorned with the crown of flames.[23]

Manoharlal Publishers, Delhi, 2016, p.37.
[20] Coomaraswamy, *The Origin of the Buddha Image*, p.32.
[21] Coomaraswamy, *The Origin of the Buddha Image*, p.29.
[22] Coomaraswamy, *The Origin of the Buddha Image*, p.38.
[23] Wilhelm Geiger, *The Mahavamsa or The Great Chronicle of Ceylon*, Book V, Asian Educational Services, Delhi, 2000, Stanza 90–94.

Chapter 22

BUDDHA AND BODHISATTVAS OF GANDHARA

The Gandharan Buddha, as he was lovingly called, had spread his roots at every turn of the Silk Road as it ran across the Indus to the Amu Darya. He lived in Gandhara as incarnations depicted in the many Jataka tales—breathing life into the exquisite schist stones of the Khyber that were carved after him, in the clay that was moulded and baked into benevolence and faith in the cities of Hadda and Mes Aynak, and in the brilliant murals that lit up the shrine walls of Bamiyan.

According to many scholars, it was sometime around the first century BC that Mahayana and the concept of the divine Buddha gained popularity and adoration of the Buddha as a deity and a supernatural divine being became the new trend of Gandhara. The historical Buddha assumed the appearance of a god, 'ageless and beautiful'. His face 'delightfully radiant' with the 'supreme knowledge of the world phenomenon' and in Enlightenment with his eyes half closed in meditation and his body wrapped in a calm and peaceful demeanour. The Buddha resembled in posture a rishi or a yogi in his different *asanas* and *mudras*. His divine observation, his transcendental nature and his compassion for humanity, all made him god-like.

As a god, the Buddha gave assurance of protection to the faithful with his right hand raised to shoulder level with the palm towards the observer in *abhay mudra*. In the *dharmachakra mudra* or the preaching attitude, he set in motion the Wheel of Law. It alluded to the First Sermon at the Deer Park in Sarnath. In *bhumisparsh mudra*, he called upon the Earth to witness the moment of his Enlightenment and in *dhyan mudra*, he meditated and observed the world from his perfumed chamber, the Gandhakuti.

SIGNS OF A *MAHAPURUSA*

The Buddha is endowed with the *laksana* (signs) of a *mahapurusa* (great man) with the *usnisa–urna*—meaning hanging earlobes—and *dharmachakra*. The *urna*, the circle in the middle of the forehead (a tuft of hair resembling the third eye of Siva—the eye of wisdom, the eye that could grasp the world in a moment) and the *usnisa*, the protuberance on the head in the form of a chignon indicated his extraordinary mental capacity. The elongated earlobes remind of his royal lineage and the princely times when he wore gem-studded *kunadala* (heavy earrings of precious stones) before embracing the ascetic life.[1]

He wears a monk's robe covering both shoulders. Without any finery, he appears unadorned. What need has he to bedeck himself with worldly jewels when he has attained the jewel of Enlightenment? He had already abandoned royal fineries and human vanities when he entered the Penance Grove on the banks of the Anuloma River.

FASTING SIDDHARTHA

As a true renunciate, the Buddha appears in great anatomical detail in the image of the 'Fasting Siddhartha' from Sikri, now located in the Lahore Museum. This rare piece of Gandharan sculpture on bluish schist stone from Sikri (in the Khyber Pakhtunkhwa province), has been dated to the second century AD, and depicts that stage of the Buddha's life when he fasted for six long years to obtain Enlightenment. The fine execution of the figure of the emaciated Buddha, absorbed in deep meditation, is a narrative in stone of the renunciation and abandonment of everything worldly. He appears withered and shrunk to the bone.

---

[1] E.H. Johnston, *Asvaghosa's Buddhacharita or Acts of the Buddha*, Book i 60, Munshiram Manoharlal Publishers, Delhi, 1995 (first published 1936), p.13. See also: G.A. Pugachankova, S.R. Dar, R.C. Sharma, M.A. Joyenda and H. Siddiqi, *Kushan Art*, Vol. II: History of Civilizations of Central Asia, UNESCO, New Delhi, 1996 and Motilal Banarsidass Publishers, Delhi, 1999, p.364.

COLOSSAL BUDDHA AS *LOKOTTARA*

In the high mountain caves of Gandhara, the Buddha appears as *Lokottara*, the 'Lord of the World'. Perched in tall caves of the Hindu Kush at Bamiyan and in the neighbouring valleys of the Kakrak at Jehanabad (located in Swat Valley in Khyber Pakhtunkhwa), in the high chapels of Takht-i-Bahi and Jamalgarhi of Mardan, and at the Kanishka Vihara in Peshawar, gigantic images of the Buddha were found.

The colossal Buddhas were part of the new trend in Buddhist thought of the Buddha's divinity, the popular idea of a transcendental being. They are a symbol of the wealth that accrued from commercial activities along the network of Gandharan trade routes. True to the words of poet Asvaghosa, the Buddha 'soars through the heaven and shines like the sun'.[2]

The most amazing colossal Buddha figures include the two 'Standing Buddha' colossi (blown up by the Taliban in 2001) the 1,000-feet 'Reclining Buddha' (so far not discovered) in the mountains of Bamiyan, and the splendid Kakrak Buddha in the Kakrak Valley (also destroyed in 2001) in Afghanistan. But these did not come up in isolation; they were part of a trend of awe-inspiring colossal statuary art in Gandhara and its neighbouring lands.

The colossi art of Gandhara also found strong appeal in adjacent and neighbouring lands. They were found at the village of Dalverzin Tepe near Arytam, in the Trans-Caspian desert monastery of Gyaur Kala at Merv, at the monastery of Fayaztepe in Termez, at Ajina Tepe near Kurgantube, at Kuva near Ferghana and at the Bezeklik Caves in the oasis of Turfan on the northern Silk Road running along the Xinjiang Province (eastern Turkestan or Chinese Turkestan).

This was an imperial style to symbolize the might and grandeur of the kingship that could have been borrowed from the 'imperial Achemenid style' that, according to M.A. Dandamayev, had spread far afield, 'creating a form of cultural unity from the Indus to the

---

[2] Johnston, *Asvaghosa's Buddhacharita or Acts of the Buddha*, Book xiv 107, p.216.

coast of Asia Minor.'[3] We have the example of the colossal Behistun Relief and Inscription of the fifth century BC of Darius the Great, symbolizing the grandeur and extent of power of the Achaemenid Persia.[4] The same picture of grandeur of lofty Persian sculptures was seen to have been replicated in the Central Asian Buddha colossi.

Of the numerous colossi belonging to the early centuries of our era on mountains, in caves and in shrine courtyards of Buddhist establishments of Gandhara, many have disappeared. As a result, we have to turn to the written records of travelling pilgrims to determine their possible locations. For example, the great shining gem-studded statue of the Buddha standing in a hall, also embellished with rare precious gems, at the Navasangharama in Balkh was seen by Xuanzang around AD 630, a little before the Arab invasion in Afghanistan.

The Chinese pilgrim Xuanzang also mentions having seen near the stupa of Kanishka in Peshawar, an 18-feet high image of the Buddha carved in white stone. Another 100-feet high carved wooden statue of the Maitreya bodhisattva, of golden colour and very majestic in appearance, was made by *arhat* (Enlightened being) Madhyantika in Swat.

The colossal Buddha statuaries represent a picture of grandeur, and are believed to be influenced by the large carved rock reliefs of the Persians that were mainly used to glorify the king. B.N. Puri writes, 'The massive bulk and frozen lifeless dignity characterizing the reliefs of Iranian kings are translated into Buddhist imagery of Gandhara.'[5]

Though the colossal Buddhas of Bamiyan and Kakrak are lost, the Buddha of Jehanabad village in Swat, carved on a cliff in the seventh century AD, was restored recently by the Italian Archaeological

---

[3] M.A. Dandamayev, *Media and Achaemenid Iran*, Vol. II: History of Civilizations of Central Asia, UNESCO, New Delhi, 1996 and Motilal Banarsidass Publishers, Delhi, 1999, p.56.
[4] Dandamayev, *Media and Achaemenid Iran*, Vol. II, p.50.
[5] B.N. Puri, *Buddhism in Central Asia*, Motilal Banarsidass Publishers, Delhi, 2000, p.299.

Mission in Pakistan. The Meditating Buddha figure depicted in a lotus position at the base of a granite cliff is about seven metres in height and is a remarkable piece of rock carving from the Gandhara region. The largest Reclining Buddhas of Asia were also recovered in Gandhara. One 1,000-feet-long Buddha was seen by Xuanzang at Bamiyan somewhere between the cave of the two Standing Buddha colossi. Another gigantic 48-feet-long Nirvana Buddha statue was unearthed in Haripur district of Pakistan during excavations near the Bhamala Buddhist site in 2017. According to Abdul Samad, director, Peshawar Museum, this Buddha is the world's oldest Sleeping Buddha and belongs to third century AD.

DEPICTION OF 'BUDDHA MAZDA'

It is said that Buddhism and Zoroastrianism peacefully coexisted in Balkh, which is considered the birthplace of Zoroaster in about 600 BC. It was the holy city of Zoroastrianism which emphasized the veneration of fire. Scholar Boris J. Stavisky mentions that cave monasteries from early centuries of our era had wall paintings of Buddhas with auras of flames and inscriptions that read 'Buddha Mazda'. Statuary art depicting worship of fire as a symbol for the Buddha in Gandharan art can be seen at the Peshawar Museum and at the State Hermitage Museum in St Petersburg. It is also seen in the depiction of the Buddha with tongues of flames issuing from his shoulders as in the 'Miracle of Sravasti'. Such images have been recovered from the monasteries of Shotorak and Paitava, near Kapisa and of Sarai Khuja near Kabul, and are now on display at the National Museum, Kabul. Similar motifs have also been found in the caves of Karatepe in Termez and in the depiction of the Fiery Pillar of Amravati.[6]

He further mentions many ruined monasteries in the neighbourhood of Balkh, especially the group of Buddhist caves across

---

[6] Boris J. Stavisky, 'Buddha Mazda' from Kara Tepa in Old Termez [Uzb]: A Preliminary Communication', *The Journal of International Association of Buddhist Studies*, Vol. III, No. 2, pp.89–91.

the Oxus River at Karatepe (Old Termez), which has its walls replete with faded wall paintings with tall bursting red flames.[7]

I was able to see the painted red walls at the entrance of a corridor of a line of serpentine caves having tall niches in their walls. I was informed by my guide that the faded paintings were those of the Buddha. The accompanying graffiti seemed to have been written by pilgrims who visited the sacred caves.

An image of the Buddha in schist, now at the Peshawar Museum, has its pedestal depicting disciples worshipping the fire. The worshippers are sitting with folded hands beside tongues of flame issuing from a brazier. Here, fire is a symbol of the Buddha. Another similar image at the Hermitage Museum also depicts fire worshippers on the Buddha's pedestal.

According to Stavisky, fire altars were used by fire worshippers and in temples of local Mazdean cults and also in early Buddhist structures, which survived up to the period of Arab conquest in the seventh century AD. Apart from being an evidence of syncretism, it also shows the struggle of religions. As we learn that at Karatepe, after the destruction of the monastic complex B, a fire altar was built in the niche which had previously held a Buddhist statue. 'It was made hastily out of materials that were at hand and symbolized the victory of some other cults [most likely Zoroastrianism] over Buddhism.'[8] The struggle perhaps explains the pile of human bones I saw at the Karatepe Cave.

Writing about the flourishing Kusana Buddhist centre of Karatepe of the second–third century AD, Stavisky points out that in the wall of one of the northern corridors there was a halo formed by the rows of stylized but clearly discernible 'tongues of flames'. A graffiti inscription in Kusana script, close to the Buddha's head read 'Buddha Mazda.' According to Stavisky, this was 'not a chance phenomenon'. It

---

[7] Stavisky, 'Buddha Mazda' from Kara Tepa in Old Termez [Uzb], pp.89–91.
[8] Stavisky, 'Buddha Mazda' from Kara Tepa in Old Termez [Uzb], pp.89–91. See also, A.H. Dani and B.A. Litvinsky, *The Kushano-Sassanian Kingdom*, Vol III: History of Civilizations of Central Asia, UNESCO, New Delhi, 1996 and Motilal Banarsidass Publishers, Delhi, 1999, p.111.

outlines the 'syncretic nature of the representation which combined the image of Buddha with attributes of the god of light or fire and syncretism of the Buddhist and local east Iranian Mazdaist cult.'[9]

It has been pointed out that the Buddhists also worshipped fire. One can see interesting representations of the Buddha as a pillar of fire, in the decoration of pedestals of Buddha images. The worship of a fiery pillar topped with a *triratna* (the Buddha, *Dhamma* and the Sangha) by the Naga people was depicted in bas-relief on stone at Amaravati.[10]

The fire cult was most widespread in Ancient India and Central Asia. The three Kasyapa brothers of Uruvela, at the time of Buddha, had a sacred fire house at their residence and were great fire worshippers. It was in their fire house that Buddha spent a night with an angry serpent that billowed smoke and fire. The representation of the Buddha, with tongues of flames rising from his shoulders in the two bas-reliefs from Kapisa (Shotorak and Paitava) displayed at the National Museum of Afghanistan at Kabul, are believed to be a representation of the 'Miracle of Sravasti', and can be traced to the same Mazdaist tradition.

A Buddhist temple thronged by fire worshippers was witnessed and experienced by none other than the Chinese monk Xuanzang when he visited Samarkand. Fire worshippers who were already inside the temple chased the monk and his disciples with burning fire. Xuanzang complained to the king who wanted to execute the fire worshippers for their evil act, but Xuanzang intervened with the king to save their lives. From monk Xuanzang's own experiences as narrated in the *Si-Yu-Ki*, we know that the two religions coexisted in Central Asia and in the contiguous region of Gandhara. The monk himself delivered discourses to the fire worshippers including the king of Samarkand, converting them to the Buddhist faith.[11]

---

[9] Boris J. Stavisky, 'Buddha Mazda' from Kara Tepa in Old Termez [Uzb], pp.89–91.
[10] Vincent Smith, *History of India*, Vol. II, Cosimo Classics, New York, 2008, p.235.
[11] Hwui Li, *The Life of Hieun-Tsiang* (translated by Samuel Beal), Low Price Publications, 1911 (Reprinted 2001), pp.45–46.

The influence of Zoroastrianism is also cited by scholars in the flaming halo of Buddhist statuaries. The halo, according to E.H. Ramsden, can be identified with the *hvareno* derived from the same root as the Persian word for sun, namely *Hvare*, from which it becomes apparent that the basis of the whole connection is light, the distinguishing characteristic of the Mazdian religion.[12]

BELIEF IN BODHISATTVAS

The 'new thought' also involved a belief in bodhisattvas and in the power of human beings to become bodhisattvas. Buddhologist Charles Eliot, writes:

> The code of altruistic ethics which teaches that everyone must do good in the interest of the whole world and make over to others any merit he may acquire by his virtues also gained ground. It involved worship of images and elaboration of ritual and a tendency to rely on formulae and charms.[13]

Edward Conze says that the bodhisattva is the ideal man of Mahayana—an 'Enlightened Being, a Buddha to be', one who wishes to become a Buddha. He finds pleasure in doing good for others. The essential quality of a bodhisattva is compassion which urges him to help human beings find way of liberation. He does not wish to attain his own private Nirvana; rather he can give up Nirvana to help suffering creatures through his acquired merit.[14]

Bodhisattvas too have the *urna* or the circle in the middle of the forehead and the nimbus, or the halo of light, around the head.

---

[12] E.H. Ramsden, The Halo: A Further Enquiry into Its Origin, 1941. Available at <www.cais-soas.com/CAIS/Religions/iranian/Zarathushtrian/halo_its> (last date of access: 10 February 2020).
[13] Charles Eliot, *Hinduism and Buddhism: An Historical Sketch*, Vol II: Bibliotheca Indo-Buddhica No.54, Sri Satguru Publications, Delhi, 1988, p.6. See also, Edward Conze, *Buddhism: Its Essence and Development*, Munshiram Manoharlal Publishers, Delhi, 2001, pp.125–30.
[14] Conze, *Buddhism*, pp.125–30.

They are adorned in rich jewels and royal robes. The bodhisattva may wear the long winding garment and the upper garment, or *uttariya*, which may be shrunk to a thread. Then his body may appear to be unclothed, draped only in jewels and multi-stringed necklaces. The same picture of grandeur in Persian sculptures can be seen in the depiction of the bejewelled bodhisattvas, especially in their stylized crowns and heavy necklaces and belts around the waist.

Some figures of standing or seated bodhisattvas are covered in a profusion of jewellery around the upper body. They have elaborate hairstyles, wearing crowns or headgears, jewelled belts around the waist and are clad in jewelled footwear. Such exhibits come from Tepe Maranjan and Kunduz (now in the National Museum, Kabul); from Sahri Bahlol and Loriya Tangai (now in the Indian Museum, Kolkata) and the Standing Bodhisattva Maitreya from Gandhara, dated second–fourth century AD (now in the Milan Archaelogical Museum, Milan and the Hermitage, St Petersburg).

> As long as there are souls groaning in pain, the bodhisattva cannot rest in Nirvana; there is no rest for his unselfish heart so full of love and sympathy until he leads all his fellow beings to the eternal bliss of Buddhahood. To reach this end he employs innumerable means [*upaya*]... [He is the bodhisattva] who feels in himself all the sufferings of his fellow-beings as his own, how can he bear the thought of leaving others behind while he is on way to final emancipation...[15]

BORROWED DEITIES

Zoroastrianism that was prevalent in Bactria and Transoxiana is also believed to have influenced many aspects of Buddhism and Buddhist art. Buddhist deities and bodhisattvas (displayed at the Peshawar Museum and the Indian Museum, Kolkata) are believed to have been borrowed from Zoroastrianism. According to Charles

---

[15] Suzuki Daisetz Teitaro, *Outlines of Mahayana Buddhism*, Munshiram Manoharlal Publishers, Delhi, 2014, p.64 and p.365.

Eliot, Amitabha, Avalokita, Manjusri and Kshitigarbha do not have clear antecedents in India, and may be borrowed from some other mythology, and if similar figures were known to Zoroastrianism, that may be their source.[16]

The most represented bodhisattva in Gandharan art is the Maitreya, or the Future Buddha, distinguishable by his coiffured hairstyle, Avalokitesvara having the emblem of a Buddha image in his headdress and holding a wreath in his hand, Manjushri with a book in his hand, Padampani with the emblem of water flask. The bodhisattvas are heavily ornamented and wear exotic turbans and different hairstyles.

Depiction of accompanying deities such as Vajrapani and Padampani are also believed to have been assimilated from Greek mythological gods and heroes. They are usually seen with the Buddha on decorative schist panels or were positioned to hold the tiers of the stupa.

MAITREYA FROM KUNDUZ

The benevolent bodhisattva Maitreya is the Future Buddha who will come into this world. He differs from other bodhisattvas as he holds the *kamandalu*, or the water pot, in his left hand.

It is significant to note that at Kunduz, the tradition of the Maitreya Buddha appears to have been strong. This was confirmed when a splendid bejewelled image of the Maitreya was found here. The people worshipped the Maitreya, who, according to Buddhist traditions, resided in the *Tusita*, or the Buddhist heaven, waiting to descend into the human realm when the time was right. He was the Universal Buddha, and with his unbounded kindness and all-encompassing love he would deliver mankind from all misery.

The beautiful Maitreya image from the Kunduz monastic centre (perhaps, one visited by the Chinese pilgrim Xuanzang) can today be seen at the National Museum, Kabul. The Buddha is seated with both

---

[16] Eliot, *Hinduism and Buddhism*, Vol II, p.219, V-3.

feet crossed at the ankles on a pedestal or a throne. He is dressed in the robes of a *bhikshu* (a monk's robe or sanghati) and decorated with heavy jewels. His earrings hang up to the shoulders and a four-layered garland with a beautifully designed pendant reaches his chest. There are bracelets around his wrist. The headdress, in the shape of a jewelled crown holds within its folds, what seems to be a conical terraced stupa, believed to be a symbolic reliquary for the holy relics of the Sakyamuni Buddha. A decorated halo with geometrical motifs on the edges adorns the back of the head.

The stupa appears to emit light or flames marked by carved bands emerging from it. It helps us to identify the image of Maitreya Buddha.

CONCEPT OF A BUDDHIST HEAVEN

A Buddhist heaven of 'radiance and glory', depicted in the soffit of the now-lost Buddha at Bamiyan, too has the essential features of Zoroastrianism as the 'boundless and infinite light' and is the abode of Ahuramazda.[17] It is the highest heaven of Endless Light. This highest heaven is also a land of pleasant music and song where angels play the *panchanada*, or the five musical instruments. There are flying celestial beauties playing the lute, dancing and offering flowers to the Buddha. They are semi-naked or wearing transparent clothing, playing various instruments. Devas wearing ornamented crowns dance in joy.

In the hands of the artiste, the schist slabs become a vast canvas for the illustration of a Buddhist heaven. The portrayal of *Sukhavati Sutra* highlights the heavenly bliss of the Buddha's domain.

Here, there is profound happiness. Darkness and ignorance have been banished by the radiance of the Buddha and all beings are equal with the potential of attaining salvation. The bodhisattva is draped in a dhoti and scarf and endowed with ornaments. Behind his head is a radiant mandala. The stupa over his head indicates that it is the figure of Maitreya. 'Buddhist Paradise' is a happy world as seen in a schist freize from Shotorak. Another schist relief depicting 'Buddhist

---

[17] Eliot, *Hinduism and Buddhism*, Vol II, pp.219–20.

Paradise' is from the site of Mohammad Nari and is displayed at the Lahore Museum.

MAITREYA: THE FUTURE BUDDHA

According to Edward Conze, a tradition about the Future Buddha, Maitreya, came to the fore in about the second century BC. Maitreya personifies friendliness. His legend was to some extent stimulated by Persian eschatology.

> When the Dharma of Buddha is completely forgotten, when the peak of sin and misery is reached and the average length of life has fallen to ten years. When the life of man reaches 80,000 years, Maitreya, at present in the Heaven of the Satisfied gods [*Tusita*] will appear on Earth, which will then be in a particularly fruitful and exuberant state. [The Earth] will be bigger than it is now. A fertile golden sand will cover its surface. Everywhere there will be trees and flowers, pure lakes and jewel heaps. All men will be moral and decent, prosperous and joyous.[18]

Conze further writes, 'Maitreya, the next Buddha, at present reigns and preaches in the *Tusita* Heaven, which inhabited by "Satisfied Gods" is a regular abode of the Future Buddha of this world system in his last existence but one.'[19]

BELIEF IN MIRACLES

The 'new thought' in Gandhara focused upon the miracles performed by the Buddha, as an increased interest in the Buddha's supernatural abilities caught the imagination of the people. Not only the Buddha, many of his disciples and other religious leaders also performed miracles. Knowing that miracles do not constitute a religious mind, the Buddha asked his disciples not to perform such feats. But despite this, the Buddha continued to perform miracles and so did

---

[18] Conze, *Buddhism*, pp.116–17.
[19] Conze, *Buddhism*, p.154.

his disciples occasionally. This is because people appreciated occult powers in the days when Buddhism gained prominence.

The 'Miracle of Sravasti', 'Ascent to Trayastrimsa Heaven', 'Subduing of Naga Apalala' and the 'Conversion of the Kasyapa brothers' became favourite themes for statuary art in the ateliers of Gandhara. The Buddha's descent from 'Trayastrimsa Heaven' after converting his mother and the heavenly dwellers who were desirous of salvation, can be seen in a schist decoration from Swat. It is today located at the Swat Archaeological Museum and dated to the tenth century AD.[20] The depiction of 'Submission of Naga Apalala' in sandstone, from Loriya Tangai, is on display at the Indian Museum, Kolkata.

Travel records of Xuanzang tell us that the pilgrim chose to carry important treasures from India while returning to China. His treasures included a model of the Buddha when he descended on the jewelled ladder from the Buddhist heavenly palace to Kapisa. Another image in his possession was after the model of the shadow of the Buddha left at Nagarhara where he subdued the poisonous dragon. This is the depiction of the 'Submission of Naga Apalala'.[21]

The National Museum of Afghanistan in Kabul displays several Buddha images in the act of performing the 'Miracle of Sravasti'. This points to an event in the Buddha's life, outside the monastery at Sravasti, when he performed the great miracle to prove his power to the heretics. This was a popular theme in the art of Afghanistan, especially at Kapisa and the region of Kabul from where several Buddha images performing the great miracle were recovered. A life-size Buddha image from Shotorak site, a few kilometres north of the old Begram city overlooking the Panjshir River, can today be seen at the National Museum at Kabul. The life-sized headless image in schist, dated second–fourth century AD, in *abhay mudra* shows streams of water issuing from the feet.

Another life-size Buddha image found at the Kham-i-Zargar site, dated from the second century AD, is also prominently displayed

---

[20] Ashraf M. Khan and A.G. Lone, *Gandhara Geography, Antiquity, Art and Personalities*, Ashiq Hussain Chaudhary, Mirpur, Pakistan, p.77.
[21] Hwui Li, *The Life of Hieun-Tsiang*, pp.213–14.

at the museum. The Buddhist complex was reportedly found near Gulbahar at the foot of Kuh-i-Kham-i-Zargar. Bearing the title 'Miracle of Sravasti', the image depicts Buddha in *abhay mudra*. It has an embossed dot in the palm of his right hand indicating *Dharmachakra* (the Wheel of Life or the Wheel of Law), while flames erupt from his shoulders and streams of water flow from his feet.

Another large schist image of the Standing Buddha in the same act was found at Sarai Khuja, 33 km north of Kabul. According to the museum notice, it was also dated to the second–fourth century AD. The Buddha's garb is in low relief and indicated by parallel lines on his body. On one side of the Buddha, mythological creatures and plants can be seen. At the bottom of the image, six figures, probably worshipping Nagas, can be seen coming out of lotuses looking up at the Buddha.

The Buddha's visit to Kapilavastu after his Enlightenment is an important event in the history of his missionary life. It is during this time that he converted many of his kinsmen to his faith. Thereafter, he came to Uruvela and converted by means of a miracle the Kasyapa brothers who were fire worshippers.

It is said that invited by his father, the Buddha proceeded to Kapilavastu with his disciples and reaching there, he took his residence in the Nayagrodharama (the Banyan Grove of the Sakyans in the suburbs of the Sakyan capital). By means of his magic powers, he rose in the air and took a long walk without touching the ground. He performed various miracles of *yamakapratiharya*, or double appearance[22] and produced flames from his upper part and clouds or water from the lower part. These performances of the Buddha removed all the doubts from the minds of his kinsmen as to his greatness.

MIRACLE OF THE SERPENTS

The Buddha was not frightened by the venomous serpent of Uruvela. He spent a night in the fire house of a hut at Gaya where the serpent

---

[22] P. Banerji, *Central Asian Art: New Revelations from Xinjiang*, Abha Prakashan, Delhi, 2001, p.24.

lived. A terrible struggle ensued between the Buddha and the serpent that involved 'smoke against smoke and fire against fire'. By the effect of the Buddha's miraculous power, the serpent's fury was subdued and he quietly coiled up inside the Buddha's begging bowl. Seeing this miraculous feat, Kasyapa and his 500 followers threw away their ritual vessels and converted to the Buddhist faith.[23]

Another serpent, Nagadanta, is a bodhisattva born as a serpent-king. As the story goes, a snake charmer catches him from an anthill and takes him to the king Ugrasena of Varanasi where the snake amuses the king. Sumana, the wife of the serpent-king, appears in the king's court and seeks her husband's release. Finally, the serpent-king shares the throne with the king of Varanasi. This tale is recounted in the *Campeyya Jataka*. In addition to this, there are several other stories about serpent kings or Naga Rajas.

At Bodhgaya, Kala, the best of serpents, whose might was that of the king of elephants, was awakened by the sound of the Buddha's feet. Hearing it, he uttered this eulogy: 'Since your splendour shines forth as the sun...today without doubt you will become a Buddha.'[24]

> And while the agents of Mara ran and leapt wildly to obstruct the meditation of Buddha sitting under the Bodhi tree, the earth-bearing Nagas, devoted to Dharma did not brook obstruction to the great sage and turning their eyes wrathfully on Mara, they hissed and unwound their coils.[25]

DEPICTION OF THE BUDDHA'S LIFE

An attempt was made to narrate the complete lifestory of the Buddha by arranging such reliefs in a chronological sequence either as stair risers or adornments on the base of the stupa at the Gandharan monasteries. Specimens at Lahore and Peshawar museums include

---

[23] Ihsan H. Nadiem, *Taxila in Buddhist Gandhara*, Sang-e-meel-Publications, Lahore, 2008, p.17.
[24] Johnston, *Asvaghosa's Buddhacharita or Acts of the Buddha*, Book xii 116–17, p.186.
[25] Johnston, *Asvaghosa's Buddhacharita or Acts of the Buddha*, Book xiii 30, p.194.

the Buddha's lifestory right from his birth until his death. There are numerous interesting episodes, such as when Prince Siddhartha goes to school on a ram, participates in sports and tames the elephant—these are all from Sahri Bahlol and are on display at the Peshawar Museum. Other episodes include the attack of Mara and the 'Fasting Siddhartha' from Sikri which can be seen at the Lahore Museum. Gandharan masterpieces include the 'First Sermon', 'Presentation of Four Bowls', marriage scene of Siddhartha and the Buddha along with his attendants—all on display at the Lahore Museum.

Queen Maya's Dream

King Suddhodana's wife, Queen Mahamaya (Buddha's mother to-be), dreamt that a white elephant had penetrated her right side. This was interpreted by sage Asita as a dream foretelling the conception of a son destined to become either a universal monarch or a Buddha, an Enlightened One.

The Great Renunciation

King Suddhodana fearing that his son would choose to give up royal prerogatives in order to become an Enlightened One increased the comforts and pleasures of palace life. But, Prince Siddhartha's fateful encounters with an old man, a sick man, a funeral procession and lastly, an ascetic in the palace gardens, awakened in him a desire to discover the reasons for the moral and physical sufferings of human beings and resolve them. One night looking at the dancers sent by his father to please him as they were sprawled out fast asleep, Siddhartha made his decision to forsake his royal life and leave his family and the palace.

Nanda's Ordination

An upright panel of a greyish-white schist depicting 'Nanda's Ordination', which originally came from Jamal Garhi, is now in the Indian Museum, Kolkata. It depicts scenes from the story of Nanda, half-brother of the Buddha, who was lured into joining the Sangha by the Buddha. Nanda leaves his lovely wife and starts out with the

Buddha's begging bowl in hand, to accompany him to his monastery. His head was shaved and he was ordained into the Order. The scene is depicted in the panel where the barber is in the act of shaving Nanda while the Buddha pours out the ceremonial water. From then on, Nanda was kept as an unwilling prisoner in the monastery and the top panel depicts his many attempts to escape. As he made his way stealthily through the wood, the Buddha suddenly appeared, advancing towards him and when Nanda tried to hide behind a tree, the tree rose into the air leaving him face to face with the Buddha.

According to art historian and Indologist P. Banerji, on the third day of the arrival of Buddha at Kapilavastu, he caused Nanda (Buddha's half-brother) to be made a monk. It is said that Buddha was at Kapilavastu at his father King Suddhodana's invitation, and was staying at the Banyan Grove of the Sakyans. He came to his stepmother, Mahaprajapati's palace to take his meals in the company of monks. After the meal was over, the Buddha handed over his alms bowl to Nanda and proceeded to his resting place. Nanda, carrying the bowl, followed him. At the end, Buddha, much against Nanda's wish, initiated him to the Buddhist faith. It was the day when Nanda was married and his wife Janapada-Kalyani (named Sundari) was anxiously waiting for her husband's return. But, Nanda never returned to family life. Asvaghosa in his *Saundarananda Kavya* has immortalized this poignant story. The manuscript fragment of this kavya has been discovered in Xinjiang. The walls of the Ajanta caves too present a painted narration of the sad story of Sundari swooning in grief at the ordination of Nanda.[26]

In a heart-wrenching tale, we learn that Prince Nanda greatly desired to return to his bride but, had to follow the Buddha much against his own will. When word was brought to Janapada-Kalyani that the Buddha had taken Prince Nanda with him, the newly married bride, with tears streaming down her face and hair half-combed, ran after Nanda to persuade him to return. But Nanda was led to the

---

[26] Banerji, *Central Asian Art*, p.63. See also, Eugene Watson Burlingame, *Buddhist Legends*, Part 2, Munshiram Manoharlal Publishers, Delhi, 1999, pp.217–19 and p.220. See also, Burlingame, *Buddhist Legends*, Part 2, pp.219–20.

monastery, and was made a monk despite his anguish.

During his monastic life, Nanda was discontented, as, besides being unable to endure the rigours of a religious life, he constantly missed his bride. The story goes that the Buddha by his power showed him 500 pink-footed celestial nymphs in whose comparison 'his bride did not come within a fraction.' Nanda fell for the promise of celestial nymphs and was won over to monastic life. Later however, Nanda is said to have released the Buddha of his promise of celestial nymphs on becoming aware of the transitory nature of love, life and beauty.

Ordination of Rahul

On the seventh day of the Buddha's arrival at Kapilavastu, Princess Yashodhara, Rahul's mother, sent Rahul to the Buddha saying: 'This monk is your father. To him once belonged great stores of treasure. From the time of his Great Retirement we have not seen him. Ask him for this your inheritance...' The story goes that the moment Rahul saw his father, he conceived a warm affection for him. When the Buddha had finished his meal, he arose from his seat and departed. Rahul followed him saying: 'Monk, give me my inheritance.' The Buddha addressed Sariputra, 'Ordain Rahul, let him share your hut with you. The elder should cut his hair. Let him be a follower of mine.' When the prince had been received into the Order, King Suddhodana was afflicted with great sorrow and requested the Buddha not to ordain any youth without the permission of his mother and father. The Buddha granted him this request.[27]

STATUARY ART IN STUCCO, CLAY AND TERRACOTTA

The great art of Gandhara brought to the devotees splendid images of the Buddha and bodhisattvas in the medium of stucco, clay and terracotta. Stucco statues and reliefs were recovered from Kafiriat Tepe and Gol Hamid monasteries in Mes Aynak, Tepe Narenj and Tepe Maranjan on the Kabul hill, from the Tepe Sardar

---

[27] Banerji, *Central Asian Art*, p.20.

monastic centre at Ghazni. In Pakistan, one can see stucco images of the Buddha at Jaulian and Mohra Moradu monasteries of Taxila. Examples of terracotta images too have been found in Hadda in Afghanistan although such medium is rare. Since stucco and clay were malleable, modelling of statues and preparing of cast was easier, cheaper and faster. Besides moulds could be carried long distances for on-the-spot production of adornments and images.

It was easy to carry the moulds for stucco and clay Buddhist art and the medium found favour in the monastic centres along the foothills of Tienshan in Xinjiang. According to P.C. Bagchi, Buddhist images and bas-relief that were found in Tumshuk near Kashgar on the way to Kuqa connect the art of this region of Kashgar monasteries and adjoining monasteries directly with the Indo-Greek art of Taxila to the extent that the same type of bodhisattvas and gods have been found at Taxila and Tumshuk. Bagchi suggests that probably, the same Indo-Greek moulds were used in both places.[28]

Apart from stone reliefs fixed on the plinth or drum of large as in Sikri, smaller votive stupas were usually embellished with stucco figures and the head of the Buddha, bodhisattvas and devotees set in niches, and with figures of Atlantes, elephants, lions and *yaksis* crouching under cornices and supporting the load of each receding terrace of the stupa base. Examples of such embellished stupas from Tepe Kafariha in Afghanistan can be seen today at the Musée Guimet, Paris.

Stucco Panel at Nagarhara

A stucco panel found at a monastery in Nagarhara shows a royal procession led by the Buddhist king of the city. The king is accompanied by monks carrying the relics of the Buddha on an elephant. The panel displayed at the National Museum recreates the scene of the Buddhist period of Afghanistan when royal processions were organized, much like the Buddhist festival and procession of images in Khotan, as mentioned by Chinese pilgrim Faxian during his stay at the Gomati Monastery. The stucco panel shows a royal personage, over whose

---

[28] P.C. Bagchi, *India and Central Asia*, National Council of Education, Kolkata, 1955, pp.181–93.

head an attendant holds an umbrella. Accompanied by monks, he leads an elephant that carries on his back a huge square-shaped carved box, perhaps holding the relics of the Buddha. The precious relics were publicly exhibited to the worshippers and common city dwellers on auspicious days. The king himself led the procession of monks followed by royal, caparisoned elephants carrying the relics of the Buddha on their back.

Clay Buddha Images from Mes Aynak

Hundreds of painted clay statues of the Buddha, bodhisattvas and donors have been discovered at the large monastic centres of Gol Hamid and Kafiriat Tepe in Mes Aynak near Kabul. New excavations at Mes Aynak in Afghanistan have recovered several clay images of the Buddha seated on a rectangular podium, which were discovered in the courtyard. There are stone reliefs portraying scenes from the Buddha's life. In one chapel were found a three-metre-long Reclining Buddha and a seven-metre-high Standing Buddha. From a second chapel was recovered a five-metre-high Standing Buddha. A wooden sculpture of a Seated Buddha was also discovered here.

Clay Bodhisattva from Tepe Maranjan

On Maranjan Hill, east of Bala Hisar, Kabul, once lay the large Buddhist monastery complex of Tepe Maranjan. Among the many sculptures found here was a life-size image of the Sitting Bodhisattva, now at display at the National Museum at Kabul. The painted clay statue titled 'Bodhisattva Siddhartha', the royal prince, has been dated to the second–third century AD. The peculiar headdress like a wreath of flowers once held a large precious stone hanging on the forehead. The neck is adorned with two layers of necklace, one clasping the neck while the second is hanging low on the chest. The posture is that of meditation. Traces of polychrome are visible on the surface.

Clay Buddha Head from Ghazni

The large Buddha head dated from the fifth–seventh century AD from Tepe Sardar, Ghazni displayed in the upper hall of the National

Museum, shows that it must have adorned a life-size image of the Buddha in *dhyana mudra*. Made of clay, it depicts the Buddha with his eyes closed in meditation, thin, long, curved brows and a finely chiselled high nose. Small volutes adorn the head and the hairline is sharply drawn.

In Fondukistan in the Ghorband Valley, the French Mission in 1936 found statues moulded of unbaked clay, mixed with straw and horse hair as a binding medium and built up around a wooden skeleton or armature.[29]

THE SMILING BUDDHA FROM HADDA

Among the salvaged antiquities from Hadda is a superb terracotta image of the 'Smiling Buddha' published by the National Museum. The image was photographed at the moment of its unwrapping at the presidential palace at Kabul in 2004, and appeared in a museum publication.[30]

Donors formed an important part of any monastic establishment. We find painted stucco images of male and female donors from Mes Aynak.

SOME FAMOUS PAINTINGS FROM GANDHARA

The sites of Bamiyan, Kakrak and Foladi valleys are renowned for their pictorial art. At Bamiyan, the marvellous paintings depicting 'Sukhavati'—the Buddhist heaven in the soffit of the Colossal Buddha Caves have been lost. The walls of cave shrines still exhibit ruined paintings of 'Thousand Buddhas' and *kirtimukhas* (glorious faced monsters) and remnants of scenes which could be from the Jatakas. Some paintings of mystic mandalas found in the caves of the Kakrak Valley have been displayed at the National Museum, Kabul. The mandalas depict the central image of the Buddha who is believed

---

[29] Puri, *Buddhism in Central Asia*, p.302.
[30] Fredrik Hiebert and Pierre Cambon (eds), *Afghanistan Crossroads of the Ancient World*, The British Museum Press, London, 2011, p.45.

to be *Vairochna* (Universal Buddha from whom all Buddhas emanate) and is surrounded by a galaxy of smaller Buddhas.

An outstanding painting from the Kakrak Valley is the 'Hunter King' who having renounced violence took refuge with the Buddha. The painting once adorned the drum of a dome at Kakrak. Now displayed at the National Museum, it portrays a royal personage, presumably the Buddhist king of Bamyan, worshipping a stupa. The sovereign, bejewelled and adorned in fabulous robes, wears a crown with three crescents, perhaps symbolizing the *triratna* of the Buddha, *Dhamma* and the Sangha.

A third centre of Buddhist art is situated in the Foladi Valley at the western entrance of the Bamiyan Caves. The caves present an excellent example of 'lantern-roof' decorations and paintings of 'Thousand Buddhas' portraying the 'Miracle of Sravasti' on the walls and edges of cave ceilings. Bright colours were obtained by grinding local mineral rock stones such as malachite, azurite, lapis and cinnabar.

Another rare painting, seen and described by art historian and Indologist P. Banerji before the Bamiyan Buddha was destroyed, from the niche of the 55-metre Buddha in Bamiyan, is the story of Rupananda of which not many representations are found, and which is now lost. According to Banerji, it illustrated the story of the Buddha's teaching to Rupananda or Janapadakalyani on the impermanence of form or beauty, at Jetavana, the grove which was presented by Prince Jeta in Sravasti for the use of the Buddha and the community.[31] A similar discourse was given by the Buddha at Vaishali at a meeting attended by the beautiful courtesan Amrapali. It had such a profound influence on the courtesan that she not only donated her mango grove to the Sangha, but also became a nun.

Buddha said, 'Beauty of form is impermanent, involved in suffering, unreal, so likewise are sensation, perception, the aggregate of mental states, consciousness impermanent, involved in suffering.' This led Rupananda to think that if she met the Buddha face to face,

---

[31] P. Banerjee, *New Light on Central Asian Art and Iconography*, Abha Prakashan, Delhi, 1992, p.26.

he would find fault with her beauty. Therefore, she avoided seeing the Master face to face.

Among the objects from Afghanistan is a niche, 66-cm high and painted, from Hadda. On stylistic considerations, the piece can be attributed to c.AD 500. According to Banerji, the niche might refer to the *Dipankara Jataka*, which was very popular in Hadda.[32]

According to the Jataka story, Dipankara was the son of the king Archimat. He renounced home and gained Enlightenment but came once to Dipavati at his father's request. At that time, a young learned brahmin called Megha (in the *Divyava Dana*, he is called Sumati) came to Dipavati, and learnt of Dipankara's visit to Dipavati from a young girl who was carrying a water pot and seven flowers. He requested the girl to give him the flowers. On his agreeing to her condition that he would accept her as wife in all future births, she gave him five flowers and retained two for her. Then both of them went to worship the Buddha. Megha threw his lotuses at the Dipankara Buddha which stuck to his halo. The girl also did the same and her lotuses remained suspended in the air. Megha then knelt down and brushed Dipankara's feet with his locks of hair and spread his long hair on the ground to cover the mud. Dipankara seeing Megha's devotion assured him that he would be born as Sakyamuni Buddha at Kapilavastu.

Painted representations of the Buddha and donors have also been found on the walls of Kafiriat Tepe Monastic Centre at Mes Aynak.

Any visitor to Pakistan and Afghanistan will notice that only a small number of Buddha and bodhisattva images are found at the monastic sites, many of which are totally bereft of any statuaries or paintings. Walls or niches that were once adorned with statues or paintings now appear dark and hollow with only some scrapings left. Marvellous statuaries of the Buddha colossi that once stood in the valley of Bamiyan and Kakrak in Afghanistan are also lost. Only models and old photographs can be seen at the National Museum, Kabul and the Tourist Information Centre at Kabul Bazar.

---

[32] Banerjee, *New Light on Central Asian Art and Iconography*, p.31.

Most Buddha images lie in the museums of Kabul, Lahore, Taxila, Peshawar, Delhi, Kolkata and Patna. Outside the subcontinent, they lie in the museums of Italy, France, Britain, Russia and the United States. A wealth of statuaries also lies inside unexcavated *dheris* or mounds of the Khyber Pakhtunkhwa province of Pakistan. At the sites of Mes Aynak and Tepe Narenj in Afghanistan where excavations continue, a large number of statuary art is being retrieved and can be seen online. The objects include scenes from the life of the Buddha, miracles performed by the Buddha, relief panels depicting bodhisattvas in acts of charity (stories from Jatakas), deities of the Buddhist pantheon, semi-divine deities, *panchanada* musicians, donors, worshippers and architectural decorations like Corinthian capitals, lotus and acanthus leaf decorations, vine climbers, playful animals and marine species.

Subjects such as cupids or Amorini (love gods), musicians playing the *panchanada*, playful animals such as monkeys, goats, deer and crocodiles, carved in relief adorn the stair risers of monasteries especially at Sahri Bahlol (displayed at the Peshawar Museum), terracotta figurines and grotesque figures, seals, stamps, relic caskets, toilet trays, ivory objects—all form decorative elements of Gandharan art.

Chapter 23

'GANDHARA IN JATAKA' AND 'JATAKA IN GANDHARA'

The region of Gandhara was immortalized and etched in the stories of the Jatakas, just as the Jataka stories themselves became a favourite theme to be immortalized in stone in the art of Gandhara. Many tales of the bodhisattvas were set in Gandhara, lending sacredness to several sites which attracted devotees from far and wide. They came from as far as Korea, China and Central Asia. Scores of pilgrim inscriptions have thus been found along Gandharan trade routes coming from the Xinjiang region.

More than 10 Chinese inscriptions mentioning names of merchants, pilgrims and royal envoys were found near Gilgit in the upper reaches of the Indus River, the territory directly adjacent to the Pamirs, indicating the Tarim Basin route through Gilgit into the Indus Valley. One inscription mentioned an ambassador Gu Wei Long from the court of the Great Wei, who was despatched between AD 443 and AD 453.[1]

Inscriptions in Brahmi, Kharosthi and Bactrian and engravings of Buddhist images and themes were also found along the old Karakoram Highway.[2] Many tales from Gandhara found narration in the travel records of pilgrims such as Faxian, Xuanzang and Hye Ch'o.

The Jatakas, or the great Buddhist tales of the Buddha's previous births as bodhisattva and adapted beautifully in the art of Gandhara, are a commentary on the achievement of perfection or *paramitas* by the bodhisattva Siddhartha Gautama through his acts of charity, love and renunciation. The Jataka, the tenth book in a collection of

---

[1] Edvard Rtveladze, *Civilizations, States and Cultures of Central Asia*, Forum of Culture and Arts of Uzbekistan Foundation, Tashkent, 2009, p.279 and p.207.
[2] Romila Thapar, *The Penguin History of Early India*, Penguin Books, New Delhi, 2002, p.222.

15 independent books of the *Khuddaka Nikaya*—the fifth Nikaya of *Sutta Pitaka* of the Pali Canon—has all 547 stories of the Buddha's past lives as a bodhisattva.

Buddhist scholar D.C. Ahir describing the *paramitas* of a bodhisattva enumerates them as '*Dana*–giving, *Sila*–moral purification, *Nekkhamma*–renunciation, *Panna*–wisdom, *Viriya*–effort, *Khanti*–enduring patience, *Sacca*–truthfulness, *Adhitthana*–resolve, *Metta*–universal love [and] *Upekkha*–equanimity'.[3]

These pious legends of the BuddhA imparted wisdom and morality through characters who were not only human beings but also birds, animals and nature spirits. In the Jatakas, the bodhisattva is born innumerable times as a fish, crab, peacock, pigeon, buffalo, elephant and so on. We have the bodhisattva born as a stag and leader of a herd of thousand deer as in *Lakkhana Jataka* (Book i, No. 11), born of a monkey's womb as in *Kapi* and *Mahakapi Jataka* (Book vii, Nos 404 and 407) or as a Sindhi horse in *Vatagga-Sindhava Jataka* (Book iii, No. 266). The stories of charity and love such as the *Sivi Jataka*, *Vessantara Jataka*, *Dipankar Jataka* and those like *Chulanandiya*, *Gandhara Jataka* and *Mahasatta* were helpful in propagating *Dhamma* amongst the masses.

The tales were not only narrated orally from generation to generation but were also carved on the walls of Buddhist monuments in Gandhara as elsewhere. Jataka panels on schist from the Khyber Pakhtunkhwa and Kabul regions are on display in the museums of Lahore, Peshawar, Kabul and Kolkata, amongst others. As many as 13 Jataka stories can be seen carved on the great stupa of Sikri (now restored and displayed as the centrepiece at the Lahore Museum). They also found narration on the stone panels that once decorated the monasteries and shrines of Shotorak, Sarai Khuja, Paitava, Karratcha, Mes Aynak in Afghanistan and at Sahri Bahlol, Jamalgarhi, Takht-i-Bahi, Sikri and Shahbazgarhi in Pakistan.

The narrations are generally carved in relief on stone in a simple and lucid style. Different scenes of a Jataka may form parts of the

---

[3] D.C. Ahir, *The Influence of the Jatakas on Art and Literature*, B.R. Publishing Corporation, Delhi, 2000, p.iii.

same panel, each divided by horizontal or vertical columns as in *Vessantara Jataka* or *Sama Jataka*, or arranged in several panels as stories of the bodhisattva Gautama during his various incarnations as witnessed on the Sikri Stupa. Here, several Jataka panels are arranged around the base of the stupa and separated from each other with the help of vertically arranged columns. The art of narration is such that stories and figures are easy to identify. Sometimes portrayal of just one crucial or main scene of the story gives cue to the Jataka as in the *Dipankar Jataka* panel on display at the Lahore Museum.

JATAKA LANDSCAPE IN GANDHARA

The important story of Dipankar Buddha[4] and his prophecy had its setting in Nagarhara. Here, Asoka built a 300-feet-high stupa to mark the place where Sakya bodhisattva met Dipankar Buddha. Xuanzang mentions in his memoir that to the west of the stupa commemorating the place where the bodhisattva met Dipankar Buddha is the 'Kia-lan *sangharama*' (perhaps Tepe Kalan) with only a few priests. South of this lay another stupa built by Asoka to commemorate the place where the bodhisattva covered the mud with his hair.

Other stories set in Gandhara include those mentioned by pilgrim Faxian whose journey took him past several stupas associated with the charity and sacrifice made by the bodhisattva. The first located in Swat Valley was where the Buddha ransomed the life of a dove with his own flesh; the second was in Gandhara where he gave away his eyes to a blind beggar; the third and fourth were in Taxila where he gave away his head to a man and his whole body to a starving tigress who was about to eat her own cubs, and finally where kings, ministers and peoples of all the kingdoms around vie with one another in making offerings.

Many stupas in Gandhara associated with the Jatakas and life of the Buddha were seen and recorded by the Chinese pilgrim Xuanzang in the seventh century AD, while on his way to India

---

[4] Samuel Beal, *Si-Yu-Ki: Buddhist Records of the Western World*, Book II, Low Price Publications, Delhi, 1884, p.91.

through Nagarhara (present-day Jalalabad) and Sakala (present-day Sialkot). The Books II, III and IV of the *Si-Yu-Ki: Buddhist Records of the Western World* mention as many as 18 colossal stupas built by Asoka as early as the third century BC to commemorate the episodes of the bodhisattva's sacrifice. In his seventh-century travelogue, Xuanzang includes stories of various supernatural events associated with Jatakas. Xuanzang arrived at Manikyala and mentioned the story of the Buddha's sacrifice to feed the hungry lion cubs.

Korean pilgrim Hye Ch'o came as far as Gandhara and Udyayana. He mentions stupas built at the places where the bodhisattva sacrificed his head and eyes to the Yakshas. Hye Ch'o also mentions the place of King Sibi's sacrifice for a dove.[5]

Pushkalavati (present-day Charsadda) was the site of the Jataka story, *Sama Jataka*, which describes the conversion of Hariti and Syama. The depiction on schist of these particular Jatakas are showcased at the Peshawar and British Museum, respectively.

Xuanzang mentions that at the side of the *sangharama* was a several-hundred-feet-high stupa (of the Eye Gift), which was built by the Mauryan Emperor Asoka. It was made of carved wood and veined stone, and was the work of various artists.

> Sakya Buddha, in old time when king of this country, prepared himself as a Bodhisattva (for becoming a Buddha). He gave up all he had at the request of those who asked, and spared not to sacrifice his own body as a bequeathed gift (a testamentary gift). Having been born in this country a thousand times as king, he gave during each of those thousands births in this excellent country, his eyes as an offering.[6]

He mentions another stupa near Pushkalavati where,

> Sakya Tathagata converted the Mother of the demons [Hariti stupa] and caused her to refrain from hurting men. It is for this

---

[5] Han-Sung Yang, Yun-Hua Jan, Shotaro Iida and Lawrence Preston (eds and trans.), *Hye Ch'o Diary: A Memoir of the Pilgrimage to the Five Regions of India*, Asian Humanities Press, Berkeley, CA, 1984, pp.49–50.

[6] Beal, *Si-Yu-Ki*, Book II, p.110.

reason the common folk of this country offer sacrifices to obtain children from her."[7]

Going north 50 *li* (25 km) or so from this place, the pilgrim mentions yet another stupa where Samaka Bodhisattva (Shang-mu-kia),

> ...walking piously, nourished as a boy his blind father and mother. One day when gathering fruits for them, he encountered the king as he was hunting, who wounded him by mistake with a poisoned arrow. By means of the spiritual power of his great faith he was restored to health through some medicaments which India (Tien-ti), moved by his holy conduct, and applied to the wound.[8]

The *Samaka* or *Syama Jataka* (and various other Jatakas stories) were also adorned on the stair risers in bas-reliefs at Jamalgarhi site, and are now in possession of the British Museum's online collection. It depicts, as cinematographic scenes, on a panel of schist, the dying Samaka after being accidentally shot by the king who was out hunting. In a thatched hut sits a bearded old man and a woman, Syama's parents, to whom the king brings their son's water pot and the news of his death. In another scene, the blind parents are led by the king to their son's body. The old man walks with the aid of stick. His hair is heaped in a top knot and he wears bracelets and garments of a forest tribal. His wife, walking behind, is wearing a long garment and has her head covered in a scarf. The final scene shows the old woman crouching at the prostrate body of her son and trying to raise his head, while the old man massages Syama's arm, trying to revive him. The king stands at Syama's feet, with folded hands. The god Indra empties a water pot over the reviving Syama, who is seen rising from the ground on his right arm with the arrow still in his chest.

---

[7] Beal, *Si-Yu-Ki*, Book II, p.111.
[8] Beal, *Si-Yu-Ki*, Book II, p.111. See also, Online Collection, British Museum, 1880.55 (Title: Syama Jataka, 2nd–3rd century AD, Material: schist).

GANDHARA JATAKA

The Jataka story especially named after Gandhara is the *Gandhara Jataka* where the bodhisattva was the prince of the Gandhara kingdom. This story was part of a discourse by the Buddha delivered at Jetavana forbidding the monks against hoarding medicines.

It so happened that people of Rajgriha, took to an elder monk five kinds of medicine. The latter in turn gave them away to the Sangha. The monks, when they received large quantities of medicines started hoarding them in pots, jars and bags. On seeing this, the people murmured, 'Those greedy priests are hoarding in their houses.' The Buddha on hearing this, declared the precept, 'Whatever medicines for sick brethren are received, must be used within seven days', and narrated the tale of the bodhisattva, the king of Gandhara, who having renounced his kingdom took to a religious life in the Himalayas.[9]

POPULAR JATAKAS SET IN GANDHARA

While many stories were set in Gandhara, many Jataka tales became the favourite theme for the stone carvers of Gandhara. The site of Polusha (present-day Shahbazgarhi) became the seat of the most celebrated of Jataka, the *Vessantara Jataka*. The bodhisattva, born as Prince Vessantara, was an 'epitome of charity' and was banished from the Sibi kingdom to Mount Vanka as a punishment for having given away his elephant, endowed with the power of bringing rain, to the brahmins of the drought-stricken kingdom of Kalinga. Vessantara left his city with his wife Maddi and his son and daughter. On the way, he first gave away his horses and then his chariot to the begging brahmins, and arrived on foot at Mount Vanka. Here, the family lived in a hermitage provided by the god Sakra. The prince then made a gift of his children to the Jujaka Brahmin, and even gave away his

---

[9] E.B. Cowell (ed.) and B.A. Chalmers Robert (trans.), *The Jatakas or Stories of the Buddha's Former Births: Translated from Pali by Various Hands*, Gandhara Jataka [6] No. 406, Book vii, Low Price Publication, Delhi, 2001 (first published 1895), p.221.

wife to god Sakra disguised as a brahmin. The latter however gave her back, and through his grace Vessantara was reunited with his father, who freed the children by paying ransom to Jujaka.[10]

According to historian Ahmad H. Dani, since Polusha is in the vicinity of the Mukam River, the area is called Mukam plain.[11] Another name for the area is Sudana plain, an ancient name that has survived from the legend of Prince Sudana who was popular under the name of *Visvantara Jataka*, narrated by the Chinese pilgrim Xuanzang.

Xuanzang mentions that on a neighbouring hill lies 'Mount Tan-to-la-kia' which, according to French archaeologist Alfred Foucher, bears the name of Mekha Sanda, meaning the female and male buffalo. This is an allusion to the supposed sojourn of Prince Vessantara and his wife Maddi.

The Buddhist remains near Shahbazgarhi are associated with different scenes from this story. The sacred sites and convents mentioned by Chinese pilgrims Sung Yun and Xuanzang at Polusha and researched by historians and archaeologists in the nineteenth and early twentieth centuries are connected with different scenes from the Jataka story of prince Vessantara.

Another famous story set in Gandhara was the taming of Naga Apalala at Swat and its depiction can be seen in schist in many monasteries. One such panel from Loriya Tangai is now displayed at the Indian Museum, Kolkata.

The *Chulanandiya Jataka* is a depiction of the fame and wisdom of Taxilian teachers and remembered by a student who is dying as a result of his evil mind.[12] The story depicts a hunter who did not keep his promise and killed a mother monkey along with her two sons. The hunter after killing two brother monkeys—Nandiya and Chullanandiya—who pleaded for the life of their blind mother, took

---

[10] Cowell (ed.) and Chalmers (trans.), *The Jatakas or Stories of the Buddha's Former Births*, Vessantara Jataka [7] No. 547, Book xxii, p.246.

[11] Ahmad H. Dani, *Shahbaz Garhi*, University of Peshawar, Peshawar, 1964, pp.1–8.

[12] Cowell (ed.) and Chalmers (trans.), *The Jatakas or Stories of the Buddha's Former Births*, Chulanandiya Jataka [9] No. 222, Book ii, p.140.

out the third arrow and shot the blind old mother monkey. He then picked up all three dead bodies and happily carried them home. On the way back home, he thought about how pleased his family would be on knowing of his valour and his having killed three monkeys in one day.

When he was about to reach home, he heard the news that his house was hit by a thunderbolt and all his family members had perished there. The loss of his family made him delirious and a lunatic. In a frenzy, he threw off his garments and ran towards his house with his outstretched hands to hold his wife and children. When he reached the house and looked for his family members in the debris, the burnt bamboo of the house crumbled and fell on his head. It is said that, as is witnessed by the people, he was lost in the smoke and a fire sprang from the hell with the yawning of the earth and swallowed him.

The eyewitnesses, however, also heard the dying man recalling the lessons of his good old Taxila guru when he had made the following utterances:

> Now I remember the lessons of my teacher,
> And now I understand what he meant,
> When he taught me to be careful;
> And do nothing to repent.

The *Chhaddanta Jataka* is the story of six-tusked elephants. It is set in the foothills of the Himalayas and was a popular theme among the stone carvers of Gandhara. The depiction of this Jataka can today be seen at the Lahore Museum. In the story, the bodhisattva who was born as a six-tusked elephant (Chhaddanta), lived in the Himalayas with his two wives—Mahasubhadda and Chullasubhadda. Chullasubhadda, believing Mahasubhadda to be her hisband's favourite, prays out of jealous rage to the Pratyeka-Buddhas, and pines herself to death. She prays to be reborn as a beautiful maiden and be married to the king of Varanasi, so that she might have the opportunity of taking revenge on Chhaddanta. In her next birth, she becomes the queen of Varanasi and, under the pretext of illness, persuade the king to engage a hunter, Sonuttara by name, to bring her the tusks of Chhaddanta. Chhaddanta, though wounded by the shaft of the hunter, pitied him and helped him saw off his own tusks. The queen, however, died out of remorse, at the sight of the tusks.[13]

Showcased at the Lahore Museum today, *Sibi Jataka* is carved on a drum-slab of the Sikri Stupa and depicts a pigeon that is the fire god, Agni, in disguise. The pigeon is seated on the left palm of King Sibi for shelter. God Sakra, disguised as a hunter, accepts King Sibi's flesh that is equal to the weight of a pigeon which had been saved by the king. When the flesh offered by the king fell short in weight, the king himself sat on the pan of the balance. On seeing this, the gods Sakra and Agni appear in their real forms to laud the sacrifice of the king (who is actually a bodhisattva).[14]

In *Tandulanali Jataka*, we read about a horse-dealer from Peshawar with 5,000 horses.[15] In *Vataggasindhava Jataka*, when Brahmadatta was king of Benares, the 'Bodhisattva was a Sindh horse, and they called him Swift-as-the-Wind; and he was the king's horse of ceremony.'[16]

JATAKAS SET IN TAXILA

We come across young brahmins being frequently sent to Taxila for their education in the art and sciences. In *Tilamutthi Jataka*, Brahmadatta, the king of Benares, had a son named Prince Brahmadatta. He wanted his son, to go to foreign country to complete his education, so that he would learn to quell his pride and endure heat or cold, and be made acquainted with the ways of the world. The

---

[13] Cowell (ed.) and Chalmers (trans.), *The Jatakas or Stories of the Buddha's Former Births*, Chhaddanta Jataka [10] No. 514, Book xvi, p.21.
[14] Cowell (ed.) and Chalmers (trans.), *The Jatakas or Stories of the Buddha's Former Births*, Sivi or Sibi Jataka [11] No. 499, Book xv, p.251.
[15] Cowell (ed.) and Chalmers (trans.), *The Jatakas or Stories of the Buddha's Former Births*, Tandulanali Jataka [12] No.5, Book i, p.21.
[16] Cowell (ed.) and Chalmers (trans.), *The Jatakas or Stories of the Buddha's Former Births*, Vataggasindhava Jataka [13] No. 266, Book iii, p.233.

king calls the 16-year-old prince and giving him one-soled sandals, a sunshade of leaves and a thousand pieces of money, says to him: 'My son, get you to Takkasila, and study there.'[17] Other Jatakas with the same theme include the *Indriya Jataka*[18] and *Harita Jataka*.[19]

In *Sujata Jataka*,[20] the Bodhisattva was born as the son of his Queen Consort. When he grew up, he received his education at Taxila, and after the death of his father, became king and ruled in righteousness. In *Nanacchanda Jataka*,[21] when Brahmadatta was reigning in Benares, the Bodhisatta was born as the son of his Queen Consort. He grew up, and was educated at Taxila. *Uddalaka Jataka*,[22] too is set in Taxila.

In *Susima Jataka*,[23] two princes grow up fair, like sons of gods and they are learnt in the sciences at Taxila. In *Parantapa Jataka*,[24] when Brahmadatta was reigning in Benares, the bodhisatta was born as the son of his chief queen. When he grew up, he learned all the arts at Taxila, and acquired a spell for the understanding of all animals' cries. In *Atthasadda Jataka*,[25] the bodhisatta was born in a brahmin family worth 80 crore. When he grew up, he learned the

---

[17] Cowell (ed.) and Chalmers (trans.), *The Jatakas or Stories of the Buddha's Former Births*, Tilamutthi Jataka [13] No. 252, Book iii, p.193.

[18] Cowell (ed.) and Chalmers (trans.), *The Jatakas or Stories of the Buddha's Former Births*, Indriya Jataka, No. 423, Book viii, p.276.

[19] Cowell (ed.) and Chalmers (trans.), *The Jatakas or Stories of the Buddha's Former Births*, Harita Jataka, No. 430, Book ix, p.294.

[20] Cowell (ed.) and Chalmers (trans.), *The Jatakas or Stories of the Buddha's Former Births*, Sujata Jataka [15] No. 269, Book iii, p.241.

[21] Cowell (ed.) and Chalmers (trans.), *The Jatakas or Stories of the Buddha's Former Births*, Nanacchanda Jataka [16] No. 289, Book iii, p.290.

[22] Cowell (ed.) and Chalmers (trans.), *The Jatakas or Stories of the Buddha's Former Births*, Uddalaka Jataka, No. 487, Book xiv, p.188.

[23] Cowell (ed.) and Chalmers (trans.), *The Jatakas or Stories of the Buddha's Former Births*, Susima Jataka [18] No. 411, Book vii, p.237.

[24] Cowell (ed.) and Chalmers (trans.), *The Jatakas or Stories of the Buddha's Former Births*, Parantapa Jataka [19] No 416, Book vii, p.249.

[25] Cowell (ed.) and Chalmers (trans.), *The Jatakas or Stories of the Buddha's Former Births*, Atthasadda Jataka [20] No 418, Book viii, p.256.

arts at Taxila. In *Darimukha Jataka*,[26] the bodhisattva goes to study at Taxila.

Several mounds in Sahri Bahlol in Mardan excavated in the early twentieth century yielded stupa courts with one or more stupas having stair risers embellished with stories of the Jatakas. These are exhibited at the Peshawar Museum and are a delight to visitors today. Attack of Devadutta hirelings which are carved in relief from Jamalgarhi, (in Mardan, dated second century AD) and the Buddha's visit to Kapilavastu, also from Jamalgarhi (dated second century AD) are on display at the Indian Museum, Kolkata.

---

[26] Cowell (ed.) and Chalmers (trans.), *The Jatakas or Stories of the Buddha's Former Births*, Darimukha Jataka, No. 378, Book vi, p.156.

Chapter 24

DECLINE OF BUDDHISM IN GANDHARA

Buddhism which took over 500 years to be fully entrenched in Gandhara from the time of the Mauryans in the third century BC to the Kusanas in the second–third century AD and continued to exist up to the period of the Turki Shahis in the ninth century, was completely wiped out from Gandhara by the twelfth century.

The first onslaught on the faith was dealt by the White Huns or the Hephthalites in the fifth–sixth century AD. The Huns destroyed Buddhist monasteries and shrines and massacred the monks. The late fifth and the early sixth centuries saw Hephthalite raids carried out by Toramana on Gandhara from his capital at Sakala. His son Mihirakula further intensified raids in the whole of northern India.

According to historian Vincent Smith, swarms of White Huns settled in the Oxus Valley and assailed the Kusana kingdom of Kabul, but were repelled by Skandagupta in AD 455. About 10 years later, the Huns reappeared in immense force and overwhelmed the kingdom of Gandhara. Starting from that base, they penetrated deep into the heart of the Gangetic plains and overthrew the Gupta Empire. About AD 500, their leader Toramana established himself as ruler of Malwa in central India and assumed the title of 'maharaja'. After his death in AD 510, he was succeeded by his son Mihirakula who established his capital at Sakala in Punjab.[1] When Mihirakula attacked Gandhara, the king was slain and a multitude of people were slaughtered.[2] The valleys of the Kabul and Swat rivers, one of the most flourishing centres of Buddhism, were completely devastated.[3]

---

[1] Vincent A. Smith, *History of India*, Vol. II, Cosimo Classics, New York, 2008, p.285.
[2] Smith, *History of India*, p.289.
[3] R.C. Majumdar, *Ancient India*, Motilal Banarsidass Publishers, Delhi, 2013, p.249.

Pakistan historians M. Ashraf Khan and A.G. Lone supporting the Hun theory, add that the Huns especially targeted Buddhist centres 'with the full support of rancorous Brahmans'. They demolished monasteries and plundered their wealth with the full assistance of local Hindus, who were deprived of royal support since the third century BC, after Asoka ascended the throne.[4]

IN DEFENCE OF HUNS

History tells us that by the middle of the fifth century AD, the Hephthalites had taken possession of the whole of Tokharistan (along with the surrounding regions of Balkh), the Pamirs and a considerable part of Afghanistan. From the mid-fifth to the mid-sixth century AD, Central Asia was ruled by the Hephthalite tribes.

During the seventh century AD, when the Chinese pilgrim Xuanzang was in Balkh and Bamiyan, he tells us that the precincts of the Naubahar, or Navasangharama (new monastery), at Balkh was attacked (not by the Huns) but by the Western Turk ruler Khan Yeh-hu (or his son She-hu) in order to obtain wealth. At Bamiyan, the pilgrim goes on to describe the prevailing religious life in the period of the Huns:

> The people are remarkable among all their neighbours for a love of religion (a heart of pure faith); from the highest form of worship to the three jewels, down to the worship of the hundred (i.e. different) spirits, there is not the least absence (decrease) of earnestness and the utmost devotion of heart.[5]

---

[4] M. Ashraf Khan and A.G. Lone, *Gandhara: Geography, Antiquity, Art and Personalities*, Ashiq Hussain Chaudhary, Mirpur, Pakistan, 2006, p.7.

[5] Samuel Beal, *Si-Yu-Ki: Buddhist Records of the Western World*, Book I, Low Price Publications, Delhi, 1884, pp.43–48 and p.50. See also, A.H. Dani, B.A. Litvinsky, and M.H. Zamir Safi, *Eastern Kushans, Kidarites in Gandhara and Kashmir, and Later Hephthalites*, Vol. III: History of Civilizations of Central Asia, UNESCO, New Delhi, 1996 and Motilal Banarsidass Publishers, Delhi, 1999, p.173.

According to eminent historians A.H. Dani, B.A. Litvinsky and M.H. Zamir Safi, the most important piece of evidence in defence of the Huns comes from the Buddhist creations at Bamiyan, where tall Buddha figures, cave paintings and monasteries attest to the progress of art in this region during their rule.[6] Also dated from that period is an entire series of artworks in the complexes at the nearby Kakrak Valley. Huge sculptures of the seated Buddha and the 'Buddha in Nirvana' have been excavated at the vast Buddhist monastery of Tepe Sardar in Ghazni, where the central stupa and many surrounding votive stupas and places of worship have been identified. Litvinsky points out that alongside monumental art, 'chamber arts' such as 'toreutics and the modelling of figurines' were highly developed during the Hephthalite period.[7]

NAUBAHAR HEADED BY HEPHTHALITES

According to Dani, Litvinsky and Safi, Balkh, a premier town in Tokharistan, was an important Hephthalite possession with the ruler bearing the Bactrian title *Sava*, meaning king. At the Buddhist complex of Naubahar of the late sixth century AD, the Buddhist community was headed by the *Barmak*, a title derived from the Sanskrit term *parmak* or *pramukh*, meaning superior or chief.[8] The Hephthalite ruler's son bore the name Pariowk (which goes back to the Buddhist title *Pramukha*) showing that Pariowk was the lord and head of the great Buddhist centre of Naubahar at Balkh. Harmatta and Litvinsky write, 'The famous Barmakid family of Islamic times were apparently the descendants of the Hephthalite pramukhas of the Naubahar at Balkh.'

---

[6] Dani, Litvinsky and Safi, *Eastern Kushans, Kidarites in Gandhara and Kashmir, and Later Hephthalites*, p.173.
[7] B.A. Litvinsky, *The Hephthalite Empire*, Vol. III: History of Civilizations of Central Asia, UNESCO, New Delhi, 1996 and Motilal Banarsidass Publishers, Delhi, 1999, pp.158–60.
[8] Dani, Litvinsky and Safi, *Eastern Kushans, Kidarites in Gandhara and Kashmir, and Later Hephthalites*, p.178.

BUDDHISM AMONG TURKS

After the Turk conquest of the sixth century AD, all the principalities of the former Hephthalite kingdom came under the rule of the Turk Yabghu of Tokharistan residing in Kunduz.[9] This included the kingdom of Zabulistan, Kapisa–Gandhara, Badhghis, Wakhan and Badakhshan. Chinese pilgrim Hye Ch'o who travelled in these lands between AD 723 and AD 729 asserts that in Gandhara, Kapisa and Zabulistan, the kings and military forces were the Turks.[10]

Xuanzang writes in his memoirs how Turks too were interested in Buddhism and after hearing his discourse, readily accepted the teachings of the Buddha along with hundreds of others. At Kunduz, monks from Balkh were in attendance on the Turk *khagan*, or ruler, to cure him of his illness. Therefore, it may be said that in the sixth–seventh century AD, Turks were favouring the religion of the Buddha. According to Smith, this was because 'Buddhism in its Mahayana form attracted the reverence of the foreign rulers—the Indo-Greek, the Kusanas and also the Turks—and they showed a tendency to favour Buddhism rather than Brahmanism.[11]

INTERNAL DEGENERATION OF BUDDHISM

By the seventh century AD, internal degeneration and conflicts were already plaguing Buddhism, and the faith had considerably weakened when the marauding Arab armies attacked Gandhara.

During Xuanzang's journey through the areas of Gandhara and Kashmir in AD 629–644, the Buddhist monastic institutions were deteriorating and while there were many Buddhist shrines and monasteries, there were also many Deva (Hindu) temples in the

---

[9] J. Harmatta and B.A. Litvinsky, *Tokharistan and Gandhara under Western Turk Rule (630–750)*, Vol. III: History of Civilizations of Central Asia, UNESCO, New Delhi, 1996 and Motilal Banarsidass Publishers, Delhi, 1999, p.371.
[10] Harmatta and Litvinsky, *Tokharistan and Gandhara under Western Turk Rule (630–750)*, pp.371–72.
[11] Smith, *History of India*, p.276.

places that he visited. He also writes about the rivalry between the Buddhists and the Hindus.

Chinese pilgrims who travelled to Gandhara in this period have given ample indication of the deterioration in faith in various cities they travelled to in Gandhara and Kashmir. According to the Xuanzang, since the anti-Buddhist 'Krityas' then ruled Kashmir, 'this kingdom is not much given to the faith'.[12] Sindh was described as a Buddhist country, but its people were said to 'study without aiming to excel'. From Sindh, Xuanzang went nearly 322 km, to Multan, where there were no Buddhists but many who offered 'sacrifice to spirits'. He also found a 'very magnificent' sun temple there.[13] During his further travels through, what is now Pakistan, he found a fair number of Buddhists and many Shaivites at some places.[14] He found several *sangharamas* where there were only few priests, while Deva temples were many as in Kapisa and Nagarhara.[15]

At Udyayana in Swat in north-west India was an important centre of Buddhism. It had 1,400 monasteries. Formerly there were 18,000 monks but their number had declined. The monasteries had turned desolate, and Xuanzang was quite unhappy to see that only a few monks lived there. Although the monks practised quiet meditation, they had no understanding of the texts they recited. Xuanzang found 1,000 monasteries in a ruinous and deserted state in Gandhara, of which he wrote: 'They are filled with wild shrubs and solitary to the last degree. The stupas were mostly decayed.' However, the heretical or Deva temples which were 'to the number of 100, are occupied pell mell by heretics'.[16]

In Peshawar, the Kanishka stupa too had been burned down and restoration was going on when Xuanzang arrived. Even the patra or the 'Begging Bowl' of the Buddha had vanished from the Kanishka

---

[12] Beal, *Si-Yu-Ki*, p.159.
[13] Beal, *Si-Yu-Ki*, Book II, p.274.
[14] Beal, *Si-Yu-Ki*, p.160. See also, Gail Omvedt, *Buddhism in India: Challenging Brahmanism and Caste*, Sage Publications, Delhi, 2003 (2nd ed., 2013), p.152.
[15] Beal, *Si-Yu-Ki*, pp.90–91.
[16] Beal, *Si-Yu-Ki*, Book II, p.98 and p.120.

Vihara and the tower of the patra was empty. Likewise at Taxila, he observes that the *sangharamas* had become ruinous.[17]

In Kashmir Buddhism soon became corrupt and according to the Rajatarangini, monks began to marry as early as the sixth century. In Sind about 10,000 Buddhists used to live and there were monasteries which were hundreds in number... As a rule [these Buddhists] are indolent and given to indulgence and debauchery...though they wear the robes of religion, they live without any moral values.[18]

Referring to the records of early Arab invasions of India, Buddhologist K.L. Hazra states that the activities of the monk and nuns were against the doctrine and discipline of the Buddhist Sangha. One of the accounts mentions that during the time of invasion of Brahmanabad by Caca, a *samani* named Buddha-Raku (or Buddha-raksita), who was a married person and an expert in magic, was able to exercise a great influence upon the life of the king of Sind. This monk even took active part in the political and military affairs of the king.[19]

Hazra also attributes the growth and popularity of Mahayanism and introduction of rituals in Buddhism as causes of its decay. The new forms of Buddhism may have resulted in the increase of the votaries of the religion, but it also brought about a corresponding qualitative decay. The Buddha was always against the introduction of rituals in Buddhism, and that is why they did not find a place in early Buddhism. However, in due course of time, they found their way into it. Gradually, Buddhism came very close to Hinduism and soon the two religions lost their own identities. It was because of this, lay people did not find any difference 'between the worship of

---

[17] Beal, *Si-Yu-Ki*, p.99, p.103 and p.137.
[18] Charles Eliot, *Hinduism and Buddhism: An Historical Sketch*, Vol. II: Bibliotheca Indo-Buddhica No.54, Sri Satguru Publications, Delhi, 1988, p.109. Beal, *Si-Yu-Ki*, Book XI, p.274.
[19] K.L. Hazra, *The Rise and Decline of Buddhism in India*, Munshiram Manoharlal Publishers, Delhi, 2009 (1st ed., 1995), p.377 and p.379.

Visnu and Buddha, of Siva and Avalokita and of Tara and Parvati', says Hazra.[20]

Referring to the tantric master Padma-Sambhava, a native of Udyayana, Charles Eliot blames witchcraft and sorcery as factors that influenced Buddhism in eighth century AD, leading to its decline.[21] Xuanzang also writes about the inhabitants of Udyayana who were devout Mahayanists, but experts in magic and exorcism. Of Kashmir, he points out that its religion was a mixture of Buddhism with other beliefs.

ARAB INVASION OF GANDHARA

As a result, when the Arab forces invaded Gandhara in the latter half of the seventh century AD, Buddhism was already in decline. History informs us that the forces of the Umayyad Caliphate (founded in AD 661) in the seventh century captured the area around Balkh where the Turki Shahis had recently displaced the Western Turks who were in control when Xuanzang visited, including Nava Vihara (Naubahar) Monastery, causing the Turki Shahis to retreat to the Kabul Valley. But the Nava Vihara remained open and functioning. The Han Chinese pilgrim Yijing (I-ching) visited Nava Vihara in the 680s and reported it flourishing as a Sarvastivada centre of study.[22]

As a consequence of the Arab invasion, the power of the Turk Yabghu was considerably weakened. Harmatta and Litvinsky suggest that after the reign of Ishbara Yabghu (son of Tatu-Shah), relations with China also seems to have soured due to the Tibetan conquest of the Tarim Basin. By AD 705, Nili Kaghan, successor of Ishbara Yabghu, had moved to Badakhshan as his capital Balkh and the central territories of his kingdom had been occupied by the Arabs.

---

[20] Hazra, *The Rise and Decline of Buddhism in India*, pp.382–83.
[21] Eliot, *Hinduism and Buddhism*, p.126.
[22] Alexander Berzin, *History of Buddhism in Afghanistan*, Study Buddhism by Berzin, 2003–19, Berzin Archives e.V Impressum. Available at <https://studybuddhism.com/en/advanced-studies/history-culture> (last date of access: 15 June 2019).

Nili Khagen was succeeded in Tokharistan by Ti-she Yabghu, king of Chaganiyan, in AD 719.[23]

We learn that both the Zabulistan and Kapisa–Gandhara kingdoms under the Turki Shahis were able to preserve their ethnic and cultural identities and successfully fought for independence against the Arab conquerors, and it was only towards the end of the eighth century AD that they acknowledged the supremacy of the Umayyad Caliph, Al-Mahdi. However, the true conquest of Kabul did not take place until the end of the ninth century.[24] In AD 795, the Muslims successfully invaded Zabul and went on to Kabul. In the subsequent eastern campaign, under Caliph Al-Ma'mun, the ruler of Kabul (known as Kabul Shah) was captured and converted to Islam.[25]

Historical accounts based on early Arab chroniclers tell us that although parts of Afghanistan were under Muslim occupation from the second half of the seventh century AD, the kingdom of Kabulistan was spared from Muslim incursions until the Saffarid invasion led by Yakub-ibn Laith, governor of Seistan and Khurasan. This was around the last quarter of the ninth century when Kabul was ruled by the Hindu Shahis who had succeeded the Turki Shahis in the mid-ninth century.

Hindu Shahis in Gandhara

Around AD 860, King Lagaturman of the Turki Shahi Dynasty, ruling in the Kabul Valley, was dethroned by Kallar (also named Lalliya Shahi) who founded the Hindu Shahi Dynasty. The Hindu Shahis wrested Gandhara and Kabul with the help of the Gurjara Pratihara king, Mihir Bhoja, who wanted to establish the Hindu Shahis in

---

[23] Harmatta and Litvinsky, *Tokharistan and Gandhara under Western Turk Rule (630–750)*, Vol. III: History of Civilizations of Central Asia, UNESCO, 1996 and Motilal Banarsidass Publishers, Delhi, 1999, pp.372–73.

[24] Harmatta and Litvinsky, *Tokharistan and Gandhara under Western Turk Rule (630–750)*, pp.381–82.

[25] B.A. Litvinsky, H.A. Jalilov and A.I. Kolesnikov, *The Arab Conquest*, Vol. III: History of Civilizations of Central Asia, UNESCO, New Delhi, 1996 and Motilal Banarsidass Publishers, Delhi, 1999, p.470. See also, Berzin, *History of Buddhism in Afghanistan*.

Gandhara in opposition to Yakub-ibn Laith. When Kabul was seized by the Saffarid Yakub-ibn Laith in AD 870, the capital of the Hindu Shahi kingdom was fixed at Udabhandapura (present-day Und), a small village on the right bank of the Sindhu River, about 24 km above Attock.[26]

The next important Hindu Shahi king was Jayapala who ruled over an extensive kingdom which comprised western Punjab as far as Sirhind in the east and Multan in the south, the Northwest Frontier provinces and eastern Afghanistan as far as Lamghan. 'Jayapala was thus guarding the gates of India when a powerful Muslim Turkish state led by Alptegin and Sebuktegin was founded in his immediate neighbourhood with Ghazni as capital.'[27]

Ghaznavid and Ghurid Attack

When Sabuktegin, the Ghaznavid king, pushed forward into the heart of India, Jayapala, the Hindu Shahi king, 'could only send a piteous appeal to the powerful chiefs of India.'[28] The imperial banner of the Rajput confederacy under the Pratiharas was unfurled in the valley of the Kurram River in the eastern frontier of Afghanistan, probably near the Gomal Pass midway between the Khyber and the Bolan passes with a direct connection to Ghazni. Jayapala was routed and Sabuktigin, the ruler of Ghazni, made himself master of all the territories up to the Sindhu.[29] According to historian R.C. Majumdar, after Sabuktigin died in AD 997, his son Mahmud, marched towards India and was met by his adversary Jayapala near Peshawar, but the latter was defeated and taken prisoner. Mahmud of Ghazni pursued his march beyond the Sutlej. According to Majumdar, what followed, took the breath of India away! Year after year, Mahmud repeated his incursions into India, totalling 17 in number. The last important expedition of Mahmud was directed against the celebrated temple of

---

[26] Dani, Litvinsky and Safi, *Eastern Kushans, Kidarites in Gandhara and Kashmir, and Later Hephthalites*, p.171. See also, Majumdar, *Ancient India*, p.300.

[27] Majumdar, *Ancient India*, p.301.

[28] Majumdar, *Ancient India*, p.306.

[29] Majumdar, *Ancient India*, p.307.

Somnath. However, he died soon after in AD 1030 in Ghazni. After Mahmud Ghazni, it was time for Mohammad Ghori of Ghor to lead a series of campaigns in India. Ghor was then a small principality to the west of Ghazni and east of Herat and a dependency of Ghazni. Like Mahmud Ghazni, Mohammad Ghori too ravaged the country from the Indus to the Ganges. He began with the existing Arab colonies on the Indus, took Multan in 1175, Peshawar in 1179 and by 1182 had subdued the whole of Sind. In 1184, he had usurped the territories of Lahore and Sialkot.[30]

DECLINE OF BUDDHISM: A PROTRACTED AFFAIR

Gandhara continued to be ravaged from the seventh to the eleventh centuries, and then again in the twelfth century by Islamic armies. The decline of Buddhism in Gandhara was thus a protracted affair that began with Arab raids in seventh century AD and ended with its complete annihilation by the twelfth century AD when complete Islamization was achieved under the Ghaznavids and Ghorids.

The conquest however faced massive revolt by the local population. Similar events took place in Central Asia where the Arab commander Qutaiba-ibn Muslim launched a campaign in Samarkand in AD 710–12. He had to capture and recapture provinces due to fierce resistance from rebellious rulers and inhabitants of Samarkand. The Arab garrisons had to maintain a stubborn fight with the rebellious natives and the powerful Turks who had joined the battle against the Arabs. On several occasions, the Arab garrisons were expelled and exterminated and the provinces reverted to the native ruler.[31]

Likewise in Gandhara, Arabs had started to invade lands east of Persia and in AD 642, the Arab armies captured Herat and

---

[30] Stanley Lane-Poole, *Medieval India under Mohammedan Rule (AD 712–1764)*, D.K. Publishers, Delhi, 1903 (reprint 2003), pp.48–49.
[31] W. Barthold, *Turkestan Down to the Mongol Invasion*, E. J. W. Gibbs Memorial Trust, UK and USA, 1928 (reprint 2012), pp.186–87. See also, Richard N. Frye, *The History of Bukhara: Translated from the Persian Abridgement of the Arabic Original by Narshakhi*, Markus Wiener Publishers, Princeton, 2007, pp.65–67.

Sistan in western Afghanistan. Nancy H. Dupree points out that as in Samarkand and Bukhara, the eastern areas often revolted and converted back to their old faith whenever the Arab armies withdrew.[32] Complete Islamization was not achieved until the tenth and twelfth centuries under the rule of Ghaznavids and Ghorids. Even after the conquest of Balkh by Qutaiba-ibn Muslim in AD 705, Korean pilgrim Hye Ch'o who visited Balkh c.AD 726 mentioned that despite Arab rule, 'the king, the chiefs and the common people respect the Three Jewels'. During his visit, he found that the place was guarded and oppressed by Arab forces. The king was compelled to leave the capital and was residing at Badakhshan.[33]

Even at this time, several monasteries were functional in Peshawar and Balkh. It is believed that the Kanishka Vihara was also still in existence in the eighth century AD when Hye Ch'o visited Peshawar in AD 726. In his description of the Kanishka Vihara, there is ample proof of the continued existence of the Buddhist centre. In fact, it was still flourishing as a place of Buddhist education as late as the ninth or tenth century, when Prince Vira Deva of Magadh was sent there to study.[34]

According to Barthold, Balkh and the Naubahar were destroyed by the Arabs during the reign of the Caliph Othman, or, according to other accounts, that of Muawiya. The Arabs built a new town in the locality of Barugan, two *farsakhs* from Balkh. But, it is significant to note that in AD 725, the governor Asad B. Abdullah restored the town at the former site, commissioning the representatives of the same house of the Barmakids to carry out this work.[35] Was this because the Arabs were finding it difficult to completely close down the Naubahar, the main monastery at Balkh, and thereby causing

---

[32] Nancy H. Dupree, *An Historical Guide to Afghanistan*, Afghan Air Authority Afghan Tourist Organization, Kabul, 1977, pp.36–37.
[33] Han-Sung Yang, Yun-Hua Jan, Shotaro Iida and Lawrence Preston (eds and trans.), *Hye Ch'o Diary: A Memoir of the Pilgrimage to the Five Regions of India*, Asian Humanities Press, Berkeley, CA, 1984, p.52.
[34] Smith, *History of India*, p.230.
[35] Barthold, *Turkestan Down to the Mongol Invasion*, p.77.

a loss of trade through pilgrimage? The Navbahar is said to have been the centre of higher Buddhist study for all of Central Asia, comparable to the Nalanda Monastery in central India. The world-famous monastery primarily emphasized the study of the *Vaibhashika Abhidharma* and admitted only monks who had already composed texts on the topic. Since it housed a tooth relic of the Buddha, it was also one of the main centres of pilgrimage along the Silk Route from China to India.[36]

In conclusion, it can be said that Buddhist institutions had considerably weakened when the Arab armies attacked Gandhara. Monasteries were in a ruinous and deserted state. Witchcraft and sorcery were rampant. Monks had become corrupt. There was introduction of rituals, much against the preaching of the Buddha. New forms of Buddhism were introduced which produced a qualitative decay and blurred its identity. Due to lost patronage of rulers and a diluted and weakened status, Buddhism could not bear the brutal brunt of a protracted Islamic attack. It was completely annihilated and wiped out of present-day Afghanistan and Pakistan as mass conversions to Islam took place.

---

[36] Berzin, *History of Buddhism in Afghanistan.*

EPILOGUE

PRESERVING GANDHARA

The treasured land of ancient Gandhara, renowned for its art and scholarship, is the custodian of Asia's Buddhist heritage. A peep into the monastic sites of Samangan, Bamiyan, Foladi, Kakrak, Takht-i-Bahi, Jaulian and Mohra Moradu, though all in ruinous condition, will give an idea of the beauty of Gandhara's architectural wealth. The rare Buddha colossi, bejewelled bodhisattvas and intricately carved Jataka stories on stair risers at Gandharan sites—now reposing in the museums of Kabul, Peshawar, Taxila and Lahore—are just a fraction of the spellbinding art discovered during explorations and excavations.

With the passing of centuries, Gandhara witnessed the waxing and waning of empires, religious beliefs, art forms, customs and traditions that gave rise to a unique cosmopolitan culture producing great art and literature. Many Buddhist stories found their setting in Gandhara. The Greek historian Herodotus from the fifth century BC writes in his *Histories* about the many riches of Gandhara, of the brave people who fought in the armies of Achaemenian rulers and of those who rallied against Alexander. The Chakravarti kings Asoka, Milind (Menander) and Kanishka also left their imprint on the Gandharan landscape in the form of gigantic stupas and viharas.

The Mauryan Emperor Asoka from the third century AD, who was in his early days the viceroy of Taxila, installed pillar and rock edicts to spread his *Dhammavijaya*. *Milind Panha*, the questions of Milind or the questions of the Indo-Greek king Menander, from the second century BC was also set in Gandhara. The Kusana king, Kanishka, from the first century AD established the magnificent Kanishka Vihara near Peshawar where he also installed Buddha's 'begging bowl'. These evidences all point to the importance and centrality of Gandhara in Buddhist world.

Sadly, down the centuries, thousands of Buddhist sites of this wondrous region have been crumbling into mounds over which village settlements have come up. Illegal mining, encroachments and trafficking of precious antiquities at the hands of unscrupulous miners, traders and builders have also been responsible for the destruction and death of the historical sites.

Even the ancient routes that bound together diverse cultural regions and along which ideas and faith travelled are withering away. The new and modern roads have completely bypassed heritage cities and new structures have buried the ancient ones.

While the UNESCO World Heritage sites of Taxila and Takht-i-Bahi are well protected, the same cannot be said about other sites such as Jamalgarhi, Sikri, Sahri Bahlol, Manikyala, Charsadda and so on. In Afghanistan, the expansive heritage complex of Mes Aynak faces impending destruction due to a copper mining lease with China, even in the face of worldwide resentment and protest.

Also, extensive construction around the monuments has suffocated these ancient sites. In the Shah Ji ki Dheri area of Peshawar and Sahri Bahlol, one is unable to find the ancient monuments due to extensive habitation on them. Following unchecked construction, the Kanishka Stupa has vanished, or is lost in a maze of a massive graveyard. Except a few patches of hardened earth, no other clear sign of any stupa can be found in the graveyard.

The cities that once made up the cherished land of Gandhara are the custodians of a fascinating history, a narrative that is evidence of Gandhara's commercial vitality on the Silk Road and its religious fervour in promoting the triple gem of Buddha, *Dhamma* and Sangha. They were not only scholastic hubs from where emerged great scholars of languages and philosophy but also ateliers from where arose great art.

It is heartening to note that the Afghan Institute of Archaeology located in Kabul and the Department of Archaeology and Museums, Pakistan are carrying out new excavations to unearth buried ancient monasteries. Marvellous specimens of Gandharan art have been recovered during new excavations in the historic Silk Road cities of Mes Aynak in the Logar province and Tepe Narenj near Kabul in Afghanistan. Similarly, new excavations at the historic villages of Sawal Dher located in district Mardan, Mian Khan in Katlang and Koi Tangey Kandaray have revealed Buddhist antiquities from the second or third century BC, putting these villages on the world's archaeological map. A couple of years ago, Pakistan unveiled the remains of a 1,700-year-old, 48-feet-long Sleeping Buddha dated to the third century AD at Haripur. According to Dr Abdul Samad, director, Archaeology and Museums Department, it is the world's oldest Sleeping Buddha.[1]

But a thousand more Buddhas are waiting to be rediscovered from the sleeping *dheris* of Charsadda and Swabi. These mounds of earth conceal rich antiquities and magnificent monasteries that are eagerly awaiting the spade of archaeologists.

Preserving Gandhara and unearthing its lost and forgotten cities are essentials tasks before the government, world heritage organizations, archaeologists, historians, researchers and media persons. Sadly, most ancient sites of Gandhara that once bustled with life and vigour and were the hub of art, history and culture are becoming object of people's greed. Encroached and built over, they are becoming a thing of the past.

This book strives to revive that past which yet lingers on in the ruins. It provides a glimpse of the people who lived through their art and the gods they worshipped.

---

[1] *The Guardian*, 'Pakistan Unveils Remains of 1700 Year Old Sleeping Buddha'. November 2017. Available at < https://www.theguardian.com/world/2017/nov/15/pakistan-unveils-remains-of-1700-year-old-sleeping-buddha> (last date of access: 10 February 2020).

ACKNOWLEDGEMENTS

In Pakistan: Prof. Mohammad Iqbal Chawla, Dean History, University of Punjab, Lahore for initiating my travels along the Silk Road of Pakistan and for inviting me to present a paper on Taxila at the History Conference of 2014. Dr Humera Naz, Assistant Prof., Department of History, University of Karachi for opening my window to Pakistan.

Dr Abdul Samad, Director, Department of Archaeology and Museums, Government of Khyber Pakhtunkhwa, Pakistan for permitting use of photos of Buddhist antiquities from the Peshawar Museum. Dr Naushaba Anjum for permitting use of photos of Buddhist antiquities from the Lahore Museum.

Zulfiqar Rahim and Dr Esther Park of the Gandhara Art and Cultural Association for providing me shelter in their home at Banigala, Islamabad and accompanying me along the Lahore–Peshawar–Mardan route. My friend Ayesha Hamid for driving me from Lahore to Manikyala on the Grand Trunk Road.

Zahoor Ahmad Durrani for guiding me through the lanes of Peshawar and Usman Mardanvi for his expert commentary on the Buddhist sites of Mardan.

In Afghanistan: Dr Fahim Rahimi, Director, National Museum of Afghanistan, Kabul for permitting me to publish some photos of Buddhist antiquities from the museum and providing a detailed history of the exhibits.

In Italy: Dr Anna Provenzali for granting me permission to publish photos of Buddhist images on display at the Milan Archaeological Museum, Italy.

In India: Rupa Publications for publishing my four consecutive historical travelogues on Asia's Buddhist Heritage. The Rupa team for their hard work on this book.

Renu Rao and Preeti Lal Verma for a critical reading of the manuscript.

Ritu Topa of Arrt Creation for designing the map of major Buddhist sites in Gandhara.

INDEX

abhay mudra, 177, 178, 183, 236, 240, 252, 253
Abhidharmakosha Sastra, 110
arhat, 186, 243
Asokan Edict, 157
Asvaghosa, 4, 29, 70, 99, 109, 192, 193, 241, 242, 254, 256
Avalokitesvara, 122, 194, 222, 249

Baodingshan Grottoes, 194
Begram Treasure, 179
bhumisparsh mudra, 191, 240
Bimbisara, 4, 5, 6, 69, 115, 116
BODDO coin, 236, 237
Buddhacharita, 4, 109, 193, 241, 242, 254
Buddha Mazda, 207, 244, 245, 246
Buddhapala, 17, 153, 182
Buddhatrata, 17, 153, 182

Campeyya Jataka, 254

DAFA, 174, 177, 180, 189, 191
Dazu Grottoes, 193
Dhamma Mahamatras, 21, 136, 137, 171
dharmachakra mudra, 176, 240
Dharmagupta, 17, 183

Dharmarajika, 133
Dharmasinha, xxviii, 17, 201, 203
Dhatuvibhanga Sutta, 4, 116
dhyan mudra, 125, 221, 240
Dipankar Buddha, 10, 150, 160, 176, 184, 266

Ekasringa Rishi, 139

Fire Buddha, 178
Foladi Caves, 195

Gandhakuti, 9, 240
Gandhara Jataka, 265, 269
Gol Hamid, 168, 176, 257, 259
Gorakhanath Temple, 103
Gor Khatri Complex, 95
Great Reclining Buddha, 191
Great Vehicle, 57, 139, 159, 180, 182, 203, 215
Guldara Stupa, 177

Hadda Monastery, 156
Hariti Jataka, 119
Hephthalite, 45, 187, 206, 208, 209, 210, 213, 275, 276, 277, 278
Hinayana, 109, 111, 202, 206

Jamalgarhi Monastic Centre, 132
Kafiriat Tepe, 176, 177, 257, 259, 262
Kakrak Buddha, 194, 242
Kanishka Stupa, 103, 104, 105, 106, 107, 111, 112, 113
Kanishka Vihara, xxviii, xxix, 99, 101, 102, 105, 108, 109, 111, 112, 118, 156, 242, 279, 287
Kashmir Smast caves, 115
Khuddaka Nikaya, 265
Khyber Stupa, 98, 99
King Pukkusati, 4, 115
kirtimukhas, 191, 260
Kumarjiva, 101, 229

lalitasana, 176
Little Vehicle, xxix, 109, 139, 180, 181, 182, 188, 203, 209, 210
Lokottara, 187, 242
Loriyan Tangai, 121, 122

Mahasthamaprapta, 194
Mahayana, 57, 108, 109, 111, 152, 160, 202, 203, 236, 240, 247, 248, 278
Maitreya, 86, 184, 203, 204, 243, 248, 249, 250, 251
Majishan Caves, 193
Manjushri, ix, 249
Manorhita, 110
Marguz Inscription, 142
Mes Aynak, xi, 91, 93, 152, 154, 168, 175, 177, 232, 240, 257, 259, 260, 262, 263, 265, 288
Miracle of Sravasti, 80, 178, 183, 244, 246, 252, 253, 261
Moksha Mahaparishad, 182

Nagarjuna, 70, 109
Nanda's Ordination, 255
Naubahar, xxviii, 198, 205, 208, 209, 210, 211, 213, 214, 276, 277, 281, 285

Padampani, 122, 249
Panj Tirath, 100
Paradise of Maitreya, 184
Parkham Yaksha, 238
Parsvika, 110
patra chaitya, 100
Prajnakara, xxviii, xxix, 17, 180, 182, 209
Purushapura, 94, 111, 118, 146, 163

Qissa Khwani Bazaar, 94, 96, 113

Ramagrama stupa, 163
Reclining Buddha, xxi, 75, 76, 177, 188, 189, 191, 220, 242, 259

Safed Koh, xiv, xxv, 42, 97, 162
Saffarid Dynasty, 189, 206
Sahri Bahlol, 76, 115, 123, 127, 128, 129, 132, 248, 255, 263, 265, 274, 288

Sanakavasa, 7, 186
Sarai Khuja, 168, 178, 180, 183, 244, 253, 265
Saundarananda Kavya, 256
Shahbazgarhi Edict, 137
Shah Ji ki Dheri, 104, 105, 237
Shankardara Inscription, 142
Sikri Stupa, 130, 266, 272
Si-ming-sse, 182
Standing Buddha, 81, 177, 178, 194, 242, 244, 253, 259
Stri-adhyaksa Mahamatras, 136, 137
Sukhavati Sutra, 250
Sundaranand Kavya, 109
Sung Yun, xxii, 42, 106, 138, 140, 145
Sutralamkara, 142
Swat Valley, 56, 64, 70, 90, 120, 139
Syama Jataka, 119, 120, 134, 268

Takht-i-Rustam, xxviii, 207, 211, 212

Tepe Sardar, 167, 215, 220, 223, 257, 259, 277
three jewels, 116, 188, 276
Three Stupa Court, 125, 126, 127
Top-i-Rustam, 207, 211
triratna, 116, 125, 195, 212, 261
Tusita, 184, 203

Upadesa, 109
urna, 241, 247

Vasubandhu, 70, 108, 110, 111
Vasumitra, 29, 109, 118
Vessantara Jataka, 139, 265, 266, 269, 270
Vibhasha Sastra, xxviii, xxix, 110, 209

Wardak Inscription, 30, 153, 159
Wheel of Law, 240, 253
White Huns, 45, 275

Yulin Caves, 193

BENGAL-BALKH TRADE CORRIDOR

Sketch map not to scale

Disclaimer: The international and national boundaries are not shown on the map

• Cities on the Trade Route

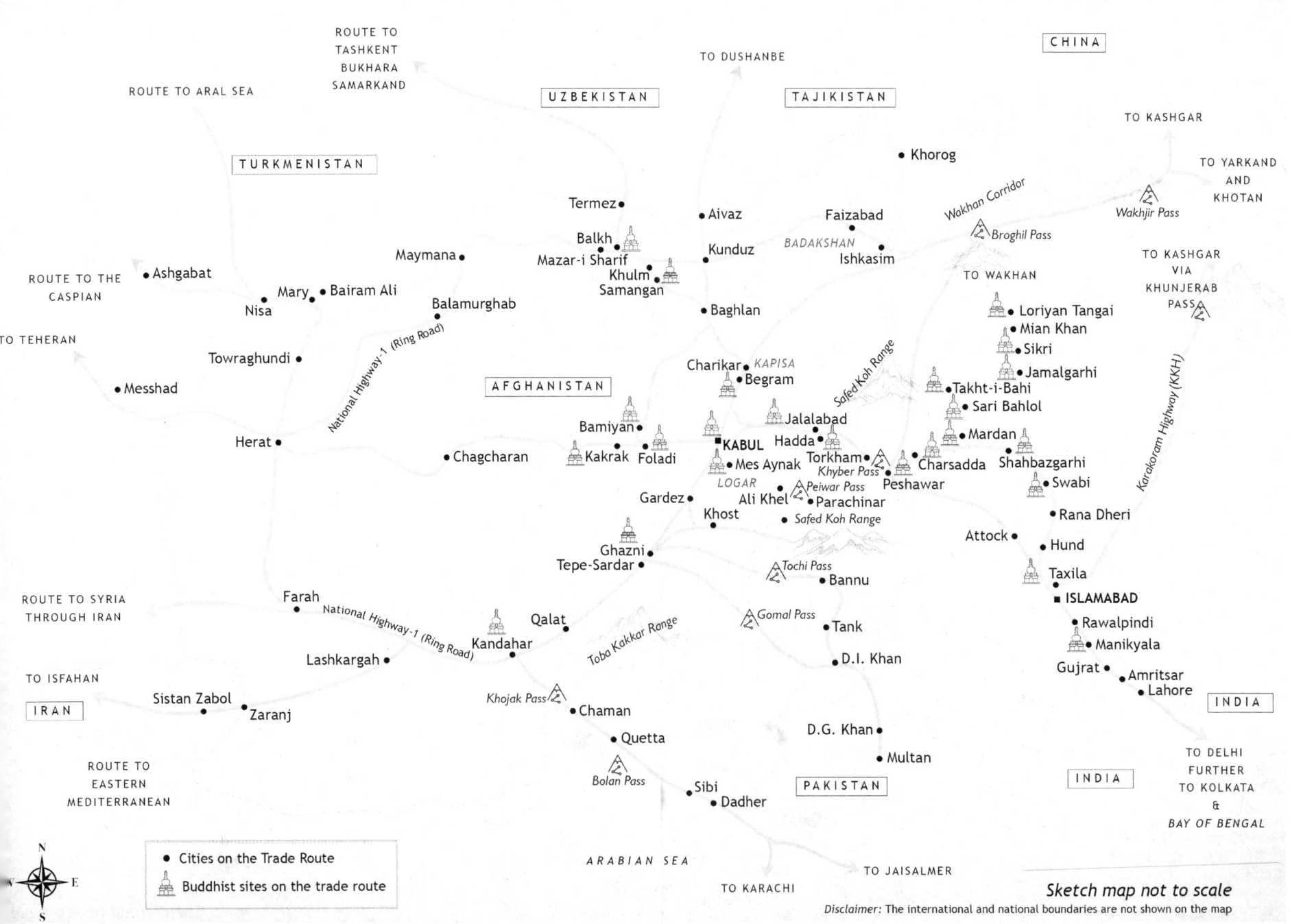